## Praise for *JobSmarts for Twentysomethings* by Bradley G. Richardson

"Richardson's book is not so much a guide to finding a job as *an operating manual for readers in their tumultuous twenties*. Plenty of titles in the career sections of bookstores can help this group of job seekers, but *JobSmarts for Twentysomethings* speaks directly to their concerns."

—*USA Today*

"In your 20s? Grab this!"

—*Mademoiselle*

"Clever. . . . Witty."

—*US News and World Report*

"Richardson is the perfect poster person for the downsized, restructured, shrink-wrapped job culture facing the 47 million or so Americans ages 18–29. Calling all you twentysomething college grads looking for, like, a job: Park the remote, get off the couch, borrow mom's car, high tail it to your local book store and BUY THIS BOOK."

—*Chicago Tribune*

"His delivery is more believable than any Prof. or parental lecture."
—*U.*, The National College Magazine

"The real life examples are very close to home for our students and appeal to their need to hear about people whose issues are similar to their own."
—Wayne Wallace, Ph.D., director of the Career Resource Center at the University of Florida

"If you're in your twenties . . . you need Bradley Richardson's practical, bottom-line advice on how to go one-on-one and slam-dunk yourself a good job. If a high-powered college education is worth $100,000, then *Job-Smarts for Twentysomethings* is definitely worth the thirteen bucks."
—Bill Strauss, coauthor of *13th Gen*

"With straight talk that young people appreciate, Bradley Richardson's creative guide will help twentysomethings prosper in a baby boomer world. As the author writes, 'This stuff really works.'"
—Donald T. Phillips, author of *Lincoln on Leadership*

"To get ahead, you'll need every advantage you can get, and taking Bradley Richardson's advice is one of the best ways to get started."
—*Skew*, The On-Line Magazine

"I was truly excited by the no BS approach you provided. I will recommend *JobSmarts* to the 2,000 plus students I teach each year."

—Dr. Roger Blackwell, professor of marketing, Ohio State University, and "Outstanding Marketing Educator of the Year"

"I wanted to let you know how much I enjoyed reading *JobSmarts*. I believe you present yourself and your viewpoint admirably, and I agree with your philosophy about helping young people find their place in the world of work. I have recommended *JobSmarts for Twentysomethings* to several of our clients already."

—Wendy Finan, director of testing, Johnson O'Conner Research Foundation

"*JobSmarts* is exactly the truth about work, our generation, and how we fit into the real world."

—Kristin Marquez, HCS Planning & Communications

"Your book has changed my entire outlook on my career search. *JobSmarts* has become my Bible. I've applied so many of the applications and they really work."

—Lisa Alexander, Houston, TX

"*JobSmarts* should be required reading, starting in high school. If your degree is only yellowing in its frame, read Richardson between your shifts flipping burgers."

—*Vancouver Sun*

"I have been haunting bookstores and libraries for years in search of such a book. I felt like it was one of my friends talking to me. This is the kind of book which can inspire people to seize the day and live with gusto. Your confidence is contagious. I am recommending it to all my friends, coworkers, and my sister."

—Whitney Brown, San Francisco State University

"Your book came into my life at a very appropriate and relevant time. I feel like I have a game plan and a goal. I have officially announced the end of my free floating, 'If you have a job I'll take it' attitude. The time has come for me to be directed. What a wonderful book."

—Kimberly Meyer, University of California, Davis

"Bradley's book is THE definitive guide to good career sense."

—Elizabeth Styron, Duke University

# JobSmarts
## 50
# TopCareers

Also by Bradley Richardson

*JobSmarts for Twentysomethings*

# JobSmarts
## 50
## TopCareers

Bradley G. Richardson

HarperPerennial

*A Division of* HarperCollins*Publishers*

JobSmarts is a trademark of The BGR Group Inc.

FIRST EDITION

*Designed by Alma Hochhauser Orenstein*

---

Library of Congress Cataloging-in-Publication Data

Richardson, Bradley G.
    JobSmarts 50 top careers / Bradley G. Richardson. — 1st ed.
        p.   cm.
    Includes index.
    ISBN 0-06-095220-2
    1. Vocational guidance—United States.  2. Occupations—United States.
I. Title.
HF5382.5.U5R49     1997
    331.7'02—dc21                                                        97-20983

---

97 98 99 00 01 ❖/RRD 10 9 8 7 6 5 4 3 2 1

*This book is dedicated to Jan and Jack Introligator,*
*who gave me a family and every opportunity to succeed.*
*You've not only shown me how to be JobSmart,*
*but smart about life.*

Whatever you dream or dare to dream, begin it.
—Goethe

# Contents

# Part III: Resources

# Acknowledgments

While it is only the author's name that appears on the cover of a book, it takes many people to write and produce it—especially one such as this. There are so many people who helped make this possible, I can't begin to thank them all for their time and insight.

However, the biggest thanks go to my wife and true companion, Meredith, who is always there for me and helps me see what is possible. To the new lady in my life, my daughter, Samantha. (Try writing a book with an infant in the house.) I can't ever thank Jack and Jan Introligator enough for all they have done for me. To my biggest fan and constant supporter, my mom, Judy Richardson. Thanks to my sister and brother-in-law, Paige and Tate Smith. My two brothers, James Introligator (finally, free legal advice) and Craig Introligator, thanks for your research. Many thanks to Steve, Shana, and Harrison Javery for always being there and putting up with my occasional (okay, frequent) episodes during this book.

Eternal thanks to my wonderful team. At the top of the list are the two ladies to whom I owe my career: my agents Pam Bernstein and Donna Dever, to whom I'm sure I gave a few gray hairs during this process. You know just when to nurture me and when to kick me in the ass when I need it. My editor, Trena Keating (she has the patience of Job), whose guidance and infinite patience make her a saint. I owe you a new car or should at least pay for your kid's college. Many thanks to Susan Weinberg and the HarperCollins staff for their enthusiasm about me and JobSmarts. I'm happy that HarperCollins is my new publishing home.

And many thanks to all the companies and professionals who were so gracious with their time, advice, guidance, and dirt. Thanks for sharing your JobSmarts.

# Introduction

You are considering a major career change or plotting out your career when a friend, family member, or even a stranger asks the following anxiety-inducing question: "What do you want to do after you graduate, change careers, or get off the couch and get a real job?" Or how about the always well-meaning but highly annoying, "What can you do with *that* degree?" This is just the type of nurturing you need after five years pursuing a degree that's left you with debt equal to the GNP of a Third World country.

When most people are asked these or similarly probing questions, they often pause, give an insightful gaze and a thoughtful sigh, and intelligently utter, "Uh, I dunno."

This year more than 1.2 million people will graduate from college, many without a clue of what they want to do with the rest of their lives. Countless others will find themselves dissatisfied or disillusioned in their current positions and will consider changing careers. The truly lost will leave their jobs and retreat to grad school, hoping to find direction in further education. (That makes sense. "I don't know what I want to do, but accumulating several thousand dollars of debt seems like a great place to start.")

People make career choices based on any number of bad reasons. A small sampling includes:

"It was my major."

"The money is good."

"It sounded glamorous." (You often hear this from those leaving journalism and the media.)

The ever popular, "My parents wanted me to go into it." (I believe that once you hit thirty, parental guilt can no longer be used as an excuse for a bad career choice. If this is the case, I highly recommend obtaining a spine.)

I've always admired people who are focused and know exactly where they want to be professionally. "I've known since I was a child that I would someday become a . . . surgeon, senator, accountant, ax murderer, etc." The reality is that most of us just aren't that focused or simply don't even know certain opportunities exist. Individuals who know exactly what they want to do and then follow through with it are the exception, not the rule. Moreover, most colleges and universities do a rather poor job of showing graduates the scope of available opportunities. Many graduates think the pool of potential employers in the Universe is limited to those who actively recruit on their campuses. Others know what they would like to do, but don't know how to go about pursuing it. After spending four or five years in college, some grads still don't have any idea of what they want to do. These are the people who flock to every assessment test and self-exploration course in the world, only to be told that the dream job they are most suited for is to work in a fish hatchery.

Let's face it, making a career choice is tough. Making the right career choice is even tougher. The smartest way to increase your chances of choosing the right career is to be informed. That is the aim of this book: To give you realistic, useful information to help you discover your options and make an informed career choice.

Parents, professors, and all the career gurus (I prefer to be called Career Master or simply Yoda) stress the importance of the "informational interview." It's just plain smart to spend time with a professional in a certain field picking his or her brain to learn the inside scoop on getting hired and succeeding in that field. It's kind of an advanced "Show and Tell," like when your dad came to school to tell everyone what he did for a living. Everyone thought the truck driver was cool. Meanwhile, no one wanted to talk with the investment banker—times have changed, haven't they?

People recommend the informational interview because it's a nonthreatening way to learn about a company or career. You don't have the added pressure of having to perform and be on your best behavior, as you do in a regular job interview.

## Separating the Truth from the Hype

As a job seeker, you're constantly being told to "sell yourself." But what you may forget is that while you are trying to sell the company on your abilities, education, and experience, the company is giving you the hard sell, too. They are trying to sell you on their company. You will hear about the opportunities, benefits, and future rewards, such as, "If you work hard, one day you can become a regional manager." Oooooh. Ahhhh.

Unfortunately, both job seekers and employers don't always paint an accurate picture. Not unlike being set up on a blind date, rarely is the person ever as good-looking or funny as was described by your friend—or ex-friend.

Think about all of the cheesy recruiting brochures, videos, and materials that companies produce. The Big Six accounting and consulting firms are notorious for producing this propaganda. They always have a trio of young men and women—as diverse as a Benetton ad—with totally fake smiles glued to their fresh young faces as they walk around a campus with rolling green hills. These slick color brochures have a cozy, "I love you, you love me, join the family and sing 'Cumbaya'" feel to them. The only thing missing is the big purple dinosaur hugging the new recruits.

I don't fault recruiters for painting this picture, but how about a little truth in advertising? I guess real pictures of haggard recruits with bags under their eyes holding their perpetually empty checkbooks might be a tougher sell. Okay, that may be extreme, but the point is that perception and reality are often different when it comes to career expectations and actual work.

## Why Read This Book?

The question you really want to ask is, "Why should I spend my money on this book when the shelves are lined with career books?" Or "I could just as easily spend my money on a CD, beer, or pizza?"

To address the pizza and beer issue, I don't have an argument for that other than you may get fat and drunk. And let me tell you, fat, drunk, and unemployed is not a pretty combination. As for the CD, it depends on what you get. If you get some romantic mood music, that's great, but if you still don't have a job, in the immortal words of Lyle Lovett, "No Finance. No Romance." That leaves you with the next logical question: Which career book should I read?

## How Is This JobSmarts Book Different?

When I first decided to write this book, I purchased every career guide on the market to see what each offered. By doing this, I discovered that there are basically two types of books: those that give dry, boring job descriptions and repeat every mind-numbing figure the Bureau of Labor Statistics has to offer and those that deal with what I call *Melrose Place* jobs. The advice was either "Accountants work in a clean, well-lit environment" or "How to become an MTV veejay" (to which my answer is, get a lobotomy and a boob job).

The majority of career guides offer a great deal of information, such as employment projections through the year 2005 and other statistics. All good stuff to know, but not the type of information that will necessarily help you understand what it's like to be employed and work in a certain field. Another weakness is that these books cover every profession under the sun. This could be seen as a positive, but I believe there are some jobs you don't need to read about in a book to know whether you want to do them. If someone wants to be a lathe operator, traffic guard, or bus driver, I seriously doubt they reached that decision from reading a book.

Machine tool operator, musical instrument repairer and tuner, housekeeper, cemetery worker, luggage repairer, and arc welder are just a few of the professions profiled in several other guides. I even saw "predatory animal hunter" listed in one guide entitled *Jobs for the '90s*. I wasn't aware that big-game hunter was a career for the nineties. Maybe they meant 1890s? Don't get me wrong, these are fine jobs, but you aren't going to read this or any other book and then quit school or leave your job to become an arc welder or a gravedigger.

## Hey, What's Wrong with *Melrose Place* Jobs?

Remember *Melrose Place* before Heather Locklear, when it had a shred of believability? Probably not, because it sucked. It's much better now that it resembles *Dynasty*. My gripe with *Melrose* is that no one has a real job. Think about it. Does anyone on *Melrose* have a normal job, like selling insurance or working as an engineer? No. Everyone is a either a surgeon, an advertising executive, a successful independent fashion designer, or a hooker.

When the show began, Billy drove a cab to support himself as a struggling writer. Now he is a power-hungry advertising executive. Sydney finally got a real job working retail, but only after she gave the world's oldest profession a try. Don't even get me started on the career paths of Amanda and Jane.

Of course, it's schlock entertainment and I'm glued to the tube on Mondays like countless other drones, but so much of the career information out there is just like *Melrose Place*. Many of the guides are devoted exclusively to the glamour industries like media and entertainment. Others cover beautiful jobs, dream jobs, adventure jobs, and how to get hired at popular companies for which everyone and their dog wants to work. The profiles of the world's most prestigious and glamorous companies are interesting to read, but Nike only hires so many people each year and there can only be a handful (thank God) of Jenny McCarthys and other annoying MTV personalities.

My favorite example of this type of useless career advice comes from no less than the series of books published by the *Wall Street Journal's National Business Employment Weekly*. While the weekly *NBEW* newspaper is a great resource for career seekers, their jobs almanac leaves a lot to be desired. The *NBEW* Jobs Almanac lists and ranks the "best jobs." Listed as the best job in America is . . . professional basketball player. Do you think this affected Michael Jordan's career choice? After reading this, I thought, "I would love to play in the NBA, but my eight-inch vertical leap and YMCA league experience might not be enough." The almanac also lists president of the United States and Indy race car driver as viable career options to consider. I'm sure that Bill consulted it before running for office.

This JobSmarts book tries to cover jobs that more than five people in the world can have at one time. For the most part, these are careers that most everyone can pursue. You won't find waifish supermodel or cohost of *Entertainment Tonight* in this book. I didn't want to write *The Top 50 Careers for Beautiful People*, *The Top 50 Careers for Left-Handed Libras*, or *The Top 50 Careers for Mensa Members*. (Mensa is the genius IQ organization. I'd show you my membership card, but it must be in my other wallet.)

## What About the "100 Best Jobs in the Universe" Books?

People are enthralled by books and lists that offer secret tips on how to get hired at "the 100 best companies in America," "the 10 largest advertising agencies," or "the 5 largest sausage makers." We're Americans, and damn it, bigger is better. If it's "hot, hyped, and popular," then it's for me.

But the job that is hot today may be rendered obsolete by technology tomorrow. Just ask the over 5 million people who have been laid off, downsized, or reengineered since 1990, and they will tell you that popularity doesn't mean best and largest doesn't mean stability.

## What You Won't Find in This Book

You won't find mind-numbing stats and unemployment figures for every profession. Why? Because they quickly become outdated. If you're reading this book six months after the original release date, there is a good chance that those employment figures would be dramatically different. For this reason, I won't bog you down with too many industry statistics and random figures that really don't tell you anything about working and getting hired in a particular field.

You also won't find a deep psychoanalysis of your character. There are no quizzes and tests to determine if you are a thinker, feeler, or analyzer. You won't find your inner child and you won't find personality assessments that determine if you are a red, blue, or green personality type, as one career guide recommends. C'mon, are you a job seeker or a mood ring? "My chart says I'm blue, but I'm feeling more indigo today." Yeah, that goes over real well with employers as they're saying, "Thanks for coming in. Next!"

You won't find flashy grids or charts that can only be deciphered by a roomful of engineers. Nor will you find confusing icons representing a mythical ratings system, like a work-o-meter or style-factor rating. If you are looking for a "Birkenstock factor," look elsewhere.

## What You Will Find in This Book

Imagine you had ten minutes with a roomful of professionals in a particular field and could ask anything you wanted about their careers. What would you want to know? How much money will I make? What is the culture like? How do people get hired? What are the typical starting positions? What are some common misconceptions of the field? What opportunities exist in this and related areas? What is the career path? Do you like your job and, more importantly, will I like your job? How do people perceive this field? Will I be able to look at myself in the mirror or will my friends think I'm a weasel? What will I really do versus the recruiting BS?

You would learn answers to many of the things you were told you shouldn't ask in a job interview but want to know before you accept the job or pursue a career in that field. Answers to these and other questions are what you will find in each career profiled inside this book.

Your boundaries will be expanded, and you will discover career options you might have never before considered. You will learn how most businesses are interrelated and what they may have in common. For example, you will learn how a field like publishing offers opportunities for people in careers as diverse as law, art, sales, marketing, and public relations, not just editing.

You will find advice on getting in, what employers are looking for, and what has worked for others. You will find information that will help you decide if a career is right for you. Each section has some useful and fun facts, as well as resources in print and on the Web in case you want to do more research.

## What If I Don't Want to Work for Someone Else or I Want to Work Abroad?

There are special sections for people considering work abroad, starting their own business, returning to school, or contemplating working for a family business. You will also find a section on how to make the most of temporary opportunities. There is even a chapter devoted to unique, unusual, or off-beat jobs. (I know it is dangerously close to resembling a *Melrose Place* section.)

## The Good, the Bad, and the Ugly

By reading this book, you will gain an accurate picture of working in certain fields, what your available options are, and what it takes to get started. The descriptions are not watered down or sanitized for your protection. This is not meant to glorify or slam any particular field, profession, or company, but to give you a realistic insider's perspective. This is also not the *Inside Edition* or *Hard Copy* career guide. If an organization was slammed, the name was changed. If you are looking for dirt on a certain company, you won't find it here. You'll have to make that judgment on your own.

## What Makes These the "Top" 50 Careers?

How did I come up with these 50 careers? Well, it started late one night with a list, a dart board, and too much caffeine. Actually, these careers were chosen for several reasons. Primarily, the fields selected are those I am most commonly asked about by graduates and job seekers nationwide. For the past two years, I have received thousands of questions about these professions at my speaking events and in letters and e-mail to my company, JobSmarts. In addition, I solicited the opinions of other professionals, educators, and job seekers on what careers students and job seekers seemed to have the most interest in and questions about.

## JobSmarts Disclaimer

Despite my desire to be all things to all people, I know that I can't possibly address every single career under the sun. So if you are bent out of shape because I did not profile the fantastic opportunities found in swine breeding or exotic dancing, I'm sorry.

This is not a ranking. I do not own a crystal ball. I don't claim to be Nostradamus, nor do I predict what the hot jobs are or will be. If I were such a prognosticator, I would be in Vegas rather than handicapping what will be the hot job du jour. These are not necessarily the fastest growing careers, the highest paying careers, or the best careers for Gen X liberal arts majors who like cheese. Accounting is not the top career. It just happens to be first alphabetically.

This is also not the final word on each profession. You may see something with which you disagree. That is fine. Please recognize that all companies, jobs, and bosses are not the same. If you were to talk with two people in the same field, you might find one who loves her job and thinks her boss is the best, while the next person is ready to purchase a weapon and is asking for a home address. No two bosses or companies are alike, so understand that this is a reflection of talking with several people in these fields. Also, by no means are these the only opportunities within these fields.

## How the Information Was Gathered

My company, JobSmarts, contacted 1,200 companies, trade groups, and professional associations in more than fifty different industries and professions. In addition, we surveyed and conducted interviews with 500-plus personal and professional contacts in each field. Information was gathered from a wide variety of people on both sides of the hiring table—both recruiters and employees. This network began to grow, and people kept putting us in touch with others who could share information about their professions.

## Who Are These People?

Some of the people are rookies who have been on the job less than three years. Others are just picking up steam and are on their second or third promotion. I also spoke with high-level executives and industry veterans, as well as people who are no longer working in a certain field for one reason or another. (Those reasons are sometimes pretty interesting.)

You will read about companies that are household names and others you have never heard of. I gave everyone the option of being quoted by name and company. Some companies and individuals chose to lend their names; others did not want their real names used. Out of respect for privacy, names were changed or withheld if requested.

## What This Book Will Do for You?

This book does the legwork of researching a profession. It will help you make a smarter, more informed career choice. Above all, this book will make you think. You will think about your options for employment, changing careers, and where you are headed. You will also think about how businesses are related and how they work together.

You can certainly read this book cover to cover if you choose. However, it is not meant to be read straight through in one sitting. Use it rather as a resource throughout your job search and career. Come back to it when you're thinking about changing jobs or need to learn about a business with which you are dealing.

## I Already Know What I Want to Do. Why Is It Important for Me to Know About Other Careers?

You may not want to work for an advertising or public relations agency, but one day you might need to hire an advertising agency, marketing firm, lawyer, or architect. You might not want to work for a hotel or hospitality company, but you may find that you are a publicist, conference planner, or executive, and you now do business with a company in the hospitality industry. Knowledge of another industry gives you an advantage in business and makes you more marketable. I started my career in the high-tech industry, but my clients were media and advertising agencies, so it helped me to understand how they worked. As many different businesses as there are, they all have elements that are interrelated. Understanding how each works will make you a well-rounded, marketable job candidate, ultimately giving you more options in your career.

## It Is All About Options

There are so many opportunities available to you, regardless of where you are in your career. A person graduating from college today can expect to change careers—not jobs, but careers—five to six times in her working lifetime. You may end up in a profession you had never dreamed of while in school, or one that has not yet been invented. You may not become aware of certain opportunities until after you begin working.

A successful career begins with knowing your options. The information and stories you will read over the next few hundred pages will help you better understand your options; make you a smarter, more informed job seeker; and give you some insight into what other people do for a living. If there is anything I hope you gain from this book, it's that you become aware of your career options. Hopefully, one or more of the profiles piques your interest enough to lead you to conduct your own informational interview and discover what it takes for you to become JobSmart in your chosen field.

Only you can decide what you want to do with your life and if a career is right for you (and you for it). As my favorite author, Dr. Theodor Geisel (Dr. Suess), wrote, "You have brains in your head. You have feet in your shoes. You can steer yourself any direction you choose. You're on your own. And you know what you know. And YOU are the guy who'll decide where to go."

This book is a map. How you read it and decide which road to take is up to you. Be smart.

# Part I

· · · · · · · · · · · · · · · · · · · · · · · · ·

# What Am I Going to Do with My Life?

# 1

● ● ● ● ● ● ● ● ● ● ● ● ● ● ● ● ● ● ● ● ● ● ● ● ● ● ● ● ●

# "I Don't Know What I Want to Do."

Do you sometimes feel you're the only person on Earth who doesn't have a direction, path, destiny, or job? Does the saying "The future is now" make you squeamish as graduation nears? Do you ever want to run to the tallest building you can find and shout from the rooftop, "I don't know what the hell I want to do with the rest of my life!"?

If so, you aren't alone. Every morning, countless people from all walks of life and every stage of their careers look themselves in the mirror and wonder, Am I in the right career? What do I really want to do? Discovering an occupation that you enjoy, are qualified for, and manages to keep you in a lifestyle you aren't ashamed of is a difficult thing that many people never achieve.

The problem isn't a lack of jobs. The economy seems to be growing and performing well. In some parts of the country, storefronts abound with "Help Wanted" signs. The problem is that many of these jobs are low-paying, unskilled service jobs. C'mon, nobody's goal after graduation is to become a server at Boston Chicken or a sales associate at the Gap.

Jobs are easy to find. Anyone can find a job by opening up the Sunday paper. Discovering a career, profession, and calling you are passionate about and then developing a career path is much tougher. It's ironic that for many people finding a job is often not as hard as choosing what you want to do.

# How Do I Know?

How do you decide what career path to pursue? It's logical to think that your major or degree would be a good indicator. Yet countless students spend four or more years and go tens of thousands of dollars in debt pursuing a specific course of study, only to realize they are in the same boat as when they entered school: Clueless.

Others may have an epiphany during their junior year and discover, "I really hate accounting, but it's too late to change my major. What am I going to do?" This clarity of thought also comes to many new professionals after about two years, when they realize, "This job sucks. I didn't really know it would be like this." Not long after, résumés begin to be updated.

Many people can't tell you exactly what they want to do, but they can tell you what they don't want to do. Sometimes knowing what you *don't* want can be just as valuable as having a clear picture of your career path (which, by the way, not many people have). Eliminating certain careers from your list can actually be a great place to start. You may have a preconceived notion of what a field is like, or you may have decided you want to work in a certain job or for a certain company. But once you try it, you might discover it's not all you thought it would be. If this is the case, don't get upset. Chalk it up to experience and consider yourself lucky that you didn't waste several years of your life pursuing something you ultimately would have hated.

Knowing what career to pursue doesn't come as a lightning bolt or message from the gods. It is a process, a journey of discovering what you like, what you don't like, and where your talents lie.

This chapter will give you some tips on how you can take the first step on that journey.

## No One Can Tell You What to Do

We look to parents, professors, campus career counselors, and other job gurus to tell us what careers to choose, but the bottom line is that it's a personal choice that no one else can make for you (though many parents try). Have your parents ever said, "You want to be a what?" Talk about pressure. Can't you just hear some father saying, "My father was an accountant, I'm an accountant, and damn it, you'll be one, too." How much bad blood and ill will has been caused by a child's career choice? We probably would have half as many accountants, attorneys, doctors, and dentists in this country if people would have looked at their own needs and desires rather than allowing their parents to live vicariously through them.

The first step in determining what you really want to do is not to let your parents or anyone else guilt you into a career. I understand this may be easier said than done in some families, but it's your career, your life, and your choice. Regardless of what career you pursue, your work will be a major part of your life. It will impact not only how you make a living, but your happiness.

## Enjoy What You Do

Work is such a big part of your life that you'd better enjoy what you do. You should believe in and respect what you are doing.

Even if you aren't a workaholic, it's tough to turn off the switch and leave everything at work. Remember, everyone gets the same twenty-four hours in a day. Some people just use their time more wisely than others. During your twenty-four hours, you might sleep at least eight a night, and you will likely work a minimum—yes, minimum—of eight hours. More than half of your waking day will be spent at work. This means you'd better enjoy what you do and the environment you work in.

### How Do I Discover What's Out There?

Don't limit yourself to thinking that the only companies that will hire you are those that come to your campus or are in the newspaper. Many companies never go to campuses to recruit and others only go to a handful of campuses (maybe twenty to fifty at most).

On the job, you will be exposed to more companies and industries than you may have ever heard of before. Take a look at who your current employer does business with. Many people change careers by going to work for former clients. Others become exposed to new industries while working in a related field and decide to make a change.

Jonathan began working in advertising and became exposed to television production. He realized he wanted to pursue a career in TV and, through the media contacts he made in advertising, he eventually went to work for several national talk shows.

You can take courses, tests, or consult counselors and psychics, but the bottom line is that no one can tell you what you want to do. It's a personal choice only you can make. This discovery process starts by doing a little personal research.

## How to Determine What You Want to Do

*The information I'm about to impart is extremely advanced and not for the weak.*

Get a pad and tear off three sheets. Divide the first page into two columns. Label one column "What I Like" and the other "What I Dislike." The next two sheets should have the headings listed below:

- What I'm Good At (Skills, Talents, and Abilities)
- Characteristics of the Perfect Job: What Do I Want from Work?

Sit in a quiet room or outside by yourself and write your answers on the three sheets. Write whatever pops into your head. Your first response is usually a genuine feeling or perception, so don't think about it or analyze it too much. You can narrow down your list later. If you draw a blank and can't think of anymore, take a break and come back to it later. This may even take a couple of days for you to complete. Answer honestly. No one will see your answers but you. Don't think about job titles, specific industries, or what you are trained for. Just think in terms of what you want, don't want, are good at, and what type of work environment you want. I know this sounds touchy-feely, but it really works. (Playing background music by Yanni, John Tesh, or any other middle-aged, overly sensitive, New Age musician is optional, but I don't recommend it.) Besides, this is what some of the assessment gurus and tests will have you do, only they will charge you several hundred dollars. You paid less than twenty dollars for this book.

## I'm Having Trouble Getting Started

The following are some questions you might ask yourself to get you thinking about what you want to do:

"Do I like working with people?"
"Do I need hands-on direction or do I work better alone?"
"Do I like technology?"
"Is money important to me?"
"How do I want to be treated?"
"Do I want an office or would working from home be okay?"
"Would it bother me to work around people who were not educated or do I want to be around people who have several degrees?"
"Do I work well under pressure or do I need a calm environment to do my best work?"
"Do I want a young, fast-paced environment or a slower more conservative environment?"

## Space Age Technology at Work

Once you have done this, you still might not know what specific position or field you want to work in (that's what the rest of the book is for), but you do have an idea of what you would like from a job and some criteria by which you can judge a potential career.

Next, using the same Space Age technology as before, take a piece of processed wood pulp and a cylindrical graphite writing utensil (it sounds more impressive than paper and pencil) and write down a list of careers or industries you might be interested in. The sky's the limit. You don't have to be trained in that field or even know anything about it, just put down about ten broad-based careers that seem interesting to you or that you would like to know more about.

Then begin to ask your friends and contacts, "Hey do you know anyone in this field that I might be able to talk to?" This is where networking, connections, and establishing contacts begins. Pick up the phone and talk with pros in these industries. Conduct your own informational interviews by asking some of the questions found in this book, or ask anything you want to know about the business. You aren't asking for a job interview, you want to learn what it's like to

work in that career. Go to their offices and see where and how they work. Feel the atmosphere, the way the office looks, the tension or excitement. Do you like it and would you want to learn more?

---

### A WORD ABOUT APTITUDE TESTING

If you are at a complete loss and don't even know what your skills and abilities are, you might consider taking a series of aptitude tests. There are many available through private companies, counselors, or college career-service offices. Some are very elaborate and expensive, while others are simple and can be taken at home.

The reason you take these tests is to determine and identify your skills, abilities, and aptitudes, *not to tell you what career to choose*. While researching this book, I took a series of tests. One of the most effective I've found is offered by the Johnson O'Connor Research Foundation. They have offices in about twenty cities across the country. It's a series of tasks and tests that are conducted over a two-day period. I had no clue what some of them meant while I was performing them. I did everything from writing anything that popped into my head for four minutes (this was to determine how many ideas I could produce in a short amount of time) to picking up pins with tweezers in a certain amount of time (this demonstrated my finger dexterity and hand-eye coordination). It may sound strange, and it felt even stranger when I was doing it, but the interpretation of my skills was right on the money. The analysis told me my strengths and weaknesses. Then they offered a list of positions that might suit my strengths. (As it turned out, I was in the right career. My other choices—based upon my aptitudes—were male model, international playboy, or pig farmer.) The test is not cheap: It costs over $1,000 for several days of testing and analysis, but it's well worth it.

---

# What If I Don't Know Anyone?

If you don't know anyone in a certain field—or even if you do—a great way to obtain contacts and learn about more careers is to keep a "clip file." Every time you read something that might interest you, cut it out and keep it in your clip file. If you aren't already reading *Fortune*, *Forbes*, *Business Week*, the *Wall Street Journal*, even *USA Today*, you should. You should also check out the local business journals and any specific trade publications in that field (some of these publications are listed in the "What the Pros Read" sections of the career path profiles).

While reading, cut out names of companies and individuals, or anything that makes you say, "That sounds pretty interesting" or "I wonder how this person got started?" The same goes for stories you see on TV or hear on the radio. Write down the person's name or company and drop it in the file.

Don't touch the file for about a month. Simply accumulate clips. After about a month of gathering information, take some time to go through your file. As you see some of the clippings, you might say, "This is stupid. What was I thinking about this career for?" or "This still sounds pretty cool. I want to learn more."

## What Do I Do Now?

Now that you have the name of the company and maybe even an individual, you have a contact you can call to learn about that field. Try to contact that person or company and explain how you learned about them. (People love to hear that someone saw them in a paper or magazine. Flattery might just be enough to get a person on the phone.) Say that you are interested in learning more about their career and hope they could spare five or ten minutes to tell you how they got started and what it's like to work in that field. You will run across some people who will say no, or whom you

---

When I was at the University of Oklahoma, I thought I wanted to be a stockbroker—prestigious job, great office, and most of all, tons of cash. I contacted a number of brokers and asked them what they did and told them what I wanted to do. "Hi, I don't know anything about your industry, but I think I want to work in your field. I would like to talk to you about it and also see if I can work for you as an intern. You don't even have to pay me. I just want to be around it and learn from the ground up." (Okay, I was sucking up, but it worked).

Some people said, "Thanks, but no thanks." Others discouraged me from going into their profession, while others praised their field. Still another group took pity on me and ultimately let me hang around for a few weeks or hired me as an intern—often for free. It's amazing how employers can get slave labor for pizza and Pepsi.

I eventually got an internship with a brokerage firm. During my internship, I talked with other brokers and learned what they did, how they got started, and about the testing and licensing requirements. I also saw the great cars many of them drove and the insane hours they worked. It wasn't the hours that got me. It was the math and the sleazy sales element that ultimately turned me off. I mean, I know what it's like to make cold calls, but these were cold calls to little old ladies who lived on a fixed income. I felt like I was hitting up someone's nana for money. It wasn't for me. Not all brokers are like that, but the experience tainted me and made me look elsewhere. Working in that environment before I graduated saved me from making the wrong choice and getting a false start in my career.

can't reach, but you at least have a place to begin. You might also call the public relations department of a company you're interested in and ask them to send you information about the company. You should also check out their Web site.

Hopefully, you now have a better picture of what you are looking for in a career. As you read the career path profiles in the remainder of this book, ask yourself if that career meets your criteria. Does it seem to match your needs, skills, and desires? Remember, it's a personal choice.

# 2

• • • • • • • • • • • • • • • • • • • • • • • • • • •

# Show Me the Jobs:
# Where and How People
# Are Working Today

Trying to determine what jobs are in demand seems to be as tough as picking winning lottery numbers. Almost every government agency, private company, magazine, and consultant with a Ouija board has an opinion on what is and will be the hot new thing. Every few months, a new ranking, survey, or listing of hot jobs and locations is released and like lemmings, people flock to them, taking them as gospel.

The job market and the workplace are constantly changing. Careers are always coming in and out of favor, but don't be a sheep and follow the crowd to the latest hot job.

## Why the Rankings and "Hot Job" Lists Aren't So Hot

1. *You might need additional training or education.* By the time you become fully trained or earn your extra degree, that career may no longer be in favor.

2. *By the time a job is considered hot by the media, it's lukewarm at best.* To take advantage of a truly hot trend, you need to be in at the beginning, not after the mainstream media has announced that it's popular. It's like discovering a great club or restaurant before anyone else knows

about it. When everyone else finds it, you can never get a reservation or the atmosphere changes.

3. *Maybe the fastest growing job isn't something you want to do.* If mortician was listed as the fastest growing job in the country, would that mean you'd want to become one? (Although, you're guaranteed steady business.)

## "The Times, They Are A-Changin'"

*Forbes* magazine and the Federal Reserve Bank conducted a survey that ranked the thirty most popular jobs from the beginning of the century through 1995. The survey found that over half the jobs ranked in the top thirty as recently as 1960 weren't in the top thirty in 1995. Many jobs that were popular when our parent's were our age either no longer exist or aren't in demand.

Companies who were once perennial Fortune 500 leaders are no longer in existence, and others who have just come to life in the past ten to fifteen years are already major players. Just this year, the Dow Jones Industrial Average replaced aging companies such as Woolworth and Bethlehem Steel with WalMart and Hewlett-Packard, companies whose products more accurately reflect the way we shop, live, and work.

I entered the University of Oklahoma in the mid-eighties, when oil was big business and everyone and their brother was studying petroleum engineering. By the time all of the petroleum engineers graduated four to five years later, the oil market was in the toilet and thousands of companies had gone bust. There simply wasn't a market for it any longer.

Three years ago, interactive CD-ROM was the latest craze in technology. Interactive CD shops were being started left and right, and major media companies and publishers were scooping them up as quickly as they could find them. Then something happened about a year later. The Web became a household name. Suddenly, anyone could go to Barnes & Noble, buy a book on HTML, and build a Web site. Today, the big companies are making different bets on the future of multimedia, and those small CD-ROM shops that managed to survive are focusing on the Web.

• • •

I went to the Smithsonian Institute in Washington, D.C., with my mom. In the Smithsonian is one of the first computers. It's bigger than my car. Instead of using software, disks, or hard drives, it was operated by punch cards—cardboard tickets with coded holes punched in them. My mom said one of her first jobs was as a key punch operator. Just thirty years later, there are no more key punch operators. Today, Mom would be a programmer. (Way to go, Mom. You're a pioneer.)

## So What Good Are the Trends and Rankings?

Realize that trends, like most businesses, are cyclical. What's in favor today may no longer be in ten years. It might then pick up again (just like trash disco). The smart way to read the trends is to look at the overall profession and determine what businesses and careers might be related to that field. This is much smarter than simply looking at one specific position.

By looking at the list of current hot job prospects, you'll notice that most of the projected growth is in healthcare and education. You can certainly pur-

## The Winners: Fastest Growing Occupations Requiring a Bachelor's Degree

Chiropractor
Secondary school teachers
Preschool and kindergarten teachers
Counselors
Instructors/coaches—sports and physical training
Management analyst
Employment interviewers
Respiratory therapists
Speech—language pathologists
Operations research analysts
Special education teachers
Occupational therapists
Human resource workers
Residential counselors
Physical therapists
Computer engineers
Systems engineers
(Source: *Occupational Outlook Quarterly*)

## The Losers: Job Categories with the Largest Projected *Decreases* in Employment, 1994–2005

Typists and word processors (Do they still make typewriters?)
Bookkeeping, accounting, auditing clerks
Bank tellers (Love that ATM card.)
Sewing machine operators and garment workers *(Hencho en Mexico.)*
Private household cleaners/servants (Not a big market for servants these days.)
Billing, posting, calculating machine operators
Duplicating, mail, and other office machine operators
Textile-machine operators
File clerks
Freight and stock movers
Farm workers
Central office telephone switchboard operators
Telephone installers and repairers
(Source: Bureau of Labor Statistics and *Nation's Business* magazine)

sue specific careers as a teacher, therapist, or medical assistant, but you will have more options by looking at the whole industry and asking yourself, "Is what I want to do related to healthcare or education?" For example, if you're interested in public relations, you might look at the trends and see that hospitals, clinics, and drug companies are going to need a way to promote and publicize their services and products. Just because the healthcare industry is hot doesn't mean you have to be a medical assistant or therapist.

Whether or not you are considering a specific job or industry, look at the big picture and how you fit into it. How do the industry and workplace trends compare with your personal needs, interests, education, experience, and values. Below are a few basic trends that indicate how, where, and why people are working today. Ask yourself how they might affect you.

## More People Are Looking for Work

A survey by executive recruiter Paul Ray Berntson and Cornell University found that 78 percent of executives revised their résumés last year and 64 percent went on an interview. This only reflects people who are currently hired. There are many people who never show up on unemployment roles because they are underemployed. These people, often recent graduates or people who have been laid off, are working in something they are overqualified for while they are looking for a better job.

## Where Are the Jobs? Not Where You Might Think

For years, people thought that success and security could be found as an employee for a major corporation. Bigger is better was the mantra. College graduates aspired to work for a Fortune 500 company and eventually become a manager. Beginning in 1989, the shape of corporate America started to change dramatically. Employees nationwide were getting the ax en masse. Although it was couched in much more friendly and politically correct terms such as "reengineering," "downsizing," or "right sizing," it still meant the same thing. "Thanks for the memories, now there's the door. Don't let it hit you in the butt on your way out."

It's estimated that between 3 to 5 million people have been laid off since 1989. The major contributors to these mass layoffs were often trusted household names that for years meant steady employment. Many of those laid off had been loyal employees for twenty years or longer. Many of these positions went unfilled. Layers of management were wiped away to form a more efficient company (in theory): One that produced better return for shareholders. Of the millions thrown into the workforce for the first time in years, the majority were middle managers, the once envied position that college graduates and rookie corporate ladder climbers aspired to. Today, no one in their right mind sets out to become a "manager."

A result of downsizing is a very different type of employer. No longer are the corporate Goliaths the nation's creators of jobs. People are looking elsewhere for work. Now the majority of hiring is done by small- to medium-sized companies with less than 500 employees. Downsizing and technology have also made it possible for small companies and even one-person shops to compete on the same level as much larger companies. Those who have been laid off are thinking entrepreneurially and starting businesses to serve larger companies who outsource the same services and projects once done by downsized employees.

## Graduate Hiring Is on the Rise . . . Finally

Just three years ago, the 1994 job market was called the worst since World War II. This topped off at least three years of record double-digit declines in college recruiting. Finally, things are beginning to look up for graduates, but don't break out the champagne yet. According to Michigan State

University's annual survey on graduate hiring, college recruitment will be up 6 percent in 1997—the third year in a row. But this doesn't mean that happy days are here again. Realize that campus recruiting is dramatically different than it was ten or even five years ago.

For starters, you're likely to see different companies coming to campus. The companies that were mainstays in the early nineties have backed off considerably and are now limiting their efforts to only a handful of carefully selected target schools. Sure, they might be hiring more students, but they are selecting those students from a much smaller pool of applicants, leaving students at schools that aren't on the choice recruiting list out in the cold.

The growth in college recruitment is coming from small- to medium-sized employers. However, many of these companies don't even go to campuses. They obtain résumés via the telephone or the Internet. Many career centers are finding ways to get their students in touch with these smaller employers. They often send résumés and refer candidates to employers.

Take advantage of all the career search tools available through your campus or alma mater. Too many graduates and alumni feel that the career center is useless, because the companies they want to work for don't recruit on campus. A lot of recruiting is going on behind the scenes. Don't miss out.

## No Shirt, No Shoes, No Service

The Bureau of Labor Statistics projects that by the turn of the century, 80 percent of salaried and wage jobs will be in the service sector. Some of these will be highly skilled service positions such as technical support and service or financial services. Others will be frontline service positions such as retail and food service.

For college students and young job seekers, this is considerably unsettling. Currently, almost 35 percent of Americans in their twenties are underemployed. College degrees are now the minimum requirement for many basic jobs. For the period from 1992 through 2005, it is expected that 18 million college graduates will enter the job market, yet only 14 million will obtain jobs that require college degrees.

## Outsourcing, Freelancing, and Temping

Don't get too comfortable with those office surroundings and regular paychecks. As companies are getting leaner and meaner, they're cutting costs by reducing overhead and permanent staff. Many duties that were once performed by full-time employees are now being done by contingent or contract workers who are brought in on a temporary basis to perform a certain task or project. By some estimates, these contingent workers make up 25 percent of the U.S. workforce.

This type of freelancing or temping was once only common in clerical positions, but now it occurs in all industries. It has produced workers who enjoy the flexibility, freedom, and opportunity for continuous learning. Many make more money when they work freelance, because skilled temps are often paid at a very high rate. It's just finding steady work or constant projects that's difficult. But it has also placed a greater burden on the employee who must now learn sales skills in order to constantly market herself to find the next position. Temps, freelancers, and independent contractors must also learn to deal with the insecurity and instability that comes from not knowing where or how long your next assignment might last, not to mention being responsible for their own taxes, health insurance, and retirement.

## You Inc.: The Rise of the Entrepreneur and Intrapreneur

More and more Americans are saying "enough" to working for someone else. They're discovering that while risky, the greatest job security comes not from a company, but themselves. This is why entrepreneurship is the fastest growing area of employment. Surveys claim that as many as 65 percent of Americans want to one day be their own boss. But it's not for everyone. Over 70 percent of new businesses fail each year, and many entrepreneurs take dramatic pay cuts to get their enterprises off of the ground. However, the freedom and autonomy that comes from running your own show is priceless to many people.

Many large employers are realizing that in order to keep employees who might have the entrepreneurial bug, they need to give them more freedom, autonomy, and ownership of projects. These people, known as intrapreneurs, have many of the benefits of being an entrepreneur without the risks. Companies who give employees this freedom are finding that intrapreneurs are more loyal, because they treat the business as if it were their own.

## You Have to Be Tech-Smart

Next time you go to a restaurant, take a look at how your waiter places your order. There is a good chance that he is entering your selection into a computer via a touch screen. Even waiting tables has gone high tech. Virtually every position in every industry will require that you be familiar with basic computer technologies. This includes the World Wide Web and e-mail. Being familiar with the Web will be even more critical in communicating and researching opportunities.

Over 90 percent of college students currently have access to the Internet and e-mail. Increasingly, technology will change how we communicate on the job. At Texas Instruments, over half of their daily communication is via e-mail. In addition, almost every college student is familiar (or should be) with word processing and spreadsheets. If you aren't, you are at a serious disadvantage.

Last year, 21 percent of Americans enrolled in some type of computer course. It is not just college students who are using technology. Who do you think is the fastest growing group of users on the Internet? The Gray Panthers. Yes, grandma, grandpa, and their friends over the age of sixty are the fastest growing group of users on the World Wide Web.

## Where You Work Has Changed

Formerly, success was measured not only by paycheck and title, but by the size, decor, and location of your office. Now, you are damn lucky if you have a cube with fabric walls that go to the ceiling. Companies are cutting overhead and reevaluating the size and effectiveness of their staff and work environments.

Many companies are adopting trendy work styles and environments—such as hoteling, flextime, job sharing, the virtual office, and telecommuting—in an effort to make employees happier and more productive. Of course, they're also trying to cut costs.

## The Virtual Office

Being tech-smart is not only necessary to find a job, it may be necessary to perform your job. Major companies like AT&T, American Express, and Compaq have put their staff in virtual offices from home or car. Over 50 percent of AT&T's staff in their Basking Ridge, New Jersey, headquarters (at least, those who are left after the downsizing) telecommute at least one day a week.

Many sales representatives and virtually (no pun intended) all drug and pharmaceutical sales reps work primarily out of their cars during the day and complete paperwork on a laptop from the road or at home in the evening.

## Just Think How Much You Will Save on Dry Cleaning: The Home Office and Telecommuting

The latest phenomenon to take place is working from home. The sixty-minute commute is out, and the ten-second commute down the hall is in. It used to be that if you were at home during the day, you were either sick, your kid was sick, or you were unemployed. Many major companies are now suggesting their employees work from home. This year, there are 24.3 million home-based businesses in the United States, according to Link Resources. Technology has made the home-based business and working from home credible.

A viable company can be run from a spare room with a phone, a fax, and a PC. One person from his bedroom or apartment can accomplish the tasks formerly done by large staffs and major companies.

These are just a few of the recent changes in the workplace that have had an impact on how we work. In some cases, the events and trends have even altered certain industries, but as you will see in the next chapter, they've also had an effect on how much money we make.

# 3

• • • • • • • • • • • • • • • • • • • • • • • • • • •

# How Much Do People Really Make?

"Show me the money."
—*JERRY MAGUIRE*

Unless you are independently wealthy or have a huge heart, most people go to work every day for the money, although your paycheck might feel like you are working for charity. Money is one of the taboo subjects in interviews. Everyone wants to know how much they will make, but you're never supposed to ask a recruiter about salary or even talk about money in an interview. It's considered bad taste, but I think the real reason is that if job seekers discovered the earning potential of certain fields, many would certainly change their career paths—putting recruiters out of a job.

## Explore the Possibilities

You might be pleasantly surprised or really let down when you learn what the starting salaries and income potentials are for certain industries. It might affect your career choice, but remember that there is much more to your career than a huge paycheck. The most important thing is to have a realistic idea of what the salary range and income potential are for the career you are looking at. Don't automatically think that because something is glamorous or high profile the people in that profession make a lot of money. By the same token, don't turn up your nose to some careers that may not traditionally be glamorous or even prestigious.

Don't scoff at certain professions or put others on a pedestal until you realize the earning power of the job. Advertising, while glamorous and exciting, was described by one rookie as "the best parent-subsidized job in the world." You may never have thought of a career in retail, let alone at a discounter such as Target or WalMart, but they both have excellent management-training programs that have produced young managers who are making over $60,000 while in their mid-twenties. How about some other interesting comparisons? An entry-level architect makes $24,000. The average librarian with less than two years of experience makes $32,000.

A senior reporter (ten years plus experience) at an average-sized newspaper may potentially earn between $50,000 and $65,000. A general manager at a Houston's Restaurant with less than five years of experience can potentially earn between $90,000 and $120,000.

## How Much Do People Really Make?

Probably a lot less than you think. I often speak to college students and rookie job seekers and ask them how much money they expect to earn five years after they graduate from school. The answer I receive the most is $100,000 or close to it. After I catch my breath from laughing so hard, I explain that less than 5 percent of Americans earn over $100,000 per year. That's about 5 million people. There are many people who will never earn $100,000 in their lifetimes. Going higher up the economic food chain, you find that—according to the latest figures from the IRS—979,626 people make over $200,000 and just over 65,000 people in America make over $1 million a year. (Of course, those are only people who *reported* to the IRS that they made over $1 million a year.)

Before you start deciding how to get your slice of the pie, realize that while some households might earn over $100,000, it often takes two salaries to do it. For an individual to consistently make $100,000 or more per year is tough. Don't let me discourage you, though. It can be done. But in some professions, the only way to make this much money is to have your own company or be one of the elite in your field.

## Who Earns Over $100,000?

Who do you think makes up the group that earns over $100,000 per year? What do they do for a living? Certainly, a large number of doctors and attorneys fall into this category, although there are a lot of attorneys who struggle to make $50,000 a year. But the profession that makes up the largest percentage of people earning over $100,000 a year is sales.

Sales? No way! You might be thinking that selling is cheesy. "I'm not selling insurance, cars, snake oil, or anything else." Sales often has a negative image to many new job seekers, but of the people consistently making six figures, over 70 percent of them are in some type of sales-related profession. They may sell financial services, industrial equipment, high-tech products, advertising, or a variety of other services.

So sales isn't your bag? What's another interesting career where you can potentially earn six figures? How about restaurant and food-service manager? Really! Not every restaurant manager or the guy managing the local Taco Bell is going to pull in six figures, but managers at restaurants such as Outback Steakhouse have incentive plans that can easily earn them over $100,000 a year. Even some fast-food organizations such as Domino's and Chick-fil-A have incentive plans that allow their managers to make more than some architects or accountants.

## So Who Really Makes the Most?

If your parents ever push you to become a doctor or a lawyer, you might listen to them. The average physician in private practice makes $218,000, while orthopedic surgeons lead the specialists with an average of $364,000. Not bad. The average partner in a law firm receives $168,000. Of course, corporate America can still pay off if you can make it to the top. CEOs of the 100 largest U.S. firms earned an average of $3.5 million in total compensation. Thank God for stock options. But the real money is still found on Wall Street, where two years ago the 161 partners of Goldman Sachs averaged $1.1 million.

The winners in the undergraduate salary lottery are chemical engineers for the second year in a row—a starting salary close to $43,000. Next are mechanical engineers, electrical engineers, industrial engineers, and computer science majors—all in the high thirties.

## Who Makes the Least?

For the second year in a row, the big losers in the salary game are journalism graduates. They take home the lowest starting salary of any college graduate, with a starting salary around $22,000, according to Michigan State University's *Annual Survey on Hiring*. According to the U.S. Census Bureau, a third of all full-time jobs pay less than $20,000. The current median wage for men with four years of high school is only $22,765. By the time an individual reaches fifty, he can expect to be making a whopping $28,084. If that is not motivation to stay in school, I don't know what is.

## What About Being Your Own Boss? Doesn't That Pay Well?

Do you think that starting your own company or being your own boss means you will make a lot of money? It can potentially. It is always better to get a bigger piece of the pie, but as we said growing up in West Texas, "One hundred percent of nothing is still nothing." Many entrepreneurs struggle in the beginning, and some don't even pay themselves a salary for the first year. Instead, they live off of savings or draw a subsistence salary far below what they were earning before they decided to start their business. When Brian, a former Andersen consultant, recently started a restaurant, his salary went from around $50,000 a year to $1,200 a month, which was just enough to pay his rent and basic expenses.

## Get Real

Before you embark on a career path or job search, get a realistic idea of what the salary ranges are. Nothing will make you appear more stupid than being unrealistic about your salary demands.

## Is There a Limit to How Much I Can Make?

Some industries are notorious for offering high starting salaries and rapid advances in the first couple of years, but plateau salaries after that. Engineers are a good example. Engineers are among the highest paid entry-level positions, but after several years, most engineers reach a ceiling where they might not be able to earn more than about $80,000. This is a good living, but does it ensure the lifestyle that you want to have? That is a personal choice you are going to have to make.

## Don't Let a Low Starting Salary Chase You Away

Some careers are often overlooked by entry-level job seekers or career changers because of

Sarah in West Virginia approached me after an event saying, "I am about to graduate with a public relations degree. I have internship experience and good grades. All of the jobs are offering $15,000, but I think I'm worth around $22,000. How do I get them to increase my salary?" The answer is: "You can't." In an entry-level position, you don't have much room to negotiate salary. The best thing to do is ask an employer what he has budgeted for this position and then take close to the higher end. You don't want to sell yourself short or cause your potential employer to have an aneurysm, screaming at you to "get a grip."

Shortly before graduating, I interviewed for a position with a sports marketer. It was a phone interview, and things were going very well until the gentleman asked what starting salary I was expecting. Being a little cocky—and knowing what amount I thought was a good salary—I casually said, "Oh, I think $35,000 would be a good place to start." I thought the man would jump through the phone and rip my tongue out. He said, "Really? Let me tell you something, kid. You are going to make $18,000 a year and you will like it." I had no idea what the salary range was for this job, and apparently I was more than a little off in my request. Be realistic before you mention a figure or discount a certain career.

Are you thinking about earning a Ph.D. and teaching on a college campus? The occupation with the highest rate of people holding second jobs is college professors, where 13.7 percent of all college professors moonlight.

In the United States, one in four women earn more than their husbands in dual income households. However, according to the International Labor Association, women are still paid less than men for comparable work in every country in the world.

the low starting salaries. The mistake in this is that they might only see the short term and not realize that some positions start low, but can escalate quickly and have unlimited potential.

This is why positions like sales and with start-up or fast-growing companies can be great opportunities for many candidates. There is certainly risk involved. A start-up company might not pay as much as a larger company, but you will gain exposure and responsibility that can lead to a big payday later in your career.

## What Motivates You?

Certainly, money is the main motivator for many people, but the older and more established you become, the more you will realize that everyone is motivated by different things. What are your motivations for choosing a career? Is it the money? How about challenge, respect, prestige, and security?

## Look at Everything

If you are early in your career or are a recent graduate, it can be easy to be seduced by a large paycheck—especially if you are swamped with loans and credit card debt or have lived in student poverty for the past few years.

While going for the highest salary may be the easy way out, there are many other things you should consider before making a career choice. How much time, freedom, and responsibility will you have? How much exposure to clients you will be given and where it can lead to is important. Remember, you will be working at least thirty years. The money you make right now doesn't matter as much as learning the ropes of your business so you can really have earning power later on.

# 4

. . . . . . . . . . . . . . . . . . . . . . . . . . .

# Moving On and Moving Up: Whether or Not to Relocate

One of the great things about a new career is that sometimes you have the opportunity to move to a new city. You might move because your job requires it or because you simply like a city and have always wanted to live there. Other times, you must go to where the jobs are. Whatever the reason, by choice or by force, at some point in your career you may have to move in order to move up in your career.

## Will I Have to Move?

In various professions, opportunities are concentrated in a certain parts of the country. For example, if you want to be in the entertainment industry, most opportunities are found in New York or Los Angeles. If you want to work in book publishing, but don't want to move to New York, you might want to choose another career. Don't worry, all opportunities don't mean you have to move to one of the coasts. In the past when people thought of the advertising industry, Madison Avenue in New York instantly came to mind. And while many of the largest agencies are still located in New York, although not on Madison Avenue, some of the hottest shops in the country are located in places such as Minneapolis, Chicago, and even Portland, Oregon, where Nike's agency, Weiden & Kennedy, is located.

Certainly, opportunities exist everywhere, but there are certain pockets where you can increase your odds. The San Francisco Bay area, Silicon Valley, and the Pacific Northwest are known for their computer, software, and high-

| Top Ten Metropolitan Cities in the United States to Live | Bottom Ten U.S. Cities in Which to Live |
|---|---|
| 1. Orange County, CA | 1. Yuma, AZ |
| 2. Seattle, WA | 2. Albany, GA |
| 3. Houston, TX | 3. Sumpter, SC |
| 4. Washington, DC | 4. Lawton, OK |
| 5. Phoenix, AZ | 5. Lima, OH |
| 6. Minneapolis-St. Paul, MN | 6. Jackson, MI |
| 7. Atlanta, GA | 7. Bridgeton, NJ |
| 8. Tampa-St. Petersburg, FL | 8. Dover, DE |
| 9. San Diego, CA | 9. Elmira, NY |
| 10. Philadelphia, PA | 10. Mansfield, OH |

(Source: *Places Rated Almanac*)

tech companies. Dallas is known as the Telecom Corridor. Boston's Route 128 is known for it's high-tech companies. Chicago and New York are both known as major financial and investment centers.

Sometimes you may just have to get real about your expectations or your desire to move or stay where you are. Not long ago, I received a letter from a woman in Austin, Texas, who wanted to work in the publishing industry. Her only hang-up was that she didn't want to move from Austin. I know that Austin has great weather and a low cost of living, but it is also not the center of the publishing universe. It is not even a rest stop on the way to the center of the publishing universe. The woman's choices were limited to working for the university press, moving, or choosing a different career.

Wanting to remain in a certain city or close to home is all right. It's just a matter of deciding what's important to you. Be realistic and find out if your profession requires you to go where the jobs are.

## What to Consider When Relocating

There are many things to consider before relocating for a job. The first thing you should do when contemplating a move is ask yourself the following questions:

"Is the job worth it?"

"If I no longer work for this company, would I still want to live there?"

"Do I know anyone?"

"What is the cost of living?"

"Are the taxes so steep that I will actually be taking a pay cut?"

"Is it a young town or am I going to be surrounded by every grandparent and blue-haired retiree west of the Mississippi?"

"What are the winters like?"

"What are the summers like?"

"Is it close to an airport? Is the airport easy to get in and out of or will I have to take a connecting puddle jumper everywhere?"

"Is it the type of place that is nice to visit, but you wouldn't want to live there?"

These may seem like basic questions, but they matter a great deal and can affect not only your bank account but your happiness. Don't base your decision to move to a new city and uproot your entire life on one weekend spent as a tourist or on a vacation experience you had during college.

## Your Bargaining Chip

In most entry-level positions, you have about as much negotiating leverage as a child negotiating his allowance: None. This is especially true for recent grads. Yet at almost every college I speak at, I am still asked, "How can I negotiate my salary?" The fact is that you probably can't. Most entry-level positions have budgeted salaries. There is a range, but not a lot of room to negotiate. Besides, if you don't want the job, there are probably ten other people working at Starbucks who would be happy to take it.

While you can't really negotiate salary, you can negotiate for assistance regarding your relocation and moving expenses. If you are moving to a city you are unfamiliar with, some companies will hire a service for you to show you the ropes, find an apartment, and make your move easier. Sometimes you can negotiate for extra time off to move or even for money to help you make the move and get established in a new city. It is not uncommon for some companies to pay for your move from another part of the country. Andrew accepted an advertising position with an agency in Minneapolis. The firm paid to move Andrew and all of his possessions, including his car, to Minnesota from Dallas. "They also gave me $1,000 dollars to handle deposits and hookups for my apartment." That is great, but the best part was that the firm also paid for Andrew to stay in a hotel for three weeks and gave him a per diem for meals until his apartment was ready.

Ask about relocation expenses, time off to move, and assistance with locating housing. This is especially helpful if you don't know the area and might mistakenly lease an apartment in the 'hood.

## How Do I Know If I Want to Move There?

First of all, try to talk with someone who currently lives there or has lived there within the past three years. It doesn't do

### Top Ten Native American Metropolitan Areas

1. Los Angeles-Anaheim-Riverside, CA
2. Tulsa, OK
3. New York, New Jersey, Connecticut Tri-State Area
4. Oklahoma City, OK
5. San Francisco-Oakland-San Jose, CA
6. Phoenix, AZ
7. Seattle-Tacoma, WA
8. Minneapolis-St. Paul, MN
9. Tucson, AZ
10. San Diego, CA

(Source: U.S. Census Bureau)

**Top Ten Hispanic
Metropolitan Areas**

1.  Los Angeles, CA
2.  New York, NY
3.  Miami, FL
4.  Chicago, IL
5.  Houston, TX
6.  Riverside-San Bernadino, CA
7.  San Antonio, TX
8.  Anaheim-Santa Ana, CA
9.  San Diego, CA
10. Dallas, TX

(Source: U.S. Census Bureau)

**Top Ten African American
Metropolitan Areas**

1.  New York, NY
2.  Chicago, IL
3.  Washington, DC
4.  Los Angeles, CA
5.  Detroit, MI
6.  Philadelphia, PA
7.  Atlanta, GA
8.  Baltimore, MD
9.  Houston, TX
10. New Orleans, LA

(Source: U.S. Census Bureau)

you any good to talk to an uncle who lived there in the seventies or someone who went to college there twenty years ago. Many cities have changed and are rapidly changing every year. Get the scoop from a native.

Next, get a copy of the *Places Rated Almanac*. It ranks cities as the best or worst places to live and gives descriptions and information you need to know about housing, activities, etc.

You should also contact the local Chamber of Commerce. Tell them you are considering moving there and ask them to send you a relocation packet. In it you should find information about the top companies, housing, and activities. This is also a great place to contact for information on local employers and the business climate. Some chambers have information about school systems, which can be helpful if you are interested in teaching. The major real estate agencies should offer a similar type of packet.

Another place to learn more about a particular area is the local business journal and Sunday paper. Local business publications generally come out weekly and cover businesses and entrepreneurs of all sizes and industries. They often go more in-depth and cover a wider variety of businesses than the local paper can. It's like a business section on steroids.

However, the best thing about local business journals and publications is the annual book of lists that most publish. The book of lists names the top employers and companies broken down by specific industry: the top 25 accounting firms, the top 25 advertising agencies, the top 25 hospitals. These books can be purchased directly from the publication for $15 to $25. They are great investments and save you hours of research.

To learn what the publication is called in your city or the city you're interested in, simply call the Chamber of Commerce and ask what the local business publication is called. You can also go online at www.amcity.com. This is the site of American City Business Publications, the largest publisher of these types of publications in the country. The site lists the publications and offers links to an online version. Check it out.

## What to Look for in the Local Paper

Traditionally, most job seekers rush out to get the local Sunday paper of the city to which they want to move. Great idea, except that the reason they are doing it is so they can check out the classified ads to see what jobs are available. Bad move. First of all, newspaper want ads are not the way to conduct an effective job search. Every Tom, Dick, and Jane who lives in that city is already scanning the paper for the same reason you are, which is funny, because over 70 percent of all available positions are not advertised in the newspaper. To make matters worse, it may be a couple of days before you get your hands on a paper from another city. Nothing is more useless than old news. By then, you are behind the other thousands of job seekers who have pinned their hopes on the want ads.

How can the want ads be helpful? By giving you an idea of what companies are in the area and how competitive the area is. The more want ads, the better the economy. People are hiring and need help. As Martha Stewart would say, "It's a good thing."

But your main goal from reading another city's newspaper is to get a feel for the community; the city; and its events, arts, sports, culture (or lack of it), and real estate and affordability of housing. By reading about the community, you can learn a lot about whether it is a place you would like to live. The only other way to get more information is to talk with someone who lives there and visit yourself.

## Don't Make a Snap Decision

Getting a job offer is exciting. You may want to answer right then. But if a move is involved, contain your excitement and take the time to think about what it involves. Talk to others and consult your family. Make sure you do your homework before jumping right in. There is nothing wrong with asking the company who made the offer if you can have a few days or a week to think about it. Most likely, you will get it. If they have an offer on the table, they won't take it back simply because you asked for time to think about such an important decision.

## Where on the Web

www.amcity.com—American City Business Publications

---

### Top Ten Asian Metropolitan Areas

1. Los Angeles, CA
2. New York, NY
3. Honolulu, HI
4. San Francisco, CA
5. Oakland, CA
6. San Jose, CA
7. Anaheim-Santa Ana, CA
8. Chicago, IL
9. Washington, DC
10. San Diego, CA

(Source: U.S. Census Bureau)

---

### *Fortune* Magazine's Best Cities for Business

1. Seattle, WA
2. Denver, CO
3. Philadelphia, PA
4. Minneapolis, MN
5. Raleigh-Durham, NC
6. St. Louis, MO
7. Cincinnati, OH
8. Washington, DC
9. Pittsburgh, PA
10. Dallas-Ft. Worth, TX
11. Atlanta, GA
12. Baltimore, MD
13. Boston, MA
14. Milwaukee, WI
15. Nashville, TN

# Part II

• • • • • • • • • • • • • • • • • • • • • • • • • • • • • •

# The JobSmarts Top Careers

# 5

• • • • • • • • • • • • • • • • • • • • • • • • • •

# Accounting

**Some Common Positions**
    CPA (certified public accountant)
    Public accountant (Big Six)
    Corporate accountant
    Analyst
    Comptroller
    Auditor

**Other Opportunities You Might Consider**
There are accounting positions with federal, state, and local government; non-profit and public agencies; hospitals; and companies of all sizes and industries. You will find accountants in banking or financial services, insurance, purchasing, and even the FBI. (They hire accountants to solve white-collar crimes. How do you think they catch embezzlers and tax cheats?).

No longer are accountants merely bookkeepers or bean counters. Accountants are now considered valuable consultants whose guidance can help determine the success of a company. An accountant is not to be confused with a bookkeeper. In fact, you can buy a software program like QuickBooks to handle bookkeeping. Accountants work with corporations, private individuals, and government organizations. They do a variety of tasks, such as performing audits and analyzing, preparing, and verifying financial data. An accountant will help you manage your money, finances, and taxes, and can give valuable business advice.

There are several different fields of accounting, the major areas being public, management, audit, and tax. Public accounting is the largest area and includes accountants who work for themselves or for a firm like one of the Big Six. (The six largest public accounting firms are often called the Big Six.)

Management accountants work in-house for a corporation or private group and monitor that company's financial information. Others choose to work for the government or an agency. These accountants may analyze the costs and budgeting of a company or organization and propose ways to make it more efficient.

Auditing is an examination and reporting of a corporation's, individual's, or organization's financial records, procedures, and assets. It can also mean examining and accounting for inventory and assets and it serves as a check and balance.

Tax accountants advise individuals and companies on the most advantageous tax strategies. They also help clients adhere to government regulations and restrictions, in addition to developing accounting structures and systems.

## Where Will I Start?

For most undergraduates, the most common starting position is that of staff accountant. This is also called an associate or analyst by most public accounting firms. Of the many disciplines of accounting, public accounting is by far the most popular for entry level candidates. According to the annual NACE (National Association of Colleges & Employers) survey, public accounting firms extended more offers to college grads than any other type of employer.

Most new recruits go through a brief training program which lasts between one and six weeks. These programs teach you the proper documentation and format that the firm uses. Most firms have a standard way of doing things. After this crash course, you will be assigned to a project with a real client.

Don't worry, you won't be sent out alone. You will work on a team that is supervised by a senior member, manager, or even a partner. Once you get up to speed and more comfortable, you will be given more autonomy, but the hand holding is there if you need it.

You will work on a variety of projects with clients in different fields. However some teams and groups specialize in certain types of business or market sectors. The large firms actually have groups devoted to special industries such as health care, technology, or manufacturing. Many people have an idea of what industry sector they want to be in, while others like to try out several before leaning toward a certain field.

## What Will I Do?

I hope you like Excel or Lotus, because during your first year you will be doing a lot of number crunching and analyzing figures. You will also help perform audits. Jessie at Price Waterhouse says, "I felt like a Lotus Jockey during my first year on the job." As a staff accountant performing an audit, you will take a client's financial statements and prove that they've documented reasonable numbers. You do this by comparing them to last year's report and analyzing developments in the client's business for that year. You will look at invoices, expenses, cash, assets, property, and equipment, vouching that they've been reported accurately and the numbers jive.

You will begin by auditing a lower-risk area or the least critical and complex accounts. For instance, you may start out auditing cash and receivables while someone else audits inventory. As you master one area, you move on to accounts of more importance.

Ross, a rookie at KPMG Peat Marwick, says, "Travel is the most difficult part of the job. You generally have to go to a client's location when you are on a project. Projects can last up to six weeks, and sometimes longer."

In addition to learning the documentation and procedures for the firm, you will prepare to take the CPA (Certified Public Accountant) exam. (See the box on the CPA exam.)

## What Is It Like?

At certain times of the year, your life can be crazy as you try to meet deadlines. You can pretty much kiss the early part of April good-bye, along with the time around any other major tax reporting deadline, such as the end of a quarter. Accounting involves extreme detail work most often done in a very structured environment. In many cases, there are significant legal ramifications to your work, so there is added pressure.

There is a huge turnover rate, with most new hires lasting a couple of years before burning out or deciding they don't want to make a career out of the firm. These people generally pursue something in their specialty area or start their own business.

Reputedly, the Big Six firms have a mentality of "We will work you like a dog for two years and then you will leave." But according to Laura, recruiting coordinator at Deloitte & Touche, that is changing. "Deloitte & Touche has led the charge in initiating the 'worklife balance' programs that are now common at most firms. Accounting has become more family friendly with flexible work arrangements, and, as a result, there is less turnover of women executives at the senior level. Public accounting has definitely changed and is less of a good-old-boy network than it used to be."

While firms talk about balance, you still hear road warrior stories from accountants who are gone for weeks on an audit. The recruiters say that the amount of travel depends on the firm's specific needs, your abilities, and your desire to travel. According to one recruiter, "On your first day, you meet the assignment director who asks if you want to travel and how much, and she tries to accommodate your needs. Since Big Six firms are located all over the country, there is not as much far-flung travel as you would think. We typically handle clients in town or within the region." However, many rookie accountants say that being away from friends and family for weeks at a time while on an audit can be a hard lifestyle.

The upside to the travel and the job in general is that you will have exposure to a variety of people and businesses. This variety is not only interesting, but it will give you insight and access to other projects within the firm, as well as exposure to other companies and industries. Perhaps most importantly, you will develop a great understanding of business.

## How Much Will I Make?

Entry-level accountants are some of the highest paid graduates. The starting salary will vary according to where you live and the size of the firm, but undergraduates going into accounting can expect to make from $28,000 to $32,000 the first year. Additionally, new recruits sometimes receive a signing bonus that can be anywhere from $1,000 to $5,000.

Because of the long hours and time away from home which are often required, some firms have overtime pay, after you reach a certain number of hours worked. Sometimes you have the choice to collect this overtime in the form of cash or in vacation time. Because you are expected to be away from home so often, some firms pick up the tab for you to return home on the weekends. In addition to your salary and overtime pay, it is standard to receive insurance, retirement packages, and expense accounts at most firms.

Experienced accountants have a median salary of $76,000. As a partner of a Big Six or with a successful solo practice, it is quite possible to make six figures, but only with years of experience.

## What Is the Career Path?

At most big Six Firms, it is customary for rookies to remain staff accountants for two years or two busy accounting periods  The next step would be to become a Senior Accountant, a position that you will be in for about three or four years until you get your next promotion. Somewhere between two to four years on the job, most people decide whether they want to pursue the partner track or if they want to leave the firm for other opportunities. Because of the exposure and contacts many accountants make within a certain industry, they often go to work for a former client in private industry or they become entrepreneurs. Since many of the Big Six firms have a reputation for providing an excellent training ground, there is a mass exodus of associates after they have spent two years on the job. They leave to pursue opportunities with clients or in their industry sector, or they start their own firms.

You don't have to practice as a CPA or work for a Big Six firm. Experience in accounting is regarded as solid business training, and once you've put in two or three years with a Big Six firm, you are highly marketable and can go into a variety of industries. In fact, many CEOs have an accounting or finance background.

**Career Path at a Big Six Firm**

Staff Accountant
Senior Accountant
Manager
Senior Manager
Partner

## How Secure Is It?

It depends on the type of accounting you choose. With a Big Six firm, it can be pretty stable, as the majority of turnovers is voluntary. It is not unlike a law firm in that you know early on whether or not you are on partner track or if you even want to be on partner track. Many see the writing on the wall that their career might flourish somewhere else. Others go the partner track and are quite secure in their positions.

For a self-employed CPA, like any other entrepreneur, success and stability depend upon your ability to generate new business and keep existing clients. While there are accountants who just get by, if you are a good accountant and a decent marketer, you will not only eat on a regular basis, but eat quite well.

## What Skills Do I Need?

It starts with a degree in accounting along with a strong business, math and computer background. At firms like Deloitte & Touche, candidates are expected to already know Microsoft Office. Since their auditing is done online, you must learn proprietary auditing software when hired.

For a long time, accountants were put in the same category as engineers—people who were very technically competent, but lacking in people skills. This is no longer true. Accountants must have excellent written and verbal skills; you will be dealing with people from line workers to managers to CEOs and must be able to communicate with people whose backgrounds are very different than yours.

Accounting is team oriented, and the teams and groups can change with each assignment. Being good with numbers is not enough. Your communication and interpersonal skills must be exceptional, since you must communicate your findings and advice to your client. You will also constantly be acquiring and developing new clients. Therefore, successful accountants must have a little "marketer" in them, especially if they want to go out on their own.

Teamwork is typically balanced with an equal amount of autonomy, so you should be able to deal with limited supervision. Even though you might work in teams, you will often be responsible for your own tasks. Almost as important as your technical ability and skills is your integrity. As an accountant, you are privileged to very sensitive information. People put a great deal of trust in their accountants. One rookie says, "People hear horror stories about accountants who stole their client's money and are now at the Rio Hilton drinking Mai Tais while the client is spending ten years in the pokey on tax evasion. People are nervous when it comes to their money."

You must develop a solid business acumen and an understanding of the client's business. This means services, operations, customers, suppliers, and competitors. Jaime, a Price Waterhouse rookie, says that quickly acquiring that knowledge is one of the most difficult parts of the job, "The client is paying us to offer expertise, and I don't always have it, because I'm young."

## CPA Certification (Certified Public Accountant)

The CPA exam is a four-part test given by the AICPA (American Institute of Certified Public Accountants). This is the most common certification, and it is a very high professional distinction. The test has a reputation for being as tough and respected as the bar exam for attorneys. Only 25 percent of those who take it pass each part they attempt, so it is not unusual for people to fail the test their first and even second time. Fortunately, you don't have to pass all four parts at once.

It is offered only twice a year (May and November), and it is administered nationwide. In addition, each state has its own requirements for education and experience, and these requirements can vary wildly. Six states and Puerto Rico allow you to become a CPA with no employment time if you have a master's degree. Others will count time with a company or government agency toward your experience requirement. Some states will only accept time worked for a public accounting firm.

Many states are now requiring candidates to have a degree that includes at least 150 hours. This means that an undergraduate accounting degree is now a five-year plan at many schools.

The CPA application deadline is generally three months before the test date. For more information about applying in your state, write or call the state board of public accountancy. Go to www.aicpa.com for a complete list of phone numbers for your state's board.

## How Do I Get Hired?

In Big Six firms, almost 90 percent of entry-level hires are obtained through on-campus recruiting. Getting in is very difficult, because the competition is tough, the grade requirements are high, and firms don't go to every campus.

Landing a position at a Big Six is only getting harder as more firms develop aggressive internship programs. At Deloitte & Touche, internships take place during the spring semester of your fourth year of a five-year program. However, the interviews take place at the end of the third year. The internship is a nine-week program where you get real experience and are treated and paid like a regular staff accountant. It is used as a test drive for the firm, allowing them to extend offers to the effective interns and weed out certain candidates. This process has become very much like internships in law school. "We expect to make offers to our interns unless something goes really wrong," says Laura, the Deloitte & Touche recruiter.

Sometimes a firm may want to hire you, but there just isn't a position at that time. One Big Six firm will try to help quality candidates by recommending them to clients who ask for referrals.

If the firm you want to work for does not come to your school, talk to your accounting professor. Many accounting professors have contacts at the firms and may offer an introduction. Otherwise, send your résumé. You can obtain the addresses and contact names easily from the firm's Web site. Most hiring is done on a regional or local basis, so if you want to work in Atlanta, don't contact the New York headquarters.

## What Will Set Me Apart?

Your grades are important, but it is your extracurricular activities that will set you apart from the other candidates. Your experience carries a lot of weight in the recruiting process. An internship or part-time job helping out a small company can make the difference in getting a job.

## Do I Need an MBA or Extra Education?

You don't need an MBA to become a staff accountant, but a degree in accounting from an accredited school is critical. In addition, once you have passed the CPA exam, most states require that you take continuing education classes or professional development seminars to maintain your certification.

David worked in public accounting with a Big Six firm for five years. He then went to work for a commercial real estate company as tax director and finally hung his own shingle. He currently has his own successful CPA practice.

*What are the main differences between the three positions you have held?*

The main difference between public accounting and private industry is that there is less pressure in industry. In public accounting, you are the service provider, while in industry, you are often the customer.

In public accounting, there is day-to-day pressure: You are always performing and trying to please many people. Someone is always watching you, and you will generally have more than one boss. Even if you have one direct supervisor, several people will determine if you move up or not. If you are asked to do something, it's tough to say no, even if it's a volunteer activity.

In a private company, you don't have as much pressure to do things for so many different people. You have one department and one boss.

Working for yourself puts you back on the firing line every day, but the difference is that you get to keep what you earn. If you work hard, you are reaping the benefits rather than a partner or the home office in New York. So the obvious cost of independence is that you can't really slow down. There is always new business to court and old business to service.

Regardless of what you want to pursue, working for a Big Six firm for at least a couple of years is the best way to learn all aspects of business. The experience you get is equivalent to an MBA.

## What Do You Wish Someone Had Told You?

Many rookies said it was hard making the transition to the working world, particularly to the fairly formal accounting-firm environment. If you have been staying out late every night, sleeping until ten, and wearing what you want, it can be a tough transition to be in a professional environment where you have to be in hose and heels or a suit and tie for ten or eleven hours a day.

Another change that many new hires struggled with was not being the best at something. Many Big Six recruits are used to being at the top of their class and succeeding at most challenges. They found school easy or comfortable. As one new employee put it, "I used to always know what was going on. Now I'm in a situation where I'm often confused, feel I don't entirely grasp a situation, and am asking what seem like stupid questions. They aren't really stupid, they're just a natural part of the learning curve. Nonetheless, it is frustrating, because they are paying me and I don't know what I'm doing." That feeling will quickly fade, says Laura of Deloitte & Touche, "The learning curve is incredibly fast, much faster than private industry."

Another misconception is that people think accounting is rigid and stuffy. In reality, while it's still quite structured, it has relaxed considerably.

New recruits say the camaraderie is a plus. "There are many people your age nearby who share your confusion, frustrations, and anxiety," says Jeremy of Arthur Andersen.

The biggest plus to the job, even if you decide public accounting is not for you, is that you will have gained experience in government, real estate, oil and gas, utilities, etc. You will be highly marketable.

## What the Pros Read

Most read the popular business magazines such as *Fortune, Forbes,* and *Business Week,* as well as any industry magazines that might be important to their client's business. Accountants constantly read updates from the associations on developing laws and tax codes. "The most important thing," says Darren of Arthur Andersen, "is to be informed about your client's business."

## You Should Also Check Out

*What Corporate America Wants in Entry-Level Accountants,* by Gary Slagel and James Sorenson. Published by the Institute of Management Accountants and the Financial Executives Institute. Phone: 800-638-4427

*Room Zoom: The CPA Source Disc*
Contact:
    AICPA
    Harborside Financial Center
    201 Plaza 3
    Jersey City, NJ 07311
    800-862-4272
(Offers information on career opportunities and CPA education.)

## Where Can I Learn More?

National Association of State Boards of Accountancy
380 Lexington Avenue, Suite 200
New York, NY 10168-0222

American Institute of Certified Public Accountants
1211 Avenue of the Americas
New York, NY 10036
800-862-4272

Institute of Management Accountants
10 Paragon Drive
Montvale, NJ 07645

### Did You Know?
Nearly one-third of accountants work for public accounting, auditing, or bookkeeping firms or are self-employed. More than two-thirds of accountants work in corporate America.

Once you have mastered the fundamentals, you can take that experience to different industries. For instance, Howard was comptroller of Fitz & Floyd, a maker of decorative ceramic figures, before leaving at age thirty to join a national paging and cellular company.

National Society of Public Accountants and the Accreditation Council for
　　Accountancy and Taxation
1010 N. Fairfax Street
Alexandria, VA 22314

## Where on the Web?

www.rutgers.edu/accounting/raw

　　Don't worry, it's not a porno site. It stands for Rutgers Accounting Web, and it's the most comprehensive resource available for anyone interested in all types of accounting. Rookies and professionals alike will benefit from this listing of all the worldwide accounting offices from the Big Six to the largest professional firms in the United States and abroad. It has contacts for all the major associations and trade journals, as well as links to specific university accounting departments.

www.aicpa.org—American Institute of CPAs

## Big Six Firms on the Web

www.ey.com—Ernst & Young
www.dttus.com—Deloitte & Touche
www.arthurandersen.com—Arthur Andersen
www.pw.com—Price Waterhouse
www.colybrand.com—Coopers & Lybrand
www.us.kpmg.com—KPMG Peat Marwick

# 6

• • • • • • • • • • • • • • • • • • • • • • • • • • • • • •

# Administration

**Some Common Positions**
>   Administrative assistant
>   Executive assistant
>   Receptionist
>   Secretary
>   Coordinator
>   Customer service representative/manager
>   Office manager
>   Personal assistant
>   Temp

**Other Opportunities You Might Consider**
There are highly specialized secretary and administrative positions in law firms and medical facilities. You should also read the "Temporary and Contract Careers" chapter of this book for ideas on how you can use an administrative position to get in the door.

If you think that administrative and customer service positions simply mean answering the phone, getting coffee, or telling a customer on the phone that she gets a set of Ginsu knives with her order, you need to wake up. Administration has become a highly specialized and quickly growing employment opportunity for people of all backgrounds.

With downsizing causing companies to run mean and lean, everyone is doing more with less. This means that administrative staff has taken on a greater role in the success of an operation. Ten years ago, administrative and customer service positions were viewed as entry-level clerical jobs with a very limited future—and rightly so.

Today, administrative assistants and customer service representatives can be found in virtually every company, regardless of size or industry. It's not just grunt work. Many have expanded responsibilities to include computer and financial skills as well as hiring and managing people.

# What Type of Jobs Are There?

Administrative positions fall into two categories: front office and support staff. Front-office jobs are on the frontline. You are the first person with whom others come in contact when they call or visit your company. This may be the receptionist or the person who answers the phone. In addition to helping to establish the impression a client has of your company and your boss, you will do administrative activities.

Support staff is the oil that keeps business running smoothly. You or your staff may support an entire department, a particular executive, or group of executives. You may be called on to do a variety of activities, depending on your company.

# What Is Customer Service?

Customer service and customer support are sometimes broken into two different categories, although the difference is not great. As a customer service rep, you may provide information to prospective clients and support existing customers. You might handle a complaint, answer a routine question, or even troubleshoot. An added element to customer service is that, in some cases, you will be called on to perform a light sales function and even place orders. (This does not mean that you will be one of those awful phone solicitors—the worst job on the planet. I did it for a few months in college.)

Customer support (often called tech support in the high-tech industry) performs largely the same tasks, except there is less of a sales element. You may provide ongoing support for problems, concerns, or needs a customer may have regarding your company's product or service. In some specialized companies, customer support is often staffed by people with special knowledge.

# What Will I Do?

Your title and duties will be determined by your seniority and the person for whom you work. As an administrative assistant or secretary, you will perform basic office duties such as faxing, filing, answering the phones, and screening calls. But as you are given more responsibility, you are likely to make travel arrangements, schedule appointments, and perform any number of computer-related activities from word processing to spreadsheets, database management, and bookkeeping.

In small companies, it is not uncommon for an assistant or secretary to double as office manager, handling payroll or paying bills. Many executive secretaries and assistants stay with an employer for years, and even change companies to work for an executive if she is promoted or leaves.

## What Will I Be Called?

There are a number of fairly useless titles that all mean the same thing: secretary, assistant, administrator, administrative assistant, and support staff. Sometimes companies will attach a fancy title to make you feel more special, like customer service "specialist" or "special assistant" to the assistant (a real title). Don't get hung up on what you're called. Gauge your work by your pay, responsibility, and how respected you are around the office.

## Isn't This a Low-Level Job That Gets No Respect?

In some cases, this is true. It depends on the company and how useful you make yourself. There are many admins and executive secretaries who are some of the most powerful people in the office. They either keep things going when everyone else is out of control or they are excellent gatekeepers and have the boss's ear. In many companies you find executives sucking up to the secretary, because they realize that he or she may have influence with the boss. They determine what he or she sees or doesn't see.

## What Makes Me Stand Out?

In sports, it is said that a referee or an official is doing a great job if he goes unnoticed. This means that if everything is working smoothly, you don't even realize that the referee is there. The same can be said for administrative staff. "It is your job to make things run as smoothly as possible for your boss or your department," says Beth, an administrative assistant at EDS (Electronic Data Systems). Lisa, who has worked for the chairman of a major hospitality company and is now executive assistant for a Fortune 500 CEO, says, "It is my job to anticipate my boss's needs and shield him from surprises."

Any additional training in customer service, communication, and computer or technical skills will be beneficial. If your company will pay for training, take advantage of it.

Kim, a marketing assistant for a software company, says, "Be willing to help make your boss stand out. If you don't know how to do something, find out." Become a resource for your boss, customer, or department. The key is to make yourself a valued asset and take initiative. Don't just wait for someone to give you a task. Look for ways to make the office more efficient.

## What About Bosses Who Make You Do Their Personal Errands?

So you think because you have a college degree you don't have to pick up laundry or lunch? Well, you shouldn't have to, but there are weird, demanding people everywhere. You may run across someone who derives some sick pleasure from telling you what to do and making you run personal errands. You may find yourself doing things that seem to be well beneath you or can't be found in your job description. I interviewed an assistant to Robert Redford, and he said, "I have to keep reminding myself that I have a college degree as I'm at the shop waiting on his car to be repaired." But at times, helping your boss's or manager's personal life run more smoothly may fall into the line of duty. However, this does not mean that you have to put up with disrespect. It is very important that you and your boss or staff outline early on what is beyond the call of duty.

The bottom line is that it all comes down to dealing with another human being, and yes, there are some jerks out there. I'm a big believer in what I call the "10 percent jerk factor." This basically means that 10 percent of the people you meet in life will be jerks for no reason whatsoever. It is no reflection on you or your abilities, and no matter how much you try, you won't change them. You can only hope it is a temporary thing that may be affected by the tides or some type of virus. Otherwise, change jobs or collect take-out menus.

## What Skills and Training Do I Need?

Having a four-year-degree is essential for advancement and salary increases after you reach a certain level. Employers want someone with a professional demeanor, technical training, and excellent communication skills. Actually, these skills are all necessary for business. Probably the most important skill any admin or assistant needs is to be well-organized. Remember, your job is to make things run more smoothly.

Professional appearance and communication skills are equally as important. In many companies, you are the first person with whom a customer or outsider comes in contact. Your appearance, attitude, and professionalism say a lot about your boss and the company. Have

Lisa, who works for a Fortune 500 CEO, said one of the most exciting parts of the job is that "I never know who will be on the other end of the phone. It is pretty interesting when a famous executive or politician calls my boss. I have to be prepared for anything." Lisa also says that since she is often privileged to certain conversations, "confidentiality is key."

you ever called a company and the person answering the phone was inept? What did you think of that company or of that person's boss?

## How Do I Get Hired?

Connections are a great way to get your foot in the door. Talk with friends and contacts who seem to enjoy their jobs. Sometimes, jobs are filled before they are even advertised. While I am not a big fan of classified advertising, this is one area where decent positions can actually be found through the newspaper want-ads.

Another smart way to obtain an administrative position and check out your future employer before you commit is to go through a temporary agency. There are temp firms that specialize in high-level administrative help. Office Team, Kelly, and Manpower are a few.

Once you apply and are asked to interview, be prepared to take a skills test. Some companies may even have you role-play a particular scenario. Employers want to see how you might handle a certain situation or how proficient you are at certain software. Anyone can claim they have special skills. Being able to perform is a completely different matter.

Kelly, the office manager for a software company, was hiring a receptionist who was also to perform some data entry and word processing. An employee said that Kelly should talk to a friend of his. Kelly met with her and liked her. Shortly after she began, it was apparent that she had exaggerated her computer experience. Every thirty minutes, she would buzz one of the programmers and ask them to show her how to use the mouse or open a file. She lasted a week. Both Kelly and the employee who recommended the person felt stupid.

## What's the Career Path?

These careers have more opportunity and potential for growth than in the past, especially in customer service. Rather than being a low-level staffer, many of these positions offer management opportunities.

While many still view these as entry-level or temporary positions until they get on their feet or find the job they want, some people are choosing to make administration a career. If you still think these are low-level positions, consider that at Microsoft more than a third of their employees are in customer service. At IBM, a similar portion of employees are devoted to customer support and service.

Many admins, secretaries, and assistants become so valued by their bosses that as their boss's career takes off, so does theirs. Many executives take their assistants with them as they are promoted.

It's still possible for administrative and support staff to use this as a way to move to other departments and get their feet wet. Ashley was a customer support rep at an information services company. After about a year of learning the product backward and forward, she saw that the sales reps were making a lot of money. Ashley was supporting their customers. So she approached the sales manager and let him know that she wanted to become a sales rep. At first, she was not taken seriously. She demonstrated her serious interest by being persistent, and after the third time talking with the sales manager, he gave her a chance in a smaller market. After two years, she became a regional sales manager.

Tim tells how he started as an administrative assistant/receptionist at an advertising agency just to get his foot in the door. Hopefully, he would move up to become an account executive. "The problem with this was that I would talk with account executives and tell them my long-term goal, and the account executives would look at me after I had been answering phones all day and say, 'What the hell do you know about advertising.' I was viewed as a staffer and could not break that stereotype."

## This May Just Be a Stepping Stone for You

Many people start out as an administrative assistant or secretary just to get their foot in the door and begin to learn the system. If your goal is to use this as a stepping stone into another department, you should try to avoid being pigeonholed. At some organizations, you are thought of as an assistant or support rep and nothing more.

## How Much Can I Make?

The salary is all over the map. You can make as little as minimum wage to upwards of $50,000 with full benefits as an experienced executive secretary. A study by the National Association of Executive Secretaries found the average weekly salary for all types of administrative staff to be $567 (approximately $29,500 annually).

Customer service and support reps are paid according to their level of expertise and experience. Customer service reps can make anywhere from minimum wage to $20 an hour. Managers for a major company or large call center can make up to $50,000 or more. Insurance, 401k, and other benefits depend upon the employer.

## What's the Toughest Thing About It?

Kristen says, "The pressure can be intense when the boss is under pressure, in a foul mood, or is trying to meet a deadline." Others say that dealing with bosses who are poor communicators or "control freaks" is hard. Melanie, support staff for a sales department, says the toughest thing is "trying to satisfy multiple people, all of whom feel their demands are the most important and should be your priority."

Kevin, a customer service rep for American Airlines, says, "It is no fun getting bitched at when you are not the cause of the problem." Troy, a tech support rep at Semantech, says, "It's difficult when you are talking with someone on the phone and they're having a hard time explaining something to you, or they don't give you all of the information you need to help them properly."

## What Do You Like the Most?

"Getting praised for a job well done and knowing that I keep things running," says Lisa. "Knowing that I am able to help someone with a problem," says Kevin in customer service.

Barbara, an executive assistant for a restaurant company, says people are wrong to think of administrative positions as "unglamorous grunt work that doesn't get any respect. What I do is critical to the company's success."

### Did You Know?

In many industries, the entry-level position, regardless of background, is assistant. Publishing, media, and entertainment are notorious for requiring people to "pay their dues" on the front lines by handling basic administrative duties. Once you have demonstrated that you are either responsible, trustworthy, or extremely creative (you can get results where others can't), you have proven yourself and are given more responsibility. Remember, even entertainment giants David Geffen and Mike Ovitz are rumored to have started out this way.

## Where Can I Learn More?

National Association of Secretarial Services
3637 Fourth Street N. #330
St. Petersburg, FL 33704-1336
813-823-3646

National Association of Executive Secretaries
900 S. Washington St.
Suite G-13
Falls Church, VA 22046
703-237-8616

National Association of Legal Secretaries
2250 E. 73rd Street #550
Tulsa, OK 74136
918-493-3540

Professional Secretaries International
10502 NW Ambassador Drive
P.O. Box 20404
Kansas City, MO 64195
816-891-6600

Office Team
Corporate Headquarters
2884 Sand Hill Road
Menlo Park, CA 94025
415-854-9700
(Ask for the branch in your area.)

You might also contact various temporary agencies. A list can be found in the "Temporary and Contract Careers" chapter of this book.

## Where on the Web?

www.nass.com—National Association of Secretarial Services
www.officeteam.com—OfficeTeam (administrative help)
www.ascs.org—American Society of Corporate Secretaries
www.nals.org—National Association of Legal Secretaries

# 7

• • • • • • • • • • • • • • • • • • • • • • • • • • • • • • • • • • •

# Advertising

**Some Common Positions**
    Account executive
    Account coordinator
    Media planner
    Art director
    Copywriter
    Art director
    Creative director
    Film editor
    Traffic coordinator

**Other Opportunities You Might Consider**
Working in-house for a company, nonprofit, or association. Other related fields include public relations, event planning and promotions, radio and television, direct mail, marketing, film, publishing, sales, illustration, and graphic design and photography.
    This section focuses primarily on the account side. You might check out the "Graphic and Commercial Arts" chapter to learn more about creatives, freelancing, and portfolios.

Many people, after seeing a great commercial like the milk ads, the Budweiser frogs, or any Levi's or Nike ad, think, "I can do that," or "What a great job." It is a great job, but it's also one of the most highly competitive and complex fields, entailing much more than creating commercials. Advertising offers many opportunities, including working for an agency, in-house for a client, or as a freelancer.

## What's an Agency Like?

There are three areas or departments that make up an agency: creative, account, and media. Each area is different in their responsibilities, but they are all related and play a huge part in making an advertising campaign work. The creatives are the copywriters, artists, and filmmakers

Sometimes you might enter as an assistant account executive or junior copywriter or creative, but this is much more common at a small agency.

One major agency requires a written commitment that you'll remain in traffic for two years. You must sign an agreement that states you will not consider moving to another agency during that period. While this sounds like indentured servitude, it's to prevent people from getting experience at the firm's expense and then moving to a higher paying job elsewhere, as is common in advertising.

The responsibilities of a traffic coordinator vary from agency to agency. Some people start out in traffic at a major agency with a good reputation and then move to a smaller agency where they can quickly reach a higher position because of their experience. This can also work in reverse if you want to move from a small to a large agency. Account executives (AE) at small firms will start as an assistant AE or even an account coordinator in a larger firm until they learn the ropes. However, because of their experience, it doesn't take them long to move up.

who actually come up with many of the ideas and create the finished product. The account side deals directly with the client or account and is thought of as the business side of the house. The media department is in charge of buying broadcast time or print space in addition to determining when and where to run an ad.

## Where Do I Start?

In most agencies, you'll likely start out as a traffic or account coordinator. Although responsibilities vary from agency to agency, this is an elaborate title for grunt. As one Leo Burnett account executive says, "The only thing below traffic is an intern." Traffic positions can be found on both the account and creative sides. You will do anything that needs to be done: run errands, get broadcast materials out to stations, and make sure artwork gets to the proper people. It's the ultimate grunt job, but it can give you a solid background necessary to succeed in advertising. Some agencies feel strongly about the type of background you get from traffic, and often require people to stay in these positions for as long as two years before they can be promoted.

## What's an Account Executive?

Like the hub of a wheel, account executives must be able to get along with each of the different spokes (departments) to get the best possible product while not upsetting the client or the creative team. You're the point person for the client. It's your job to convey the client's needs to the creative and communicate the creative's vision back to the client. Much of what you'll do is make sure that things run smoothly. To be successful in advertising, you have to adapt to other people's businesses.

Account executives say they must be second-best in everything. They must know the client's business almost as well as he does. Matt at Grey Advertising says, "I must be second-best in copywriting, research, media, and financial. Account executives and supervisors are the people answering the client's questions regarding media, creative, financial, and budgeting. You must be able to answer those questions, but you must also be smart enough to defer to the experts when it really comes down to it. Your expertise is in coordinating these efforts and departments. You're responsible for pulling together materials and managing the process. You'll make sure the creatives are getting their work done and that the production department is getting materials finished on time and on budget."

Account executives set themselves up to be the heroes or the goats. When things go well, you appear to be the winner, because you're right there with the client. By the same token, when something goes wrong, you're the first one at whom the client yells.

## How Much Can I Make?

Depending on what you do and the agency you are with, you will either make a whole lot or not much at all. In an agency, creatives tend to make the most money, followed by people on the account side, and finally media. A few major agencies reportedly pay their entry level creatives and account staff in the low to mid-twenties. Media planners and buyers make less, generally in the high teens. Overall, however, advertising is a low-paying profession in the beginning. Once you have experience, you can advance rapidly. Top creatives and account executives at major agencies can make close to six figures within five years, yet some people in advertising work other jobs on the weekend so that they can afford to live in New York.

Starting salaries, especially in New York, are notoriously low. Many rookies in advertising say they can't live in New York on what they make, so they get help from their parents.

The way most people increase their salary is to change jobs and hop from agency to agency. Advertising is a very connected industry where your relationships and networking ability play a huge role in your success and advancement.

## What's the Career Path?

Since you will likely start out as a junior or assistant something or other, anything is a move up. In large agencies, there are several levels of seniority. You base your advancement on your exposure and responsibility more than your title. Tenure doesn't matter as much as talent and the needs of the agency. It's a young business, and you can advance very quickly if you hit a home run.

## Does Age Matter in Advertising?

No, it doesn't. If anything, being young is an advantage, because it demands so much energy that people burn out early. The CEO of DDB Needham Southwest recently resigned, citing burnout as a reason for leaving the industry. "This is a young person's industry, and I no longer have the energy it takes." He is forty-two.

Age makes no difference on the creative side. You can be a young hot-shot, but it's harder to earn your stripes there, because it's so competitive. Once you've proven yourself, your work stands on its own.

Age matters more on the account side, since you're dispensing advice to clients who are often spending hundreds of thousands—if not millions—of dollars. You may appear less credible if you even look too young. Alexis of Foote Cone says, "In advertising, your glory years are from age twenty-five to forty. After thirty-five, you're living off your wins." To me, "living off your wins" sounds like a surefire way to fall on your ass. When you're ready for the rocker and denture cream at thirty-five, it's likely you'll not be as involved in day-to-day production activities and will have more management responsibilities.

## What Skills Do I Need?

If you are an account executive or account planner, you need to have solid business and marketing acumen. Since you will be dealing directly with clients, you must be a great communicator and have excellent presentation skills. You need to be able to understand a client's needs and convey them to your creative department. By the same token you need to convey your creative department's vision to your client without anything being lost in the translation.

Media planners or buyers must be organized and comfortable with numbers and quantitative research.

As you might expect, being creative is a prerequisite to working in a creative department. Backgrounds and training can vary, but generally artists have special training and may be graduates of an art program. Writers, on the other hand, come from all walks of life. There are copywriters who have business or science backgrounds. Talent plays a greater factor in a creative's success than education. Both artists and writers need to have a portfolio or book to show potential employers. (See the graphic and commercial arts chapter to learn more about portfolios and how to make sure your work is seen by the right people.)

Because advertising is created by a team (client, account, creative, and media) you need to be able to work well with others. This can be rough sometimes, because advertising can be subjective and your fabulous idea may be crushed by a client. Sometimes your ego has to take a backseat to the whims of a client.

## Is an Advertising Degree Necessary?

No, but any coursework in advertising or marketing can't hurt. Combine coursework with practical experience such as an internship with an agency, and you'll have a definite advantage over someone who only has an advertising degree and no experience. Many agencies hire their own interns. Majoring in advertising doesn't mean you're qualified to work in an agency.

Agency experience is best, but experience or special knowledge related to the business of an agency's client can be as valuable as agency experience and better than an advertising degree.

## How Do I Get Hired?

If you think that sending your résumé and a few copy samples will get you plucked from the ranks to help create the newest Nike ad, keep dreaming. Advertising is one of the most competitive fields to break into. Think about it: Who wouldn't want to get paid to be creative? Major agencies like Grey Advertising can receive hundreds of résumés a week. Most of these are destined for the "round file." Agencies rarely do any type of campus recruiting, and the handful that do only go to certain campuses. Most entry-level positions, other than secretarial or administrative, are found through connections, networking, and word of mouth. If you want a job, start making contacts right now, long before you need a job.

Hiring at agencies is generally a slow process. There are several steps and interviews before someone is hired, and it takes about a month between each step at most of the agencies. Alexis says, "It wasn't a speedy process. I started my search in November of my senior year and was hired just as I graduated in May." The best thing you can do is to have fifteen to twenty résumés continually moving. If you have your hopes pinned on only one agency or dream job, you'll drive yourself nuts waiting to hear anything from them.

Every aspect of advertising involves networking and relationships. It's a small and incestuous industry in its hiring practices, whether you're a freelancer or with an agency.

Maybe you have tried to reach a creative director for months, but can't seem to charm her assistant enough to put your call through. At an ad club meeting, you might find yourself standing next to her at the bar or sitting next to her at lunch. People at these meetings are accessible. Volunteer and get involved to increase your exposure to these professionals.

A great way to establish industry contacts is to join your city's ad club. Most cities have an ad club or similar group. The best thing about ad clubs is the opportunity to network with high-level agency professionals whom you might otherwise never be able to reach.

## Bigger Is Not Always Better

The major agencies such Grey, Leo Burnett, and Young & Rubicam are great, but a big agency might not be the best place for you to start. It depends on your personality and what you're looking to gain from your first job. An AE at Campbell Mithun Esty, a mid-sized firm in Minneapolis, says he interviewed a person who was leaving one of the top three agencies because he was stuck in traffic (no pun intended) and wasn't getting any hands-on experience or opportunity to move up. The agency and what it offers must be compatible with your goals, experience, and personality.

## How Do I Get Experience?

Internships are the best way to get practical experience and pay your dues as painlessly as possible. It also dramatically shortens your learning curve. If you're in school, try to have at least two internships at different agencies before you graduate. This will make you more well-rounded and give you a better idea of your strengths and interests and what opportunities exist. No two agencies are alike. If you still lack experience after you graduate or if you're looking to make a career change, you may have to bite the bullet and take an unpaid internship. While traffic is a common starting point, several agency veterans quietly said, "You don't want to get stuck in traffic or as an account coordinator for long."

They also said that you're better off being an unpaid intern than starting as a secretary just to get in the door. People get labeled very early on, and it's tough to shed the secretary image. It's better to have an internship to gain experience and then enter at a higher level with a different agency.

---

### How Should I Choose an Agency? Should I Apply to All?

No. Agencies vary greatly. There are some basic differences in the personality and philosophy of each firm. When deciding what type of agency you want to work for, you should first decide whether you are a creative or an account person, then look for agencies that are strong in your chosen area.

Agencies are driven by a basic philosophy. It's generally established by the owners and directors of the agency and reflects their training and background. Agencies are either account-driven or creative-driven. Each is highly effective, but the overall cultures, who makes decisions, and what is important can be very different. It basically determines where the center of power lies.

---

Just make sure that your agency experience is real, practical experience and not just secretarial tasks. Says Matt at Grey, "Sometimes I see bright, energetic people working as a secretary in an agency for a year and a half, after which they don't have any experience except as a secretary."

There is such competition for jobs in New York that agencies can pick and choose. At a major agency, it's rare to jump right into an account executive or a decent creative position. Many of the New York agencies ask people to start in an administrative position. Once you have experience and are looking for a permanent position, you need to be focused and know exactly which area you want to pursue. Steve, a twenty-four-year-old AE at DDB Needham, says, "If you have experience, say that you're not willing to take an internship."

## What About Job Stability?

Advertising and job security are two things not often found in the same sentence. Generally, if a company decides to change agencies or move its business in-house, everyone working on that account is out of a job. Only the largest agencies have the resources to shift people from one account to another, but there's no guarantee. People tend to move frequently among agencies to advance and increase their salaries. Rikki at Ogilvy & Mather says, "Always keep your résumé current and save copies of what you're working on."

Sometimes your job security has nothing to do with you or the quality of your work. If a client hires a new advertising or marketing director, that new person might want to shake things up simply because he wants to make his mark. Political BS? You bet. Does this really happen? You bet.

## What Makes a Candidate Stand Out?

"If someone can't tell me why they want to be in advertising, I don't want to talk to them," says one Grey Advertising executive. Those who don't have an answer or say something stupid—such as "I like commercials"—generally get shown the door pretty quickly. Those who make the cut are truly excited and passionate about advertising. The word "passion" was used frequently by every advertising person with whom I spoke.

You should practice your interviewing skills to become polished. How you handle the interview is crucial. Your résumé might get you in the door, but after that, they want to see how you handle yourself and how knowledgeable you are about the industry, the agency, and their clients. It also doesn't hurt to know the supermarket backward and forward. Know the

Matt at Grey Advertising tells about one of his first interviews with another agency. The interviewer asked Matt, "Why do you want to be in advertising?" Matt says, "I gave a canned answer saying how I wanted to get involved in the company's business, become an expert in that field, and carry that experience to related fields." The man looked at Matt and said, "You know why I got in advertising? Because you get people to do what you want. It's a real power trip."

Matt was a little taken aback at the time, but now he realizes that this guy had a point. Marketing and advertising is about getting people to do something. It's about motivating another person to take action, to buy your product. Matt says that to be an account executive, "Part of your psyche has to enjoy being the person who is responsible and in control."

categories. For example, know their competition and where certain brands and products are located. This is potentially important if you interview with an agency that has a consumer or packaged goods client—and many will.

Before you go into any interview, you should have a favorite and least favorite advertisement and be able to articulate why you like or dislike it. You should also know who the agency's main clients are and research the client industries. How do you find this information? Call the agency ahead of time. If you know the name of the person who will be interviewing you, ask what account she works on and do some homework on that account. The people who rise above other candidates are the ones who have better knowledge of the industry.

## What's the Difference Between Those Who Succeed and Those Who Fail in Advertising?

There is definitely a fast track and a slow track in advertising. Once you get on that slow track, you're trapped. People label you quickly, and you're either a prospective leader of the agency or you're not.

You should decide if you're going to make this your career or if it's just going to be a nine-to-five job. In advertising, the nine-to-fivers don't move ahead. "It's an early night if I leave at eight o'clock," says Amy of DDB Needham. "People who get into advertising because they think it would be fun and they'll work with cool people either get shell-shocked or they get comfortable, relax, and don't move ahead very quickly."

Most agencies aren't going to hold your hand. They're not going to say, "You should be on this account," or "You should be taking these courses on the side," or "You should be developing your writing skills." Once you're in the business, the key to making it is to act smart and be proactive, says Tom at the Richards Group.

Another thing that separates the winners from the "also rans" is attaching yourself to the right people. Having a mentor is crucial to being successful in this business. People move around so much that if you can build a relationship with superiors whom you respect and admire, chances are good that you can grow with them.

## What Are the Differences Between Working for a Large Agency Versus a Small Agency?

Depending on the agency, you'll have different support networks. In a small shop or satellite office of a major agency, you're on your own more than at a large agency. You don't have as many resources, but it can be a great opportunity to build your skills and potentially to mature in the business more quickly than at a big shop.

On the other hand, at a big shop you have every possible resource available to you, and it doesn't hurt having big agency experience on your résumé. Matt, who has worked at both large and small offices, says, "In a large agency, you're learning the right things from the right people. You're also networking with and getting exposure to the heavy hitters of the industry."

You don't have to work for an agency or in-house to be involved with advertising. The publishing, broadcasting, and film industries often overlap with the advertising field. Steve, twenty-eight, floats between the publishing, journalism, and advertising worlds as an editor and reporter for *AdWeek* magazine.

## Where Are the Jobs?

You may be asking yourself, "Will I [have to or get to] move to New York?" While people still think of New York and Madison Avenue as the advertising Mecca, there are major agencies in Chicago, Los Angeles, San Francisco, and most other major metropolitan areas. New York, however, is still the reigning champ.

Surprisingly, a number of the most successful and cutting-edge agencies are far away from New York. Do you like Nike ads? They're created by Weiden & Kennedy, located in the advertising metropolis of Portland, Oregon. Other hot agencies located outside of New York can be found in Minneapolis, Boston, and even Dallas. You will also find major agencies in Detroit, close to Ford, GM, and Chrysler. If an agency isn't located near its clients, the agency may open a branch office in their area.

Agencies come in all sizes, and bigger is not always better. Choose an agency according to what is right for you and the type of work the agency does. Agencies are not always consid-

> ### Don't Forget the Web
>
> Advertising on the Internet is arguably the most profitable use of the Web today. Like print or broadcasting, the Web provides another medium. Don't overlook small Web developers in your job search. They're currently taking a lot of business from the big ad agencies. In fact, they're doing such a good job of finding a target market that many major agencies have set up internal divisions devoted to interactive advertising.

ered large because of the number of employees; they are judged according to their billings or revenue. To learn what agencies are in your area, or the area to which you want to move, check out the Agency Red Book. Its formal name is the Standard Directory of Advertising Agencies, and it can be found in your local library.

## I Don't Care, I Still Want to Work in New York

This is like going from high school to the major leagues. It can be done, but it takes a special person or special circumstances, like your parents knowing someone.

First and foremost, to get anything besides a form letter saying "Thanks, but no thanks," you must know advertising. The largest New York agencies receive several hundred résumés a week. To even get someone to talk to you seriously, you must know something about agency life. That can only come from experience. Julie, a former media buyer at Young & Rubicam, says, "Thank God I had an internship. There is no way I could have been hired unless I knew how an agency worked."

Jenny at BBDO says, "In my experience, the only people who have started off in New York either started in an internship, are related to somebody who has pull, or started off in a different city." Matt, an account supervisor at Grey Advertising who started his career in Detroit, says, "The fact of the matter is, you can get to New York pretty quickly if you plan your career path wisely."

If you absolutely have your heart set on working in New York and are prepared to pay New York rent on your entry-level salary of less (far less) than $22,000 before taxes, go right ahead. Julie, the former media buyer at Young & Rubicam, describes working for a New York agency right out of school as "the best parent-subsidized job in the world."

If you don't have the parental parachute to save you or you simply want to get hands-on experience quickly rather than be a secretary for a year, I suggest that you pay your dues outside of New York. If you still want to move to New York after you have some experience under your belt, go for it. Just realize that while New York is still thought of as the epicenter of advertising, there are many fantastic shops doing extremely creative and meaningful work in other parts of the country.

## What Does In-house Mean?

Rather than hire an outside advertising agency, sometimes companies will have an advertising department made up of

### You Might Also Consider

Other advertising-related opportunities exist in direct mail, promotions, special events, and newspaper insert and specialty coupon companies such as Val-Pak or Catalina Marketing.

company employees. Often these "in-house" departments or people work closely with and serve as a guide to an outside agency, while others handle everything "in-house" on their own. Companies such as Calvin Klein, Levi's, and AT&T all have in-house advertising departments.

## What's It Like to Work in Advertising?

It's much harder work than people imagine. Outsiders think of advertising as glamorous and fun, full of brainstorming sessions, huge client dinners, and special parties and events. While there is some glamour—although much less than in the past—there is research and behind-the-scenes work that the public never sees. Alexis of Foote Cone says that she was prepared for the world of work, but she was not at all prepared for the grueling work and hours of agency life. "I'm working seventy to eighty hours a week, including weekends," she laments. It's an intense business that leads to burnout. Generally, the people who are left at the end of two years are the people who want to succeed and really enjoy advertising.

It's incredibly stressful. There are deadlines and client demands that must always be met. You have to take your job seriously, but it's equally important to decompress and have a life outside of the office.

It's a highly creative business. You're dealing with very bright and creative people, and sometimes that means dealing with giant egos. It's further complicated because evaluating creative work is highly subjective—there often is no right or wrong idea. Consequently, people can take criticism personally. Alyssa, a San Francisco-based artist who has worked for several agencies, says, "Sometimes the client doesn't know what he likes and we as creatives must tell him." I thought it was the client that paid the bills? Maybe that's why Alyssa has been with several agencies?

One of the great things about advertising is being able to see the results of your work. In fields like accounting, you never see the results of your effort (unless your client gets audited by the IRS). In advertising, you might turn on the TV or open a magazine and see a piece on which you or a friend worked.

Advertising is also an environment that's constantly changing. Andrea, a copywriter at the Richards Group, says, "I'm never doing the same thing. I have not had a day where I haven't learned ten new things."

Amy is a copywriter for DDB Needham. During one very intense period when Amy was trying to meet deadlines, she was losing sleep and getting sick to her stomach. Recognizing Amy was a wreck, her boss pulled her aside and put everything into perspective by saying, "Don't worry about it. You aren't saving lives, you're selling f---ing advertising."

You're rarely bored. If you get tired of working on one piece of business, you can switch and work with a completely different client. One month you might be working on a food account, and six months later, you're working on a car or telephone account.

One of the great misconceptions of advertising is that it's free and loose. Actually, it can be very bureaucratic. Andrew, an assistant account executive at a major Minneapolis agency, says, "I fill out forms all the time. I also do an unbelievable amount of paperwork and number crunching."

Advertising agencies are like law firms in that they bill the client. Everyone must keep meticulous records and time sheets. You have to be a people person: You have to want to go and talk to people. You work hard, but unless you really show how hard you're working, it won't count. It's political.

## Who Are the Big Agencies?

The top ten agencies, according to the latest *AdWeek* Agency Report Card, are:

1. J. Walter Thompson—New York
2. Leo Burnett—Chicago
3. Grey Advertising—New York
4. Foote, Cone & Belding—Chicago
5. McCann-Erickson—New York
6. DDB Needham—New York
7. Young & Rubicam—New York
8. BBDO—New York
9. Saatchi & Saatchi—New York
10. Ogilvy & Mather—New York

## What the Pros Read

There are two major publications devoted to the advertising industry. *Advertising Age* is a weekly magazine devoted to the national advertising scene and is considered the Bible.

*AdWeek* is the other industry publication. It's broken down into several regional issues that cover national topics, but it also devotes coverage to local and regional campaigns and agencies. This is a great resource for leads, contact names, and to learn what type of work is being done. Both magazines have job listings and classifieds.

People in advertising also read what their clients read. Alexis at Foote Cone in San Francisco says that she must be as knowledgeable about her client's product as he is. That means studying the market. "If we are creating advertising for orange juice, I need to know everything there is to know about oranges and every other citrus fruit known to man."

## Where on the Web?

www.commercepark.com—American Association of Advertising Agencies (the main trade association for the advertising profession)

www.adweek.com—*AdWeek* magazine

www.adage.com—*Advertising Age* magazine

A current trend in advertising is to become a total marketing partner of the client. This means helping with every aspect of creating, launching, marketing, and advertising a new product. It also may entail finding new media outlets such as Web sites. Large agencies like Grey Advertising have developed entire departments devoted to interactive media.

In the era of full-service agencies, you may help with more than advertising a product. You may even help develop one. Rachel, an AE in California, tells how she acted as marketing partner for one client. "Our client was thinking of making soap, and they've never been in the soap market. My job was to do an entire review of the soap market. I went to the supermarket ten times in a week. I bought every kind of soap. I found out what the sales were, what the trends were. I became a soap expert in two weeks. I created a report detailing how soap would fit into their existing business and then presented my findings to our client."

# 8

• • • • • • • • • • • • • • • • • • • • • • • • • • • •

# Aerospace

"I feel the need, the need for speed."
—TOM CRUISE IN *TOP GUN*

**A Common Position**
   Staff engineer

**Other Opportunities You Might Consider**
Since aerospace is such a broad and diverse industry—encompassing commercial, freight and cargo, and defense—there are many diverse job opportunities: engineer, flight attendant, cargo pilot, sales, marketing, government affairs, publicity and media relations, lobbyist, and human resources. All of these departments can be found in the aerospace and airline industry.

Do you like to fly or are you fascinated with things that fly? Are you interested in space and cutting-edge technology? Would you like to control or create multimillion- or even billion-dollar machinery? Do your friends often mistake you for a rocket scientist? (Yeah, me too.) Well if you're as smart as a rocket scientist—and even if you're not—there are many opportunities in this rapidly changing field.

## What Does It Mean to Be in Aerospace?

The aerospace industry encompasses all elements of the design, manufacture, sales, service, and operations of commercial, private, and defense-oriented aircraft, spacecraft, and systems.

When people refer to the aerospace industry, they typically think of airliners—companies like Boeing that actually construct commercial airliners—but aerospace also includes a large portion of defense, systems work, and commercial technology.

Companies like Lockheed Martin—the nation's largest aerospace firm—not only build planes, they also build electronics, software programs, and systems integration for both the military and commercial customers. These commercial customers are increasingly outside the aircraft arena. Of course, companies like Lockheed Martin support aircraft companies with flight controls and the like.

A huge growth area for aerospace companies is commercial spacecraft. In fact, Lockheed currently has sixty spacecrafts on order, including some intended for use in communications and imaging by commercial clients worldwide.

## It's Much More Than Airplanes and Spaceships

The aerospace community is aggressively pursuing more commercial business these days. Defense spending is considerably down, and there's been a lot of consolidation among the major aerospace firms. Companies are looking beyond traditional markets for commercial opportunities that may not even be aircraft- or space-related.

Aerospace companies have developed much of the image-generation technology for military trainers, flight simulators, and tech trainers, and are now starting to commercialize that technology. Lockheed Martin has an arrangement with Sega to create video-game software, and some of Sega's bigger arcade games already run on Lockheed Martin software.

Currently, the aerospace industry is applying its expertise to adjacent markets. These markets may not be traditionally aerospace, but they can benefit from the technology. You won't see companies like Boeing, McDonnell Douglas, or Lockheed begin to build refrigerators or computers, but both will ultimately benefit from their design and technology.

Mike, a recruiter for Lockheed, says, "We are taking expertise we gained by creating huge information systems for the government and using it to develop systems for commercial clients like Federal Express and Fieldcrest Cannon."

## It's Just Another High-Tech Business

Aerospace firms are taking a cue from companies like EDS and expanding into the high-tech market that deals in general industry. There are still the major players that focus on building aircraft, but at companies like Lockheed Martin, aircraft business is a very small portion of the $30 billion in annual sales.

## How Do I Get Hired? What Type of Degree Do I Need?

Now is the time to go into this field. This year Lockheed Martin will try to hire 2,000 new college grads with degrees in engineering, and a surprising few will have their degrees in aerospace engineering. Sixty-five percent of those hired will be electrical engineering and computer science majors.

This represents a significant shift in the traditional hiring for aerospace companies. While they used to go after a lot of mechanical and aerospace engineers, both are now in the minority for two reasons. The first relates to what I said before: Aerospace companies are expanding into information technology and systems engineering. The second reason is that the industry is no longer supported by big-ticket defense contracts. There are still some large contracts out there, but aircraft-related business now comes more often from systems integration or electronic upgrading than from replacing a plane.

## Where Will I Start?

The typical starting position is staff engineer.

## What Will I Do?

Lockheed's manager of entry-level programs says he is asked that on campuses all the time. "We have seventy separate businesses and a couple hundred contracts, so it's pretty hard to specify what a recruit would be doing." Typically, a new college grad is matched with more experienced engineers to work on a team project. Common assignment areas for new graduates to go into are programming, systems engineering, software development, or database management.

## How Can I Be a Stand-Out Candidate?

While grades are important, several recruiters said grade point average is not a dominant factor. Recruiters are more interested in well-rounded graduates with good interpersonal skills, because they will be working in a team environment. As with most businesses, any type of relevant experience is a huge plus—getting it is the hard part.

## How Hard Is It to Get Hired?

Engineers are in demand. Based on current college enrollment, the engineering workforce commission says engineering class size for the next several years is not going to increase, whereas more companies are recruiting engineers.

Aerospace companies are competing for recruits with firms that are not historical competitors. Lockheed, Boeing, McDonnell Douglas, and Rockwell are now competing with banks and consulting firms for the same students, because other businesses are beginning to look at different majors.

## What's the Typical Career Path? How Long Would Someone Be a Staff Engineer?

There are typically three or four levels. You would enter as an associate engineer and remain there for two years. Next, you'd be an engineer for three or four years, then a senior engineer for three or four more. At the eight- to ten-year mark, you would either be an "individual contributor," because you have developed a specialization, or move into management.

## How Stable Is It?

The aerospace and airline industries are in a period of huge transition right now. Since it reached a peak in employment in 1989, the aerospace industry has lost 41 percent of its workforce. This is mostly a result of defense budget cuts and a downturn in the civil transport market. Some industry analysts are saying that business is beginning to improve. International revenue from passenger miles are expected to double between 1995 and 2005. However, it's still safe to say that, depending on which area you go into, your stability and job security depend on many variables completely outside your control. In the defense and space community, companies' futures depend upon government contracts that often fall prey to the political environment.

## What's the Prestige Factor and Quality of Life?

Many aerospace companies have a regimented and bureaucratic corporate culture, which is natural since many executives and employees are former military. Like many engineering-oriented fields, aerospace is still male-dominated.

## What Are Some Pros and Cons?

Engineers say that the opportunity to deal with state-of-the-art technology is the best. You may be working on projects that really are "top-secret" or that seem like they belong on *Star Trek*. Others like it because it's a diverse business. You can work on spacecraft, launch vehicles, or airplanes. There's a wide variety.

Mike of Lockheed Martin says, "There's also a real sense of pride and excitement in working on various programs like Mars Global Surveyor, which is a spacecraft that's going to Mars. Another team just won the contract for Venture Star, which will be the next generation shuttle. There's a lot of pride in seeing what we do in the news."

## Am I Assigned to an Area or Can I Say, "Hey, I Want to Work on the Shuttle"?

You won't be placed anywhere you want to go, but most companies try to cross-train and educate recruits on the different types of business.

## Where Are the Jobs?

Depending on your area of emphasis, it's either feast or famine. In the space industry, it's lean—very lean. When I called NASA's representative while researching this book, he simply said, "We have a hiring freeze for the next *two years*, so it wouldn't even be worth talking." Tight times with the space program seem to have trickle-down effects for suppliers and other venders dependent on the space program. On the defense side, production should not increase until after the turn of the century.

## If Defense and Space Are Not Hiring, Where Are the Jobs?

If you want a career in aerospace, your best bet is in the commercial arena. Commercial transport fleets worldwide are expected to grow by 4,642 aircraft from 1996 to 2005.

## What Are Some of the Misconceptions About This Industry?

One of the real misconceptions is that people don't realize that aerospace companies write software. Lockheed Martin probably writes more software than anyone in the world. Some of the programs run a million lines of code. It takes 15 million lines of code to run a Sea Wolf submarine.

Many new engineers become disappointed that they aren't moving through the ranks more quickly. There's much to learn and experience is crucial to becoming a good engineer. Recruiters say there are no real prodigies in engineering. Your learning curve and advancement can be accelerated if you work exceptionally hard, but experience can't be bypassed. It's like being a prodigy trial attorney—you don't get good until you've done it.

## What the Pros Read

*Aviation Week & Space Technology*
*Aerospace Daily*
*Flight International*
*Defense News*
*Space News*

## Where Can I Learn More?

American Association for the Advancement of Science
American Defense Preparedness Association
Aerospace Industries Association
American Institute of Aeronautics and Astronauts
National Security Industrial Association
National Space Foundation

## Where on the Web?

www.lmco.com—Lockheed Martin
www.aerospace.net—Aerospace.Net.
www.csn.net/aeac/table/airsalary—Careers in Aviation
www.aiaa.org—American Institute of Aeronautics and Astronautics

# 9

●●●●●●●●●●●●●●●●●●●●●●●●●●●●●●●●●●●●●●●●

# Airline Careers

## Commercial Airline Pilot

**Some Common Positions**
> Pilot/captain
> Copilot
> Flight engineer

**Other Opportunities You Might Consider**
American Airlines, Continental, or Southwest aren't the only ways to fly the big jets. Freight and cargo companies like FedEx and UPS also hire pilots, as do fire-and-rescue departments and crop dusting and agriculture companies. There are also opportunities to fly as a private or corporate pilot. Other airline-related opportunities are air traffic controller, mechanic, or ground crew.

It doesn't take a rocket scientist to figure out what a pilot does. I have flown hundreds of thousands of miles since I began my career, and for the longest time I never knew what it took to become a pilot. I thought these guys were just bus drivers in the sky. I would steam and stew whenever my flight was late. I would somehow think the pilot was responsible. Then a friend of mine who had spent the better part of his career on an airplane said, "Remember, they also have a family they want to get back to." It put it all in perspective for me, and I began to learn more about these incredibly skilled professionals. Whether you want to become a pilot or you simply fly a lot, I think this will give you a new respect for the people who get us where we need to be.

## How Do I Become a Pilot?

You don't simply go to flight school. Becoming a pilot at any level takes a long time and a significant amount of training. You should already have several thousand hours of flying time. But to fly the big jets for a major airline, you must meet very tough minimum requirements, which vary slightly from airline to airline.

First, you must have a United States FAA Airline Transport Pilot Certificate. It must reflect "type rating" to fly a certain type of aircraft, like a 737 for example. Think you might call up the FAA and have them send you one of those certificates, huh? Save your pennies first. The certificate costs about $10,000.

You must also have significant flying time. Taking the Cessna single engine around the pasture won't quite cut it, but your time does not have to be in the 737. Airline pilots must have 2,500 hours of total air time in any airplane or 1,500 hours as the pilot in command of a turbine aircraft.

The majority of airline pilots are former military. The military offers a great opportunity to acquire hours. At Southwest Airlines, 80 percent of the pilots are former military. The nonmilitary route would be to log hours as a flight instructor or flying charters, progressively moving up to bigger aircraft. Many pilots also earn their hours as corporate pilots.

In addition to your certification and flight-time requirement, most airlines require you to pass an FAA class-one medical exam and have at least three letters from people who can attest to your flying skills. A four-year college degree is preferred, but not required. This is because so many pilots choose the military instead of college.

## Where Will I Start? Will I Automatically Fly?

You'll certainly be able to fly, but whether or not you're the pilot depends on the airline. In a commercial airline, the typical career path can take several years and begins in the third seat as a flight engineer (navigator). You may do this for several years before moving over to the right, or second seat, as copilot. Here, you'll do much of the same thing the pilot does. Moving over to the big chair, or (you guessed it) the left seat, can often take a long time, as many as ten years on some airlines. Once someone is in the big chair, they are often reluctant to give it up. It's extremely competitive to move into that spot, and it doesn't open up easily or often.

Some airlines like Southwest shorten the time their pilots must spend as a copilot. Sandy Sombrano, coordinator of pilot recruiting for Southwest, says it takes their pilots "three to five years to move into the left seat."

There is generally very little turnover among pilots. "At Southwest, they don't leave unless they retire or die. The company makes a big investment in people. We will do anything we can to help them out, professionally and personally," says Sandy.

# What Are Some of the Pros and Cons of Being a Pilot?

"The pay is good, you have flexibility, and you get to fly with pretty women" were the three benefits listed by the Southwest Airlines "People Department." (That's what they call their Human Resources Department.) This is still a very male-dominated field—as of June 1996, Southwest Airlines had 73 female pilots and 2,217 male pilots.

Commercial pilots average sixteen days off per month. They generally fly four days on and three days off. The hours are very flexible. You can often trade, give away, or pick up shifts with other pilots. The downside is that airlines never shut down, so you'll have to fly weekends and holidays. It's also a heavily unionized field, although there are a few airlines whose pilots don't belong to a union.

## What Will I Do Besides Fly?

A pilot may have a number of nonflight or ground duties, depending upon the airline. If you're with a major commercial airline, you don't have to do much. However, if you have ever flown a white-knuckle puddle jumper, you know the guy loading your bags is often the same guy flying the plane.

## Misconceptions About Pilots

Kevin, a ten-year veteran pilot at American Airlines, says pilots have an image of being "egotistical fly jocks." A reputation, he says, which is untrue. Even if they are, who cares? If you're one of the small class of people on the planet who can move that much machinery and take responsibility for the lives of hundreds of people each day, you have the right to be proud of yourself.

## How Much Can I Make?

Commercial airline pilots make more than other pilots, averaging $80,000 annually, according to the Future Aviation Professionals of America. Your salary depends upon the airline, your experience, and the type of aircraft you fly. Like most things, bigger is better. Flying jets pays more than flying props. Pilots have a union that negotiates their labor contracts, which may vary from airline to airline.

## Where Can I Learn More?

Airline Pilots Association International
1625 Massachusetts Avenue NW
Washington, DC 20006

Southwest Airlines
Pilot Recruiting
214-792-5088

## What the Pros Read

*Airline News*
*Professional Pilot*

## Where on the Web?

www.americanair.com—American Airlines
www.iflyswa.com—Southwest Airlines
www.nbaa—National Business Aircraft Association
www.propilot.com—Captain Bob's Pro Pilot Aviation Page (stupid name,
    great site)
www.air-transport.org—Air Transport Association

# Flight Attendant

For those who aren't pilots or engineers, another great flight-related opportunity is flight attendant (if you call them stewardesses, you may incur their wrath and miss getting peanuts). "It is a great job if you like travel and dealing with people," says Kelly, in-flight recruiting coordinator for Southwest Airlines.

## What Are the Requirements?

Most airlines have certain height and weight requirements. Recruiters say the physical requirements are proportionate for height, weight, and age. (Don't worry. You don't need that waif-like Kate "I'm in need of a good meal" Moss look.) You must be able to reach seventy-five inches (the standard overhead bin height) and lift at least fifty pounds (although most people's carry-on baggage weighs ten times that amount).

## What About Work Experience and Education?

Southwest Airlines, known for their spectacular service and fun corporate culture, requires applicants to have at least two years of customer service experience. This experience may come from retail, a restaurant, or even child care. "We have many former teachers who become flight attendants," says Kelly of Southwest. "We look for anything that demonstrates that they have dealt with the public before."

At Southwest, you must be at least twenty years old and have a high school diploma or GED. Other airlines' age requirements may vary.

## How Do I Get Hired?

Rarely is recruiting for flight attendants done on college campuses. Airlines have recruiters around the country, usually located in the airline's hub cities. Applications can also be picked up at ticket counters or ordered through job hot lines. Some airlines don't even accept applications unless they are hiring at that time.

## What Makes a Good Candidate?

Someone who is well-groomed, a team player, and can work well under stress. Recruiters also look for people who are flexible with their schedules and transferable. "We don't ask anyone to move to a certain place. You may live in Utah, but be based in Chicago and commute when you are on duty. You're not required to live where you're based, but it sure is easier," says Renee, an American flight attendant.

---

### Did You Know?

Most airlines charge a small application fee when you apply—generally around $20. Applications can be picked up for free and you are not guaranteed an interview.

Beware: There are some disreputable private companies that claim to help you complete the airline application and guarantee you an interview with the airline of your choice. Run away! They charge $150 and up and do nothing that you can't do on your own.

---

## How Can I Stand Out in an Interview?

Recruiters look for good communication skills and a solid reason of why you want to be a flight attendant. Whatever you do, don't say you are becoming a flight attendant for the free trips, says Kelly of Southwest.

## How Competitive Is It?

Very. Recruiters warn applicants to make sure they understand and meet the basic requirements.

## What About Training?

Training programs vary among the airlines, but most last several weeks and are generally *unpaid*. Southwest Airlines training lasts four and a half weeks and always takes place in Dallas, where Southwest is based. The airline flies trainees in from around the country and arranges for accommodations and two meals a day.

Check out what is provided before you begin training. Some airlines don't even pay for their trainee's accommodations.

## What Is the Best Thing About Being a Flight Attendant?

Many say the best things are the flexibility and the chance to meet and help people, but the number-one thing that flight attendants (and their families) say is the best part of working for an airline is the free travel. In most cases, you and your family can fly free. You just have to pay the tax.

Another factor that has a lot to do with job satisfaction is the culture of the airline. At Southwest, flight attendants say that they love the fact that they can dress casually, often wearing shorts. (On Halloween, all Southwest employees—flight attendants, gate agents, etc.—dress up in costume. CEO Herb Kelleher is known for roaming the halls as Elvis.)

## What's the Worst Thing About Being a Flight Attendant?

The long hours. The jet lag. Being away from your family and friends. Debra, a Continental flight attendant, says the toughest part is "dealing with rude passengers who don't realize that it isn't your fault that their flight is late." Renee at American says that even though you are going to many different cities, you don't always have a lot of time to be a tourist. "Sometimes you are bored to death because you are in a hotel room." The low pay and physically draining work is a drawback as well.

## What Are the Greatest Misconceptions?

Oddly enough, many flight attendants enter the field thinking that because they're flying in and out of cities, they will be back home at night. Actually, there are lots of layovers and overnights, even for an airline like Southwest that only flies in the United States.

The other stereotypes that flight attendants say are absolutely not true is that you have to be a beautiful young blonde or that you are just a glorified "waitress in the sky," as one flight attendant for American put it.

## How Much Will I Make?

Let's just say that most airlines hope that you will think the free travel is enough to make up for the low pay. Salaries vary from airline to airline, but they start between $15,000 to $22,000 a year. With experience you can expect to make in the mid-twenties. At one major airline, the recruiter said, "I even heard of someone making around $30,000 . . . once."

You don't get paid a straight salary. You get paid according to the number of flights you make. You may also make a per diem for meal expenses. Many flight attendants save their per diems to boost their income. You will also be paid when you are stand-by or on call to fly.

In addition to free travel, there are great benefits including insurance, profit sharing, and 401k. Some flight attendants belong to a union.

Flight attendants are responsible for some of their expenses. Most flight attendants (and pilots, too) must pay for their own uniforms. This can add up quickly, especially when you are just getting started.

## How Do I Get the Best Trips?

Before you put in your request for working the flights to Hawaii or the Caribbean, realize that you might have to spend a lot of time flying to Newark or Cleveland first. Scheduling is done on a bidding system each month, with the most senior staff getting first pick at the best trips.

# 10

· · · · · · · · · · · · · · · · · · · · · · · ·

# Architecture

**Some Common Positions**
 Registered architect
 Intern architect

**Other Opportunities You Might Consider**
With a design background, you're prepared to go into a number of specialties and related fields dealing with the construction of buildings and dwellings and designing landscapes, golf courses, furniture, and special structures like churches. Some related positions and fields are: landscape architect/designer, construction/home builder, developer, interior designer, and surveyor.

Have you ever noticed that when an architect is portrayed on TV, he or she is either drawing or standing in front of a model of a skyscraper or massive shopping mall? In reality, this is a minor part of what an architect does. Architects do much more than simply draw or provide design, and only a handful ever get the opportunity to build a skyscraper or shape a skyline.

In addition to design, architects specify all elements of a building or facility, including the structure, air-conditioning, heating, electrical, plumbing, landscape, and even the interior. These specifications must often meet building codes and zoning laws. An architect must oversee each project to make sure it's functional, safe, and meets the client's needs and budget.

There are several types of architecture. Commercial, industrial, residential, and universal are the most common.

## Where Will I Start?

First, you must earn a degree in architecture from an accredited school. Most architecture schools have gone to a professional degree program, which means you spend five years in school.

Once you graduate, you'll get a job with an architecture firm and begin an intern development program. No one starts out as a full architect right out of school. The common entry-level position is an intern architect. You'll remain an intern architect for three to seven years before you're experienced enough to take your exam to be a fully registered architect. Most states require you to spend at least three years as an intern, apprentice, draftsman, or researcher before you can apply for accreditation.

The architect registration exam is a difficult twelve-hour, multipart, nationwide exam given once a year. It's a professional test on the level of the bar exam for attorneys or the CPA exam for accountants. To be a registered architect means you're allowed to sign on your work and are legally responsible for it. If your building is a few inches off or is structurally unsound and collapses, you're on the hook.

Architecture is becoming a practicing profession, requiring as much education and experience as a lawyer or a doctor. The whole process to become a registered architect—including education—averages about nine years.

## What Will I Do?

It'll be a long time before you actually get to design anything. You'll likely start in production as a CAD draftsman (computer aided design) drawing on the computer. This is the grunt work in architecture. "As an intern, you do CAD, CAD, and more CAD," says to Michelle, an intern architect in Kansas City.

However, according to most intern architects, the bulk of your time will be spent on the phone, preparing documents, researching zoning and building codes, pricing material, and site planning. Dave in Chicago says there are a lot of negotiations between contractors, engineers, and the client. "I often help with the bidding and negotiating of the costs of materials." Kelly, an apprentice in Atlanta, says, "We work with all sorts of people. We work with a lot of interior designers and decorators, and, of course, we work with the government, with the ADA [Americans with Disabilities Act] reviewers, and the construction and contract administrators."

As an intern, you'll likely specialize in your own area of expertise. But some firms want their architects to grow and develop, so they cross-train interns in various areas to expose them to different studios like interiors, residential architecture, and industrial or commercial architecture.

---

### How Much Actual Drawing Is There?

There's not much manual drafting anymore. Most of the drawing is CAD production, because time and efficiency are so important. There is a CAD production staff, usually consisting of intern architects or unregistered architects. The senior or registered architects actually design and direct the CAD draftsman on what to draw.

Architects, builders, and construction managers have a great deal of overlap in their jobs. They often work closely together on a project.

## What Skills Do I Need?

Drawing is an important skill, but great drawing talent is not critical. CAD makes drafting easy, but you still need basic drawing skills so you can understand design.

Good architects have the ability to conceptualize and are excellent communicators. In many cases, you'll be the liaison between the client and the builder, so you must be a good manager, facilitator, negotiator, and mediator, as well as being able to supervise others. You must have a knowledge of zoning, construction, and engineering.

## Is Architecture Similar to Engineering?

They're equally hard, but different. Engineering is more quantitative, requiring analytical and logical thinking to solve a problem that has a definite answer. And since it's quantitative, it will have only one answer.

Architecture is a more creative, multifaceted process. To design something, you must come up with new and innovative ideas. There's never actually a right or wrong answer when you're being creative.

## What Is the Career Path?

Once you're registered, you're a fully capable, legal, and working architect. However, you aren't automatically given your own project. Once you're a registered architect, you're allowed to sign your name to a document, which means you're liable and legally responsible for that project—including it's safety. Depending on the firm, it may take a year before you get to that point. You will still work with registered architects as a team, but you will probably be given much more responsibility.

"Basically, if you're not a registered architect these days, you can't get anywhere," says Richard in Los Angeles. "You acquire a certain status, prestige, and respect once you become registered."

## How Do I Get Hired?

The best advice is to find a mentor and serve an internship while in school. It's an extremely competitive field, so getting experience early is important. Many of the larger firms recruit on campuses that have large architecture schools. Contact your professors and ask if they have any contacts. Some intern architects recommend going to different architecture firms and introducing yourself. Some partners say they have hired graduates they have met at conventions or trade shows.

## What Do Employers Really Look For? Is It Based Upon Your Grades, Experience, Portfolio?

All of the above. You're better off if you have work experience. However, because this job is about much more than drawing, you're also judged on how well you work with people and your communication, organizational, and leadership skills. You must also show initiative and be assertive.

## The Perfect Candidate Needs to . . .

Understand the importance of work experience. "Architecture is so fast-paced, firms don't have time to train someone and hold their hand," says Michelle. "They would rather hire someone who at least has office experience in an architecture firm or understands the terminology and the implications of the codes and regulations."

## How Much Can I Make?

Not much. Even though the professional training and education is similar to that of a doctor or attorney, the salaries couldn't be more different. The median salary for an intern architect is $24,500. Registered architects make in the high thirties to mid-forties. Most firms offer a standard benefits package, including insurance and a 401k. If you're a partner or own your firm, you'll make over $50,000. Some make well over $100,000.

It makes you wonder how Mike Brady of the Brady Bunch could support six kids and a maid—who never really worked.

## What's the Culture Like?

Architecture is a very male-dominated profession (almost 80 percent). Architects say there are two types of architects: Those steeped in theory and abstract aesthetics and the technical types who think like engineers. Often they are paired together to play on each other's strengths. "Designers can be cocky, even a little elitist," says Richard in Los Angeles. "Image is everything. Architects can be very intense and take themselves and what they do very seriously. Outsiders to architecture find it hard to see how seriously architects take their profession."

## How Stable Is Architecture as a Career?

It's cyclical. When the economy goes down, architecture goes down; when the economy goes up, architecture goes up.

## What Do You Enjoy Most About This Field?

Dave in Chicago says, "I enjoy taking someone else's creation, someone else's image of what they want and dream of, and making it a tangible thing. It's incredibly exciting to take something that is completely in the mind and make it a reality that you can touch, see, and feel."

## What Are Some Misconceptions About Architecture?

People think that they'll be able to design as soon as they get out of college. Not true. Architecture is more than just creating new designs. There are a lot of structural aspects to it. Michelle says, "Actually, that's the only part I don't like about it. In order to design something, you have to know how it's built, what it takes to make the structure stand." Dave says, "If you want to be the next I.M. Pei or Frank Lloyd Wright, keep dreaming." It's unglamorous, tedious, detail-oriented work dealing with issues like codes and zoning.

Another common misconception is that popular opinion says you have to draw well. Drawing is not as important as communication and people skills. One architect said, "This is ultimately a business, and architecture school doesn't prep you on the elements of running a business and making money."

## Where Are the Jobs?

Anyplace with active construction and development. One advantage to this career is that you are not limited to a certain location. The only thing that may affect where you live is your specialty. However, more architects are taking on renovations, since the cost of building from the ground up is so expensive.

One-third of all architects work for an architecture firm or are self-employed. Others work for builders, construction firms, developers, and the government.

According to several architects, "The current market for residential architecture is nil."

## Shop Talk

If there is one acronym architects need to be familiar with, it's ADA. It stands for the Americans with Disabilities Act, and it affects every element of architecture today.

The ADA requires architects to use a universal design that accommodates everybody at any stage of life, regardless of disability. "It has changed architecture 180 degrees," says one architect. It requires more involvement with laws, codes, ordinances, and the government. Once you create a design, it must be approved by the city and state in which you're building. You have to pass the variance for ADA. This includes making enough space to accommodate a wheelchair and making sure there is a ramp from the parking lot to the entrance.

## Why Isn't There a Strong Market in Residential?

Residential design is being taken over by contractors and large home builders that use standard models. There are plenty of architects who design houses, but many choose to focus their business on another area of architecture, because the growing influx of home builders has saturated the residential market.

## Are There Any Current Trends?

Many architects are seeing growth in institutional areas like schools, hospitals, and specialized healthcare. In corporate architecture, you're seeing a lot of larger clients renovating rather than building from the ground up. They're consolidating, downsizing, and reengineering. They can't afford to waste any space or have an inefficient work environment.

## You Might Also Consider

Space planning
Historic renovation
Interior design
Urban planning

## What the Pros Read

*Architecture*
*Progressive Architecture*
*Architecture Review*
*Architecture Digest*

## Where Can I Learn More?

American Institute of Architects: Careers in Architecture Program
1735 New York Avenue
Washington, DC 20006
202-626-7472

## Other Associations

National Association of Home Builders
American General Contractors
American Society of Landscape Architects

## Where on the Web?

www.aia.org—American Institute of Architects

The site for the main professional association for architects. It offers information on careers, education, current events and trends in the field.

# 11

· · · · · · · · · · · · · · · · · · · · · · · · · · · · · · · · ·

# Child Care and Development

**Some Common Positions**
- Nanny
- Child care director
- Caregiver
- Au pair

**Other Opportunities You Might Consider**
Teaching is a closely related field. You might also take a look at special education, child psychology, or even counseling. Many of these opportunities often require an advanced degree.

With so many dual-income families in America needing to make ends meet, it's impossible for many couples to have one parent stay at home with the kids. It puts many working families in a financial and emotional bind. Just ask any parent, and you'll find there's nothing more precious to them than the safety and care of their children. This is one reason for the recent growth in the childcare field.

## What's It Like?

Do you have nieces, nephews, or friends who have a couple of rug rats? Ask to baby-sit and invite about six of the child's friends over for an eight-hour period. You'll get the idea. It's intense. It's loud. It's hectic and tiring. It's also very rewarding.

## How Do I Get Hired?

For a day care position, there's generally no special training or certification you need to go through other than *not* having a criminal record. (This still doesn't mean you can't get hired. I find that pretty scary.) Most centers do thorough background checks and criminal investigations. Day care traditionally has high turnover. It's fairly easy to find a job, because there's such a shortage of high quality caregivers. People tend to leave this profession after a few years because of burnout, so day care centers are always hiring. Call and ask to speak with the director or owner to see if there are any openings.

Nannies are generally hired through special placement agencies. They prescreen candidates and match qualified nannies with families. These agencies are often paid a flat fee by the family or up to 10 percent of a nanny's first-year salary as a finder's fee.

If you're placed through an agency, you're generally contractually required to remain in the position for at least a year. If there's a newborn involved, you may be asked for a longer commitment lasting up to three or four years.

## What Skills or Experience Do I Need?

Becoming a nanny requires more experience than is required at a day care facility. Most agencies require you to have a minimum of one year child-care experience. You can expect to go through thorough background checks, including criminal, drug, credit, and otherwise. In some cases, there may be psychological testing. You must also have personal references who can vouch for your character.

It shouldn't come as a big surprise that all of the nanny placement agencies said clients want someone who "likes children and pets." I guess saying you hate kids and think rabbits make great stew would make a parent nervous.

There's a shortage of American and English-speaking nannies. While many nannies are from other countries, clients generally require they be fluent in English and able to drive. Being a nonsmoker also helps. My wife and I had a chain-smoking Russian nanny for about two days. As if not being able to communicate with her wasn't bad enough, after the woman left, my daughter smelled like the Marlboro Man.

Requirements for nannies may be detailed and specific and are generally spelled out by the family. There are no standardized requirements or skills.

## What Will I Do?

As a nanny, you'll take care of kids all day long. It may involve infant care or transporting kids to various activities after school. In some cases, you might even help prepare lessons at home. You may also be asked to perform some housekeeping or even cooking duties. When these employment contracts are structured, all of these details are stated specifically.

In a day care setting, you'll do more of the same thing: taking care of kids. However, since it's more of a school environment, you'll also plan activities for the kids. One of the neat things about day care centers—or the good ones anyway—is that kids are broken into age-appropriate groups for activities. There are state regulations that mandate the child-caregiver ratio and how many children can be in the same room.

## What About Education?

For nannies—unless a client specifies a college degree—a high school diploma or GED will be enough. It's also helpful to be certified in CPR and first aid. A degree in child development is certainly a plus, though often not required. The exception is if you choose to open a day care center. Requirements and certifications vary from state to state for home child care and child care centers. Call your state's human services or child welfare office for more details.

## How Much Can I Make?

Nanny's salaries depend upon the family and the duties. Find a rich family, and you can expect to make anywhere from $12,000 to $24,000. The highest paid nannies can earn $750 a week. This may not sound like much, but remember, in some cases you have no living expenses. On the other hand, you may not have insurance or retirement benefits.

Day care salaries can vary widely, too. Most day care centers do not offer benefits or paid vacations.

## What Do You Like the Most?

If you like kids, what more could you ask for? You get paid to spend time with kids and play a major part in developing good human beings. Nannies say both the travel and being able to earn money without having to pay living expenses are a plus. Many people do this for a while to earn money before returning to school or deciding what they want to do with their lives.

Nannies and day care providers alike say that the greatest thing about their job is watching a child grow and discover things for the first time. Kara, a day care provider in Albuquerque, says being able to watch a child go from crawling to the first steps is really wonderful. "I feel that I have a big part in their development."

## What Do You Like the Least?

Janice, a nanny in Chicago, says, "Sometimes clients don't live up to their promises. There's a hard sell to get you in the beginning, and then you work harder and do more than was negotiated or described to you." She also says, "The kids may be tough to discipline, and you get no support from the parents. Some parents expect you to do everything or to be a surrogate parent. Nothing replaces a parent."

Others say that as a live-in, you still feel like a guest. "You might not have the privacy you're used to. The hours are long. You never get downtime, because the kids still need care. Donna, a nanny for a wealthy Florida family, says, "I get to travel with the family and go to places I might not otherwise be able to go, but I'm working the whole time."

Day care providers say it's difficult when you're dealing with sick kids. Kara says, "You want to help them feel better and sometimes you can't." You also get sick easily, because you're working in a giant Petri dish. "You're always around runny noses, so you regularly catch colds and flus."

## What's the Career Path?

You can make a career of being a nanny or caregiver if you choose, although not many people do. There's a lot of turnover. There are a number of people who eventually open their own center or placement agency after working as a nanny or day care provider.

## Where Are the Jobs?

Everywhere—small towns and big cities. Another perk is that there are no geographic boundaries. As a nanny, your best bet is to contact one of the national placement agencies. In most cities, you'll find one of the large national day care providers such as Kindercare or Children's World. To learn of local agencies or providers, contact the university in your area. Ask for the child development department. If they have such a program, they should be able to steer you in the right direction.

Jobs aren't just with private families or day care centers. Don't forget that many corporations have in-house day care for their employees. Churches, temples, and mosques also provide day care programs that need quality caregivers.

## Where Can I Learn More?

Call your state's Department of Children's Welfare Services or any similar department. You might also visit the local library to look in its listings for child care services and talk with workers there.

## Where on the Web?

www.assoc-mgmt.com/users/nafcc—National Association for Family Child Care

www.careguide.net—CareGuide

http://ericps.crc.uiuc.edu/nccic—National Child Care Information Center

# 12

● ● ● ● ● ● ● ● ● ● ● ● ● ● ● ● ● ● ● ● ● ● ● ● ● ● ●

# Consulting

**Some Common Positions**
The most common position is simply that of consultant. However, there are many different types of consultants. Consultants generally work in one of three very different settings: a large consulting firm (such as Andersen Consulting), a small specialty boutique, or that of a solo practitioner or independent consultant.

**Other Opportunities You Might Consider**
Consultants can be found in virtually every industry. Although traditionally thought of as management consultants, they can have a variety of specialties and expertise. Other fields and tasks closely related to consulting include training and development, professional speaking, writing books and articles, or being an expert media commentator or columnist. For many in this field, consulting is only one of many things they do.

Whenever I speak on a college campus, there always seem to be several students who approach me and say, "I want to be a consultant." My response to them is, "Great. What type of consulting do you want to do?" They either say, "I want to be a management consultant and work for Andersen Consulting" or they get a glazed look and say, "Uh, I dunno. I hadn't thought about it." Hearing this always cracks me up, because as I see it, there is one small problem these people overlook. To be a consultant, you must first have expert or unique knowledge that your client is willing to pay for. Many people just starting their careers don't have any specialized knowledge or experience (unless you consider making fake IDs specialized knowledge).

Why does everyone want to be a consultant? C'mon, who wouldn't want to be paid a lot of money for dispensing advice like you're the Oracle at Delphi? But consulting is much more involved and difficult than simply giving advice.

There are several types of consulting firms and innumerable different types of consultants. Consulting is a nebulous field that is defined according to the specific situation. It used to be a code word for unemployed. "I'm doing some consulting" just sounds better than "I'm between jobs."

## Types of Consulting

The most recognized type of consulting firms are the major companies like Andersen Consulting, McKinsey & Company, or Bain & Company. Consultants and consulting practices work with many different industries. Some firms have specialty consulting units devoted to different business services and industries. What do the major consulting firms, consult their clients on? Some areas include: management issues, strategic planning, customer service, dealing with change, information systems and technology, manufacturing processes, customer service, or mergers and acquisitions, among others.

Many of the large consulting firms have teams that specialize in certain industry sectors, such as telecommunications, or health care, retail, or financial services. Some firms may be known for their expertise in a special area. Some are known for management expertise, while others are known for their systems knowledge. There are also major technology companies such as EDS that are creating consulting units that develop large systems and controls for clients.

Boutique or specialty firms consist of only a few people whose expertise is in a certain area. These small shops usually overlap on issues and areas with the big firms, but the small firms typically have a very narrow focus or area of expertise. Many consultants in small boutiques started with large firms and decided to branch out on their own or pursue a specialty. Others are former employees and executives from various businesses whose contacts and industry experience are valuable. A large firm is not necessarily better than a smaller one. It depends upon the situation and the client's needs.

Finally, there are the solo practitioners. This is the fastest growing area of consulting. This new breed of consultant often comes to the profession with prior experience in a field. As a result of downsizing or a choice to leave a large company, many are taking their experience, knowledge, and connections and becoming entrepreneurs. They are similar to free agents in the sports market. These consultants may work alone or with a small support staff or assistant. It's not uncommon for them to work from home. The issues they consult on and clients who utilize them are as diverse as you can imagine. There are consultants whose expertise is in healthcare benefits, investments, import/export, customer service, getting products to market, product development, sales, cultural issues and diversity, and Web site development. I even know a consultant who makes an incredible living teaching salespeople how to have better manners. (She makes $250,000 a year offering pearls of wisdom like, "Chew gum, people don't want to deal with you if you have bad breath.")

Not just anyone can say, "Poof, I'm a consultant." Actually, there is nothing to prevent you from doing that, because there is no standardized certification required to become a consultant. Consultants are supposed to be experts in their field or have unique knowledge or experience. At least, that's the idea. There are plenty of schlocks out there who give consulting (and themselves) a bad name.

## Where Do I Start?

Typically, the starting position for someone with a bachelor's degree is analyst. Andersen Consulting, Deloitte & Touche, and other Big Six firms offer business analyst or systems analyst positions for those with bachelor's degrees. Sometimes, this is called an associate consultant. The Big Six firms don't like their employees to leave the firm for an MBA. They feel that their "ongoing internal training is so good and extensive that an MBA is unnecessary and removes valuable players from the firm." At Andersen, if you're going to stay with the firm and head down the partner track, they discourage you from leaving the firm for an MBA program. Only the strategic consulting firms (like McKinsey) require that you have an MBA or that you get one after two to three years to move beyond associate consultant or analyst.

In smaller firms, it's much more difficult to get a position right out of school. Many people enter a small firm after they have gained experience in a particular field or with a large firm.

Many solo practitioners start out in another business—gaining experience and contacts—and consult part-time on the side. Others make sure they have some clients lined up before quitting their day jobs and making a full-time commitment to consulting. When you hang your own shingle, you'll think you've been put in a one-man life raft. You'll do it all. You aren't just a consultant, you're the secretary, marketer, presenter, design staff, analyst, and janitor.

> Some of the larger firms such as Bain have summer intern and associate programs that allow you to gain experience before you graduate. These are often ten- to twelve-week programs. Contact a firm's regional office for details.

## What Will I Do?

It varies from person to person, company to company, and specialty to specialty. You might think consulting is simply dispensing your sage advice to paying clients, but it's much more detailed and complex. It involves research, reading, interviewing, and analysis. Your activities will depend on your firm's specialty and the client's needs. Regardless of what type of consultant you are, you'll work closely with your client to learn her business.

Consulting is commonly used as a blanket term when people are really referring to management consulting. As a management consultant, you may be involved in financial analysis, business reengineering, strategic planning, competitive assessment, cost management, productivity improvement, analyzing the client's corporate culture, or helping clients implement the recommended strategies. There are different "competency groups," such as process (which is systems integration), technology, change management (restructuring), strategic services, and practice management (HR). As a new grad recruit in process, you're taught new computer languages (C++ and COBOL) in the office, and then you're sent to school outside Chicago. At school, you're put on a team and given a mock assignment where you get a design, do the programming, build a small system, and test your work. You also have sessions where you learn what is proper behavior at a client site—what is and isn't acceptable. They want to see that you can do the work and that they can throw you on a team and you'll work with others. They test you on the technical aspects and give you a feeling of a day-to-day client environment. They also work you overtime so you can get an accurate picture of the job. A number of new recruits quit after this six-week training period.

As an associate, you'll do a lot of research and quantitative analysis.

## What Does That Mean?

If you're still cloudy on what management consulting means, a corporation will basically hire an outside consultant or firm to observe the company's procedures, manufacturing, morale, finances, or whatever issue or area is of concern, needs improvement, or is not performing properly. The consultant is brought in as an objective, expert third party who can look at the company, its people, and its procedures without emotion or fear for his job. The consultant will do a variety of tasks, surveys, and studies to learn the organization and determine first if there is a problem, and second, what the source of that problem might be. Based upon those findings, the consultant or firm will prepare a report or analysis of the situation and provide these findings to the client often with a recommended strategy. In some cases, this is all that's required. In others, the client looks to the consultant or firm to help implement the recommended strategies.

Some specific tasks consultants perform to arrive at the point where they can dispense advice are:

- Conducting focus groups with employees, vendors, or customers.
- Conducting a competitive analysis of a certain market that your client wants to enter into.
- Filling in as an employee to better understand how certain procedures and processes work and how they might be improved.

## What Is the Environment?

You'll most likely work on a project or case team at a client's location. This can be for several weeks or months at a time. Consulting at any level requires a great deal of travel, because the best way to understand your client and his needs is to be on-site.

In a large firm and some boutique shops, you'll work on a project team, which may consist of three to ten colleagues. The team is made up of people with different levels of seniority and expertise. As an associate consultant or analyst, you'll do the bulk of the frontline research, information gathering, or number crunching.

Consulting is a fast-paced and demanding environment. It is a highly professional setting where your exposure to and experience in many different fields will help you throughout your career.

## How Much Can I Make?

Salary depends upon where you live, your education, and experience with an established firm. The average is between $30,000 and 40,000 for those with a bachelor's degree and slightly higher with a MBA. Consultants usually make another $10,000 in overtime. The good news is that the larger firms also offer standard benefits packages that include insurance, a retirement package, and a travel and expense account. Some firms offer new recruits between $2,000 to $5,000 as a hiring bonus.

Every year when the *Business Week* ranking of business schools and MBA programs comes out, there are reports of grads going into consulting and receiving six-figure starting salaries. Remember that's *not* for undergrads. The people who get the stellar offers are at the top of

---

### Specialize

Consultants can specialize in a variety of fields other than management. A few include:
- Aviation
- Environmental issues/OSHA requirements
- Jury selection
- Human resources
- Political strategy and campaigns
- Computer networking
- Ergonomics and design

their class at a top tier school, and they most likely have prior work experience.

## How Do They Make Money?

Many firms charge a set fee for a project or bill a client an hourly or daily rate for a consultant's time. These fees vary wildly according to the consultant's expertise and reputation, the nature of the business, and what tasks are required. Fees may run as low as $75 an hour to several thousand dollars a day. That may appear to be a steep rate, but realize that you may not be working every day. And if you don't work, you don't eat. Consultants should also be fair to themselves and their clients when estimating how much time a project will take. If you're charging by the hour or day and extend the project's length, you can get a bad reputation. By the same token, if you establish a set fee and then spend twice as long as you had expected on the project, you can lose money.

Other consultants charge their clients a retainer or an annual fee instead of an hourly or daily rate. This is good for the consultant, because she has consistent revenue. Clients benefit by having unlimited access to the consultant and don't watch the clock worrying what it will cost them to use the consultant.

In addition to straight consulting or advising, consultants sometimes supplement their income by providing the client with a variety of value-added tools or services such as designing and licensing training materials and workbooks, conducting focus groups, preparing research reports or surveys, and selling training materials, books, and tapes.

## What About Solo Consultants?

A consultant who is a one-person shop or works from his or her home is no less credible than and can make just as much money as someone in a firm with several partners. There are many solo practitioners who are on the road 150 days a year and easily make $500,000 or more. Many individual consultants are former high-level executives who like the flexibility.

Good consultants are not looking for ways to charge their client for every little thing. You don't want the client to wonder, "Should we call Bradley? How much will it cost us?" You want to become a resource for your client to turn to. How you price your fees does a lot to help determine how much of a resource you'll be. A flat rate per project or retainer is attractive to many clients and goes a long way toward making you a valuable resource.

## What's the Career Path?

At a large firm, you can go the partner route—similar to an accounting firm. The larger consulting firms have many similarities to accounting firms. Some of the Big Six firms, like Andersen and Deloitte & Touche, have both consulting and accounting departments. Generally, you're an analyst for two years and then you're a consultant for two to three years. The goal is to become a manager in five years. But many consultants don't want to become managers, because while you get a salary increase, you lose your overtime. After manager, you can become an associate partner and then a partner.

In these firms, it's often an "up or out" policy. If you're not on the partner track or it's evident you'll not make partner, it's expected that you'll leave. This is similar to law firms. Many people choose to take their experience and then work in-house for a client or become an entrepreneur.

## What Skills Do I Need?

Some of the major consulting firms require that you have an MBA. Just passing doesn't cut it; you need at least a 3.0 or better. However, recruiters want more than good grades—they want people who have demonstrated leadership, drive, commitment, maturity, and the ability to work well with others. Your campus and extracurricular activities are looked at very heavily. Recruiters also look for technical ability, communication skills, and previous work experience. As a recruiter for Deloitte & Touche says, "We aren't looking for certain skills as much as we are looking for candidates with talent."

## What's It Like?

It's different at every level. People have a misconception that it's a cool and easy job. Although the money is great, the hours are extremely long, and you're away from your family and home for weeks at a time. Sometimes you're seen as an outsider and can

John Arnold Smith used his experience working in France and Asia to begin a consulting firm that helps executives and employees doing business abroad become acclimated to another culture. His work takes him to South America, Asia, and Europe. He talks with foreign executives about U.S. customs and ways of doing business. He also helps companies solve cultural conflicts within their organizations. This sometimes means spending time at a client's site and observing communication patterns and how employees and managers of different cultures get along. Other times, he will conduct focus groups to determine the specific challenges.

Three former Big Six consultants in different parts of the country said that their firms had a policy that consultants were not to bring their lunches or eat at their desks. They were expected to have lunch outside of the office where they would be seen—and that did not mean the McDonald's downstairs. These consultants—who were in markets other than New York and Chicago, where people commonly take public transportation—were also told not to take public transportation.

A key to being a successful consultant is to constantly market yourself and make people aware of you and your expertise. People have heard of Andersen Consulting and hire them based upon reputation. However, they might not have heard of Joe Blow Consulting, so it's important that people become familiar with you. If you don't like selling, you're in the wrong business. Until you develop a reputation and client base, much of what you'll do is marketing.

appear threatening to some employees. (What can this guy tell us about our company?) You must be careful not to inflict your personality and will on a client.

If you're with a small firm or on your own, you may be hired on a contract basis, which means that you must always hustle and look for new business—although once you become established, much of your business will come from existing clients. It's hard to get bored as a consultant; there's a lot of variety. You might work on several projects at once or move to a new project or client every few months.

You're largely free to live wherever you want. Unless your firm is based in a certain location, as an individual consultant, you're free to live anywhere. Sam Horn speaks, writes, and consults on communication. She lives on the beach in Maui. Not bad.

Firms often move you to a new state or country to work on a project. The relocation can last for several months to a year.

Consulting is a very professional environment, and your image and reputation matter a lot. Sometimes, a little too much. There is a high amount of turnover in the big firms. This is generally due to burnout or people taking advantage of other opportunities. It's a great training ground for almost anything you want to do. If you have consulting experience with a large firm, you're highly marketable. The major consulting firms are still considered one of the best all-around business training grounds available. Once you have major consulting experience, you're highly in demand.

## Who Are Some Top Firms?

Most of the Big Six firms also have consulting divisions. Some are household names, such as Andersen Consulting. Others are Bain & Co., McKinsey & Company, Booz Allen, Boston Consulting Group, and Gemini Consulting. If you want to work in a particular office of a large firm, such as the Atlanta, Dallas, or San Francisco, you should contact that office directly, since some firms don't have centralized recruiting.

## What The Pros Read

Everything. Good consultants probably read more than anyone except editors. Why? They must stay up on current events, news, and trends within their specialty. Some consultants read two or three books a week in addition to general business publications such as *Fortune, Forbes,* and the *Wall Street Journal.* They also read any trade journals that might be relevant to their or their client's specialty. Many also spend a lot of time on the Net.

## You Should Also Check Out

*Million Dollar Consulting,* by Alan Weiss. Published by McGraw Hill. If you're thinking about starting your own practice, this is the Bible. This guy is a dynamic one-man show who makes a million dollars a year working with Fortune 500 companies. Alan tells you everything from setting your fees to setting up an office. You name it, he covers it. It works.

ACME—The Association of Management Consulting Firms
230 Park Avenue, Suite 544
New York, NY 10169

### The Coaching Craze

Consultants are like junior high girls. They are slaves to the latest trends and fashions. A recent craze among the consulting community is a phenomenon called "coaching." Here is the basic idea: Athletes have coaches to guide and motivate them, so why not employees or individuals? For that matter, where can a CEO turn when he or she needs a little kick in the butt? People don't need to be managed anymore, they need to be coached. So many consultants are shedding the consultant title and adopting the coach moniker. Many people are coaching outside of an office setting and becoming personal "life" coaches. It just sounds softer and friendlier, doesn't it? I wonder if you get to trade in your suit for a pair of those really cool polyester coaching shorts?

What does a "life" coach do? Good question. Several coaches have told me that they meet with a client in person or on the phone to help establish goals and "training" programs, talk through any problems, motivate them, offer a different perspective, and act as a sounding board.

There are some very qualified, intelligent people out there performing a real service. The downside is that every Tom, Dick, and Joe Bob with an opinion thinks he can be a coach. Last summer, I received a call from a woman in Seattle. She read a newspaper article about me and said that she felt that I could use a coach. "What would you do?" I asked. She was vague, saying things like she would help me reach my peak performance. When pressed for details, she said, "We would talk on the phone once a week, and she would give me someone to talk to and help motivate me." For a small fee, of course. Some coach. I was fired up already. I said, "Thanks, but I already have people who I can talk to. They're called friends, and they don't charge me $125 an hour. And as far as motivation is concerned, I get motivated every month when I have to pay my mortgage."

There are some professionals, speakers, authors, and counselors who provide a great one-on-one service, but there are some losers, as well. If you're interested in learning more about becoming a coach or being coached, there is a "virtual gathering" of these coaches who trade ideas on the Internet at a place called—what else—Coach U (www.coachu.com). This is a great concept when used properly by respected, credible experts who can act as high-level advisors, but make sure you get what you pay for. Check the WWW.

ASTD—American Society of Training and Development
1640 King Street
Alexandria, VA 22313

AMA—American Management Association
135 W. 50th Street
New York, NY 10020

## Where on the Web?

www.imcusa.org—Institute of Management Consultants
www.cob.ohio-state.edu/~fin/jobs/mco—Careers in Management Consulting

# 13

• • • • • • • • • • • • • • • • • • • • • • • • • • • • • • • •

# Cops

"Bad boys, bad boys, what ya gonna do?"
—FROM THE THEME SONG OF *COPS*

**Some Common Positions**
Patrolman
Police officer
Detective/investigator

## What Type of Background Do I Need?

Well, not being a convicted felon is a good start. All major police departments begin their prescreening with extensive background and criminal checks and psychological testing. You must have a driver's license with a good driving record (this weeds out a lot of folks) and pass a written civil service exam. There are also physical requirements and tests of strength and endurance.

Most police departments require you to be a U.S. citizen. Age requirements vary, but can start as young as twenty in Los Angeles. (Great, you can't buy beer, but you can pack heat.) The age requirement is older in some cities—twenty-three in Chicago, for instance.

## What About Education?

Most major cities require that you have between forty-five and sixty hours of college credit. Military experience with an honorable discharge also counts. Los Angeles, however, only requires a high school diploma or GED, in addition to passing written exams. (And you wonder why the LAPD gets a bad rap?) All candidates then attend police academy.

## How Much Will I Make?

Starting salaries range from $27,000 in Dallas to a high of $36,900 in Los Angeles. Veteran cops can expect to earn a top salary of between $38,000 to $50,000, with the highest salaries found in New York and Chicago. You don't do this for the money. Most departments offer great health insurance and retirement plans. You might even get a cool black-and-white company car. In some cities, cops are allowed to take their squad cars home. It serves as a neighborhood deterrent.

## How Do I Get Hired?

There's no standard procedure. Every city is different. Some cities—Los Angeles, for example—accept constant walk-in applicants. They expect to hire over 1,000 new police officers this year. Others cities—New York, for one—have an open testing period twice a year. If you're a college student, you can apply for the cadet corp program, which serves as a police internship. In any department, the hiring process can be quite lengthy, taking several months. Contact your local police headquarters to learn about their application process.

## What's the Career Path?

It's largely up to you. Everyone starts out as a uniformed police officer, but then may choose to specialize in an area such as investigations, drug enforcement, crime scene analysis, or forensics, among others. Police officers generally have great retirement packages. In New York, you can retire at half your full salary for life after twenty years of service. That means that in your early forties, you can pull half your salary and pursue something else. Making it to twenty years is the challenge. Some cops choose to go into the FBI or private security.

## What Are the Misconceptions About Being a Cop?

The biggest misconception is that all cops love donuts. The second is that it's all action and danger. It's certainly a dangerous job, but there are many cops who have never had to draw their weapons. You have to be prepared nonetheless. Officer Tim of the Chicago PD says there's much more paperwork than people think. "It seems like I am always filling out reports."

## What's the Most Dangerous Situation Cops Find Themselves In?

Cops say the most dangerous thing is stopping a car or dealing with a volatile domestic situation.

## Where Can I Learn More?

Call your local police headquarters.

## Where on the Web?

There are many law enforcement–oriented sites on the Web. If you go to Yahoo! or any search engine, there are categories devoted to cops and law enforcement. In addition, many police departments have their own Web sites.

### NYPD Cadet Corps

In New York, there's a unique program for college students called the NYPD Cadet Corps. If you're in college and know that you want to pursue a career with the NYPD, they will provide you with up to $20,000 in total compensation for full-time summer and part-time school-year employment. It's basically an apprenticeship or internship program for the police. In addition, they will give a you a $4,000 student loan that will be considered paid in full after two years of police service upon graduation.

During the junior and senior years in the program, you'll have varied assignments. You'll be assigned to a neighborhood precinct, police service area, or transit district. (Talk about hands-on experience!) To apply, contact the NYPD or see if a similar program exists in your area.

# 14

# Education

Although a career in education generally means being a teacher, professor, or administrator, it does not mean being a professional student. Traditionally, education is broken into several categories: elementary, secondary, and higher.

**Some Common Positions**
Teacher
Coach
Professor
Administrator

**Other Opportunities You Might Consider**
Plenty of jobs in education aren't related to teaching at all. For instance, there are administrative positions that are also found in virtually every business. Some of these administrative positions include financial aid and financial services, public affairs, media relations, counseling, facilities management, and development or fund raising. These positions are found at all levels, but are more plentiful in a college or university setting.

There are also educational opportunities outside of the traditional school systems, including vocational education and trade schools, as well as adult education facilities. Other paths educators tend to follow are consulting, counseling, training, publishing, or sales. Don't overlook opportunities in the fastest growing part of education: Special education and languages.

You're probably thinking, "I just spent the past sixteen years in school. Why would I want to go back?" The answer might be, "For a rewarding job." Careers in teaching and education are not only noble professions, but, depending on your specialty and which part of the country you live in, they're professions in high demand.

Traditionally, you might think working in education means being a teacher, but there are many administrative opportunities that exist in a school, school system, or university. It's not unlike any other large business or organization. It takes many resources and departments to make it operate smoothly. This means plenty of opportunities for people from all backgrounds who do not necessarily want to teach or become a principal or superintendent.

There are three basic categories of education: elementary or primary, secondary, and higher education. Teaching opportunities exist in all levels, as do administrative positions. However, there's a greater variety of administrative and operational opportunities within higher education. This section touches on all three levels of education, yet the main focus will be on teaching in K–12.

## Where Will I Start?

When you graduate from college and obtain state certification, you're qualified to teach. You'll start out as a full teacher, ready to mold little minds. In K–12, there are no real levels or degrees of teachers. Any apprentice or assistant work is done while you're student teaching.

Administrative positions in K–12 are a little tougher to come by. It's rare that anyone begins as an administrator without teaching experience. Most administrators are former teachers. It's recommended that you have a minimum of three years teaching experience before considering any type of administrative positions.

Then you might begin as an assistant principal or administrator of a certain department or area such as food service, facilities, or curriculum. Many administrators have advanced degrees, often a master's in education.

## What If I Want to Be an Administrator?

Being a school or an education administrator is like managing any other business. In small schools, there are really only two administrative positions: principal and assistant principal. When you get into a larger school system, there are other administrative- and superintendent-oriented positions.

For administrative positions in higher education, you simply start working in a certain department such as media relations, development, housing, or student activities, to name a few. You advance as you grow in experience, although in many cases you must have an advanced degree (master's) to advance past a certain level.

## What Will I Do?

If you think teaching is simply standing in front of students, you're in for a shock. Certainly, the bulk of your time will be spent teaching kids. Just what does that mean? It means that you'll create lesson plans, make sure that your lesson plans closely follow the curriculum recommended by the state or local school board, and take care of disciplinary problems.

But that is only half the job. Teaching is not an 8:30 to 3:30 job. Teachers easily work over 50 hours a week. The average teacher spends 36.5 hours a week in the classroom, another 9 hours preparing lessons and grading papers, and an additional 10 hours on other nonteaching school-based activities such as dealing with parents. You'll take a lot of work home with you.

Coaching demands even more time because of games, practice, scouting, and travel—all in addition to regular teaching duties.

## What Education and Training Do I Need?

To become a K–12 teacher, you need to have at least a bachelor's degree and should be certified to teach in your particular state. Requirements for teacher certification vary from state to state. To learn what those requirements are, contact your state's or college's education department.

While it's possible to teach without an education degree, it's a much longer and complicated path to become certified. The smartest degree plan is to obtain your bachelor's degree through your school's education department. Through the education department, you can graduate with a general education degree, specialize in elementary education, or obtain a degree in your core subject. Regardless of your specialty, choosing to graduate from the education department is much easier, because it's structured to offer you additional education classes necessary to obtain certification and pass the required competency exams.

Before you get too far into your education, you should decide whether you want to teach elementary or secondary school. The paths are similar, but the type of degree you obtain is slightly different. Elementary education is considered a general discipline, which is reflected by the required degree and courses. Most elementary teachers teach all subjects until about the fourth-grade level.

Secondary teachers are rarely generalists. They usually stick with one particular subject. If you choose secondary education, you'll likely graduate from the education department, but with a degree in your core specialty, such as math, science, or history. In

---

### What If I Want to Teach Several Subjects?

Secondary (junior or senior high school) teachers are often only qualified to teach one subject. There are various exit or competency exams for specific subjects. Exams are usually given upon graduation, and they vary from state to state. Once you're certified, it's possible to take the competency exam for other subjects in which you wish to specialize. Upon passing this exam, you're then qualified to teach that subject without having to return to college or take additional coursework to gain a specialty. For example, if you're an Earth science teacher and you also wanted to teach biology, you would take the teacher's test (names vary from state to state). If you pass, you're then qualified to teach biology.

addition, you'll take four educational classes dealing with child psychology, curriculum development, class assessment and evaluation, and classroom observation. Finally, you'll student teach for fourteen weeks. Student teaching is the last thing you do: They don't let you loose with the animals until you're prepared.

Upon graduation, you'll take an exit exam in both your core specialty and general education. If you pass the exam, you'll send your results and fees into the appropriate state education department or agency. You will then be granted a teaching certificate. Certification is state by state, but several states have reciprocity (like the legal profession), which means that if you're certified in one state, you're automatically certified in another. Others require you to take that state's certification exams.

## Where Are the Jobs?

Teaching is feast or famine. There are school districts and areas of the country that are in dire need of teachers, while others must turn away people who want to teach. Of course, upscale suburban school districts don't have a hard time attracting candidates. The pay in top schools is often above average, and the work environment is fairly nice. Moreover, disciplinary and safety concerns that may be inherent in many inner city schools exist to a much lesser degree. However, these are also the schools that have the stiffest competition when it comes to getting hired.

There is great need for teachers in urban and rural areas. There is also high demand for teachers who are speakers of foreign languages, primarily Spanish. There is a dearth of teachers of English as a second language, male teachers, and teachers of color. According to the Clearinghouse on Teaching and Teacher Education, public teachers are 73 percent female, 87 percent white, and 48 percent under forty years old. These percentages are even higher in private schools.

Many schools need men who teach science or math and are willing to coach sports. If you teach special education, you can write your own ticket. Special education means teaching kids who have physical or learning disabilities or who are emotionally challenged. It's estimated that there will be a 53 percent increase in the amount of special education teachers in the next eight years.

## How Do I Learn About Teaching Jobs?

If you're still in college, you should sign up with your school's career services office. Many school districts recruit on campus. Other school districts ask the career services office to send résumés of qualified candidates.

Some schools even have online and telephone services that allow school districts to automatically screen applicants by viewing their résumé on screen or listening to a profile on the phone. Whatever services your college provides, you should make sure your that your information is available in all forms. The most frequent way graduates obtain teaching positions is by word of mouth and contacts from their department or college.

## Career Fairs

Another popular way to learn about teaching positions is through career fairs. In general, I am not a big fan of career fairs, but educational career fairs are one of the few industries where a significant number of people actually get hired as a result of attending. Career fairs are a great way for you to learn about positions in areas you might not be familiar with or have not before considered. Veterans of education career fairs say the smartest way to work a career fair is to obtain in advance a list of which school districts will be attending the career fair. You can request a list weeks ahead of time. Simply call the sponsors of the career fair and ask them to fax a list to you. Once you know who will be attending the fair, call the school district and ask for an application. Have the application completed before you attend the fair. Many job seekers wander aimlessly from booth to booth at a career fair, picking up applications to send in later. If you're smart, you'll already have a completed application ready to turn into recruiters at the career fair. This will let recruiters evaluate you on the spot and give you an opportunity to properly sell yourself.

Another way to obtain a teaching position is by simply applying to various schools for which you would like to work. If you don't know where to turn, call your city's school district or education department and ask for information and an application. If you're considering relocating, you should contact the local Chamber of Commerce and ask for a relocation packet. They should have a list of school districts in the area.

You can also contact that city's local business journal or newspaper. They often publish an annual list of local school districts with contact names, salary, and education and experience requirement information. If you have a hard time locating any of this information, contact the education editor of the local newspaper.

## It's Who You Know

Even in education, it doesn't hurt to be connected. Many people establish their contacts while student teaching and some even obtain full-time positions at the school where they student taught. Ask your friends and contacts at other schools if they know of any openings. Your contacts may learn of job openings long before they're posted. They can tell you when something might come open so you can apply before the rush. Ask your contact to recommend you for the job.

## Why Do You Like Teaching?

Every teacher I spoke with—elementary or high school—said the same thing, "You don't go into teaching for the money. You teach because you know you can make a difference in a child's life." You must like dealing with and influencing children. Many people go into teaching because they were influenced by teachers or coaches as children and feel that teaching is their chance to give back. Others say they enjoy having an impact on society. Some simply enjoy watching children learn. Sarah, a second-grade teacher, says, "Everything is exciting to the little ones."

Teaching, of course, has other benefits, like three months off for summer, a week off for spring break, and two weeks off at Christmas. But vacation time is the wrong reason to go into teaching. Many teachers take second jobs during the summer months because they're bored after a few weeks of inactivity or they need the money.

## What's Hard About Teaching?

Teaching means spending your days shaping eager young minds who thirst for knowledge and hang on your every word. Yeah, right. If you think teaching

### How Do I Become a Substitute Teacher?

If you were anything like me as a kid, think of the hell you put substitute teachers through. Well, if you want to be a substitute, remember that payback's a bitch, as they say. In order to become a substitute teacher, you do not need any type of certification or even a degree. Depending on the school district, you only need from sixty to ninety hours of college credit and a pulse to qualify to substitute teach.

To apply, call the school district in your area and ask for a substitute teaching application. Once your application is completed, you must attend an orientation meeting to learn about that district's discipline, rules, and procedures. You're then put on the substitute list. As needs arise, the "substitute coordinator"—or whoever is in charge of scheduling—calls people on the list. The substitute coordinator goes down the list and chooses people who are certified in the core subject needed for that day. If no one meets that criteria, he then looks for anyone who is certified. If no certified teacher is available, they check the list for people who have college degrees and finally a warm body with some college credits.

Subbing is very tough according to Craig, who has subbed for over a year on the high school level. "Even the bad teachers have some form of discipline. Substitutes don't have any real way to discipline kids, and that makes it tough to gain respect."

You can really work as often or as little as you would like. If you would like to work a lot, you should put your name on the substitute list in several districts. Pay for substitutes depends upon the district, but can range from $45 to $65 a day before taxes. Being a substitute is a great way to earn extra money, so it attracts a lot of college students and recent graduates who have yet to find a job. There are also a number of retired people who substitute teach because they like to be around kids.

To keep your sanity as a substitute teacher, you must be flexible and able to deal with change and the unknown. "I never know if I'll work from one day to the next. I have to be prepared for the call at 5:30 A.M. telling me where I'll be that day," says Craig.

Jessica, a junior high science teacher, says, "Sometimes I'll come up with a lab or a lesson that I think is a great idea, and the students just can't understand the project or they just don't care. It can really be frustrating and disappointing. It really bursts my bubble. I had to realize that not all students enjoy school or like learning as much as I do."

is just talking in front of kids or creating exciting assignments that make kids want to learn more, you need a little reality check. Kids don't respond well to traditional teaching methods like lecturing or using overheads. They want to be entertained. You can't stand in front of students and simply lecture anymore. Kids are much more sophisticated and require more exciting ways to learn. "You can't get up there and BS your way through things. Kids pick up on that in a hurry, and when they do, you'll lose control," says Louisa, a high school biology teacher. Sometimes it's discouraging, because you work hard to plan an assignment that you think is fun and will allow your students to grasp an idea, and they just don't respond.

It's a far cry from *Dangerous Minds* or *Welcome Back Kotter*. Television sitcoms and movies portray teachers as being able to create innovative teaching styles and curriculum. This is the exception, not the rule. Teaching is much more structured and regimented than you might imagine. Curriculum is often dictated by a school board or state board of education. Some states, such as Texas, require students at all levels to take a standardized test to determine proficiency in certain subjects. The curriculum is geared entirely toward passing that test, not toward students strengths or interests.

There's been much debate over this type of education. Teachers argue that it has become more difficult to address students with special needs, interests, or aptitudes, because they must follow the state-mandated curriculum. A teacher's performance is sometimes evaluated according to how they follow the curriculum and how well their students perform on the standardized test. It's easy to become frustrated, because the curriculum is not always exciting or appropriate.

## This Isn't Day Care

Sometimes you'll feel like a baby-sitter. Karen, an elementary school teacher, says, "The toughest part is dealing with parents who don't care. Sometimes I'll contact parents, but I usually reach a grandma, aunt, or other relative with whom the child is living." There has been much debate on whose job it is to discipline kids and who should teach kids values, morals, and right from wrong. Kim, a first-grade teacher, says, "Some parents think, 'I'm dropping my child off at your door, and he is your responsibility.' They want us to mold their children and teach them manners and morals. The problem is that we spend most of the day with these kids and make progress, but the moment they go home, these values aren't reflected in the home, so everything we did that day is wasted."

## All Bark, But No Bite

Several teachers stated that school systems have made it harder for teachers to discipline kids. Corporal punishment is a thing of the past at most schools. If it's used, it's only allowed if the student's parents give written permission. Even teachers who don't believe in corporal punishment or are not strict disciplinarians say they feel that their hands are tied in many ways and that it's sometimes difficult to maintain control of the classroom.

This is most evident in schools with gang problems. An increase in gangs and troubled youth in the classroom has made teachers' jobs more difficult—and in some cases, more dangerous. Gangs and troubled children are no longer a problem restricted to teachers in the inner city. Gangs are becoming a problem for teachers in all areas, including suburbs and small towns. It makes teaching the kids who do want to learn much more challenging. Chad, a high school science teacher, says, "Many of these gang kids don't expect to live to age twenty-five, so they don't see the need to study. They could care less about school, and it adversely affects the other students and the learning environment."

Another challenge for teachers is an increasingly multicultural environment. Teachers are encountering some major cultural differences, which affect how kids learn and how teachers should approach them. Jason, a high school coach in an ethnically diverse urban school district, says, "Each ethnic group has a different learning style. Especially with high school–aged kids, you must be in tune with those cultural differences and know how to approach each one. Many of these kids are at risk. As a teacher, I must be able to know which buttons to push, or I risk losing them for good."

## When the Kids Go Home, You Go to Work

In addition to the work in the classroom, there's a lot of after-school and prep work at home. If you coach, you can easily expect to be at school until 6:00 P.M. every day. At smaller schools, it can be even more demanding, because you may have multiple duties. If you're in a large metropolitan area, chances are that most extracurricular activities are also in the area. However, if you're in a rural area, you'll have to travel to compete with other schools or participate in activities.

# How Much Will I Make?

Not much. People don't become teachers to get rich. Your perks and personal satisfaction may far outweigh any monetary rewards. Last year, the average salary for all teachers was $36,933. Starting salary for beginning teachers was $23,915. Traditionally, private school teachers are paid less than public school teachers.

Salaries vary from state to state and district to district. Some school districts' pay scales depend on the demand for teachers. Districts in a nice suburban area with no gang problems and a wealthy tax base will have no problem finding teachers. However, there's also stiff competition for these jobs. Schools in less desirable areas might pay considerably less. An interesting trend among some rural schools or schools that have a difficult time attracting teachers is to offer considerably higher salaries, which one teacher called combat pay.

Salaries rise according to experience and additional education, but an advanced degree does not mean a giant increase in salary. In fact, the difference in pay between having your masters versus only a bachelor's degree is negligible. According to figures given by the Houston Independent School District, the difference in pay between two people with ten years of experience—one having her master's degree and the other possessing only a bachelor's degree—was

---

## What's It Like to Be a Coach?

I know, you want to be a coach, because you get to wear those really cool polyester coaching shorts. If you only want to be a coach and not teach, I've got bad news. Unless you coach in the college ranks, you'll be a coach *and* a teacher. There are no special requirements or certifications necessary to become a coach, although many are former athletes or studied physical education in college.

A coach's main salary comes from teaching, but they receive additional pay in the form of a coaching stipend. This coaching stipend depends on what you coach, where you're located, and sometimes how good you are. In what may seemingly be one of the great injustices in America, the varsity football coach often makes more than the volleyball or track coach.

One of the special benefits of being a coach is that you get to relive your former athletic glory. It's nice to still be associated with a sport, but more importantly, you're helping young people build self-esteem. Tate, a junior high football and basketball coach, says, "It's fun to see kids succeed and build self-esteem. In an athletic situation, I have a better chance to teach kids about manners, morals, values, and discipline than I have in a traditional classroom setting. It's also nice to see a kid who can't succeed in anything else find something he or she is good at. That kid may be dumb as a post in the classroom, but when he succeeds in athletics, you see him begin to feel better about himself."

Other coaches say they entered coaching because sports played such a big role in shaping their lives when they were young. They see coaching as a chance to create those same memories for other kids. Tim, another junior high coach, says, "Many of these kids aren't good enough to ever play in high school or college. For them, this is the high point of their athletic career. For some of these kids, participating in sports will be one of the special memories they cherish about this time in their lives."

Of course, there's a major downside to coaching. You often have to deal with pushy parents who yell at you because their kid is on the bench or who feel they're qualified to coach.

approximately $3,000. (In case you were wondering, the maximum salary for a teacher in Houston with ten years experience and a master's degree is approximately $47,000.)

Administrators have the potential to make over $50,000, and a few might even crack $100,000, but only in the largest or wealthiest school districts and with many years of experience.

> Tate, a junior high coach and biology teacher in a town of 250,000, was offered a position, sight unseen, in a small town of 2,000 people. The closest major city was three hours away. In addition to the school district's offer to pay for his family's move, the starting salary was $4,000 more than he was making. If he decided to coach in addition to teaching, he would be paid an additional $6,000.

In higher education, the money varies greatly and depends upon your department and institution. You can actually make decent money in administration and managerial positions in a university setting. It just takes a long time to reach that point. Top development officers might make between $40,000 to $60,000. Public affairs and media relations staff might make in the $30,000 to $50,000 range. If you're a dean or full professor, you might make over $100,000, but it depends upon your specialty and your school.

## What The Pros Read

*Education Week*—A weekly newspaper that focuses on K–12 and includes
   ads for teacher placement agencies
*Chronicle of Higher Education*

## Where Can I Learn More?

*The Job Search Handbook*. Published by AAEE (American Association for
   Employment in Education), which can be reached at 847-864-1999.
Teach for America: The national teaching corps of recent graduates who
   commit a minimum of two years to teaching in rural or underre-
   sourced areas. It's the Peace Corp for teachers.
ERIC Clearing House on Teaching and Teacher Education
ERIC Resources Information Center: A federally funded information net-
   work designed to provide access to education literature.

## Overseas Teaching Opportunities

To teach abroad, you usually need a minimum of an undergraduate degree, state certification, and two or three years of experience. Requirements may vary. There are teaching opportunities through private organizations or government agencies. The following organizations are a good place to start:

## Did You Know?

Sea World in Orlando looks for job candidates with education degrees. Many of the programs they provide at the park involve educating guests and the community about sea life. So appropriately, many employees are former teachers.

Friends of World Teaching: 800-50-FRIENDS

The U.S. State Department publishes a list of American-sponsored Elementary Schools. For details and contact names, call 703-875-7800.

International Schools Services (ISS) runs schools abroad for American industry and business contact. They can be reached at 609-452-0900.

U.S. Department of Defense: Opportunities in schools on military bases around the world. They publish a booklet entitled *Overseas Opportunities for Educators*. They can be reached at 703-696-3033.

## Where Can I Learn More?

American Federation of Teachers

National Education Association

Pi Lambda Theta

National Clearing House for Bilingual Education: 800-321-6223

National Association of State Directors of Vocational Education: 202-737-0303

The Council for Exceptional Children (Special Education): 703-264-9476

TESOL—Teachers of English to Speakers of Other Languages: 703-836-0774

National Council of Math Teachers: 703-620-9840

National Art Education Association: 704-860-8000

## Where on the Web?

www.teachforamerica.org—Teach for America

www.ericsp.org—ERIC Clearinghouse on Teaching and Teacher Education

www.academploy.com—Academic Employment Network

# 15

· · · · · · · · · · · · · · · · · · · · · · · · · · · · · · · ·

# Engineering

**Some Common Positions**
> Civil Engineer
> Chemical Engineer
> Petroleum Engineer
> Mechanical Engineer
> Electrical Engineer
> Industrial Engineer
> Computer/Software Engineer
> Geek

**Other Opportunities You Might Consider**
Many engineers use their technical background to go into sales or technical support. Others become analysts or consultants, helping companies develop systems or troubleshoot problems. There are more than twenty-five different types of engineers. They each work in their own specialty, but have basic training applicable to many different areas.

## What's Engineering?

As a kid, I belonged to the Cub Scouts and, like every other kid, I tried to earn my merit badges. When I came to the engineering badge, I just skipped right over it. I thought it meant you had to build engines. In college, I still had no real idea of what engineers did, but I was jealous nonetheless, because they seemed to get all the high-paying job offers. Meanwhile, my colleagues in liberal arts and I were contemplating whether we should take the low-paying advertising job or just sell our plasma. So here goes a brief description of what engineering really is.

Whether it is the computer you use, the car you drive, or the pen you write with, an engineer probably had a large part in its design and creation. Engineers basically design, create, and implement processes, machinery, and systems. They determine how things work and work together. Part of their job also involves evaluating design, cost, safety, and reliability of a product or project.

Engineers can be found in such diverse areas as design, manufacturing, or quality control. Some work in a design studio, while others work in production or in the field. Many people traditionally think of engineering as design or manufacturing, but increasingly you are finding engineers in areas such as sales, consulting, customer service, and technical support. An engineer may find himself called on to evaluate specifications, troubleshoot a production line, or consult with a manufacturer on their procedures.

## Where Do I Start?

You will likely start out as a junior or associate engineer, although occasionally some people start out as full engineers. Training varies from company to company. You may be paired with a senior engineer or team member to learn the ropes and be their shadow, or you may go through weeks of formal training to learn the company's procedures. You are likely to start as a member of a team. Rarely do engineers work alone. More typically, you have one task on a piece of a project. You might also go through a rotation of various departments to see what you enjoy and so the company can determine where you would best fit. Other times, you simply go where there's a need.

As a rookie engineer, much of your learning will be done on the fly. Many of the situations you encounter will not have a clear-cut solution that can be found in the manual.

## Who Hires Engineers?

Nearly every company hires engineers, including manufacturers of food, consumer goods, textiles, computers, and software, as well as oil and gas companies and the government. Even consulting firms such as Andersen or Ernst & Young hire engineers. Employers love the way engineers are trained to think critically and analytically.

## What's the Career Path?

Engineering does not have a specific career path. Some people choose to make a career with one employer and rise through the ranks, while others develop their skills and then take what they learn at a large company and move to a smaller company or specialty engineering firm. Others open their own businesses. In a large corporation, you can expect to move up every eighteen to twenty-four months. However, you may be on a project that lasts for an extended period.

## What About Education?

A bachelor's degree in one of the engineering fields is the minimum requirement. Many disciplines will accept a degree in computer science or math. Many of the degrees can apply across several fields. For example, a high-tech or computer company might take engineering degrees in electrical, computer, mechanical, industrial, chemical, etc.

Grades are very important, because many companies use that as a first screen, so study hard. If your grades are not up to par, make sure you have phenomenal work experience or internships. This is a discipline where your technical proficiency is important. Starting out, the best way to demonstrate your competence is though your grades. After that, experience is all that matters. Some people go back for master's level work and graduate degrees, but it's not a requirement. More engineers are boosting their skills with classes or even an MBA.

Recruiters say not to overlook math courses and pure science. Many young engineers narrow their focus, but employers want someone with a broad focus who can understand physics, chemistry, and the sciences.

## Learning Doesn't Stop Once You Graduate

Jeff at Texas Instruments says he sees a lot of new employees who think that learning ends when you earn the degree and begin your career. "Learning accelerates once you being working, especially in this industry where technology is changing so rapidly. There is always something new to learn."

## What Skills Do I Need?

Regardless of your discipline or industry, you must be comfortable with computers and extremely comfortable with complex math. Since engineering is much more than design, you will be often be called on to deal with coworkers, contractors, and clients. Engineers with good communication skills really stand out from the crowd. It doesn't matter how great your design is if you can't explain it to the people who have to build it. Jeff Goodwin, staffing director at Texas Instruments, says, "Communication skills and the ability to work collaboratively are the qualities we value the most, yet they are the skills that engineers appreciate least in themselves. If all you have to offer are technical skills, we will pass. We need engineers who have both."

You should also be creative, analytical, and detail-oriented. Engineers are analytical and logical by training. They can think in very precise terms. Many are great with math, can think spatially, and work well with their hands.

Recruiters say they want someone who is innovative and "agile." (Agile? Are they going to make you run a forty-yard dash?) Actually, they mean that you must be able to handle change and chaos, because technology is changing so rapidly.

## How Do I Get Hired?

To find entry-level candidates, most private firms and public-sector organizations use career fairs and on-campus recruiting as the main way of hiring people. Many also use their summer internship programs as mini recruiting sessions. "At Union Carbide, it's not uncommon for us to extend offers to more than half of our summer interns," says Don Gatewood, college relations manager. Many engineers participate in co-ops while in school and remain with their employer after graduation.

Sad but true, many technology and engineering companies rely so heavily on campus recruiting at select schools that if you don't go to a place where they recruit, you're out of luck. They'll say you can apply, but you can also buy a lottery ticket. You stand about the same chance. The good news is that some companies like Texas Instruments can go to as many as 75 to 100 schools. Union Carbide might go to 20.

While many engineering positions are listed on the Internet, not that many people are landing jobs on the Internet. A recent survey by *Electronic Engineering Times* found that only 5.5 percent of those polled have actually found a job using the Internet.

Once you're hired, employees learn of other jobs through word of mouth, clients, and internal job postings. In a large organization with several divisions, it's common for job openings to be posted so employees from other divisions might apply for a transfer.

### JobSmarts Top Career Pick: Electrical and Computer Engineer

According to *Forbes* magazine, the top ten semiconductor companies have 12,000 open positions, and the pay of computer engineers has risen by two-thirds over the past ten years. Some companies are even offering cash bonuses as finders fees if an employee recommends someone who is eventually hired.

## Everyone Wants Engineers

Companies that have traditionally not hired engineers—such as banks and consulting firms—are beginning to compete with high-tech firms and others who have historically been the main employers of engineering grads. "There isn't enough engineering talent in the world to support everyone's interests and endeavors," says Lynn Davis, a Senior VP at

SDC Telecommunications. Employers can't hire them fast enough. John Chambers, CEO of Cisco Systems, says, "We're growing at a thousand people a quarter."

## How Much Will I Make?

Entry-level engineers generally earn between $30,000 to $40,000. Salaries depend upon area of expertise, grades, and what part of the country you are located in. Most companies that hire engineers offer standard insurance and benefit packages.

Engineers traditionally have the highest starting salaries of any college graduates. This year, chemical engineers are the highest paid graduates. Engineering is a popular career choice because of the high starting salaries, but many don't realize that they never make as much as people in some other fields who may start at a lesser salary. Salary increases slow down after about three to five years and can often top out in the $80,000 range. The average salary for electrical engineers, one of the fields in greatest demand right now, is $65,100. The way to really make more is to go into management or start your own company.

### What's a Civil Engineer?

An engineer with exceptional manners? No. Civil engineers oversee the design, building, and maintenance of bridges, roads, buildings, rail systems, highways, airports, and other structures that are utilized by the general public. They primarily work for a public or government agency or with a private firm.

## What Will I Do?

Everything. Most new recruits are rotated through different departments to get an overall look at how everything fits together. You may also be placed on a project team with experienced engineers. Depending on the organization, you might get hands-on experience writing or reviewing code or performing experiments and tests. You might also end up doing mundane activities.

A lot of what you will be doing is crunching numbers on an engineering database or modeling software. Computers have completely changed the way many engineers do their jobs. "You will devise experiments and test. You will spend a lot of time working on a PC with design tools or Excel or other databases," says Kirk at Texas Instruments. "You will spend a lot of time sending and responding to e-mail." In many organizations, e-mail is *the* primary method of communication. "I spend about an hour a day taking care of e-mail. Using it is an absolute requirement," says Kirk.

For civil engineers, training may consist of building mock bridges and roads for the first few months so that you can learn all of the design stan-

Scott, who began his career at a large computer manufacturer and now owns his own software firm, says, "For the first six months, I drove a truck and delivered parts between two plants. I was the most educated truck driver they had."

dards. There are certain standards and codes for buildings, electronics, and systems, which you will learn on the job.

According to Kirk at Texas Instruments, there's a lot of interfacing with other engineers on a project team. "We might have a daily formal meeting to exchange ideas and information."

If you're a designer, you might communicate with people on the line and work closely with people producing the work you design. You have to be able to translate a written or pictorial idea into layman's language that an operator or line worker can use.

## What's the Culture Like?

Engineers and culture are two words not often found together in the same sentence. If you have ever read *Dilbert*, you pretty much have it. Okay, that might be stretching it a bit, but some engineers agree with the stereotype that, in general, they lack communication skills and fashion sense. This is still a very male-dominated field. (In some disciplines, such as mechanical engineering, only 10 percent of engineers are women.) Certain disciplines have a bureaucratic or military feel to them, while others are loose and casual. The culture will depend largely on the company or organization. You may be in a corporate headquarters setting such as EDS or Texas Instruments. Other companies might have you in the field at a client's location, plant, or construction site. You may have an office or you might even office out of a mobile trailer.

## What About Working for the Government?

The state and federal government hire a huge number of engineers. As in most professions, you won't make as much money working in the public sector as you would working for a private company. The benefits can be good, and you will have job security. Contact the OPM online at www.usajobs.opm.gov for more information on job openings.

## Intellectual Property: What's Mine Is Mine and What's Yours Is Mine

### Did You Know?

The largest branch of engineering is electrical engineering. The highest paying branch is chemical engineering, due largely to its complexity and demand.

The companies that hire you to design, invent, and create new products and processes that may potentially be worth millions often may lay claim to all that is in that noggin of yours. They do this by asking you to sign agreements that relinquish your rights and ownership of all patents or ideas born while employed there. This can also mean things that you do on your spare time and at home. How do you get around it? Sometimes you can't, but several engineers said to either not sign it or calmly tell your employer that you must speak with your attorney. "Sometimes they'll just drop it if you drag your feet and don't sign it."

## Public Versus Private Sector

Public-sector employees say that the biggest disappointments are that your salary is significantly lower than it would be in the private sector and you sometimes have to do things that are sometimes beneath you. Yeah, well who doesn't? But the training is excellent, and many engineers take advantage of this to move into private industry. There is also greater job security in the public sector than in private industry.

---

**You're a Problem Solver**

Steve was trained as a field engineer in weapons systems at Texas Instruments. He could say what he did, but he would then have to kill you. He also worked in a special area of technical purchasing with the company. Seeing how defense spending was being cut, he changed companies and is now a senior business analyst for CompUSA. His engineering and purchasing background help him as he and his team build and troubleshoot a new inventory control and warehousing system.

---

## What's the Worst Thing About Engineering?

Rookie engineers claim they were a little disillusioned during their first six months. Brandon, a rookie mechanical engineer, says, "I thought that I would be designing, inventing, working on projects, and making an impact. I didn't realize that I would have to wait so long before getting to do significant work. I thought, "This is what I went to school for?" This is not the case at every company. There are many who put you right into the fire, working on actual projects from day one.

## Where on the Web?

www.ieee.org—Institute of Electric and Electrical Engineering
www.ti.com—Texas Instruments
www.nspe.org—National Society of Professional Engineers
www.iienet.org—Institute of Industrial Engineers
www.pitt.edu/~slcst19/women.html—Women in Computing and Engineering

# 16

●  ●  ●  ●  ●  ●  ●  ●  ●  ●  ●  ●  ●  ●  ●  ●  ●  ●  ●  ●  ●  ●  ●

# Entrepreneurship

Are you sick of the rat race? Tired of slaving away nights and weekends only to watch your boss go to Aspen for the weekend? Tired of listening to the company president talk about the problems that come with decorating a beach house? Life's rough, isn't it? If you've had enough of being the worker bee, consider what more and more Americans are doing each year: starting their own businesses.

There is a growing trend in America for people to become entrepreneurs. Technology has made it possible for a one-person shop to compete with much larger companies. Colleges are taking notice of this trend, too. As recently as ten years ago, there were only a few programs devoted to entrepreneurship. Today, there are over 500. People are beginning to take the plunge into business for themselves at a much earlier age. According to *Forbes* magazine, almost 65 percent of Americans under thirty-five years of age plan on owning their own business or being their own boss. This compares with only 35 percent of Americans over the age of thirty-five. Twentysomethings and young adults have been called the most entrepreneurial generation in history.

You may dream of being the next Bill Gates or discovering the next Netscape, Yahoo!, or other fast-rising company, taking it public, and making millions of dollars overnight. But it's important to realize that not every entrepreneur is financially successful, and most work harder than they ever did when someone else was picking up the tab. Below are some tips and information that may help you decide whether or not to start your own business.

Anyone can become an entrepreneur, regardless of education or economic background. Even inner-city kids in the Bronx have discovered entrepreneurship through programs like NFTE (The National Foundation for the Teaching of Entrepreneurship), which teaches business principles to inner-city youth and helps them start businesses in their neighborhoods. There really are no barriers that can't be overcome, but it starts with being creative and working hard.

## Why Do People Become Entrepreneurs?

People become entrepreneurs or decide to work for themselves for a number of reasons, many of them personal. However, the rise in small business and entrepreneurship is a direct result of the downsizing and restructuring of larger companies and the steady decline of campus recruiting by major corporations. More students and young adults realize that they're going to have to invent their careers. Many experts believe that the ultimate job security is not with companies, but rather in your own skills and abilities, as author Cliff Hakim says in his book *We Are All Self-Employed*. Even if you are working for a company, you are still ultimately responsible for developing your own career.

A number of people turn to entrepreneurship or start their own business to fulfill their need for more freedom and autonomy. They're tired of working for someone else and playing the political games present in working for a larger company. Others turn to small business because they might not have the desire or personality to make it in a large bureaucratic company.

Yet the most common reason that people become entrepreneurs is to make more money. It's certainly risky. You could lose everything you own, but there is always a greater chance of making more money if you're the owner rather than the employee.

## Be Prepared to Wear a Lot of Hats.

Getting your first business cards that read president, CEO, king or queen, or whatever title that indicates you are in charge has to be one of the greatest feelings in the world. That title says, "I have arrived." Enjoy that feeling, because it lasts about five minutes before you realize that in addition to being president or CEO, you are also the secretary, printer, data entry person, manager, market-

### Top Three Reasons People Become Entrepreneurs

1.  To earn more money.
2.  For more freedom and independence.
3.  To work in an area that fascinates them.

(According to a U.S. Trust *Survey of Entrepreneurs*)

ing and sales department, referee, human resource specialist, bookkeeper and accounts payable department, janitor, and coffee jockey. If something needs to be done, it's up to you.

Having your name on the door is cool, but it doesn't mean that you can kick back and think, "I'll have other people do that. I don't have to do that now that I own the company." You will do everything, *because it is your company*. Even if you delegate a task, the ultimate responsibility is with you.

Most small businesses are a one-person show. The U.S. Census Bureau recently found that of all American small businesses, 81 percent have no paid employees. The only workers are the people or families who own the company. "One-person shows" are a very common and smart way to get a company off the ground. Many small companies hire temps, freelancers, or contractors to produce work instead of keeping a full-time employee.

## What Type of Business Should I Start?

Before you rack your brain trying to come up with a super idea that no one has done before, look around to see if there is a need that is currently not being met or an existing product or service that could be improved upon. Almost everyone has sat around with their friends at one time or another and said, "I have a good idea for a business," or read a story about an entrepreneur and said, "I thought of doing that years ago." There are millions of good ideas out there. Many never come to fruition, because people talk about it, but never act on it. Many people also think that a good idea is all that it takes. A good idea is the first step, but it's a baby step when compared with what it takes to create a successful business.

## You Don't Have to Reinvent the Wheel

First of all, truly original ideas are a rarity. (Okay, Bill Gates excluded.) Certainly in technology, people are making fortunes creating revolutionary products, but for every entrepreneur with a brand-new idea that has never been seen before, there are at least five who have created successful businesses by taking an existing product or service and finding a way to make it better or capitalizing on a market that wasn't being served adequately.

A great example is Wayne Huzinga, former CEO of Blockbuster. I realize that the movie rental business may not be brain surgery. Huzinga certainly didn't come up with the idea of renting movies on his own, but he saw a way to make it better. It wasn't as if he had a long track record in the video business, either. Huzinga made his first millions in the trash-hauling business. His current venture involves the used-car market. His company, Auto Nation, is finding a better, more palatable way of selling used (sorry, previously owned) cars.

Many entrepreneurs start businesses based on something they love. They take a hobby or passion and turn it into a business, or they take a personal need or observation and tailor a business around it. Tomima Edmark was trying different ways to put her hair up other than a basic ponytail. By playing with some wire, she discovered a way to put her hair into an elaborate design. The piece of wire that she used was to become the Topsy Tail. She made a few more and sold them to some stores. It took off, earning her tens of millions of dollars. It's not rocket science. Look in your everyday life and see if there is something that you could turn into a viable business. Remember, you may have a great idea, but the true litmus test is if people are be willing to pay for it.

## What's a Franchise?

Franchises are chains, like restaurants, retail outlets, or services. As a franchisee, you pay a franchise fee to the parent company or franchiser. This is often a substantial amount, ranging from tens to hundreds of thousands of dollars. There are also royalties, which are based on a percentage of revenues or profits to license the name from the parent company. Amounts and structures vary. Franchises such as McDonald's are among the most expensive to start up, costing several hundred thousand dollars.

As a franchisee, you have the right to operate your business under the parent company's name. The parent company may offer support in obtaining products, purchasing and distribution, materials, signage, training, and advertising. They may even help you build your location. There may be restrictions on what you can and cannot do, since you are licensing the name from them. It can be much more complicated, but essentially you are buying a business. Franchises can be very lucrative, but are difficult to make succeed. It generally takes much more money than people may imagine. A good place to learn more is the International Franchise Association, which can be reached at 202-628-8000. You can also read more about franchising and particular companies, including franchise costs, in *Entrepreneur* magazine and *Entrepreneur Online* at www.entrepreneurmag.com.

## How Do I Find a Reputable Franchise?

Call your local Better Business Bureau or state attorney general's office to see if there have been any complaints filed against a certain franchise. Next, contact the Federal Trade Commission's division of marketing prac-

## Two Common Types of Businesses

*Those That Provide a Service*. Services range from advertising and consulting to painting or dry cleaning. A service business can be one with very little overheard and initial expense, such as a public relations firm, where it's just you, a phone, and a computer, to something requiring a great deal of start-up money, such as a dry cleaners or self storage garages.

*Those That Sell or Manufacture a Product*. A product can be anything, large or small, high-end or discount. You might have costs associated with creating the product or buying inventory. You can sell your product retail, wholesale, mail order, over the phone or Internet, or directly.

tices at 202-326-2222 and the International Franchise Association at 202-628-8000. They should be able to give you reports on certain companies.

## What Do I Need Start a Business?

Money. Don't worry if you don't have a lot of money, not many people do. Some great companies have been started with less than $1,000. Among them are Logo Athletic (makers of sports and team apparel) and Joe Boxer (boxer shorts). Both companies are worth millions today. Start small and think big. Every year, *Inc.* magazine comes out with an issue touting entrepreneurs and business who started with less than $1,000. I recommend that you get a copy. You'll see that you don't need a fortune. You just need to use it wisely.

## Where Can I Get Money?

That's the tricky part, but here's the rundown on a few traditional and not so traditional sources of financing:

*Banks.* Banks have money. You need money. Sounds like a good fit, right? It's not that simple. Banks want a guarantee that they will get their money back, and since over 70 percent of all start-ups fail in the first year, they're reluctant to give money to an unproven commodity. Even if you are proven, they sometimes make it tough to get money. It doesn't matter if you're a swell person with the best idea in the world, banks want you to put something up to guarantee that they will be repaid. You have to put up collateral such as assets, products, inventory, machinery, stocks, property, or equipment they can confiscate and sell if you default on your loan. Banks are one of the last places to go for financing a new business.

*Small Business Administration (SBA).* The SBA is a government agency dedicated to helping small businesses. One way they do this is by guaranteeing loans to small businesses. It is a great resource, but there are some very strict guidelines for obtaining an SBA loan, and the application must still go through a bank. There are also restrictions on how much money you can borrow. The SBA helps many entrepreneurs, but the process is still similar to going through a conventional bank to get a loan.

*Venture Capital Firms.* There are companies who have a ton of money to invest. Rather than leave it in a bank or play the market with it, they invest in fledgling companies. Venture capital firms can be large or small, and they are located all over the country. Many invest only in certain industries or types of companies. Some very successful companies got their start through venture capital financing, including Compaq Computer. However, venture capital financing is extremely difficult to obtain, because the investors want a far better return on their investment than they could get by playing the stock market.

Now for the kicker. Where a bank charges you interest on your loan, venture capital firms take an equity stake in your company in exchange for the funds. The venture capital firm now owns a piece of your company—often a significant piece. Since the venture capital firm owns part of your company, they want you to succeed so their investment pays off. This means that they want some control over how the company is run and may even replace managers or try to influence day-to-day operations. Lisa, who started an online service with venture capital money, says, "The biggest drawback is giving up control of my company. Even though it's my company, I still have to answer to people just like when I worked for someone else."

Venture capital firms look at dozens if not hundreds of deals a year and only select a handful. They review business plans and have extensive meetings with management before investing. The process can take a long time.

*Credit Cards.* While financial planners might not advocate it, using credit cards is an increasingly common and effective way to obtain cash for your start-up. One loan officer at a major bank told me that if an entrepreneur is seeking less than $25,000, he or she is better off getting the cash advance on several credit cards and paying it off rather than trying to get a loan from a bank. Think about all of the credit card applications you get each week. If you're a student, you're set. College seniors are bombarded with sometimes five or more credit card applications a week, all with ridiculously high credit limits.

All you do is apply for several credit cards and obtain the cash advance. It's an expensive way to obtain financing, because the interest rates are usually very high, but if you have nowhere else to turn, it can get you started.

*Friends & Family.* MCI isn't the only one with a friends-and-family plan. The majority of entrepreneurs obtain their financing from friends and family. It's not uncommon for a company to be founded with investments and loans of up to $10,000 from several relatives or close friends who believe in you and your project.

If you borrow money from friends or family, explain the risks to them. Please tell them that there is the possibility

> Tom recently started a restaurant with two buddies. They obtained over $250,000 in start-up capital by having over 100 different people invest small amounts of $1,000 to $5,000 each.

that they will never see their money again. It's a risk. It's also smart to draw up a legal agreement. This can protect both you and the lender from any tax or legal problems. (If there is no agreement, any money over $10,000 can be considered a gift, in which case, the person loaning it to you will be have to pay steep taxes on the money they loaned to you.)

Before you borrow from a friend or relative, ask yourself if the relationship can stand bringing a financial element into it. Money changes everything. Besides, if a banker gets mad at you because your business failed, big deal. If you lose your Uncle Bob's money, it can make for a pretty ugly Thanksgiving holiday.

## Building Your Team

There is a saying that only a fool represents himself. While you might be a one-person show, you still need the counsel of a few people. This starts by finding a good attorney and a good accountant. Spend the money to meet with these two professionals before you get started. It may seem expensive in the beginning, but their advice can get you started on the right track and save you many headaches and thousands of dollars down the road.

## Should I Incorporate?

Incorporating makes your company a legal entity. Even if you're a one-person shop, incorporating allows the company to stand on its own and not as an individual doing business. The advantages to incorporating are primarily for tax and liability purposes. If something goes wrong with a product or service that you provide, the company is liable. However, if there's no corporate structure, you may be personally responsible, which means you can be sued and potentially wiped out. Good-bye apartment, hello park bench.

There are several types of corporate structures, each having different tax implications. For example, one type of corporation, a C corporation, allows the company to stand on it's own and pay a corporate tax rate. A sub chapter S corporation allows company losses to flow through the principal individual and are paid at his or her personal tax rate. Tax laws are confusing, and how you establish your company can make a big difference in the long run. Consult with an accountant to learn more about the different corporate structures and which one would be right for you.

Having an attorney complete and file all of the appropriate incorporation paperwork for you will cost around $1,000. To have an accountant consult with you on how to structure your company could cost between $100 to $500. It sounds like a lot, but it is money well spent.

You should also obtain a federal tax ID number. This is like a Social Security number for your business. You will use it often. Call your local IRS office, and they can help you obtain one.

## Should I Start a Business Right After I Graduate? What About a Business I Have Never Worked in Before?

There are plenty of success stories about people who started a business while in school or took a chance in a business they were unfamiliar with. However, most entrepreneurs say to learn a business on someone else's nickel. According to U.S. Trust, over half of entrepreneurs started as employees for another corporation. Learn a business and then use what you learned to start your own company.

Let's face it, you're going to screw up. Everyone does. There is no way you can be prepared for every contingency. Why not let someone else pay for your early mistakes. Learn the ins and outs of a business—the problems that might arise and how to solve them—while you are working for someone else and they are paying you.

Jessica was marketing director for a large law firm before starting her own marketing communications company. She used what she learned at the law firm to help get her company off the ground. Her first major client was her former company. They were unable to find a suitable replacement.

## How Much Will I Make?

Being an entrepreneur could mean you are either riding a Schwinn or hopping on your plane. It can be feast or famine, but as an entrepreneur, you have a greater chance of becoming very wealthy (if that's your goal) than most other fields. Entrepreneurs are the richest 1 percent of Americans, but if every business were easy to start and successful, everyone would be doing it.

Some entrepreneurs won't pay themselves a lot of money during the first couple of years of the business. Instead, they put all profits (if any) back into the company.

Others don't even pay themselves a salary. They chose to live off of savings until the company can sustain a salary and the paperwork and payroll taxes that go with it. Payroll tax is

> Hank and his wife began a neighborhood ice cream store. It is a small business that allows him to take about a $45,000 a year salary. Some entrepreneurs businesses generate just enough for a subsistence salary. Why continue to do it? Hank says, "Because working for myself and making less is better than having to answer to anyone else."

very expensive, often a third to half of your monthly net income. So if you are paying yourself $3,000 every month, you will also cut a check to Uncle Sam for over $1,000. That's why it's important to think about whether you really want employees or whether you should hire temps and contractors.

Another perk you might miss during the start-up phase is insurance. Health insurance is prohibitively expensive and hard to get as a new or small company. Many entrepreneurs buy COBRA or continue their coverage from their former employer, often at a much greater expense than when they were an employee. Others will put themselves on their spouse's insurance plan if the spouse works. There are a growing number of consortiums that allow small businesses to purchase insurance at the same cheaper rates of big companies.

You might miss that 401k plan, too. However, once you can afford it, set up retirement plans for yourself and your employees if you have any. Consult with your accountant on what's best for you.

## What Are the Biggest Mistakes Entrepreneurs Make?

There are many, but one of the most common and most deadly mistakes that rookie entrepreneurs make is that they mismanage their cash flow. As an entrepreneur, you should test yourself every time you consider buying anything for the company. "Do I need this or do I just want this?" "Is this a must-have item or an 'it would be nice to have' item?" If something isn't an absolute necessity, you might think twice before buying it. Remember, cash is the fuel that keeps your business running. When you run out, you stop going.

Another critical mistake is hiring people before you absolutely need to. Ask yourself, "Is this person going to help me increase revenue more than enough to pay for their salary? Will they help me grow the business or give me the freedom to focus on growing the business?" If not, you might hire a temp or use contract employees on an as-needed basis. Having employees means that you must pay payroll tax on your employees in addition to filing all of the necessary paperwork and reports. It is an expensive and time-consuming pain, so make sure that you are getting value from your employees.

## Should I Work At Home or Get an Office?

It depends on the nature of your business and the size of your ego. Ask yourself if you really need an office. Is it something that would just be nice to have?

*Office Space.* Office space is expensive. If your business relies on customer traffic or if customers come to visit, you might need an office. One inexpensive solution is an office suite or executive center. These are groups of offices that you can rent at a greatly reduced price that share common facilities such as a conference room, copiers, receptionists, etc. This arrangement takes advantage of the economies of scale. With an executive suite, you don't have to pay for a full-blown office with a receptionist. While it is more expensive than working from home, you will have a professional place to meet clients. (Asking a client to step over your dirty laundry and your kid's toys doesn't exactly create the right image, does it?)

*Home Office.* If you travel a lot or work primarily on the phone or computer, you might consider working from home. Technology and changing attitudes toward home offices have made this a popular and relatively inexpensive choice for many people. According to Link Resources, there are currently over 24 million full- and part-time home-based businesses in America.

As recently as three years ago, the idea of working from home had a very negative image. "Oh, you work from home. So you're unemployed." I worked at home for a while. For months, my neighbors believed I was either out of work or a drug dealer, because I was always around during the day.

Shortly after Susan started her company, she negotiated a lease on a beautiful contemporary office space. She spent a fortune decorating the office. It was very impressive. The only problem was that most of Susan's business was done out of town or at her client's office. In the first year that Susan had the office, she met only two clients there. After realizing that she had wasted tons of money, she moved her business back home.

## Home Office vs. Office Building

A good thing about an office building you must drive to is that you leave work at work. You may spend a lot of time at the office, but your work is not overflowing out of a spare bedroom as a constant reminder that you have stuff to do. You also have more space and feel more professional going to work or meeting clients. The main negative against an office is the expense. Is it necessary to have the office or is it for your ego? It's good for the ego to have people visit a stylish office or to have prestigious address, but when you're a start-up company, money in the bank is better.

Home offices are less expensive, but can be more stressful. The ten-second commute down the hall isn't bad, but you can never leave work, because you live there. You might think there would be all kinds of distractions (and there are), but it's not like you will say, "I think I'll watch HBO all afternoon." It's the opposite. If you walk by the office (spare room) at 10:00 P.M. and you have something to do, it's easy to walk in there and work until 1:00 A.M. It can be counterproductive, because you tend to work too much. It takes a lot of discipline. You also need to schedule some time outside of the house with living, breathing human beings. Otherwise, when you see your spouse, roommate, or the FedEx driver, you will be like a puppy who has been locked up all day.

## How Can I Make My Business Successful?

I wish I had the magical answer to that. If I did, I'd be on late-night infomercials right after Tony Robbins. The main thing is to manage your cash flow. Don't pay for things in advance unless there are substantial discounts for doing so.

It may sound simple, but tell everyone about your business. You have to be the biggest cheerleader for your business. If you aren't, who will be? You can let people know about your business without spending a lot of money or producing an elaborate advertising campaign. Become involved in the local business community, join the Chamber of Commerce and all of the civic business clubs and groups.

Don't overlook where business can be found. You should have plans, but your plans should be flexible enough to adapt and change according to what the market wants and your customers demand.

Ken in Atlanta owns a remodeling business. One of the first things he did was to join several local associations where he could obtain leads and share information with other small businesses. One of the groups he joined was a local organization promoting gay or gay-friendly businesses. It didn't matter that Ken was straight with a wife and a son, he knew that the gay community have a lot of disposable income and are loyal to business who provide good service and treat them fairly. After attending one trade show, he began to attract a phenomenal amount of business. Word spread about Ken's business, and now he doesn't do any advertising at all. He has to turn away business, because he is too busy. All of his business now comes from word of mouth, and over 80 percent of his business comes from the gay community.

According to U.S. Trust's Survey of Entrepreneurs, the top two factors leading to the success of entrepreneurs were a willingness to work hard and a willingness to take risks. Education was ranked eighth, right above luck.

## Think Big!

I recently had the opportunity to meet Pat Williams, president of the Orlando Magic. He is one of the truly successful executives in professional sports and is a phenomenal businessman to boot. On Mr. Williams's voice mail is a message that says, "Each year over 70 percent of small business start-ups fail. So I have a great idea. Start a large business." It may be a corny play on words, but his point should be well taken. It's true that over 70 percent of new business start-ups fail each year. They fail for any number of reasons, but if there's a common thread among companies that fail, it's that they all failed to have a business plan.

You may have heard stories about entrepreneurs who are wildly successful one minute and then go out of business a few months later because they grew too quickly or couldn't handle sales. As a small or emerging business person, you must plan for rapid growth and realistically ask yourself if you are prepared for it. As strange as it seems, there may actually be a time when it is in your best interest to turn down business.

## Are You Ready to Take the Plunge?

Think about your options and what it means to start a business before diving right in. The dumbest thing you can do is to quit your day job, take your life savings (or worse, your parents' or friends' money), and start a business without any experience or thought as to what might happen.

Smart entrepreneurs may test the waters by trying something part-time or on the side until it develops or generates enough revenue to support them. You're ready to switch when your part-time income begins to equal or exceed your full-time income.

A few questions you should ask yourself to determine if you are really ready to start your own business or work from home are:

- Am I motivated enough to work without a boss, any supervision, or any colleagues to urge me on?
- Am I aware of and willing to do what it takes to make my business successful? Do I realize that this means I will wear many different hats and perform any task that needs to be done, no matter how unglamorous?

## Do I Need A Degree?

A degree and education can never hurt your chances for success, but it's not required to start or run a company. According to the U.S. Trust *Survey of Entrepreneurs*, 29 percent never went to college, 27 percent went to college but never finished, and 33 percent say education was important to their financial success. Over half of entrepreneurs put themselves through school in some way.

## What Type of Economic Background Do Most Entrepreneurs Have?

Not many trust-fund babies in this crowd. According to U.S. Trust, almost 80 percent come from poor or middle-class working families.

## What Are the Pros and Cons?

Easily, the biggest perk is having the freedom to do what you want when you want. Now don't start thinking that you will have all of this free time to play golf and go to movies during the day. Kevin, who owns a California Closet franchise, says, "I work harder and longer now that my name is on the checks than I ever did when someone else was paying the bills." But being an entrepreneur can offer the flexibility of being able to make your own schedule without having to answer to your manager or be talked about by your coworkers when you take time off.

Sometimes if I am about to go out of town for a while, I will pop into my daughters day care in the middle of the afternoon to play with her before I leave. At first, my daughter's teachers asked me, "So you have the day off?" I said, "Nope, I'm the boss." That freedom and flexibility are priceless.

The cons are that you tend to work too hard and there is added pressure. Before, it was your boss who worried about paying the bills, meeting deadlines, and any other problems that crop up every day. Now those problems belong to you.

## What's the Most Important Skill an Entrepreneur Needs to Have?

Depending on who you ask, you are likely to get a long list of great answers, but among the people I spoke with, discipline and motivation were the top traits. There is no boss to watch you, encourage you, or kick you in the butt when you need it. It will be tough, lonely, and even depressing at times, but the ones who make it are persistent and have an unbelievable belief in themselves even when no one else does.

## What the Pros Read

Once you are an entrepreneur, you will read whatever the trade publications are for the field you chose. There are also several great magazines devoted to entrepreneurs and small business:

*Inc.*
*Entrepreneur*
*Success*

## Where Can I Learn More?

YEO—Young Entrepreneur's Organization
703-527-4500

NFTE—National Foundation for Teaching Entrepreneurship
212-232-3333

Center for Entrepreneurial Management
212-633-0060

The SBA Answer Desk
800-827-5722

Women's Business Development Center
312-583-3477

## Where on the Web?

www.franchise.org—International Franchise Association
www.inc.com—*Inc.* magazine
www.nftebiz.org—National Foundation for Teaching Entrepreneurship
www.sife.org—Students in Free Enterprise
www.yeo.org—Young Entrepreneurs' Organization
www.entrepreneurmag.com—*Entrepreneur* magazine
www.successmagazine.com—*Success* magazine

# 17

• • • • • • • • • • • • • • • • • • • • • • • • • • • • • • • • • • • •

# The Family Business

*"Nothing personal, it's strictly business."*
—LINE FROM THE MOVIE *THE GODFATHER*

Should I work for the family business? Choosing a career is tough enough without having the added pressures that this situation can bring. On the one hand, what a great deal. You don't have to really look for a job. On the other hand, it may not be a choice as much as it's expected that you will join the family business (whether you want to or are qualified doesn't matter). Guilt can be a great motivating factor, "Damn it, I paid for four years of school. The least you could do is help."

Working for your family is tough, regardless of what type of relationship you have. It changes how your family and others treat you. In any other business, you can tell your boss to go to hell (although I don't recommend it) and walk away from the job, never to be bothered by the incident again. Say that to a family member and walk away, and you'll have mom, dad, and big brother giving you the evil eye at Thanksgiving.

It's not an easy choice, and it takes a special individual, relationship, and circumstance to make it work. Following are a few things you should consider if you are contemplating—or being pressured into—joining the family business.

## Is This a Permanent or Temporary Career?

Is your working for the family business a permanent career choice or is it a temporary solution. Temporary could mean you are helping the family business through a tough period or they are helping you out until you find your true calling, get into law school, or whatever choice you make. Knowing this is important so everyone can have the same expectations from one another.

If you are approaching the family business as a long-term career choice, then your attitude will be very different than if you know it's a temp job. Your choice will affect how others treat you. If employees know that you are only there on a temporary basis, you may find a lack of respect from coworkers, even if you're the owner's kid. Workers know you won't be around forever, so why should they listen to you?

Decide ahead of time what your goals are and discuss them with your family members.

## How Will I Be Treated?

People who've worked for the family business say that it will generally go one of two ways:

1. Your parent or family member will feel that they can show no amount of favoritism at all, so you must pay your dues and work harder than anyone else. As a result, they are much harder on you than if you were a regular employee.
2. You're given a choice assignment or position, because you won the lucky gene pool contest. Naturally, you're resented by everyone who had eyes on that job before you came around.

### Beware of Spoon-feeding

There is a tendency among employees to think that a family member who joins a business isn't qualified or didn't earn it. It's important for you to fight your own battles and avoid having your parent or relative spoon feed you. It can be tough to fill your relative's shoes. You must bring something unique to the table, as in special skills. And if you don't have it, you had better develop it, even if it means going back to school or working somewhere else and then coming back to the family business. It is also good for you to have a skill that is different than other family members. This is not only good for the business, but good for you, since you'll have a specialty in which you won't have to compete with anyone.

Brenda went to work for her father's company. He was grooming Brenda to eventually take over for him someday. However, Brenda's father tried so hard to protect Brenda that he wouldn't let her make mistakes or take the time to teach her. "Dad just thought that I would learn by watching him. I learned a lot, but when it came time for me to do something, he would get frustrated and say it is easier to do it myself. Employees started to look at me as if I were helpless. It would have been better if Dad would have let me fall on my butt once in a while, but I should have spoken up."

## How Will My Coworkers and Other Employees Treat Me?

Those in family business say you will either:

1. Have coworkers and underlings kiss your butt in an effort to endear themselves to management. This results in you never knowing who you can really trust.

2. Have a coworker or manager who feels threatened and may have it in for you. It doesn't matter if you are the brightest or nicest person in the world, you're still the boss's kid. You'll be talked about, vilified, judged, and scrutinized harder than anyone else in that office. You may even be scrutinized by customers.

## What About Working for Someone Else's Family Business?

It's very common. Almost 60 percent of the American workforce work for a family-owned business. Every environment is different. Success, failure, and happiness depend on the company. But realize that it's likely that you may never be the boss. It's cliché but true: Blood really is thicker than water.

## Keys to Making It in a Family Business

- Lay out specific goals, targets, and expectations.
- Do it for you, not for someone else.
- Make your own mark and bring something of your own to the table. That might be an extra degree or education. It might be certain experience in another field.
- Set your boundaries. Set clear guidelines of what's "off-limits" outside of work.
- Leave personal business or conflicts at home and leave work at the office.

## What About Nepotism?

No, nepotism isn't the tricolored Italian ice cream. It's the hiring of family members within a company. It can have a negative meaning, because many people think of it as displaying favoritism to a family member.

Some companies allow it, but have a policy stating that there cannot be a direct supervisory relationship. Others say that spouses or family members may not work in the same department or division, and others just say "no way."

Among some companies, there is a move to encourage family members to work together. Companies think, "If we have one quality employee who is bright and has a good work ethic, others can't fall too far from the vine. The JobSmarts Most Incestuous Company award must go to Cisco Systems, which employs over 400 married couples. They even have their own school for employees' children.

## Should I Work with a Spouse, Lover, or Someone I'm Dating?

Sometimes it can't be helped. In some situations, the people you work with are your only social outlet, and when people work closely together, it can be natural for there to be some romantic sparks or an attraction to develop.

That said, my advice is: If you can help it, don't date coworkers or work in the same company as your spouse. I don't care who you are or what your company policy says, I think it is a bad idea to date someone you work with. This goes double if you are with a small company or you're involved with someone in your division or department.

I don't want to be bombarded with letters saying, "Look here, JobSmarts guy, Pookie Bear and I met working at Blockbuster, and we are in luv." Great. I'm happy for you. I acknowledge that sometimes it can work out well, but it takes a special situation and two special individuals.

If you begin dating a coworker, join the company where your significant other works, or, worse yet, relocate or accept a position based upon your lover's location, you'd better be prepared to marry. Why? Because if or when it ends, every little quirk, weird habit, and personal secret you have will be exposed for all of the office's enjoyment. Meanwhile, your credibility will be spiraling down the toilet faster than you can blink an eye.

Steven in Atlanta went to work for the same food brokerage business his father had been with for thirty-five years. While his father didn't own the business, he was one of the top officers in the company. Steve was persuaded to join the company and follow in his father's footsteps. Steve didn't exactly want to go into this business, but reluctantly agreed to join the company.

Shortly after Steve began working, his father had a falling out with the company's owner. Steve began to hear some bad things about his father through the grapevine, and shortly thereafter, his father was fired from the company at which he had spent almost his entire career. As for Steve, it was only a few months later that he received his pink slip.

# 18

## Federal Bureau of Investigation (FBI)

Let's just clear this up at the beginning. The FBI does not have an X-Files division. If you want to investigate paranormal behavior or space aliens, you pretty much have to stick to watching Fox. However, even without space aliens, the FBI is still one of the most fascinating and diverse areas of law enforcement.

### What Does the FBI Do?

The FBI enforces over 260 federal statutes and conducts investigations for national security issues. The FBI investigates organized crime, white-collar crime, financial crime, copyright matters, bribery, fraud against the government, interstate criminal activity, bank robbery, terrorism, fugitive matters, and extortion, just to name a few. Sorry, space aliens do not fall under their jurisdiction.

### What Type of People Does the FBI Hire?

The majority of FBI employees are called special agents. However, they also hire a number of scientists and lab technicians, forensic specialists, accountants, lawyers, language specialists, and engineers.

## Where Will I Start?

When you join, you'll become part of a class of special agent trainees. You'll then spend fifteen weeks at the FBI academy in Quantico, Virginia. After your training, you'll be assigned to one of the fifty-six FBI field offices, although your first assignment will generally be in a major metropolitan area like New York or glamorous Newark, New Jersey. These assignments are based upon need, but you can request a preference. You're automatically on a probationary period during your first two years with the Bureau.

## Do I Get a Gun?

Yes. All special agents have a gun or must have ready access to one. But some agents have never pulled their weapons in their entire careers.

## How Long Before I Advance?

You can expect to be on your first assignment for at least four years.

## How Much Will I Make?

Since you're a federal employee, you'll be on the GS scale. You'll start as a GS10 (mid-thirties) and can advance to a GS13 (low-fifties). All agents start at the same salary, regardless of experience or background. In addition to their base GS10 salary, agents are paid overtime, which amounts to a preset 25 percent of their base salary. This 25 percent is adjusted for cost of living according to where you're stationed. Every agent gets this. This is because the FBI can't pay hourly overtime, and as special agent John Scholtens says, "You can't tell the bad guys that it's time to go home for the day. You stay until your work is done." The 25 percent overtime bonus usually allows agents to make in the low forties during their first year. If you become a supervisor, manager, or executive, you can become a GS14 or GS15. (Check out the "Government and Politics" chapter to see a GS table and compare salaries.)

## What Are the Qualifications?

You must have a degree from an accredited four-year college. Your major doesn't matter that much. Don't think that being a criminal justice major gives an advantage. Some agents have advanced degrees. There are attorneys, MBAs, and other specialists in the FBI. You don't need an advanced degree unless you want to pursue something in forensics or behavioral profiling. You must be a U.S. citizen between the ages of twenty-three and thirty-six. If you're older than thirty-six, sorry grandpa. You must have good vision—no worse than 20/200 uncorrected and 20/20 corrected in one eye and 20/40 in the other. You must also be available to relocate. This is absolute.

## How Do I Get Hired?

Getting the process started is very easy, but actually getting hired is another story. It's a long, comprehensive process involving many interviews and levels.

Start by contacting your local FBI field office to ask for an application. The FBI is constantly hiring due to the attrition of agents. They'll ask you a few questions to see if you're eligible. Once you complete the application, you'll begin a barrage of tests and interviews over the next few weeks. You'll go through a one-hour interview, a one-and-a-half hour writing sample prepared with nothing but pen and paper, a drug test, polygraph tests, credit checks, background checks, and physical agility tests. If you fail any part along the way, you'll be thanked for your time and told of the wonderful opportunities in the food service industry. Agent Scholtens says the application process is like a track race with hurdles. "Hit any of the hurdles along the way, and you're out of the race."

If you're able to make it past all of that, you'll then be sent a letter informing you that you've been selected to become a member of the next FBI training class. New classes start at the academy every two weeks. You have two months to wrap up your life before moving to Virginia for four months of training, although sometimes you don't even have that luxury. Some trainees have only a couple of weeks to decide if this is what they want to do, move their families, and make arrangements to start another life.

## What Is the Strangest Part of the Application Process?

If you're married, it's not just you who the FBI is checking out. For married couples, the FBI wants to interview the spouse. This is largely to see if the spouse supports his or her partner's decision to become an agent. "You would be surprised how many people make it this far and then their wife says, 'This is not a lifestyle I'm willing to lead,'" says Agent Scholtens.

## What Can I Do?

There are four main areas for entry-level programs. These are law, accounting, languages, and diversified. A legal background helps, but is not necessary. The FBI has a legal department. The FBI also has attorneys in the field.

Because of the increase in computer fraud and white-collar crime, the "forensic accountant" has become a popular position. The FBI uses accountants and MBAs to help uncover white-collar crimes.

## Other Types of Detectives, Investigators, and Snoops

Why can't it be like *Magnum PI*? Hanging on the beach, driving a Ferrari, and solving crime in a bad Hawaiian shirt. Instead, the hottest type of detective or investigator today deals with "competitive intelligence." This doesn't mean stealing Cold War secrets or weapons plans. This new type of spy is a high-tech researcher who digs for the latest information on new products, deals, and acquisitions—rummaging through people's trash is part of the job.

Many companies have in-house units that keep tabs on what the other competition is doing. There are private companies that do much of the same thing. One of the largest investigative and research firms is Kroll Associates in New York. On a less glamorous level are companies like Find SVP, also based in New York. They have a huge staff devoted to researching and generating reports on any topic. Find SVP uses almost every database and online service known to man, in addition to other techniques.

**Did You Know?**

If you have something to hide, either don't apply or admit it early on. Agents say it's better to explain something ahead of time, even if you think it's not a big deal, because they will find out. You claim, "I never smoked dope," and then it comes out that ten years earlier as a zit-faced punk in junior high, you did. You're automatically out. No questions asked. Why? Because you smoked pot? No, because you lied. The FBI, surprisingly, has a pretty reasonable drug policy. Agents can't have used marijuana in the past three years and can't have used anything harder in the past ten years.

They also check your credit. This doesn't mean that if you've ever bounced a check, you can't be an agent, but if you have bad credit, you should clear it up before you apply. And if you've ever defaulted on a student loan, you can just give up ever becoming an agent. That's the one cardinal sin.

## What Are the Pros and Cons (No Pun Intended)?

The best thing about being a special agent is that it's never routine. "You drive to work expecting your day to be routine, and it ends up totally different. You never know what you'll be asked to do," says agent Scholtens.

The downside is that sometimes you can be in over your head. "There are resources available to you, but once I was assigned to a white-collar crime and I did not have any accounting or business skills. And I had to finish the case. It can be frustrating and stressful when you are given something and told to handle it and you have to rise to the task."

## Is It Dangerous?

Of course it can be, but it depends on what department you're in. White-collar crime and language specialist aren't at risk that often. The most dangerous area is dealing with reactive crimes, such as bank robberies and fugitives.

## What's the Closest Thing to the *X-Files*?

Drop it, okay. It's just a TV show. If you're hell-bent on getting near the weirdos, your best bet would be the behavioral sciences unit (*Profiler*- and *Silence of the Lambs*–type stuff). These positions are generally filled by people with advanced degrees in psychology and the sciences.

## Where Can I Learn More?

Call your local field office.

## Where on the Web?

www.fbi.gov

# 19

• • • • • • • • • • • • • • • • • • • • • • • • • • • • • • • • • • • • • • • •

# Film Industry

**Some Common Positions**
  Production assistant
  Agent
  Director
  Producer
  Production manager
  Location scout
  Writer
  Actor/actress
  Waiter
  Unemployed

**Other Opportunities You Might Consider**
There are opportunities in film for artists, drivers, publicists, marketers, writers, construction workers, computer graphics specialists, camera operators, animators, makeup artists, costume and set designers, sound technicians, distribution and logistics experts, attorneys, accountants, and, of course, actors and actresses. (This section does not cover being an actor. For information regarding acting, try looking in the "Performing Arts" or "Food Service" chapters.)

The film industry covers much more than making movies, music videos, and documentaries. Producing television commercials and corporate, training, or promotional videos is also a major part of the film industry. Television and advertising are closely related fields.

Who hasn't thought about being in the movie business at some point in their life? You're checking yourself out in the bathroom mirror or at the stoplight thinking, "I'm as cool as Tom Cruise or Val Kilmer." (Sorry, I was sharing a personal moment.) Or maybe you think, "Hey, I look as good in a baseball cap as Ron Howard or Steven Spielberg. Maybe I could be a director." Whether you want to be the next George Lucas, write a screenplay, produce a feature film, be an agent, make a commercial, or design costumes, the cliché is true: Opportunities in this field are endless. The catch is this: Film is the most competitive and most difficult profession to break into.

# What Can I Do?

There are several career tracks you can pursue. Traditionally, when people think of the film industry, they think of either the production, technical, or creative end. Believe it or not, not everyone is an actor, writer, producer, or director. There are plenty of technical, artistic, labor, and office positions that play an important part in making movies and television programs. Many of these are union jobs.

When I think of unions, I tend to picture either a bunch of swarthy guys from New Jersey hanging out in a warehouse or Jimmy Hoffa and the Meadowlands. Certainly not Hollywood. However, there are no less than 44 local unions involved in the motion picture industry, each representing different classes of employment in entertainment ranging from acting to technical trades.

There are locals for cartoonists, script supervisors, story analysts, publicists, scenic and title artists, editors, costumers, makeup artists, technicians, projectionists, script writers, ornamental plasterers, modelers, and sculptors—get the picture. There are unions for trades and skills that you may never have known existed.

Union positions don't necessarily mean labor or construction jobs. There are unions and guilds for performers and "above the line" people. An example is the Directors Guild, which represents directors, assistant directors, and production managers. They also represent television directors and floor managers in broadcast facilities. There's also the Screen Actors Guild, which represents actors and extras. There's even a union for stunt performers (remember Lee Majors in *The Fall Guy*)? And if you are really lucky, you might find yourself a member of the Brotherhood—the International Brotherhood of Teamsters, that is. Location managers and animal wranglers belong to the Teamsters. I have no idea how animal trainers get into the Teamsters.

## Are Some Areas Easier to Break Into Than Others?

There simply are no "easy" places to break in. It's a damn tough industry. In most places, there's a glut of wannabes. What you hear about MBA's in the mailroom is every bit true. The computer graphics and animation field is one of the only places right now where there's a real shortage of qualified people.

## Where Will I Start?

I think it's pretty safe to say at the bottom. There's not one specific place to get started. It all depends upon the type of job you want and the lucky breaks you get.

Regardless of the area you choose, you will likely start out as an assistant or intern—often for no pay. No one comes in as a producer, director, agent, or any other position of consequence. You need to learn the business from the ground up. Even film school doesn't completely train you in how this industry works.

On the production side (which is what this chapter mostly addresses), most people start as a production assistant or PA. As a PA, it may feel like you are working at Starbucks, because you will be coffee person and grunt extraordinaire.

## How Long Will I Be a Production Assistant/Indentured Servant?

It depends on how good you are. If you're really good, you'll only do it once. This is completely a business of relationships. If people like your work and get to know you, they'll say, "Remember that kid we had, that gopher on our last shoot. I really liked her." You must be willing to do anything, and I mean anything, with a smile and a great attitude. Because this business is about relationships, it's important you use the opportunity of being on a set or shoot to make contacts. Who you know is not always as important as who knows you.

## Should I Move to Los Angeles?

Some people move straight to LA without having any experience and connections, thinking, "I'll find something when I get there." It's not the smartest move you could make, and it's pretty risky. I caution you that if you do decide to make the move, make sure that you at least know some people or have some connections you can call before you go west. I can't stress enough that this is a business of relationships above all else. Try to establish some connections and production experience before you go to Los Angeles.

## How Do I Start Working in Film Outside of Hollywood?

It's possible to get experience, meet people, and even work on a movie in or near your hometown. Many college students get started this way so they have experience and connections before they move to LA.

Another way to enter the movie and film business is by working in a related industry. The most common way to get into film production is by working for an advertising agency or production house that creates music videos, commercials, or documentaries.

You can work as a PA on a production in your area. Every city has commercial production houses. They may be large or small, but that is where you will get a good understanding of production.

## What Type of Experience Helps in Producing and Where Can I Get It?

Any activity that requires you to, well, produce something. It might be producing a catalog, newspaper, or special event. These are things that you can do in school or as a volunteer activity. It may even be an entirely unrelated business, just something that shows you can coordinate multiple things and people.

## What Does a Production Manager Do?

This is an operations position. You're responsible for calculating budgets, hiring the crew, and keeping the project moving. You handle scheduling, sorting gear, and purchasing equipment, as well as logistics and finance. You're an office manager on speed. Shelly, a former production manager who worked at Paramount, says, "When my mom used to ask me what I do, I'd tell her, excuse my French, when the shit hits the fan, I'm the fan!"

Being a production manager is a great place to learn the business and elements of what goes into a production. Production managers can also be found in television.

## What Type of Education or Background Do I Need?

To work in the movie or film industry, at least on the production side, you really don't have to have a film degree or any degree at all for that matter. Just look at any MTV cast member and you'll realize that you not only don't need a degree, sometimes you don't even need a brain. A degree will help you in terms of knowledge, but it's not a requirement. Everyone pretty much starts out the same—at the bottom.

## How Do I Get Hired?

It depends on what type of job you want. The film and entertainment business is no different than any other business in that there are plenty of office or administrative jobs like secretaries, accountants, lawyers, and contract coordinators. These positions can generally be found through the human resource departments.

Production jobs (which is what most people think of as the "movie business") aren't found through the personnel department, and there's virtually no campus recruiting except at a handful of film schools. If film positions did recruit like other companies, can you imagine students signing up for interviews? Hmm . . . which interview should I sign up for? Pharmaceutical sales rep or movie producer?

> "No one ever asks about GPA or where or even if I went to school," says Alex, who worked on the movie *Quiz Show* and is now working for a production company in LA. "I went to an expensive liberal arts college, and it simply doesn't matter out here. There's an assistant in my office in her early thirties with a degree from Columbia."

## How Do People Learn About Production Jobs?

Almost entirely by word of mouth. They rarely get advertised. You learn about production jobs by banging on doors and making as many contacts as you possibly can. The exception to word-of-mouth hiring would be union or "below the line" jobs, which are required to post job openings.

## What If I Don't Have Any Connections and Don't Live in NYC or LA? What's the Best Way to Get Into the Business?

Every city and state has a film commission. They know of almost everything and everyone related to production in that region. The best way for someone to get started is to contact the film commission and ask to see or purchase a copy of their lists, directories, or film guides to the region.

In it, you should find the names of local producers, production houses, and other businesses and individuals related to film. Call the studios, producers, and others listed in the books and say, "I'm interested in getting started in film. This is what I'm good at. I'd love to intern or see if you have some kind of position open." Remember, you will likely be working for free. You may even offer to work for free simply to get exposure, work on some shoots, and meet people.

## What's the Likelihood of Talking with Someone? Is It Difficult to Get In?

It depends on who you are trying to see and what connections you have. If you have a contact who says to call someone and "drop my name," or if the person you are trying to reach is not a major player, you might have a chance. On the other hand, if you're thinking about contacting someone like Spielberg, Cruise, Redford, or any other major star, director, or producer, remember these Cruise-related words—*Mission Impossible*.

Alex, who is an assistant for Robert Redford, helps screen outsiders and says he hears friends talk about sending a script or résumé directly to someone like Spielberg. Alex tells them, "If it will make you feel better, go ahead, but he will never see it." Everyone is trying to get into this business. There are so many layers of assistants, secretaries, and gatekeepers that 98 percent of unsolicited material is either immediately sent back or tossed.

## Have Something to Offer

Todd, who produces commercials for the NFL, says, "If someone wants a job with me, they need to tell me what they can do for me. If someone says, 'I want to work, but really don't know how I can help you—but I'll do anything,' it's not as appealing as someone who comes in and says, 'I can do this, I can do that, I've done this before.' The key in this business is doing as much as you possibly can and taking on responsibility beyond what you're asked to.

## I've Never Worked in Film Before. What Do I Have to Offer?

A great production assistant is someone who is a great organizer, someone who says, "I'm a great people person. I'm great on the phone. I have no problem cold calling people, dealing with people, asking them to do me a favor, or making deals." A lot of producing and coordinating is learning to make deals, trying to stretch your budget and find bargains. Say, "I'm not afraid to tackle numbers and try to put together a budget. I'm a great scheduler. I'm fast, I can get anywhere you want and back in no time. I'm a responsible person." These are all things that will grab a producer's attention and set you apart from others.

## How Much Can I Make?

In many cases, nothing. The movie business is so competitive, people line up to do anything, including being a production assistant for free.

Those production assistants who actually get paid start off at around $75 dollars a day. This can go up to $150 to $175 a day. Freelance production managers probably make $400 to $500 a day, and producers make

$750 to $1000 a day. Of course, you don't work every day. However, a good producer could be working two jobs at one time, and might work up to 200 to 250 days a year.

There are some salaried positions. Staff coordinators, often found in production companies, have a starting salary of about $400 a week and the salary moves up from there. Pay for many union jobs, technicians, and "below the line" positions varies. Check out the Industry Labor Guide on the Web at www.laborguide.com to learn about wages, contracts, and working conditions.

## What Is Production? What Does a Producer Produce?

While many jobs in film are difficult, the producer might have the hardest. Production includes every element of producing or creating the project. There's deal-making, seeking financing, coordinating locations and equipment, and picking out the proper creative people for certain projects (like the director, director of photography, and talent).

In some cases, production entails executing and enhancing an existing idea. Sometimes it means developing an original idea. Producing means taking an idea from thin air and coordinating everything necessary to make that idea become a reality.

## Are Production Companies Made Up of Directors and People on Staff?

Many production companies have a small staff. Production crews are brought in on an as-needed basis and may be local depending on the location of the shoot. Directors and directors of photography are often on retainer to a production company or with an agency.

These directors are like freelancers, except they're under agreement to a production house for a certain type of project. For example, a director might be free to do anything film related except make commercials.

## What Does the Production Staff Do?

The production staff puts a job together. Some staff might help develop the project prior to shooting, and others will coordinate on the shoot itself. This may mean putting together a crew, selecting a site, and choosing a director. It can be very complicated, especially if you are dealing with different locations. You might have a job shooting in a different location every weekend, so during the week you would put together crews in all the cities.

## Did You Know?

Production companies often have someone who is responsible for sales. Their job is to develop new business leads and projects. They do this by getting into advertising agencies, coming up with clever marketing ideas, and getting the company known and recognized.

### ON THE JOB WITH A PRODUCER

Todd, twenty-six, is the founder of Mad House Entertainment, a company that produces commercials for the National Football League. If you have seen any of the NFL's "Feel the Power" advertisements on *Monday Night Football* or Fox, you have seen Todd's work. He has also worked with some of the hottest advertising agencies and produced spots for Nike. Todd worked on major feature films and music videos before starting his own company.

*How did you get started?*

After I graduated from Temple with a communications degree, I went to Atlanta to become a production assistant on the film *Philadelphia* with Tom Hanks. I got that job through a contact at school and worked for free. While there, I became friendly with one of the producers. When Jonathan Demme, the director, and his crew were coming to Philly, they called and asked me to help them set up their offices. I was in charge of getting office space, making calls, and dealing with anything they needed while in Philadelphia. I was more of a coordinator for that project. I dealt with setting up all the trafficking of people coming into Philly. I then went to New York to help with post production. I was on that project for about eighteen months.

*What made you turn to commercials instead of features?*

I was able to get experience as a producer more quickly in the commercial world. In the feature world, I could have climbed the ladder, but you're such a small cog in a huge machine. I wanted to have creative opportunity and control. So I decided to branch out and do my own thing. I was able to jump right into producing commercials and music videos based on my experience on a feature. Now, as a result of the success of my company, I have the funds to dive back into independent features.

*What's different about working in commercials versus feature films?*

The main differences between the two are the time involved in filming and the amount of control you have as a producer. Commercials are obviously shorter and there are more people to answer to. The client, the advertising agency, and many others have a say in your work. A commercial shoot might last a day or two, with big commercials taking longer. Features shoot for a period of six to ten weeks, sometimes more. It's much more intense, and you are shooting longer days.

*What do people in a production office do?*

It's a huge undertaking. On a commercial shoot, there can be up to 100 people working on a project. Feature films can have many more.

## How Do Directors and Other Creative Types Get Hired?

There are different agencies that represent directors and other creative types. Producers look at hundreds of reels and demo tapes and determine who might fit the project? Then the production company calls their agent and books them for particular jobs.

## Where Are the Jobs?

You guessed it, most are based in New York or Los Angeles. However, there are production and film jobs all over the country. There are always shoots for films and commercials going on. As stated above, almost every major city has a film commission. There are also state film commissions. These are great places to contact to discover what is going on in your area and learn about production houses in that city.

The buzz among industry pros is that there's some production activity in San Francisco (a lot of multimedia) and Orlando. Vancouver was also mentioned as a current hot spot

for production. A look at the
1997 Academy Award nomi-
nees and winners illustrates
that there are great films
being produced outside of
the major film studios in LA.

## What Are the Benefits of Working in Film?

It depends on the area in which you are involved. Producers said they liked the business challenge as well as the creative challenge. PAs and other production staff like the flexibility of it. "Working in corporate America, you get your two weeks of vacation. As a freelancer, I can work hard for four months and then take a month off to lay on the beach, and it won't hurt my career. No one will look at me funny," says Steven, who has worked on three movies.

Another positive thing about working in film and entertainment is that age doesn't matter. This is a very hectic, fast-paced business, so there are a lot of fresh young people in it. People in this business tend to have good attitudes, because they're doing something that they have passion for and enjoy. This is not a field where people say, "My parents told me I should be in film and now I'm miserable."

It's also fulfilling because you're seeing a final product. You start with a loose idea and then develop it into a massive, completed product.

## What Are the Keys to Making It?

Making it in this business is all about luck and working your butt off. It's also about knowing what you want, putting yourself in the right place at the right time, and taking advantage of all opportunities. This is not a business for the weak, unambitious, or mealy-mouthed. It's too competitive. At every level, it's a business about relationships. The friendlier you are and the better attitude you have, the more people will want to work with you.

Being intelligent is a given, but another key to standing out is to be incredibly energetic and willing to work the hours. You not only have to show people that you want to be in this business (so does everyone else), but you have to show them that you are willing to do whatever it takes to make yourself available. This may mean taking a night job, second job, or asking for help from Mom and Dad so you can work a free internship or be an unpaid production assistant.

Another key to success is being ambitious and not waiting around for people to tell you what to do. Success comes from asking a lot of questions. The more you ask, the more you learn and the faster you will advance.

## What Are Some Misconceptions About Working in Film?

A common misconception is: "Hey this is a fun, glamorous business just hanging out making movies." The reality is that it's a lot of hard work with many tight deadlines. Steven says, "It's not a nine-to-five thing. Sometimes I'm working twenty-four hours a day for days on end just to get a project done." Other complaints are the fierce competitiveness in the industry.

## What the Pros Read

*Variety*

## You Should Also Check Out

There are several excellent film schools in the country. You can pursue a degree in film or take extension programs, evening class, or continuing education courses to learn more about the industry and gain valuable contacts.

The University of Southern California (USC), New York University (NYU), and the University of California, Los Angeles (UCLA) have three of the best programs in the country.

There are also several excellent books that industry pros recommend to rookies:

*How to Make It in Hollywood,* by Linda Buzzell
*The Complete Guide to Animation and Computer Graphic Schools,* by Ernest Pintoss
*Getting in Film* and the follow-up *Making It in Film,* by Mel London

## Where on the Web?

Many of the print directories for the entertainment industry are also available on the Web. You'll find information on job descriptions, job openings, and working conditions for just about every possible position in film, TV, multimedia, and music.

I highly recommend that you go on Yahoo! or your favorite Web browser and search for "film industry," "music industry," or "television industry." Take advantage of what is on the Web.

The sites listed below are national and general in scope, but there are plenty of sites devoted to certain states and even cities. There are sites devoted to film jobs in Florida, Chicago, Texas, and even Cleveland.

www.edweb.com—Entertainment Directory
www.hollyvision.com—Hollywood Creative Directory
www.talent.infep.com—International Network of Film and Entertainment Professionals
www.mediapages.com—MediaPages
www.filmfolks.com—Film Folks
www.showbizjobs.com—Entertainment Recruiting Network
www.vine.org—The Vine
www.directorsnet.com—Directors Net
www.laborguide.com—Industry Labor Guide (Excellent for production jobs)

# 20

• • • • • • • • • • • • • • • • • • • • • • • • • • • • • • •

# Finance and Banking

**Some Common Positions**
The banking and financial services industries are made up of several separate career paths, a few of which include banking, investment banking and brokerage services, venture capital, corporate finance, mortgage banking, pension and fund management, and trading and sales of equities, bonds, commodities, and other financial instruments.

> Loan officer
> Branch manager
> Credit analyst/manager
> Financial analyst
> Mortgage banker
> Private banker
> Investment banker
> Trader
> Salesperson
> Retail brokerage/stockbroker
> Institutional salesperson
> Securities analyst
> Portfolio manager
> Controller
> Financial planner
> Money manager

**You Might Also Consider**
Real estate, insurance, and venture capital (providing capital/money to start-up companies, entrepreneurial endeavors, or expanding companies). These fields deal in all elements of money and investing. Credit card companies such as American Express or Visa, as well as the major issuers of cards such as First USA or MBNA, have great opportunities as well. Customer service is also one of the fastest growing areas of financial services. Companies such as Fidelity have several major customer service centers located throughout the country.

Companies in these fields also have positions in accounting, marketing, legal departments, personnel, human resources, and training. Since the industry has become so dependent upon computers and technology, there are great opportunities for programmers, engineers, network administrators, and other high-tech folks.

It used to be that insurance companies only sold insurance, banks stored and loaned money, and brokers sold stocks. Today, the financial services arena has thousands of new products and services and everyone is getting into the mix.

The lines are no longer clear. This is a field with a great deal of opportunity, but it is still under construction as companies try to stake their claims. While investment banking, working on Wall Street, and becoming a young Gordon Gecko in training is sexy, the truth is that the majority of entry-level positions and opportunities exist in lucrative but less glamorous areas such as banking and financial planning. C'mon, not everyone can get hired by the top investment firms and move to New York.

What is clear, however, is that last year the first of over 100 million baby boomers turned fifty. By the year 2010, it is estimated that over half of the population will be over fifty. Retirement is right around the corner, and boomers are thinking about where to put their money so they can live comfortably in their old age. It certainly won't come from Social Security. (A recent survey found that more twentysomethings believe in UFOs than believe they will ever see a penny of Social Security.) This race to grab the retirement bucks of the boomers (and everyone else for that matter) has everyone from banks, mutual fund companies, insurance companies, and traditional brokers and financial planners throwing their hats in the ring to hire people.

## Where Will I Start?

First, you must decide which area of banking or financial services you want to go into. Depending on the organization, you may begin as an auditor, analyst, or trainee. Where you start and what you are called depends upon what area of finance you go into. Generally, you will go into a some type of training program.

To be in banking means much more than being a loan officer or a teller. In banking, you are likely to start out in a management training program. This program may last several months to a couple of years. You will be exposed to all areas of the bank and may even be briefly assigned to a teller or frontline position before you may move to a specific area of interest or need. Among some of your choices are the loan department, credit department, auditing, investments, operations or administration, corporate finance, and systems.

As a financial planner, you will become a system financial analyst and go into their training program, where you will learn the products and sales process and study for your licensing exams. You might shadow a manager for several months. During this time, he or she may help you to establish a client base that you will eventually take over. While most areas of banking and financial services offer excellent training programs and courses, there will still be a lot of OJT (on-the-job training). Much of this type of training is on-the-job. You will gradually be weaned off the training and begin selling and counseling clients of your own.

In brokerage and investing, you may spend the first year training and studying for your certifications and licensing. (You must be licensed to sell certain securities and financial instruments.) At other investment houses, you will be part of a rigorous training program and will be assigned to a department where you might crunch numbers in Excel or research and gather information on companies or stock performances.

## What Will Technology and Automation Mean to Banking?

Much has been said lately about electronic banking, PC banking, and home banking. From an employment perspective, the rise in technology is good news for programmers, network administrators, and designers, who will become the architects and managers of this new way that people conduct financial transactions. However, for some it means they had better update their résumés. This is primarily at the lower-level or branch positions.

Many institutions make it easy for you to apply for a loan or any other transaction or service right from the phone. In the future, it will not even be necessary to go to the bank.

The teller job is going to be a thing of the past, according to many analysts. Some banks are now charging a premium fee to have contact with a live human teller. (I guess you get a discount for a dead one.) Sadly, this not only affects the quality of customer service, but it affects the employees themselves. Many tellers are having their hours dramatically reduced as banks steer customers toward using automated services like ATMs and "in-store" branches in grocery stores or malls. (Maybe it's just me, but when it comes to my money, I don't feel very secure making my deposit at the same place I get my toothpaste.)

Even though the teller position may be a thing of the past, there are a ton of job opportunities in this field. One of the fastest growing areas of banking is in teleservice. Community Credit Union, the largest regional credit union in the United States, has a whole department devoted to teleservice. They not only handle traditional customer service issues that a teller in a branch location might have, but they also have specialist who can process a loan, establish a line of credit, or most any other service you require. And these aren't entry-level positions, either. "We put our most skilled people in the teleservice center, because they can handle anything," says Cindy, training manager for CCU.

As face-to-face tellers become extinct, there will still be a need for back-office support that your local checkout person at Kroger can't answer.

Sure, the high school kid bagging your groceries can tell you what aisle the soap is on, but he can't counsel you on a loan or help you set up an IRA.

Jobs in branch locations are quickly becoming extinct. According to a study by Deloitte & Touche, about 30 percent of bank employees (850,000 people) work in branches. Due to technology and consolidation, it is estimated that 450,000 of those jobs will disappear by the year 2000

## Banking Is Undergoing Many Changes

Currently, banks are going through a period of consolidation, resulting in mergers, acquisitions, name changes, and layoffs. They are trying to compete with insurance companies, discount brokers, and mutual fund companies. People aren't putting their money into CDs and leaving them in the bank anymore. People are using ATMs and the electronic services.

## What Are Investment Banks?

Investment banks are very different from your corner NationsBank branch. Investment banks handle a variety of activities: They issue and trade securities for investors and provide financial advice to corporations and extremely wealthy individuals. Investment banking is one of the highest paying career fields in the world. It is also one of the most competitive. Generally, only the top students at the top schools are selected. It is a relatively small field.

## Where Do I Stand the Greatest Chance of Getting Hired?

College career counselors nationwide have said that the number of financial planning companies recruiting on campuses has increased considerably.

Most entry-level recruiting is done on college campuses. If you want to work for one of the top New York banks or investment firms, your best bet is to find a contact at one of the firms. The top New York investment firms only go to the top-ranked schools.

High-level investment houses recruit at the top business schools or often steal other firms' talent. It is not uncommon for top brokers or traders to change firms if they receive a better offer.

Dan at Merrill Lynch says that if you don't want to work in New York, you should contact the branch office in your area. "Contact the local managing director. Most hiring is done on a regional level."

Some surveys indicate that the financial planning industry has some of the greatest potential for growth. Think about it. Since fewer companies are offering pensions, more and more people have multiple jobs that don't offer a retirement plan. They don't work long enough to become vested in a program. It's not surprising that many people are taking their financial security and retirement into their own hands.

## How Much Will I Make?

You can make an unlimited amount of money, depending on the field you choose. Bankers and financial planners can make six figures after they have years of experience or have built a good clientele, but they won't make millions. Most entry-level positions start in the low thirties with benefits.

Traders and investment bankers make the most, with many making millions. It can be lucrative for the partners. It is reported that all of the partners of J.P. Morgan earn well over $1 million a year. An average trader or investment banker would make at least six figures.

## What's the Career Path?

In financial planning and brokerage, some people train and establish a client base and then move locations or open their own firms. Some organizations (investment houses) have a partner track similar to a law firm.

## Do I Need to Be Licensed, Certified, or Have an MBA?

Different disciplines require certification and licensure. These are often state or national tests that you must pass in order to sell certain products. An MBA can be helpful and is required by some companies and professions.

## What Skills and Education Do I Need?

Skills, background, and even personality may differ depending on which area you go into. A couple of things are consistent, though. Regardless of what field you go into, having a strong business and math background will be helpful. There are plenty of people who don't have business backgrounds. Adam was in advertising before be became a commodities trader and later a salesman for Bear Stearns. Dan was in commercial real estate for seven years before he became a financial planner. And Bobby graduated from the University of Texas with a biology degree and was prepared to go to medical school before he went to work for a brokerage firm and eventually become a very successful (and wealthy) bond trader.

It is still recommended that you have a business degree or at least a strong business background. For management and many investment banking positions, you need an MBA—preferably one from a top school.

You need to be technically competent, but this doesn't mean you have to be a math or finance whiz (although it helps). The two most important skills you need are sales and customer service skills.

Being able to work independently is critical. Many financial planners are one-person shops that may operate from home or a single office. Even if you are with a major company at their branch office, you are extremely autonomous. Many actually have independent contractor arrangements.

## What Are the Pros and Cons?

People who are fairly new to this field, especially younger adults, claim it is tough to get new clients. People like to see a little gray hair and experience when it comes to investing their money. Newcomers run into many of the same problems that young insurance agents have. Most of your contacts and connections don't have any money to invest. You may find yourself hitting up your friends and family, who might not have much money, but if they did, they wouldn't be comfortable investing it with you. This is a business built on relationships.

Natalie said that she has lost at least five friends because of the overaggressive tactics of some firms. "It always starts out with, 'I want to take you to lunch.' Then I get this hard sell from my friend. I felt used. This was a college roommate who knew I was just starting out. I also knew this person couldn't balance her checkbook and now wanted me to invest money with here."

You must be self-disciplined. Realize that your young friends either a) Aren't going to have any money to invest, b) Don't give a damn about retirement, or c) Will blame you forever if they lose money.

## Where Are the Jobs?

It depends on what field you want to go into. The nation's financial centers are New York and Chicago. While Boston, San Francisco and Los Angeles also have major players in certain disciplines, the largest investment banks, brokerage houses, and, of course, the exchanges are located in New York. However, most national firms have an office or branch in nearly every major city. While some banks recruit on a national basis, the majority of them hire on a local or regional basis.

## What The Pros Read

*American Banker*
*Wall Street Journal*
*Financial Times*
*Investors Business Daily*
*Institutional Investor*
*Financial World*
*Financial Planning*

## The Top Ten U.S. Banks

1. Chase, New York
2. CitiCorp, New York
3. BankAmerica, San Francisco
4. NationsBank, Charlotte, NC
5. J.P. Morgan, New York
6. First Union, Charlotte, NC
7. First Chicago, Chicago
8. Bank One, Columbus, OH
9. Fleet Financial Group
10. Shawmut National, Providence, RI

## Where Can I Learn More?

American Bank Directory
404-448-1011
(Listing of banks by state.)

American Banking Association
202-663-5000

*Moody's Bank and Finance Manual*

*Liar's Poker,* by Michael Lewis
(It's a novel, but it gives you an interesting insight into the former high flyers of the industry.)

## Where on the Web?

www.financialjobs.com—FinancialJobs.com
www.financialjobnet.com—Financial Job Network
www.cob.ohio-state.edu/dept/fin/overview.html—Virtual library/finance
www.smithbarney.com—Smith Barney
www.wellsfargo.com—Wells Fargo
www.fid-inv.com—Fidelity Investments
www.bankamerica.com—Bank of America
www.jpmorgan.com—J.P. Morgan
www.salomon.com—Salomon Brothers
www.nyse.com—New York Stock Exchange
www.nasd.com—National Association of Securities Dealers

# 21

· · · · · · · · · · · · · · · · · · · · · · · · · · · · · · · · · · ·

# Firefighter

**Other Opportunities You Might Consider**
Being an emergency medical technician (EMT) or paramedic is closely related to firefighting. Actually, many firefighters are required to be trained as paramedics. Firefighters can be employed by cities, counties, airports, corporations, and private firefighting companies (for example, those who handle oil rig fires). If you don't want to risk life and limb, but still like the rescue-and-safety field, there are a number of companies that manufacture and sell safety products and firefighting equipment.

As a kid, firefighter may have been on your short list of career options, right after cowboy and astronaut. As an adult, firefighter is still on the short list of many people, especially adrenaline junkies.

## What Education Do I Need?

The requirements vary from city to city. In some cities, you need only a high school diploma or GED. In Cleveland, you need to have a GED and you must pass a civil service exam, while in Dallas, you must have at least forty-five college credit hours or a BA and pass the civil service exam. Chief Frank Ravka of the Houston Fire Department says, "More departments are requiring at least some college hours or even and an associate's degree. Firefighting has become a more technical job, and you simply need to know more." Check with your local department for specific educational requirements.

## What Skills Do I Need?

First of all, you have to be in great shape. This is a physically demanding job. Your endurance and agility are among the first things you're tested on. For many candidates, this is often the hardest part of the application process.

John of the LA Fire Department says, "It doesn't hurt to be a little cocky." This job, like being a cop, requires a good deal of self-confidence. You also need to be able to work well in a team environment. You're going to be living closely with other people whose lives may depend on you someday.

## How Much Can I Make?

The salary varies from city to city, but the average firefighter can expect a starting salary of between $27,000 to $32,000. Benefits are included. Most firefighters have a pension available to them after twenty years. As one firefighter put it, "This is a career where you won't get rich, but it will take care of you. It's steady. You don't hear of cops and firefighters getting laid off."

## Where Do I Start?

In many departments, you go through a six-month training program at the fire academy. You might then be assigned to a firehouse, where you'll be on probation for up to a year. In some cities like Houston, the probation period lasts eighteen months. This is because in Houston and other cities, rookie firefighters are now required to spend six to eight months training as paramedics before they begin firefighting. "Our priority has shifted from having non-medically-trained firefighters to wanting a highly-trained person," says Chief Ravka.

## How Do I Get Hired?

It can be a long process. In many cities, you start by going to the local civil service office to complete the application and schedule a civil service exam. All civil employees from postmen on down have to take this exam. If you pass the civil service exam, you're called to take other aptitude tests, as well as math and reading exams.

If you make it to the next level, you take a physical endurance and agility test. This is generally the washout for many applicants. Next, you take a polygraph test, drug test, and go through extensive background checks. Are you beginning to understand why it takes so long? If you jump all of these hurdles and pass all of the exams, you're asked to become a member of a rookie class. Cities might vary, but there may be only two or three rookie classes per year. These classes may have up to forty people.

## What Will I Do?

Obviously, you'll respond to fires and emergencies when you're on duty. The hours are tough. You may work a schedule of anywhere from forty to fifty-six hours a week. It may be broken up into a variety of shifts. For example, you might work two shifts of twenty-four hours on and twenty-four off and then get five days off. In a small town, there can be some downtime, but if you're in a major metropolitan area, you're always busy. You may not be out on calls, but you'll be training or maintaining the engines and equipment.

Other non-accident-related activities include getting cats out of trees (it really happens), checking gas meters and smoke alarms, unlocking car doors, and performing public relations activities such as talking with schoolkids about fire safety.

## You Might Consider

Chief Frank Ravka of the Houston Fire Department recommends that someone who enjoys the life but isn't hell-bent on being a firefighter become an EMT. Some cities have EMTs stationed in the firehouse as part of a unit. Other EMTs work as part of a separate ambulance service.

## What Do Firefighters Like the Most?

Firefighters cite the obvious benefit of saving lives and helping people, but they say it's also a great job because of the adventure, excitement, and competitive spirit. Sounds like one big testosterone kick to me, but that's okay. I don't want any wimps who might hesitate when it's my home going up in flames.

There's also a lot of camaraderie, because you stay at the firehouse when you're on duty. "You really feel close to your team." The staggered schedule can be demanding when you're working, but it can also leave you with the free time to pursue other interests or even have another job to provide additional income.

If you were wondering if firefighters really get to do it on top of the fire trucks like they do in the movie *Backdraft*, no one was willing to disclose that information.

## What Are the Negatives?

I can think of a few negatives right off the bat. How about danger, loss of life and limb, or even death? While these negative factors are certainly ever present, most firefighters commented on how physically and emotionally demanding the job is. Frank in Houston says, "You're constantly seeing death, destruction, and violence."

Firefighters also say the money and hours could be better. Others say being away from your family is tough. Brian of the LA Fire Department says, "You have to be able to deal with your family after being on duty for twenty-four hours."

## Are There Many Women Firefighters?

The numbers are increasing. And it's not just for single women. The Houston Fire Department firefighters say they have several firefighting moms.

## What's the Turnover Rate?

Very low. People who get hired generally stay and make a career of it. One fire department estimated up to 90 percent of their firefighters stay and make it until retirement, which can be twenty years.

## What's the Career Path?

After the basic firefighter position, advancement is by rank. The names and titles vary from department to department, but they are basically sergeant, lieutenant, captain, then district or battalion chief, deputy chief, and fire chief. Many firefighters choose to pursue advanced or special training in an area such as rescue or hazardous materials.

The Phoenix Fire Department has a trail-bike rescue force. They patrol over seventy miles of trails in the city's South Mountain Park. Members ride bikes packed with bandages and splints to treat people for broken bones or help riders who have suffered from heat exhaustion in the 100-plus-degree heat. Some members make over $40,000 a year.

## How Can I Advance?

Diversify your talents. Many firefighters seek advanced medical or rescue training. The rescue training might include rescues in swift water, vehicular, underground, or high-angle or above-ground rescues.

## Where on the Web?

www.fire-rescue.org—Fire-Rescue.org

www.fire-ems.net—Fire and EMS Information Network

www.ifpra.com—International Fire and Police Recruitment
  Administration

## Shop talk: "Off the Tower"

When someone is finished with training, they are said to be "off the tower."

# 22

● ● ● ● ● ● ● ● ● ● ● ● ● ● ● ● ● ● ● ● ● ● ● ● ● ● ●

# Food Service

"Would you like fries and a hot apple pie with that?"

**Some Common Positions**
Server
Manager
Kitchen manager
Bar manager
General manager
Food and beverage director
Chef/cook

**Other Opportunities You Might Consider**
Food service is part of the much larger hospitality industry, which is made up of both hotels and restaurants. There are a variety of related industries that help make a restaurant or any food service organization work. A few examples of people involved are the food brokers, suppliers and sales people, restaurant decorators and designers, real estate and property managers, trainers, and human resource staff.

Don't forget the food and nutrition sciences, either. Food manufacturers such as a Gerber, M&M Mars, or Nabisco have opportunities for people with scientific backgrounds to help produce and develop new products. Many of the restaurant chains also have test kitchens where they prepare new dishes.

If you're thinking, "I spent my youth working in a fast-food restaurant and anything involving a hair net is not a viable career option," think again. The food service industry is much more than burger flipping, hair nets, and hourly wages. It's one of largest and fastest growing fields in America. Food service is among the largest of U.S. industries. It represents 5 percent of the U.S. GNP. Approximately 5 percent of the nation's workforce is employed at eating and dining establishments.

## What Does It Mean to Work in Food Service?

Working in the food industry can mean anything that involves the preparation and serving of meals to the public. It also involves supplying, management, and marketing of restaurants and food service operations for institutions such as hospitals, universities, or corporations.

## It Isn't Just Fast Food

There are several segments that make up the food service industry:

*Fast Food*: The industry's largest segment

*Full Service Restaurants or Dinner Houses*: National chains like Chili's or T.G.I.Friday's, as well as fine "white tablecloth" restaurants. This isn't one of the best areas of opportunity for college graduates.

*Hotels, Resorts, and Lodging Places*: A popular area, but difficult to get in unless you have a hospitality background. You generally must go the hourly employee route and work your way up.

*Institutional or Contract Food Service:* Many institutions are outsourcing their food service areas to private companies. This is the industry's fastest growing segment.

*Healthcare:* Hospitals and nursing homes.

*Education:* Universities, colleges, and other school cafeterias.

*Recreation:* Public stadiums, ball parks, and auditoriums.

*Employee Food Service:* Companies with on-site employee cafeterias.

*Transportation:* Airlines (nothing like airline food).

*Retail Stores:* Cafes in stores such as Nordstrom.

## Where Are the Jobs?

How about every street corner in America, or so it seems. More than one in four retail outlets is an eating and drinking establishment. Opportunities aren't limited by location. There are restaurants of all types in virtually every urban or rural area.

Just like the Gap and Starbucks, many restaurant chains have begun to dominate the landscape. You can't go to any suburban corner in America without seeing a Chili's, a T.G.I.Friday's, or an Olive Garden. There's even a Chili's in the Atlanta airport. This is a far cry from the days when your only choice in an air-

The fastest growing opportunities in food service actually have nothing to do with restaurants. They're in institutions such as hospitals, nursing homes, prisons, and universities. The people running the food service for airlines or cafeterias for large company headquarters are often outsourced to institutional food preparers.

### JobSmarts Top Career Pick: Food Service Manager

Don't laugh. More Americans are eating out than ever before. Restaurants have traditionally had a hard time attracting people to the industry, but are now offering salary packages that make it possible for a restaurant general manager to make $100,000 plus. Combined with the growth in outsourced food service by institutions, the food service field looks to be a smart choice. The opportunities keep coming. The number of food service managers is expected to increase 44 percent by the year 2005 and the need for cooks will increase 38 percent.

### Categories of Service

1. Fast food
2. Casual dining
3. Fine dining
4. Institutional food service

port was paying $8 for a cold hot dog. When an Olive Garden went up in Times Square, I knew their quest for world domination was complete.

Oddly enough, the fastest growing area of the food service industry has nothing to do with restaurants. Institutional feeding is another way to describe food service in hospitals, universities, or even prisons. The number of chef and cook positions in hospitals and universities is supposed to increase by 86 percent by the year 2005. This also includes serving meals and food in stadiums and arenas, as well as on airplanes.

## Institutional Feeding (Doesn't the Name Sound Appealing?)

Institutional food services serve universities, hospitals, nursing homes, and even private companies and outlets like airports. When you fly, the meals for those airlines that still serve meals are run by food service companies. There are several large institutional food companies. Two of the largest are Host Marriott and Aramark. They're hired by organizations that choose to outsource their food service operations. Host Marriott serves a number of facilities such as airports, stadiums, and arenas. They may have even been hired to prepare that great dorm food for your campus. Institutional feeding operations can also be found on-site at many corporations. They run corporate cafeterias at companies like EDS and Texas Instruments, where thousands of employees are at one location.

Geographically speaking, anywhere tourism is big, there will be opportunities in food service. California, New York, Texas, and Florida are the states with the most eating and drinking establishments.

## How Much Will I Make?

Probably a lot more than you think. Of course, wait staff and servers don't make a fortune. But don't make the mistake of thinking this is just $5.50 an hour and a few tips. There are opportunities for people who have degrees and are willing to work hard to make between $60,000 to $120,000. And these aren't necessarily at big ticket, high-end restaurants.

If you're in a management training program with a national dinner-house chain like Houston's, you'll start in the mid-twenties to low thirties. This is about $10,000 more than advertising, public relations, or media jobs. In addition, many companies will pay for your relocation costs.

Most restaurant chains offer full benefits found in other fields. You also get free meals. Some managers have performance tie-ins and bonuses that can be up to 20 percent of their salary. Some also receive stock options.

Managers are generally in charge of a certain part of the restaurant, and the general manager oversees the entire operation. There's a bar manager, night manager, assistant manager, and kitchen manager to name a few. These managers can earn between $30,000 to $50,000. At Houston's, once you become a general manager—which can take from four to six years—it's realistic that you can oversee operations for a facility with gross sales of $3 to $5 million and easily be earning six figures. Not bad considering you could be as young as twenty-seven or twenty-eight.

## How Stable Is It?

Traditionally, there's unbelievable turnover at the hourly and entry level. However, if you get into a management training program with the right organization, it's very stable and you can have a long career with a company if you choose. Pack your bags, though, because in order to move up, you must move around. This is a field where unless you're in a single-unit establishment or a local chain, you'll have to move around. It's almost guaranteed in any multi-unit chain.

## Where Will I Start?

I've got good news and bad news. The good news is you probably won't have to wear a hair net. The bad news is that you don't start out as corporate, either. If you're to take a management track, it's likely that you'll start out as an assistant manager. This may last for a couple of years. In most companies, you'll begin by spending time working in all sides of the "house," as it's called. All managers start out entry-level. In this business, it's critical that you understand all sides of the house and not have a superficial overview.

In companies like Houston's, you'll start out learning service procedures, bar operations, and administrative procedures. You'll have exposure to payroll, recruiting, purchasing, cost control, and inventory. And most importantly, you'll polish your people skills.

When your back-of-the-house training begins, you'll work hands-on in a kitchen. You'll learn how to prepare each dish, and you'll train at each line station. This will give you an understanding of "cook times" and how things can run smoothly or go foul in a kitchen when you're "in the weeds" or swamped.

While training time varies from restaurant to restaurant, this may last between four to nine months. You might also take courses or train in employee and guest relations, floor management, recruiting, or profit and loss management.

## How Fast Will I Move Up?

Don't you mean, "How long will I be serving food?" Not long if you're smart and you hustle. There are few industries that allow you to become the boss of a restaurant within a year of graduation and realistically make six figures within five years. Food service is one of the few fields where age does not matter. In a training program, you'll spend several weeks or months at various stations (bar, kitchen, server) before moving into a management position overseeing one of the areas of the restaurant. It takes between two to three years to go from manager to general manager.

## What Do Managers Do?

Restaurant managers and GM's have a variety of duties, not unlike managers in any other business. They recruit, hire, train, schedule, and motivate employees. They resolve food quality and service complaints. They develop marketing strategies and promote the restaurant. They're in charge of increasing sales, purchasing supplies and equipment, and monitoring the budget and cost controls.

In addition, there are the chefs or kitchen managers who plan the menu and are responsible for the safety and cleanliness of the kitchen.

# I Want to Cook

If you want to be a cook or chef, you might see if the restaurant you're considering has a traditional setup, which means they have a chef, a sous chef, and cooks. (Otherwise, they might have a kitchen manager system, which is most common.)

## How Do I Become a Chef?

There's no one certain way. You can just start cooking. Many begin cooking as a hobby or start in a low-end restaurant and work their way up to better restaurants with no formal training. On the other hand, you can go through a culinary arts program or attend a culinary arts school and become highly trained. You don't have to become certified to become a chef. Regardless of which path you take, there's some form of training, whether it's a mentoring process, a structured program, or an educational institution.

According to the National Restaurant Association, there are 170 four-year programs in hospitality management and more than 700 two-year or associate's degree programs.

> **JobSmarts Food Service No-No**
>
> It bears saying that if you're considering a career in the food service industry you want to avoid scaring the customers as one employee at a Roy Rogers fast-food restaurant in Washington, D.C. reportedly did. The worker, upon spying a rat in the restaurant, corralled the animal behind the counter and proceeded to pummel the rodent as diners watched in horror.
>
> (As reported in *Training & Development* magazine)

## What Are Some of the Best Culinary Schools

Culinary Institute of America, Johnson and Wales, or the California Culinary Academy are a few of the top programs.

## Do I Need a Formal Education or Restaurant Degree?

It depends on the restaurant. A restaurant degree or participation in a food service program at school will certainly help, but it's not a requirement. This is still one of the few industries that allows someone without a formal education to work hard and rise through the ranks to become a manager and possibly advance further.

## What About the Hours?

This is not a nine-to-five job. Management trainees work between fifty and sixty hours a week. You may be there to open and/or close.

## What Skills Do I Need?

It's a cliché in many fields, but it's very true for this industry: You must be enthusiastic and have a great attitude. Recruiters say that you also need maturity and empathy. "You'll be dealing with all types of people, and you'll need to understand their needs and be able to communicate with them," Susan Mills of the National Restaurant Association says. "Food service is a high touch trade."

Having a knowledge of safety, sanitation, food chemistry, nutrition, and appearance is important as well.

## Do You Want to Work Abroad?

This is a great industry for opportunities abroad. More and more, companies are expanding into foreign markets. An Outback Steakhouse was recently opened in Cancún, Mexico. You'll find Chili's restaurants in Asia. There are Domino's Pizzas in Israel, the Netherlands, and Japan. According to the National Restaurant Association, the Pacific Rim is where most companies are planning their foreign expansion.

## How Do I Get Hired?

There are as many ways to get hired as there are restaurants. Some restaurants, food organizations, and chains actively recruit on college campuses. If you don't have connections or are not involved with a formal program, contact the restaurant directly if it's independent or locally owned. Ask for the owner or GM. If it's a chain, you should contact that company's headquarters or regional manager.

Not every company has centralized recruiting. Inquire about management training programs. Realize that not every restaurant may call it that. Some may not even have a training program. If they have a management training program, you may still start out in an entry-level position and work your way up as you demonstrate responsibility and skill in various areas. You might also check out any of the trade publications.

## What Makes Me Stand Out As a Candidate?

Education is helpful, but when it comes right down to it, experience, attitude, and a realistic view of what working with food and others is all about is what counts. You're working with and helping to serve other people and make their experience pleasant. You have to be energetic. While these are qualities that could apply to any field, in the food service business, they are essential and you're judged on them. It doesn't hurt to be involved in activities where you have demonstrated people, crisis, and team-building skills.

## What's So Great About This Field?

Some people like the entertaining, bon vivant aspect of it. Others truly enjoy food or grew up around restaurants. It's very common for people to enter the food service industry if their parents were involved in it.

Others say it's like being a CEO, but with other people's money. You know that you can turn to headquarters for support and advice. You're responsible for sales, marketing and promotion, costs, and employees.

## What Are Some Misconceptions?

It's not just waiting tables or cooking. It's like any other business in that you may deal with the financials, products, marketing, and employees. It's also a misconception that there's no money in this field. You might receive a lower starting salary, but the opportunity for growth—financially and professionally—can double or triple in a very short period of time.

Tanya, manager of a Chili's in Atlanta, says not to underestimate the amount of politics and people skills involved. "You really need to learn to deal with people who not only have different backgrounds, but different ideas as well. You really need expert people and management skills, with particular strengths in delegating and being able to motivate and hold people accountable."

The other misconceptions have to do with being a chef or owning a restaurant. It's easy to romanticize being a chef when on TV you see the chef as a celebrity and "god" who spends time in the kitchen and schmoozes with guests. While it's true that good chefs are part entertainer, chefs I interviewed said that regardless of how romantic you think it may be, it's damn hard work. Cooking can be physically demanding, and you'll work exhausting hours.

## What Are the Greatest Concerns for Managers?

While service, staffing concerns, and, of course, food quality are important, safety and sanitation are probably the biggest concerns that chefs and food service professionals must face.

## What's the Worst Thing About This Field?

It's an intense business. You may find yourself doing anything and everything. Most of it isn't glamorous. Tanya says, "Taking care of minor crises such as cleaning up the flooded bathroom. When you're shorthanded for the night, you have to do whatever it takes to keep the restaurant running smoothly."

## Where Can I Learn More?

NRA—National Restaurant Association
1200 Seventeenth Street NW
Washington, DC 20036-3097
202-331-5900
(The main trade group for this field. They also have student benefits and services, as well as regional and state chapters you can join to learn of opportunities in your area.)

American Culinary Federation
10 San Bartola Drive
St. Augustine, FL 32086
904-824-4468
(The nation's largest association representing 25,000 chefs, cooks, bakers, and educators.)

*Food Work: Jobs in the Food Service Industry and How to Get Them*, by Barbara Simms Bell. Published by Advocacy Press: 800-676-1480.
*FoodService USA*. Published by the National Restaurant Association and geared for young adults considering careers in food service. Call the NRA to get a copy: 202-331-5900

## Where on the Web?

www.restaurant.org—National Restaurant Association
www.acfchefs.org—American Culinary Federation

# 23

• • • • • • • • • • • • • • • • • • • • • • • • • •

# Freelancing

If you're sick of playing politics and dealing with the bureaucracy often found in an agency or corporation, you'll love freelancing. Freelancers are self-employed and work for their clients on a project-by-project or contract basis. The information here is geared for artists, photographers, and illustrators, but the elements of freelancing described here are the same for many fields, particularly freelance copywriting. (You should also check out the graphic and commercial arts chapter.)

## What Will I Do?

Most freelancers work out of their homes or apartments. Occasionally, you'll work in the client's office or meet at the agency that hired you. You'll usually meet at your client's location to discuss the project and pick up any materials. You then complete the project at home. There's also a lot of communication via e-mail and fax.

One of the great things about freelancing is that you have the freedom to live anywhere you want. You can set your own hours. You can work as much or as little as you like. The downside is that if you don't work, you don't eat. Your income will vary from month to month, depending on the number of projects on which you're working.

When you meet with a client, you'll discuss what the need is for the project and what they expect of you. Sometimes the client will give you a great deal of information and direction; other times you'll be asked to come up with something from scratch. If you're hired by an agency to work on a project, you'll be partnered with an art director (if you're a copywriter), and you'll work on the project as a team.

Troy, a copywriter in Chicago, says, "Sometimes I work directly with the art director to come up with a concept and then we both go off and do our separate things. Other times an agency just says, 'Here is an idea we had, now go write this brochure.'"

## What's It Like to Freelance?

You have to realize that freelancing can be a lonely business. You're no longer just a creative person, you're a businessperson who is responsible for the marketing, billing, and administration of your freelance business. It takes a certain discipline to sell yourself and work alone from your home. You must treat your home office like a real office. Many people have a hard time making the transition from working in an agency and being surrounded by people to working alone. They miss the camaraderie and being able to bounce ideas off other people quickly.

Ellen, a freelance illustrator, says she enjoys freelancing because, "Your work really does speak for itself. In some cases, you might just drop your book off and a decision will be made solely on your work. You might not ever have the chance to charm someone, because you might never meet him until he calls you for a job."

## What About Job Security?

Yeah, right. If you want stability, do not freelance. Job security depends upon your own talents and sales abilities. That scares a lot of people. However, many freelancers love the challenge and the unpredictability. Chris, a copywriter in Atlanta, says, "The only thing I'm certain of is the uncertainty. I also know that I'm not going to be laid off."

There's an ebb and flow to freelancing as well. There will be lulls where you might be bored out of your mind, and then you'll be swamped with several projects at once.

## How Do I Find Business?

No matter how creative you are, being a freelancer means being a salesperson. Finding business is a combination of research, networking, and cold calling.

Business just doesn't come looking for you. You must actively seek it out by making phone calls. You should start by reading the advertising publications such as *Ad Age* and *Adweek*. You should also keep up with trade journals and local publications to find out who has and who lost certain accounts. It's important to keep up with who is working on what account.

## Who Would I Cold Call?

Start by contacting the art director or creative director of an agency. Ask the director if you could come by to show her your book. Many agencies simply ask you to drop your book off, or they have a specific "drop policy," such as they only review freelancer books on Fridays.

Another way to get business, especially when you're just starting out, is to walk into a local business you think could use some advertising help and ask if you can create ads for them. This may be a restaurant, hair salon, insurance company, or mom-and-pop store. It doesn't matter if they have a giant budget or not. Your goal is to have produced work for your book. When creative directors are looking at portfolios, they prefer actual produced pieces rather than student work or samples. You can also build a nice little business in your community.

## To Whom Do I Drop My Book Off?

If you're an illustrator, you should target art and creative directors. Some large agencies have actual art buyers, but usually it's the creative or art director.

## Never Let Them See You Sweat

Ellen recalls a meeting where she thought she was only supposed to meet briefly with the art director to drop off her book. When she arrived, there were six people who worked on the account ready to review her work with her. Always expect the unexpected and be professional.

# 24

● ● ● ● ● ● ● ● ● ● ● ● ● ● ● ● ● ● ● ● ● ● ● ● ● ● ● ● ● ● ●

# Government and Politics

**Some Common Positions**
There are no common positions, since government and political jobs are so diverse. Positions are found at all levels (federal, state, and local) in almost any profession you can imagine. Don't forget the many opportunities working for your state and local departments, agencies, or commissions.

Whether you are out to change the country or simply collect a paycheck from Uncle Sam, you have plenty of choices in working for the government. Basically, there are three categories of government and political jobs: city, state, and federal. To many people, the most obvious thing that comes to mind regarding the government is working on Capitol Hill for a congressman or senator. However there are an incredible number of departments, agencies, think-tanks, and nonprofit organizations that are either a part of the government or associated with it, so there are unlimited possibilities. Some of the most common jobs that people think of when working in D.C. involve working on the "hill." These may be working for a senate or house office or committees, such as the Republican or Democratic National Committees. Off of the hill you can work for a lobbyist, trade association, or even the executive branch or one of the federal agencies.

## Where Do I Start?

Where you start your career depends on where you are employed. If you are working on Capitol Hill, you will likely start as a legislative correspondent or legislative assistant. An assistant is a little more senior than a correspondent. Assistants may go by different names depending on the department. In committees, assistants are called professional staff members. Because of the competition for jobs, it is possible that you might have to start as a receptionist simply to get your foot in the door. People get hired largely through connections and networking. Your relationships also help you advance in your career.

## Do I Have to Move to Washington, D.C.?

If you don't want to move to Washington, D.C., an area you may want to explore is state or city government. This may be an easier route to gain experience and exposure than trying to crack the competitive beltway scene in Washington. One Hill staffer says that the federal bureaucracy is so huge it can take a while to understand how the process works. A state government is of a manageable size, so you can get a feel for how things work and take that experience to Washington if you choose.

Washington D.C. has plenty of government-related opportunities that aren't political and for which you don't have to be a government employee. For example, if you're an attorney or paralegal, Washington has more attorneys per capita than anywhere else in the country. D.C. is also headquarters to more associations and trade groups than anywhere else in the nation. Associations and special interest groups have positions in marketing, sales, public relations, and finance, just like any other company. Washington is also a good place if you're interested in public relations, media and journalism, or speech writing.

## What Will I Do?

It depends on where you're employed. If you're working on Capitol Hill, each office is organized a little differently. Traditionally in a congressperson's office, the staff is pretty small (around ten people). It's divided into two sections: legislative staff and general support staff. These two groups are known as the member's "personal" staff.

Legislative Aides/Assistants (LA) and Legislative Correspondents (LC) perform many of the basic activities such as responding to letters from voters, writing statements, and

### Common Entry-Level Positions on Capitol Hill

Administrative assistant/staffer
Legislative correspondent (LC)
Legislative aide/assistant (LA)

tracking legislation. There is a lot of time spent writing and talking with people on the phone. You'll generally have particular legislative issues you're responsible for tracking and researching. You also keep track of where other congresspeople stand on certain legislation and keep your boss aware of what proposals and issues are being talked about and will become important for him to know about.

Before you can do the cool stuff like track legislation and inform your boss on issues, you have to do a lot of grunt work. Nothing comes easy on the Hill. Without experience you have to be willing to do anything just to get in the door, and often for free (or next to it). "This is not the place for you if you are above doing grunt work or think you are a prima donna," says Trent, who works for a congressman.

Rick says that during his interview he was asked his position on a variety of issues. "It's important that you fall in line ideologically with your boss. I'm not saying you should be a mindless clone, but you might have a hard time if you're a Democrat working in a very conservative Republican office. And if you have experience working for a Democratic office, you'll have a hard time switching to a Republican office, unless you can demonstrate that you had an epiphany."

## What's It Like Working on the Hill?

There is a huge learning curve as you become acclimated to how things work in Washington. Hill veterans say that many recent graduates come to D.C. idealistic and full of ideas that can change the world, and quickly realize that it's hard to make a difference.

Some Hill workers and government staffers say that there is not as much support in the public sector as there is in a private company. Trent says, "I'm the support staff. There is no one to do anything for me, whereas I have friends in other fields who have secretaries and other people to take care of things for them. You fend for yourself a lot."

Some LCs are asked to prepare statements and even speeches that their boss is to read to the media or on the floor. Cameron, an LC for a congressman, said he had a great opportunity to learn about speech writing. "Sometimes you prepare an entire statement that a congressman will read verbatim, or you just provide notes and fact cards to which he can refer. It depends on what he prefers."

## How Much Can I Make?

Two words: civil servant. If you are looking to make a lot of money, this is not the field to go into. Salaries are considerably higher in the private sector. Entry-level salaries vary according to what area of government you are in. For workers on Capitol Hill, the starting salary range is between $10,000 to $20,000 a year. Receptionists and legislative correspondents would be on the

## What's It Like Working for a Congressman?

Chris served as legislative assistant for a California congressman for three years. His uncle had helped campaign for the congressman and told Chris about a summer intern position. Chris enjoyed his internship, so after he graduated from Hamilton College, he contacted the congressman and was offered a position as legislative assistant. It was unusual for someone to start out in such a great position, but his experience as an intern helped.

"A lot of what I did as an LA was scan through the mountain of paper and information that came into the congressman's office and condense it into a form that he could understand. The problem with 'the Hill' is that you must stay abreast of vast amounts of information that are vital to the congressman.

"My typical day started at 8:00 A.M., and for the first hour and a half I would go through the in-box. Then in the afternoon, we would get faxed newsletters from the Republican leader's office telling us what action happened that morning on the floor and what we could expect later in the week.

"The Democratic and Republican leaders' offices would also hold a weekly meeting for staff members, preparing everyone for what would happen the next week. This is how LAs learned about information in other offices so we could brief our bosses.

"It's a tough job, and it took a long time to learn what type of facts my boss needed. He was very knowledgeable on some issues and simply needed a status report. On others, he needed to be fully briefed.

"I just can't get over how busy congressmembers are. Almost every minute of my boss's day was scheduled. Sometimes, when he was unable to meet with constituents, I would meet with them as his representative. I would also sit in on meetings with him and take notes to make sure that we did not forget anything. It's a job where you grow up very quickly."

lower end of the pay scale. Regarding Senate versus House, staffers say that the Senate pays better, but also requires more experience.

Salaries off the hill tend to be a little higher; however, it depends on the lobbying firm, department, or association. Generally agencies and firms representing private industry pay better than non-profits. (Hey, I hear the tobacco guys have a few bucks.)

If you're hired by the federal government, your pay will be determined by a scale based upon your tenure, job description, and where you live. The GS, ES, and EX (general, executive, and senior executive) pay schedules outline salaries for everyone from secretaries to FBI agents to Bill Clinton himself.

## What's the Career Path?

Career paths vary from person to person. It depends upon their individual goals. Some people hop from office to office and use each position as a way to advance their career, while others stay at one office or with one member for a long time. Some people use their experience and connections working on the Hill or for an agency or department, to help them launch a career in private industry. Your advancement comes from your experience and the responsibility you have been given.

Trent says that breaking into a government position is like being an actor. "It is hard to get in, but once you are there and have a reputation it is easier to get around." Many people say that careers are made simply by being in the right place at the right time and being very aggressive. "Take advantage of every contact you make and really build your network," advises Trent.

Working on the Hill, it's easy to get burned out in a particular office. Sometimes after a couple of years, you might need a change of pace, so it's not uncommon for people to move from one office to

another. However, most movement is to gain more responsibility. A common career change is to go from working on a personal staff for a congressperson or senator to working on a committee staff. Committee jobs are some of the most coveted. They are better paid, you get your hands in juicier policy issues, and you can develop a single focus.

Other people who start out on a personal staff sometimes make a move to a department or agency. This is also considered a move up. The lifestyle is slower and more comfortable, and the pay is better.

Another thing that people do after working on the House side is to try and move to the Senate. These jobs are more difficult to come by and are often staffed by older and more experienced people.

## What Skills Do I Need?

There is no prerequisite. There are people with a variety of degrees and backgrounds. Just because you have a political science degree doesn't guarantee you a job or mean that you will like it. Pros recommend that you volunteer or intern before you pack your bags and move to D.C. or make a career decision. Amy, who works for a Senator, says, "You have to love the whole political process."

It helps to be a good communicator and able to work well with people. You also have to be aggressive and a little opportunistic.

## Do I Need a Political Science Degree?

No. Your major or degree doesn't matter at the entry level. Many people who are senior staff members have advanced or even law degrees.

## What Are Some of the Pros and Cons of Working for the Government?

You mean you really have to ask? C'mon, government holidays. Just like banks, the government and its offices seem to shut down for everything except Groundhog Day. Although it's not as true on the Hill or in legislative positions, the hours are pretty easy. Most agency and department jobs are eight to five.

Going to parties and meeting powerful and influential people are only a couple of the perks of working on the Hill. Other intangible perks include being informed on current events and issues as well as being in a center of power.

Government employees also seem to love the benefits packages. Government employees are offered great health benefits and retirement packages, sometimes with your employer picking up all of the premiums. Remember that in the private sector, most employers only pay a portion of your insurance and you must pick up the rest.

One of the things frequently heard from people in government, especially city government, is that they feel like a part of the community. They feel they are really justifying their existence and making a contribution. It's the whole Jimmy Stewart, *Mr. Smith Goes to Washington* thing. Rent the movie sometime.

While some government jobs offer a nice environment, job security, and great benefits, a potential negative is that, because it's a safe environment, you have people who are not challenged or who are content to simply show up and collect a paycheck. Sometimes, the work can be mind-numbing. Agency or department jobs might be stable, but working on the Hill or for a legislator is very unstable. If your candidate gets voted out of office, as a staffer, you too are out of a job. Other complaints are the low pay and the limited potential for advancement.

Shana is an attorney with a state agency. While many attorneys put in ridiculous hours, Shana's office must close at 5:30. There's no staying late. Her job prevents her from having any sort of overtime, except several times a year on specifically mandated dates. Why? Because the state and its agencies don't want to pay overtime. Shana says, "The good thing is that I am home by 6:00 and have a pretty regular schedule."

Make sure that you believe in the person you work for. Chris, a former legislative aide, says, "Working on the Hill is hard enough when you believe in the person. It's too hard if you're spending all of your energy and don't believe in what you're doing. Sometimes, the only thing that keeps you going is knowing that you're doing something good."

## Where Can I Learn More About State and Federal Jobs?

In addition to their fantastic Web site (see below), the OPM operates the Career America Connection, a telephone-based system, that you can call to learn about federal jobs. Call 912-757-3000.

You can also access job information from touch-screen computers and interactive kiosks located in most major cities with OPM career transitions centers. These are often located in federal office buildings. You can contact your state's workforce or employment commission to learn of similar services they provide.

## Where Can I Learn More About Jobs on the Hill?

There are several resources that list job announcements in D.C. and on the Hill. A couple you should check out are *Roll Call*, a weekly newspaper covering events on the Hill, and *The National Journal*, another weekly newspaper. Both list job openings and career moves.

Michael Berone's *The Almanac of American Politics* profiles all congress-members and senators and gives a several paragraph description of their biographies and views on certain issues.

## Where on the Web?

For general information about the government and its branches and agencies, I recommend that you go to Yahoo! and search under the "Government and Politics" section. It has over 800 different Web sites devoted to government and political issues. It has great information and links to specific state and federal offices.

www.dol.gov—Department of Labor (It has some great information about working for the government, including a *Federal Employees Survival Guide*.)

www.usajobs.opm.gov—Office of Personnel Management (Absolutely the best resource for finding a job with the federal government. The USAJOBS site provides worldwide job listings that are updated daily. You can tailor your search by pay, geographic location, and job category. You'll find job listings and information on jobs at all levels, as well as information on how to apply for federal jobs, the presidential intern program, student employment and summer jobs, salary and benefit information, qualification requirements, and information about working overseas. If you ever doubt that there are opportunities for anyone to work for Uncle Sam, check out the section on this site that lists eight pages of federal jobs broken down by major. It will blow you away to learn about all the jobs that the government hires for. You should study this page just to learn about opportunities in any field pertinent to your major.)

# 25

. . . . . . . . . . . . . . . . . . . . . . . . . . . .

# Graphic and Commercial Arts

**Some Common Positions**
Graphic artist
Illustrator
Art director
Graphic designer
Freelancer
Photographer

**Other Opportunities You Might Consider**
Advertising agencies are probably one of the largest employers of graphic and commercial artists. Corporations and nonprofit associations also hire artists and designers to work in-house rather than hire a full-service advertising agency. Graphic artists are also self-employed or work in design firms. Illustrators and artists are hired by magazines, book publishers, newspapers, television stations and production houses, greeting card companies, packaging firms, and record companies. There are also specialty fields such as technical and medical illustration.

Another growing area for artists and designers to consider is multimedia. Web site developers are constantly in need of people to create content and graphics. Don't worry, you don't have to know HTML or be a programmer.

There are two basic types of artists: fine and commercial.

## Fine Artists

Fine artists include painters, sculptors, or other artists who create art for beauty or enjoyment. However, since people have to eat on a regular basis, artists often accept a commission from individuals, companies, or organizations to create specific works of art. Some fine artists support themselves by selling their work through galleries or artist's representatives. Others support themselves through grants and endowments. It's very difficult to make a successful living as a fine artist, and it's common for fine artists to supplement their incomes by doing commercial art.

The goal of many fine artists is to sell their work in a gallery. Galleries make their money by taking a percentage, generally 40 to 60 percent, of the sales price of an artist's work. Galleries often specialize in certain styles of art. In addition to displaying and selling the work, galleries actively promote and publicize the artist and their work.

## Commercial Artists

Commercial artists create art that is intended for sale or a specific use. Commercial artists are either self-employed or freelance their services on a contract or project-by-project basis. They're also hired as staff by advertising agencies, corporations, design firms, magazines or newspapers, book publishers, film or television studios, multimedia firms, and fashion houses.

Graphic and commercial artists design the artistic elements and layout that we see in books, newspapers, magazines, annual reports, advertisements, billboards, logos, packaging, labels, CD covers, greeting cards, brochures, and direct mail and promotional pieces. Even the bottles and containers we use or the graphics we see on our favorite sports program were created by a graphic artist or designer. The medium can take many forms, including print, multimedia, television, and film.

## What Does a Commercial Artist Do?

It depends upon the position. You'll likely start as a staff member at an advertising agency or design firm. You'll perform grunt work, like preparing storyboards or mechanicals, creating basic marker sketches, doing layout and pasteup, coordinating, and getting material ready for print.

In an agency, one of the top jobs is art director. Art directors act as supervisors and managers of projects or campaigns, and they may oversee the creation of advertising, magazines, brochures, and layouts. They're similar to film or TV producers. Art directors don't get involved in much of the production or dirty work, but they must understand how all elements of photography, illustration, and film fit together. Art directors also select and purchase artwork from freelancers.

One of the main differences between fine and commercial art is the direction and freedom of expression of each artist. Fine artists can create whatever they want. No one tells them what to create or how it should look. Commercial artists, illustrators, and designers are creative, but they don't have as much freedom, since the project must meet the needs, expectations, and budget of the client.

In an agency art department, you might work with the client, art director, or copywriter to determine what the project's needs are and brainstorm on a rough layout. Artists then produce storyboards or rough drafts. The rest is a refining process until it actually goes to production.

In-house or freelance, you'll talk with your client to determine the project needs. You may have free reign to create. Other times, the client may have a basic idea or concept and you will simply refine and produce that idea. It may be as simple as designing a logo and stationery for a new company or creating a direct mail piece from scratch. You might work closely with printers and other vendors or negotiate the print price for the client.

> Debra, a graphic designer for a small software company, does anything that's asked of her one-person department. She may create a training guide for the HR department, design a new brochure for the sales staff, or lay out a proposal for the CEO. She also takes care of routine tasks like designing and ordering new stationery and business cards.

Design has changed dramatically in the past few years. Outside of illustration, much of the work is done on computers (artists love Macintosh) with programs such as Quark. Freelancing requires you to constantly market yourself in addition to producing work. (Learn more about freelancers in the freelance chapter.)

Have you ever noticed window displays or product displays in a store? Department stores and merchandisers hire visual designers and artists to design in-store displays or catalog pieces.

## Happy Groundhog Day

Greeting card companies employ many artists and designers. Hallmark leads the way as the largest employer in this field. Hallmark relies heavily on in-house or staff artists. Your best bet for freelance employment in the greeting card industry is with one of the smaller greeting card companies. They tend to hire more freelance artists. If you want to learn more about career options in the greeting card industry, you might want to check out *Greetings* magazine, the main magazine for the greeting card industry.

## It's Not Just Copies Anymore

Major print shops like Kinko's and AlphaGraphics are attempting to become one-stop shops for many small businesses. In doing so, they're beginning to hire in-house graphic designers.

## What About Education? Do I Need a Design or Art Degree?

Your grades and academic history don't really matter. What matters is your portfolio. Some people have special training or attend special design schools like Parsons School of Design or Rhode Island School of Design (RISD). Many freelancers and artists say no one ever asks to see your grades or your diploma. They don't care if you went to school. Emily, a Parsons grad, says, "If you attend design school, it may impress a few people. But if your work sucks, it doesn't matter. A degree looks good on your résumé, but it still comes down to your portfolio. School teaches technique and skills, but not the business end of being an artist or illustrator."

Kristen is the marketing coordinator for a regional telephone company. Her position involves designing materials not only from an artistic perspective, but from a strategic marketing view. As a commercial artist, your work is communicating a certain message. Kristen does not produce any materials, only the design. Production is done by an outside firm.

## What Sets Me Apart?

Experience and a good portfolio are the keys to finding work. If possible, get experience as an unpaid intern while still in school. An agency is a great place to get experience. This will give you a chance to build your book. Use the opportunity at an agency to make industry contacts and show your book to other people so you can get some constructive feedback.

## How Do I Let People Know About My Freelance Work?

Another good idea for getting into an agency is to choose an ad that you like and find out which agency created it. Then contact the agency and ask for the person who wrote or designed the ad. Once you get through, tell her you're just starting out and would like to show her your book and get her feedback. This can lead to a great contact or even a mentoring relationship. Ask her opinion of your work and ask her what she thinks sells in a portfolio.

This business is very competitive, so it's important that you let people know about you and your work. One way to do this is to print color postcards of your work and send them to art directors. Freelancers say that creative directors really save these cards and will call when there's a need for your style of work.

You should have a clear idea of your style and the type of work you want to do. Sherry, a Los Angeles–based illustrator, says, "Employers want to know what you have done before and how it applies to their clients." But it's also important to demonstrate diverse skills and style in your book.

Ellen, a freelance copywriter and illustrator in San Francisco, says, "Illustrators can get labeled as doing only a certain type of work. Even

> It's important to have produced work in your portfolio. Employers want to see real work instead of student projects and samples, although sometimes that's all you can provide. It's tough to do in the beginning. Even if you have to do free work for a local company, restaurant, or store, do it to have real work for your book.

though this is supposed to be a very creative, innovative industry, people tend to go with what is proven. If you want to work on a credit card account but don't have credit card experience in your portfolio, people tend not to hire you for those accounts."

Some experts say to take the first job you can find, but remember that it should be the right type of experience. Your first job can often determine the next several years of your career.

If you're an illustrator, you should consider sending your work to one of the many illustration annuals or art magazines. *Communication Arts*, one of the most popular industry publications, publishes a design and advertising annual. There's a fee to display your work in many of these annuals, but it can be a great way to showcase your work to millions of people. Industry publications like *Communication Arts* and *Graphis* also give a good idea of what type of work others are doing and how yours stacks up.

## How Much Can I Make?

You'll become familiar with the phrase "starving artist." According to a survey by the Graphic Artist Guild, 68.5 percent of commercial artists earned between $17,400 and $26,000. Only 10 percent earned more than $40,000. If there's big money, it's at advertising agencies either as an art or creative director. Top creatives at advertising agencies can easily make six figures.

As a freelancer, pay varies according to the type of work being performed. Typically, illustration work for a magazine tends to pay less than advertising or corporate work. Even though you're an artist, it's still a business. If you're serious about making money as an artist, your first purchases should be the *Graphic Artists Guild Handbook*: *Pricing and Ethical Guidelines* (513-531-2222). It's the Bible for many illustrators and artists. In it you'll find pricing and ethical guidelines to help you value and protect your work. It has information for all types of graphic artists from medical illustrators and cartoonists to art directors. It's based upon surveys of Graphic Artists Guild members. It gives you a good barometer of what the market is for certain types of work.

## Protect Your Work

As an artist, you need to protect your work. Several illustrators recommend retaining your original artwork when contracting on a project. Usually artists and illustrators (like writers) only sell the rights for a one-time use of a work. This prevents someone from taking your work and using it over and over or making a poster or T-shirt out of it. If the client wants to keep the original artwork or have multiple uses, that's an additional fee. Some artists are uncomfortable with contracts, but it's always best to get things in writing.

Your fees should be based on the project and your experience. Some projects may have a standard fee or the client may only budget a certain amount for that type of job. You might get a call from a publisher or magazine saying, "We want you to design a book cover or magazine illustration for us, and this is what we pay."

## What Are Some Misconceptions?

Ellen, a San Francisco based illustrator, says, "People think artists are so lucky to be able to do something they love. They forget that we are trying to make a living at this. People sometimes think artists are a little spacey and not good with money. I've seen many of my friends who are graphic artists get taken advantage of." Some artists are uncomfortable discussing money or placing a value on their work, but it's like any other job—you're providing a service and you should charge for your service.

Ellen is a successful illustrator because she hustles. She not only attracts business, but seeks it out. "You have to treat it like a business. I have so many friends who get cheated. I ask them what happened, why haven't you been paid? They just look at me and say, 'We never really agreed on an amount.'"

It's difficult for many artists to put a price tag on their work. If you're uncomfortable with the business end and don't want to deal with contracts, negotiating, or even selling your work, there are artist's representatives who agent for various types of artists and illustrators. They're similar to agents in music, publishing, and entertainment. They serve a great function, but realize that you'll be paying them a significant percentage of any money you make.

One of the best aspects to this job is that you're always doing something different. It's tough to get bored. One day you're selling, and the next day you're talking to the printer or meeting with a client. One day you're on a beer account, and the next day you're working on a project for a nonprofit group. It's a great career for someone who thrives on variety and change.

Start building your portfolio as soon as possible. Jannelle, an illustrator in Houston, began taking her portfolio to magazines and publishers while still in school. She immediately got several freelance jobs from magazines. "It was kind of cool getting people to actually pay me while I was in school."

## Artists on the Web

Many artists are making the transition to multimedia. With the explosion of Web site developers, artists are in great demand to provide graphics for these sites. Many Internet developers are hiring graphic artists to remain on staff, while others use them on a freelance basis. As I said before, don't worry. This doesn't mean that you need to know HTML or be a programmer. Just think of the Internet and multimedia as another outlet for your work and the computer as another tool.

Many of the larger advertising agencies are also creating entire multimedia or interactive departments devoted to providing their clients with Web sites. This is a great opportunity for fine artists, photographers, graphic artists, and illustrators.

To start your art career in cyberspace, it's a good idea to create a digital portfolio in addition to your regular portfolio.

> Remember to factor in the amount of time a project takes when pricing your work or preparing a quote. If you agree on a price and the project takes three times as long as anticipated or your client requests change after change, you might be making less than minimum wage after you determine total hours worked.

## What the Pros Read

*Communication Arts*
*Graphis*

## You Should Also Check Out

*Artist's Market*
F&W Publications
1507 Dana Avenue
Cincinnati, OH 45207
513-531-2222

*The Design Firm Directory*
Welfer & Associates
P.O. Box 1591
Evanston, IL 60204
312-454-1940

## Where Can I Learn More?

ASCAP—The American Society of Composers, Artists, and Publishers
IABC—International Association of Business Communicators
National Cartoonists Society: 212-617-1550

Society of Illustrators: 212-838-2560

SPAR—Society of Photographers and Artists Representatives: 212-779-7264 (nationwide organization representing photographers and illustrators)

## Where on the Web?

www.aiga.org—American Institute of Graphic Arts
www.nmaa.org—National Multimedia Association of America
www.gag.org—Graphic Artists Guild

# 26

· · · · · · · · · · · · · · · · · · · · · · · · · · · · · · · · ·

# Healthcare

**Some Common Positions**
>Registered nurse/licensed practical nurse
>Clinical and lab technician
>Hospice care worker
>Therapist (speech, physical, occupational, rehabilitation)
>Home healthcare aide
>Physician's assistant/medical assistant
>Case manager
>Medical imaging technician
>Healthcare administrator

I could go on and on. Healthcare probably has a greater variety of positions available than any other field. A whole book could be devoted just to special healthcare jobs, from technicians to nurses to therapists to the entire business staff necessary to run the facilities. This section will give you a general idea of the industry and the more popular options that don't require going to medical or nursing school.

**Other Opportunities You Might Consider**
There are dozens of positions related to healthcare that don't require you to go near a hospital, nursing home, or doctor's office. Among them are nutritionists, trainers, counselors in all fields from eating disorders to alcohol counseling, psychologists, and even athletic trainers. There are also opportunities for biologists and chemists with private companies who are developing drugs.

Don't forget that healthcare is (or has rapidly become) big business. It takes a lot of people to make it all run smoothly. Most of the positions found in any other major company or industry can be found here. In addition to hospital and healthcare administrators, opportunities are especially good for people in accounting, insurance, and finance.

I'm not going to cover being a doctor, dentist, psychologist, pharmacist, or any of the super specialized fields that require the highest level of education. Why? Because if you want to be a doctor or are considering medical or dental school, you already have an idea of how to get in. If not, there are some very good resources devoted to these professions and the entrance process.

You can't pick up the paper or watch the news without hearing about changes in healthcare, the importance of healthcare, or careers in healthcare. According to the Labor Department, among the top ten fastest growing jobs in

America, seven are in the healthcare field (chiropractors, counselors, respiratory therapists, speech-language pathologists, occupational therapists, residential counselors, physical therapists). Healthcare is an incredibly important and sometimes volatile issue. It is undergoing great changes due to the influence of insurance companies, HMOs, and managed care providers that, many argue, are putting price and cost containment ahead of quality of care.

Regardless of what "big business" does to the healthcare field, it will only grow and become more important in the coming years. One reason for continued growth is the aging of the millions of baby boomers. By the year 2000, there will be more people over the age of fifty in America than under the age of fifty. All of these baby boomers are getting older. They are going to need someone to care for them—namely us. Boomers are accustomed to a certain level and standard of care, and, believe me, Medicare won't cut it.

## What Can I Do?

What can't you do? There are several different routes you can take. You can become a caregiver such as a nurse, medical assistant, or physician's assistant, all of which often require a special degree. You can become a lab or clinical technician, which often requires training, but not an additional degree. You can work in the business or administrative area of a hospital, healthcare facility, or large healthcare services company. But according to healthcare executives and pros in the field, the greatest need is for skilled therapists (speech, physical, occupational).

## Where Can I Work?

The number of places you can work has increased significantly in the past few years. You can work in a hospital, nursing facility, physician's office, outpatient clinic, or home health or managed care agency.

Probably the two fastest growing areas are home healthcare and skilled nursing facilities (nursing homes). It all comes back to money. The insurance companies and HMOs are trying to contain costs, and it is much cheaper to have a person in a home with care available or, better yet, in their own home where a caregiver can go to them and reduce costs even more.

## What Types of Facilities Are There?

There are basically six types of facilities:

1. Acute care facilities (hospitals/intensive care units)
2. Transitional care units (detailed nursing care often found in hospitals)

3. SNF—skilled nursing facility (nursing home)
4. Rehabilitation (speech, physical, and occupational therapy)
5. Assisted living (apartment complexes with care available)
6. Home health agency (home care)

## SNFs—Don't Call Them Nursing Homes

When most people think of nursing homes, they think dark, depressing, smelly. If you're like me, you're thinking, "Not for my nana!" But as managed care providers push for cost-cutting measures, nursing homes are big business in an aging population. Some companies like Beverly Health Care are changing the way the old-style nursing homes are run. They are also providing one of the greatest sources of jobs in the health-care industry.

Beverly Health Care is the nation's largest operator of nursing homes in the country. Beverly has over 650 facilities, $3 billion in revenue, and over 30,000 employees. They hire therapists, case managers, nurses, and technicians in addition to administrators, accountants, and computer specialists. At Beverly and some of the other larger healthcare companies, hiring is done mostly on a regional basis or at the facilities themselves. To learn of facilities in your area or the name of the contact person, call the headquarters or check out their Web site.

## Who Are the Major Players in Healthcare?

Four of the largest healthcare providers and facilities managers are:

- Beverly Health Care
- Manor Care
- Vencor
- Integrated Health Services

## What About Education?

Most of the positions in healthcare will require at least a college degree, with the exception of the technician positions, which sometimes require only simply training. They all require additional training, licensing, or certification. Certain nurses and all therapists must have additional schooling, a specific four-year degree, or a master's.

## What Is Healthcare Administration?

It's the business of healthcare. Administrators deal with issues that are not health-related, including staffing and personnel, public relations, operations, insurance, and expenses.

## How Do I Get Started in Administration?

Few people go straight into administration. Those who do studied it in college, usually in one of the few schools that offer programs in hospital administration. A common path is to work for one of the Big Six accounting firms, either as a consultant or accountant. Most of them have a department or specialty area that focuses on the healthcare sector. After gaining experience in the industry, they make the move to a hospital or larger healthcare provider. Tom, director of finance for Beverly Health Care, began his career as an accountant for seven years with Ernst & Young.

## How Much Can I Make As an Administrator?

The average starting salary for healthcare administrators is $30,000.

## What Are the Pros and Cons of the Health Care Industry?

Regardless of the profession, people in the industry say they like the growth and opportunities available to them. Ron, an administrator for Columbia Healthcare, says, "I like doing something different every day. I also feel like I am making a contribution and helping others, even if I am not dealing directly with patients. "

Most caregivers, therapists, and others who have direct contact with patients feel they are making a direct impact on someone's life. Shani, a speech therapist, said, "I really enjoy seeing someone regain their independence after a stroke or being able to tell their children 'I love you' when they thought it might never again be possible."

The toughest thing for everyone to deal with is the constant change in the industry and how it has become driven by dollars and big business. There is a great deal of consolidation among healthcare companies and hospitals.

Those who deal directly with patients face the threat of infectious diseases, long hours, and hard physical work, such as moving patients.

## How Much Can I Make?

It depends on the job. Increasingly, not every doctor makes big bucks. There are doctors, primarily those with managed care facilities, who may make less than $100,000 a year.

Registered nurses will start in the low to mid-twenties and can make up to $45,000 with eight to ten years of experience. Managing nurses earn more.

Assistants and technicians make a little less, although it depends on your field and level of experience. Many at this level are hourly employees earning anywhere from $7 to $15 an hour.

## What Is Therapy?

There are many types of therapy, but the three most common in a health-care setting are speech, physical, and occupational. Depending on your specialty, you are helping an individual regain or develop speech, motor skills, or the ability to care for himself and function independently in the day-to-day world after an accident or disability.

## Common Types of Therapy and What They Treat

- Physical therapy: motor skills, muscular, and tissue rehabilitation
- Occupational therapy: fine motor skills used for daily living (commonly with stroke patients)
- Speech therapy: language, communication, swallowing

## What Will I Do?

You will help diagnose and treat patients who suffer from a disability. You may have to reteach them how to swallow, speak, feed themselves, or move their legs. Many of the patients have had accidents or diseases. It may also have been a condition since birth.

## Where Will I Work?

You can work in a hospital, facility, or clinic. However, many therapists work directly in patients' homes.

## What Type of Education Do I Need?

To practice as an OT (occupational therapist) or PT (physical therapist), you need a bachelor's degree in that field. These are industry-specific bachelor's degrees, and getting into a program is very difficult—especially physical therapy school. "Even once you get it, PT is one of the tougher and more competitive disciplines," says Kelly, who is a PT in Miami. You will also have to be licensed by your state. Speech therapy is a little more complex. It requires a master's degree in speech therapy or pathology.

## What Does a Speech Therapist Do?

Speech therapy encompasses much more than speech. It covers language, breathing, and voice training. You may help a person who has a stuttering problem or a lisp or someone who lost their language function after a stroke. There are a number of exercises you help them with in addition to analyzing their condition.

## What Are the Pros and Cons?

Kelly says that the best part about it is that "I can work with someone who has lost so much and give them part of their life back." The money and the hours are pretty good, too. Many therapists have their own businesses after gaining experience working for a major provider. "It is like being an entrepreneur," says Andrea.

The toughest part is easily the emotional drain. Ten percent of therapists leave the industry each year, many citing depression as the reason. "You get screamed at a lot. Your

### JobSmarts Top Career Pick: Occupational Therapist

Any position as a therapist guarantees a great future, but OT looks particularly promising, since the large insurance companies are looking to reduce disability claim payouts by having employees get back to work quickly.

Andrea is an occupational therapist who has her own practice. She works with people who are disabled or have been injured and helps train them to get back on the job or retrain them for new positions for which they may qualify. She also works with employers to help find positions for these individuals. Her incentive is that she is paid by the state or insurance company (whoever her client is at the time) if the candidate stays on the job for a certain period of time. "I save them money over the long haul, because I help this person get back to work and take care of himself rather than the insurance company continuing to pay a disability claim for the next twenty or forty years."

### The Worst Job Title Ever

How would you like to tell your date that you are a phlebotomist? A what? No, it is not someone who collects phlegm, but it's not too far off. A phlebotomist is someone who specializes in drawing blood for lab testing. They work for hospitals, labs, and clinics. It requires state licensing and several weeks of specialized training. Training requirements vary from state to state. In addition to being saddled with a title no one understands, you only make $10 to $14 an hour.

patients are struggling, and you have to be the hard-ass," says Kelly. "Sometimes I can't encourage them or motivate them to do something I know they are capable of," says Shani. "You have to be patient."

## How Much Can I Make?

Salaries vary according to specialty. Starting salaries are between $25,000 and $30,000. After at least ten years of experience as a salaried therapist, you can earn in the high thirties and low forties, although many in private practice earn much more.

## Where Can I Learn More?

American College of Health Care Administrators
325 S. Patrick Street
Alexandria, VA 22314
703-549-5822

Association of University Programs in Health Care Administration
1911 N. Ft. Meyer Drive #503
Arlington , VA 22209

National Association of EMTs
120 West Leake Street
Clinton, MS 39056
800-346-2368

National Health Council
1730 M Street NW, Suite 500
Washington, DC 20036
202-785-3910

American Speech-Language Hearing Association
10801 Rockville Pike
Rockville, MD 20852
301-897-5700

American Physical Therapy Association
111 N. Fairfax Street
Alexandria, VA 22314
703-684-2782

National Rehabilitation Association
633 S. Washington Street
Alexandria, VA 22314
703–836-0850

American Occupational Therapy Association
P.O. Box 1725
Rockville, MD 20849

American Association of Medical Assistants
20 N. Wacker Drive, Suite 1575
Chicago, IL 60606

## What The Pros Read

Every discipline has its own trade publications. Below are a few for the
career paths described in this section:

*Health Managers Update*
*Health Care Management Review*
*Modern Healthcare*
*Clinical Administrator*
*EMT Update*
*PT (Physical Therapy Journal)*
*Speech Therapy*
*The Journal of Speech Therapy*

# 27

· · · · · · · · · · · · · · · · · · · · · · · · · ·

# High Tech: Computer and Software Technology

**Some Common Positions**
Analyst
Programmer/coder
Software/systems designer
Software/systems/quality/computer engineer
Computer scientist
Software developer
Technical writer
Contractor/consultant
Permatemp
Billionaire geek

**You Might Also Consider**
There are a number of careers in high tech that never involve writing code. There are opportunities in sales, marketing, public relations and communications, customer service and tech support, accounting, and finance.

You can work for a large technology company like Microsoft, IBM, Compaq, Oracle, AT&T, or Texas Instruments, or you can work for a small start-up or niche player such as Trilogy, which makes sales and distribution software.

You can also work for a company that has nothing to do with technology as an end product, but utilizes it to make their business run better. Banks and financial institutions, consulting firms, retail organizations, trucking companies, and food processors are all beginning to hire people to work in-house maintaining or developing their systems.

The technology field is also one of the fastest growing areas for entrepreneurs. Other closely-related fields you may want to look into are engineering and Web site development.

Did you see the movie *Apollo 13*? I loved the scene where the roomful of engineers and scientists are trying to determine the spacecraft's trajectory on a slide rule. I can't balance my checkbook without a calculator. We've come a long way in thirty years.

Do you think you want to go into high tech so you can be the next Bill Gates or Marc Andresson, founder of Netscape, who became worth over $50 million literally over night? The PC came into existence twenty years ago and has changed almost every aspect of our lives.

There are incredible opportunities in the high-tech and computer-related fields. Yet even though there is more demand than there are talented bodies to fill the positions, not everyone makes a fortune. This is a business where in one corner there are highly-skilled people making incredible amounts of money and in the other corner there are equally skilled and educated people working for a lower hourly wage.

This is such a broad field. It is constantly changing, and there are no constants or typical positions. Even though there are companies who design and develop systems and software, they may serve completely different markets or conduct their business in very different ways.

## What Background or Education Do I Need?

A degree in computer science, math, MIS (management information systems), or electrical engineering all are very helpful. Actually, most engineers of any type do well in this field. At least as important as your education is your experience and skills. Technology is changing so quickly that by the time someone graduates from college, what they know is obsolete. People learn on the fly. "If you rely only on your education, you are going to fall behind," says Chris, a systems engineer at Texas Instruments.

Sarah, a recruiter for a specialty software company, said she likes candidates to have some business background as well. "You need to know how things work in the big picture, since you will be thrown into new industries."

## Where Will I Start?

It depends on your specialty, industry sector, experience, and whether you are with a large company or a small niche player.

If you are a programmer, you will start as a junior or entry-level programmer. Analysts might start out as associates. Your title may not even accurately describe what you do. Chris at AT&T is an analyst, yet what he actually does day-to-day is reverse engineering.

In many positions, you will work on a project team. Instead of having a whole program to yourself, you may be responsible for analyzing or testing one small piece of the code. As you advance, you will be given bigger pieces and may eventually oversee a team. "You are one piece of the puzzle," says Carlos, an entry-level programmer.

You may do all types of work ranging from dealing with hardware, software, systems such as UNIX, networks, mainframes, client servers, and languages such as C++ and Visual Basic.

## What Will I Be Called?

It depends on the company. Some companies are loose and not really into titles. Others say they aren't into tittles, then give their employees abstract generic titles that don't mean anything, but still have rank. At AT&T, you might begin as an A1, A2, or A3. These are various salary bands. Peter is an analyst at AT&T, although his official title is senior technical associate #2. "My next promotion, I will be a technical staff member, whatever the hell that means. You generally have two years to prove yourself and rise at least a couple of salary bands."

Chris, an AT&T analyst, says, "On the corporate food chain, programmers are at the bottom, because they are dispensable. That is why AT&T hires so many programmers on a contract basis. 'Contractors' are looked down upon around here. They are just skilled temps." One programmer said that the big programming houses are the sweatshops of today.

On the corporate food chain, contractors and programmers might be toward the bottom, but in some industries such as video games, the coders are the kings.

## How Do I Get Hired?

The computer, software, and technology fields generally offer more career fairs than any other any industry. Employers frequently hire people from technology career fairs. Schedules of many of the high-tech career fairs are listed on the Internet. Many firms seeking programmers, analysts, or engineers actively recruit on campuses. This is also a field that practices what it preaches. Companies not only post positions on the Internet, but aggressively hire people from many of the sites where people have posted their résumés. (A good site to find high-tech jobs and post your résumé is www.gradquest.com.)

## What Sets Me Apart from Other Candidates?

Debra of Systems Engineering Services says she looks beyond a candidate's technical ability to his or her maturity and professionalism. "We are dealing with Fortune 500 clients, and our employees must present a professional image and be able to communicate well. Sure, there are many programmers who might fit the mold of the disheveled office and Pepsi cans everywhere, but our employees are dealing inside organizations whose culture might not foster that. I want someone who can handle themselves well in any situation."

"Thank-you letters make a huge impact," says Chris, a manager at Sterling Software. "I only get two to three thank-you letters for every 1,000 candidates I interview. They are rare and precious, because I know if they would do that with me, they would do that for a client."

David Pritchard, director of recruiting for Microsoft, says, "We look for smarts and experience. Are they flexible? Can they learn new concepts? In this industry, things are changing on a daily basis, and if you're not capable of learning new things, you won't be successful."

Since the industry is changing so fast, you have to stay current on languages. Many people who worked for years on mainframes are having a hard time now that mainframes aren't as popular as smaller systems that use different languages. Experience is key.

## What Is the Career Path?

In a large company, you can become a project manager and then rise in management levels from there. Many companies, however, are flattening their organization, so there are fewer levels of management. Once you're hired, you have a couple of years to prove yourself and rise at least a couple of levels. Promotion may not be noticed in title but by pay scales or salary bands.

## How Much Will I Make?

Starting salaries for analysts and similar positions are in the high thirties to low forties. They also include the usual perks and benefits such as insurance and 401k. Some people are lucky enough to get stock options. There is the potential to make very good money. Coding superstars (usually found in the video game industry) can easily make six figures. On the other hand, the grunt workers (programmers) may be paid an hourly wage between $7 to $15 an hour.

## Where Will I Live?

You can live wherever you want. If you are a contractor or freelancer, you can work from anywhere, but you might have to travel for projects. If you work for a company, there are opportunities all over the country. There are pockets where there are high concentrations of technology and computer-related jobs. Obviously, the San Francisco Bay Area, including Palo Alto and Silicon Valley, is the most densely populated. Boston's Route 128 is known for a high concentration of tech companies, as is the Pacific Northwest. Don't think that you are limited by a major metropolitan area either. The once sleepy south Texas city of Austin has become a hotbed of computer activity. Companies such as Dell have their corporate headquarters there.

Something to keep in mind before you pack up and move to Palo Alto or even Austin: Because these are rapidly growing areas, they often aren't prepared for the influx of people. The infrastructure can't always handle it. Austin now has traffic problems that rival much larger cities such as Houston. Not to mention the cost of housing. According to *USA Today*, the median home price in Palo Alto is $1 million, and rent in Austin is among the highest in Texas.

## Is It a Stable Career?

No. This industry is constantly changing and evolving. Much of what you learn in school will be obsolete by the time you begin working. As a matter of fact, you will have to constantly learn new skills and technologies, even once you are on the job.

People do tend to job-hop frequently. Many enjoy the challenge and want to learn different businesses, so they freelance or contract their services.

## Life As a Contractor

Temping and freelancing is a way of life in the high-tech industries. Independent contractors (high-tech temps) are often called consultants, but there is a big difference. Some consultants work on big projects, are paid like kings, and are really respected. They actually have a lot of industry experience. Regular contractors (also known as contract programmers or coders), on the other hand, are basically skilled temps.

High-tech employees are the new migrant workers, shifting companies, bosses, and loyalties. In Silicon Valley, the number of temporaries is twice the national average. Many temp positions area administrative or clerical, but skilled technical temporary positions account for one of every ten jobs in Silicon Valley. At some companies, the temps outnumber the regular employees. Many work on short-term projects that may last only a few weeks or months. Others may be a "permatemps," working at a company for years without ever being considered a full employee. They enjoy the benefits of regular employees, such as insurance or retirement plans.

Maurice began his career in marketing with a small video game company. He says, "If a small company is hot, it can be a revolving door. People come, in grab experience, and then move on to the next thing, because they are now a commodity. Everyone is looking for that next job. Then you have people who are looking for the next hot shop so they can try to land stock options and time it right."

## How Much Can I Make As a Contractor?

Salary varies greatly according to your skills and the project's necessity and urgency. For experienced or skilled employees, the hourly salary ranges from $30 to over $100 per hour. Some entry- and low-level coders may make around $10 an hour.

Some experienced contract employees easily make over $100,000. Pay is one of those things that is very personalized and individualized. There are also performance bonuses tied in with some contract houses. At Systems Engineering Services, a programmer gets between $100 to $1,000 if a commendation letter or acknowledgment arrives from a client. "It goes a long way toward making our programmers do a better job," says Debra, technical recruiter for SES.

Because you are a contractor, you will receive your 1099 at the end of the year. You are expected to pay your own taxes, Social Security, and Medicare. You also get the joy of dealing with the paperwork. As an employee, your company deducts taxes, so you never have to think about it. Now it is up to you entirely. You are also responsible for your own insurance and healthcare.

## What Is the Worst Thing About It?

The worst thing about being a contractor is that the employer can let you go with only an hour's notice, according to Debra of SES. "Traditionally, there is no loyalty whatsoever from contractors. We have tried to change that by offering them benefits and security not often found at most contract houses."

Contractors are paid very well, but Vickie, a contract programmer, says, "The companies don't value you at all. As long as you can fog a mirror and fill a seat, they don't care, just do your job. It sucks when you have all of the responsibility as the person next to you, but none of the perks like insurance."

Another complaint contractors have is that they feel they are always bidding for the next job. "Even while I'm on a project, I still have to kiss ass and set myself up for the next project so I can continue to work," says Michael, a contract developer.

On the positive side, people in this field tend to value their freedom. Contractors especially like the freedom to come and go as they please. When a project is over, you are gone. The ability to constantly acquire new skills and work in different businesses is also a plus, not to mention the money.

Companies love it, because they aren't out the added expense of insurance and other benefits. The downside for companies is that they end up paying about twice the salary they would for a regular employee. However, there are no unions to get in the way. This also means that contract workers don't always have the same rights as regular employees.

## How Do I Get Hired As a Contractor?

Of course, your own industry connections are the best way to learn about positions and projects. There are a number of "contract houses" that serve as placement or temp services. They have a pool of candidates and match them with companies with special projects that don't want to have to search for employees.

They negotiate everything for you and pay you directly. You do not pay them a commission; they obtain that from the client company.

## How Do the Contract Companies or Employers Know What My Skills Are?

They test you before you begin. You will also go through technical interviews, where you will talk with employees who quiz you to check your skills and level.

## Where Will I Work?

You might work for a technology company. Many, such as AT&T hire low-level coding and programming out to contractors and consultants. However, much of your work may come from working in the technology or computer department of a company that has absolutely nothing to do with technology. Many frequent employers of contract employees are banks, insurance companies, and healthcare companies.

You may work alone or on a project team. Once inside a client company, you are generally in the MIS or IS (information services) department.

## What Happens When the Project Is Over?

You are free to move on to the next job, no questions asked. Many have projects lined up; others try to remain with that company by seeing if they have any additional projects that need contract services. If you are with a contract house, you go on what is called "bench time" when a project is finished. (I guess it's like an athlete riding the bench.) When you're on the bench, you are paid your regular hourly salary by the contract house, even though you're not working. Meanwhile, the contract house is trying like hell to "sell you" to another client or place you in another project. Bench time often gets a bad rap, because a number of contract houses will drop an employee if they are unable to place him in a few weeks. (No wonder employees aren't considered loyal.) SES is one of the few contract houses that will keep its employees on bench time for up to six months.

## Where Can I Learn More?

American Society of Information Services

## Where on the Web?

www.hightechcareers.com—*High Technology Careers*
www.systemsengineer.com—SystemsEngineer.com
www.networkengineer.com—NetworkEngineer.com
www.asis.org—American Society for Information Sciences

# 28

• • • • • • • • • • • • • • • • • • • • • • • • • • • • • • •

# Hospitality: Hotel and Lodging

"We'll leave the light on for you."
—TOM BODET OF MOTEL 6 FAME

**Some Common Positions**
> Desk clerk
> Front office manager
> Rooms manager
> Club manager
> Food and beverage manager
> Sports director
> Dining room manager
> Convention and meeting planner
> Sales

**Other Opportunities You Might Consider**
Working in a resort, casino, or on a cruise ship. Related fields you might want to check out are food service and the travel industry. You might also think about meeting and convention sales. Many hotels have conference service managers and sales staff who are responsible for attracting group business and conventions to their property. There are also plenty of finance, accounting, marketing, and human resource positions.

When people think of working in a hotel, they generally picture a sleepy, bleary-eyed front-desk clerk in a fleabag hotel or something resembling the glamour of the old Aaron Spelling show *Hotel* (the *Love Boat* in dry dock). The hotel and hospitality business can certainly be glamorous and exciting, but it does take a lot of hard work behind the scenes to make it all run smoothly.

## What Is the Hospitality Industry?

The hospitality industry is a huge field that's actually made up of several very large industries, including lodging and hotels, food service and restaurants, clubs, and travel. It's the world's largest industry according to the American Hotel and Motel Association.

## Aren't Most Hotels the Same?

In the United States, there are 44,700 hotels and motels representing 3.1 million rooms. There are several types or classifications of hotels. Each differs in the services they offer and the guests to whom they cater. There are city center hotels; resort hotels; airport hotels; freeway hotels; casino hotels; full service, economy, or budget hotels; and a new trend, the extended stay or all-suite hotel.

## How Is a Hotel Set Up?

Most hotels and guest properties are broken into several departments or "sides of the house." Each side is different, yet each plays an integral part. Choosing which side you want to work in is similar to choosing between account and creative in advertising. They are interdependent. The departments found in most hotels are sleeping and meeting rooms, sales and marketing, reservations sales, front office, food and beverage catering, housekeeping, security, and PBX and phones. Also included are the hotel's concierge, restaurant, banquet, and room service. The administrative offices, of course, include human resources, management, and accounting to name a few of the most common.

Rooms and food and beverage are the two most popular among college graduates.

## Where Will I Start?

It depends upon which area you want to work. Most people begin by working in either the rooms or food and beverage side. For a general understanding, the best place to start is the front desk. Sometimes, you may not have a choice. Some of the major hotels like the Fairmont Hotel in Dallas have programs that train you in all sides of the house. You rotate departments, spending several months learning each. These programs used to last about a year, but with the hospitality business becoming more competitive, it's critical that hotels get new employees up to speed as quickly as possible. "You're almost expected to be trained and experienced before you begin," says Richard, a graduate of Penn State's hospitality program and now a trainee with Marriott. "That's why internships are so important."

## What About Sales Positions?

While sales is exciting and lucrative, most hotels want seasoned staff to sell their property. Although some companies like Marriott are beginning to hire for entry-level sales positions.

## Do I Need a Degree in Hotel Management?

There are many schools that offer degrees in hotel and restaurant management, or hospitality as it's most commonly called. Some of the best programs are at UNLV, Cornell, Florida State, the University of Houston, and the University of North Texas. While a hospitality degree is preferred—especially for management training programs—it's not required. There's no formal certification or licensure needed.

## What Will I Do?

Some hotel companies have structured management programs that rotate you through different departments. This can take up to six months to complete. After your training period—when you're familiar with the different departments—you can choose.

### Rooms

As a management trainee on the rooms side, you'll work the front desk and serve as a front-desk clerk. You'll learn the necessary software for checking people in and out, as well as take reservations, deal with customer complaints, and learn how to use the PBX (phone) system.

### Food and Beverage

On the food and beverage side, you might go into catering, banquets, restaurant management, room service, or other related areas. You would schedule employees and handle customer relations and quality control, making sure that service and food follows the operating procedures.

---

**You Might Also Consider: Conventions or Group and Conference Services**

Most hotels have a department devoted to the scheduling and planning of meetings and group functions at their hotel. This is big business. The conventions, meetings, weddings, bar mitzvahs and the like can be planned well over five years in advance. The problem is you're the "go-to" person. You make sure everything runs smoothly. It can be a logistical nightmare, and you won't have weekends or nights free.

---

## How Much Can I Make?

It depends on the type of property you're with. Starting positions at airport, full service, and city center hotels are among the highest paying. Starting salaries at these properties can range from $21,000 to $27,000 for graduates with hotel experience. It used to take about a year to get your first evaluation or raise, but now you may be evaluated after three to six months.

## How Do I Get Hired?

The best route to getting hired is through an internship. "It's pretty common for someone to get an offer from the hotel where they interned," says Jennifer, a UNLV grad who now works for Hilton.

Many hotel companies recruit on college campuses, particularly at those schools that offer hotel management degrees. However, if you do not have access to a university career center or if hotel chains don't recruit on your campus, you should contact a hotel's regional office.

More and more hotels are moving away from a national or central recruiting structure and are utilizing regional offices. Send your résumé to the regional director of human resources or identify a specific property at which you would like to work and approach the general manager.

## What If I Want to Change Careers?

According to Dr. Richard Tas of the University of North Texas School of Merchandising and Hospitality Management, "It's easier to break into this industry fresh out of school than it is to make a career change from another industry." If you already have a degree and experience in another field, it's recommended that you obtain a master's degree in hospitality.

## How About Job Stability?

This is a very mobile industry. There's such demand for competent, quality employees that there's frequently floating from company to company—and even "pirating" of employees. If you're on a career track with a major chain, you may be asked to relocate. Advancement often means gaining experience at different properties. To be promotable, you must be mobile. Managers typically do not stay at one hotel for their entire career.

Stephanie began her career as an intern with the Fairmont in San Francisco. Since graduation and accepting a full-time job, she has moved two times, gaining experience at other properties. "The goal for me is to keep moving to larger and larger properties."

## How Can I Stand Out?

As a job applicant, experience is the key. "Degrees don't mean anything without experience," says Don, a management trainee with Marriott. "Once you're on the job, a key to advancement is recognizing and taking advantage of opportunities," says Jerry Dickenson, a veteran club executive and board member with ClubCorp, the largest owner and operator of country clubs in the world. "Everyone is shorthanded at some time or another. One night when someone is out, jump in there and take up the slack. Use that as your opportunity to shine and show what you can do." It's a service industry, and the better you help people and solve their problems, the more successful you'll be.

## What Are the Pros and Cons?

Hotels are a fun environment. You'll meet many different people and maybe even some celebrities. You get free or half-price meals at hotel restaurants, and some offer employees a free week per year at any of their other properties.

The negative things about the industry have to do with the working conditions. The hours are long. Hotels are always open, including nights and holidays. Guests can be rude. Jennifer of the Fairmont says, "It's tough, because you're dealing with people who may have very different backgrounds and education." Anthony, an F&B trainee in Orlando, says, "It can be tough. You're in this wonderful environment where people are relaxing, yet you're working."

People in the club industry say it can be very political. If you're with a club that's not owned by a company, you're held at the mercy of the board. "You piss some guy's wife off or tell his kid not to run near the pool, and the next thing you know, this guy is president of the club or on the board and has a vendetta," says Brian, a young club manager in Miami.

## What Are the Misconceptions?

People perceive it as a vocation, not a career. "People think of hospitality and food service as something they don't want to do. They would rather go make $10,000 a year less working at a job they believe is more prestigious," says Stephanie. Jerry says, "Everyone wants to work in the corporate headquarters, but for every 1 job in corporate, there are 500 in the field. In the field is where the opportunity is."

## Who Are the Major Hotel and Lodging Chains?

Check out the AHMA Web site—www.ahma.com—for a comprehensive list of the top fifty companies and their properties. You might not be familiar with some of the parent companies, but the properties will ring a bell.

| Company | Properties Owned (ranked by number of properties) |
| --- | --- |
| 1. HFS, Inc. | Days Inn, Ramada Inn, Super 8 |
| 2. Holiday Inn | Holiday Inn |
| 3. Choice Hotels | Comfort Inn, Quality Inn, Clarion |
| 4. Best Western | Best Western |
| 5. Marriott International | Marriott, Courtyard, Residence Inn |
| 6. Hilton | Hilton |
| 7. Sheraton Hotels/Inns/Resorts | Sheraton |
| 8. Motel 6 | Motel 6 |
| 9. The Promus Corporation | Hampton Inn, Embassy Suites, Harrah's |
| 10. Carlson Hospitality | Radisson |

## Where Can I Learn More?

American Hotel and Motel Association
1201 New York Avenue NW, 6th Floor
Washington, DC 20005
202-289-3100

## Where on the Web?

www.club-mgmt.com—Virtual Clubhouse
www.hospitalitynet.nl—Hospitality Net
www.restaurant.org—National Restaurant Association
www.ahma.com—American Hotel and Motel Association

# 29

. . . . . . . . . . . . . . . . . . . . . . . . . . . . . .

# Human Resources

**Some Common Positions**
    Human resources director
    Personnel manager
    Recruiter
    College relations director
    Benefits administrator
    Trainer

**Other Opportunities You Might Consider**
Executive search firms, headhunters, personnel or temporary agencies, and out-sourcing firms all fall under the human resources or HR banner. HR departments and personnel can be found in virtually every industry. Human resources frequently deal with and even hire people with insurance, training, and legal backgrounds. Some HR professionals work in college career services offices, while others work alone and capitalize on their experience, sometimes in another field such as consulting or individual career counseling.

## What Will I Do?

It depends on your company and your specialty. Most HR managers and departments handle a wide variety of tasks and responsibilities that go far beyond hiring people. HR departments are often responsible for continuing education, training and certification of employees, forecasting, budgeting, staffing needs, performance appraisal and management, compensation and benefits administration, union/labor relations, career development, continuing education, and organizational development.

## How Do I Get Hired?

Very few people go straight into human resources as an entry-level position. Most people move into HR from another department. Companies like to bring in people who have line or management experience and a solid understanding of the business.

The American Society for Training and Development (ASTD) recommends a couple of ways to become involved in the HR field. The first is to look for opportunities to transfer into the HR department at the company where you are currently working. You already understand the business, so you are at an advantage.

Next, they say, work part-time or volunteer as an intern. While you are there, work your ass off as if it were a high-paying full-time job.

If you possess specialized experience in training, sales, customer service, compensation, or retirement and benefits packages, you can sell your services as an independent consultant. Many companies use a combination of internal employees and outside professionals.

## What Are the Educational Requirements?

Some people have undergraduate degrees in HR. While this degree is helpful, it is not a requirement. Another discipline that does well is psychology (especially organizational psychology).

## Where Will I Start?

Since no one really starts out in HR management, it is typical for people to begin their career in a specialty of HR, such as testing, recruiting, interviewing, benefits administration, or training. From there, you will begin to learn the other aspects of HR.

## What Are the Misconceptions About HR?

Bob Orndorf, career services director at Moravian College, says he sees that many people want to go into HR because they think they will be working with people all the time. There is a lot of paperwork involved.

Doug, HR director for Today's Kids, a large toy manufacturer, says, "HR deals with a lot of situations, but it's not our job to fix the problems. Rather, we analyze, diagnose, and offer recommendations to fix the problems."

Rob began his career in sales for an information services firm. As part of his job, he was also to train the customers on the systems. He enjoyed the training aspect a great deal and eventually began training new customers more than selling. In addition, Rob would tinker with different software programs and learn the shortcuts. Coworkers began going to Rob for answers, because he was knowledgeable and could demonstrate in a helpful way. The company was growing rapidly and needed consistent training and evaluation, so they asked Rob to create the training department. Today, he has a staff of five who create, evaluate, and purchase programs regarding new employee orientation, continuing education on existing products, customer service, and software.

Virginia works in the training department for a Philadelphia brokerage firm. According to the law, brokers at her firm must complete a certain amount of continuing education. "I assist the training director in researching and finding different vendors [training programs] that we can bring in to teach our brokers." Virginia says her job is made more difficult because many brokers resist training. "The brokers, even though they know they have to take the courses we provide, think it is time-consuming, so they only do the bare minimum that is required. They aren't very happy about being there, and it is reflected in how we are treated."

## What Are the Pros and Cons?

The pros are that you are dealing with people, although maybe not as much as you would like. In some cases, you are helping them to reach their potential. You will also become exposed to every department and area of the business. Other people in HR say they enjoy creating and developing programs. "I like spending time on the computer developing PowerPoint presentations [overheads and slides] and newsletters," says Sonya, who is in the HR department at a major hospital.

The downside to working in HR is that while what you do is so important to the success of a company, you have no real authority. "You have all of the responsibility, but no authority. You are essentially a cheerleader," says Doug. Other HR professionals voiced similar concerns that they really didn't carry as much weight at the company as they had imagined.

## I'm a People Person

If you are ever tempted to go into human resources because you're a people person, don't. The name is misleading. You will not always deal with humans. You may dealing with issues that affect humans: legal issues, safety issues, disciplinary or morale issues, diversity issues. "There is more paperwork and research than I imagined," says Lisa, who is in HR with a regional bank.

## How Much Will I Make?

You won't get rich working in the human resources department. Starting salaries are in the lower twenties, and management positions average in the high forties, although that can be higher if you are a senior VP or manager in a large company.

## What's the Career Path?

If you ever have aspirations to climb the career ladder (if there still is such a thing) to become CEO or a real mover and shaker in a company, HR is not the way to go. There are very few CEOs who have HR backgrounds. (Most come from marketing, sales, or finance.) Once you have HR experience, it is easier to move to another position or industry. Some HR professionals who specialize may go into private practice as consultants or trainers.

## Where Can I Learn More?

There are several excellent professional organizations in the HR field. They offer great information about organizations and career options. They publish great magazines for their members.

SHRM—Society for Human Resource Management
606 N. Washington Street
Alexandria, VA 22314

ASTD—American Society for Training and Development
1640 King Street, Box 1443
Alexandria, VA 22313

Association of Human Resource Systems Professionals
P.O. Box 801646
Dallas, TX 75380–1646

Human Resource Planning Society
317 Madison Avenue, Suite 1509
New York, NY, 10017

## Where on the Web?

www.shrm.org—Society for Human Resource Management
www.astd.org—American Society for Training and Development

**Did You Know?**

Employment law is a growing area of concern for many companies. With a number of discrimination and harassment issues, employers must be careful of how they treat, hire, and fire employees. HR professionals will have to be familiar with the many laws affecting the workplace. Some companies have in-house counsel (attorneys) who work primarily on HR issues.

# 30

· · · · · · · · · · · · · · · · · · · · · · · ·

# Independent Filmmaking

**Other Opportunities You Might Consider**
Waiting tables, tending bar, maybe working at the Gap. Seriously, many people work several jobs, often unrelated to film, simply to earn enough money to make their film or be able to have the free time necessary to write and develop their project.

Aspiring filmmakers do related film work, perhaps freelancing as a commercial, corporate, or music video director. Others obtain work as freelance writers or production assistants on other people's projects. Some may develop and produce segments for television.

If you watch *Mad About You*, you know that the lead character, Paul Buckman, is a "filmmaker." He makes a nice living directing and producing documentaries and independent films. Living in New York, Paul and his wife look as if they are living a cozy, comfortable little life. The only problem is Paul Buckman is a fictional television character.

You may hear success stories of people discovered at the Sundance Film Festival, but the reality of independent filmmaking is that it's a damn competitive business littered with many failures and wannabes.

Independent film has recently experienced a boom in popularity and is enjoying attention in the mainstream. Recent success stories have inspired every young filmmaker to be the next Quentin Tarantino and make a fantastic feature-length film. Only a handful will. I don't want to squash your dream—feel free to invite me to the premiere of your feature film to prove me wrong and rub your success in my face—but realize that in order to eat on a regular basis, you may have to resort to making documentaries, commercials, and other types of film work.

## Why Make a Short Film?

People make short films and enter them in festivals so studio executives and other film bigwigs will be able to see their work. That film is like a portfolio or demo. If an executive or someone fairly powerful sees your short and likes what you do, they might approach you and say, "Tell me what else you have in mind or are working on." This is how filmmakers "get discovered." Of course, there are plenty of people who simply make films for the joy of it and really don't have any major career aspirations.

## How Do I Get Started? Do I Need to Go to Film School?

Many people earn degrees in film and begin to produce their own work while in school as part of a project. Others come from different fields, but learn about filmmaking by enrolling part-time in classes at a film school or continuing education program. Another way to break into filmmaking is by coming directly from the entertainment field and learning on the set as a production assistant or writer. You also see people from advertising getting into filmmaking.

Brian in New York has made two short films (fifteen and thirty minutes) and is now collaborating with a partner on his first feature film.

"I started out in corporate America working for Apple Computer when I got the film bug. I started taking classes at NYU in screenwriting, editing, directing, and independent producing." Brian then left Apple to pursue film full-time. He took an unpaid internship with a screenplay doctor and supported himself by working in a photography shop. "I saved some money and made my first short film. I basically pushed it for a year, distributing it and getting it into festivals. I was lucky enough to get some money from sales of that film to make another short." Brian is now collaborating with a classmate on his own feature film, but is still working odd jobs and freelance projects to pay the bills until he "hits it." This whole process has taken him five years.

## Will I Be a Starving Artist or Just a Very Hungry One?

If you're talking about money from sales of your film, I hope you like toast. There is not much, if any, cash unless you're a superstar or incredibly lucky. If you count income from ancillary activities and odd jobs, you might just survive.

First of all, you have to produce, promote, distribute, and sell your film. This can be as cheap or as expensive as you want. Robert Rodriguez shot his first film, *El Mariachi,* for around $7,000. It was discovered by a major studio, earned him hundreds of thousands of dollars, and became a cult classic. He's now earned millions more on subsequent pictures like *Desperado* with Antonio Banderas. Another success story is Ed Burns, who wrote and directed *The Brothers McMullen* while he was a staffer for *Entertainment Tonight*. These are the exceptions.

Then you have people like Jeremy, a New York "indie filmmaker" who works several freelance jobs in TV production (manning control boards and doing a lot of PA/grunt work) trying to make ends meet. Jeremy, like countless other independent film-makers, constantly talks about how once he does a feature film, he will "have it made." Yeah, and if I could hit a hanging curveball, I would have it made, too. If making movies and hitting baseballs were easy, there would be more than only a handful of people on the planet making a nice living at it. Features are sexy and everyone wants to make them, but the reality is that no one gets paid until the movie is produced or sold.

Brian, the New York indie filmmaker mentioned earlier, says he was contracted to write a half-hour short film for another indie director. It turned out to be a six-month project, for which he was paid $3,500. "It was just a part-time gig." (For six months of work while living in New York, Brian might have made more money checking out videos at Block-buster a la Quentin Tarantino.) Brian has now taken on the task of writing a feature film project that is scheduled to last for six months. He will make $12,500 for six months of work. This is while he is trying to produce his own feature works.

## I Hope You're a Good Fund-raiser or a Trust-Fund Baby

Making your own film is not just about writing and directing. It is about raising money, and much of your time will be spent trying to seek funds for your production. Unless you have a rich uncle who is about to pass away, you will take your finished script around to agents, actor's agents, conventions, festivals, and wealthy individuals trying to obtain private funding. "It's just one of those things. You keep at it and hopefully some kind of lead or contact will hit and you'll get your film made," says Jeremy.

# 31

• • • • • • • • • • • • • • • • • • • • • • • • • • • • • •

# Insurance

**Some Common Positions**
   Agent
   Broker
   Underwriter
   Claims adjuster
   Actuary

**Other Opportunities You Might Consider**
Insurance is closely related to many other businesses, particularly financial and investment services. In addition to insurance sales and brokerage, there are many opportunities in marketing, communications, government, and regulatory issues. Large insurance companies also manage investments, so there are opportunities for money managers and pension planners. You can be an entrepreneur and work as an independent agent or for a large company.

When you think about it, insurance is such a great industry. Why? Because everyone at some point in their lives will need insurance. Whether it's an individual needing insurance for his car, home, or life or a company needing to insure its inventory, protect against liability, or offer its employees health coverage and benefits, people will always need to protect things and people they care about.

I used to think life insurance was simply a sales job with two products, selling life insurance (which I didn't need, because I was young and unmarried) or auto insurance (which was a necessary evil I couldn't afford, because I was young and had dozens of tickets).

## How Has Insurance Changed?

A few years ago, insurance agents had only a limited number of products to sell. There was property and casualty insurance (home, auto, fire, etc.) and life insurance (your family cashes in when you cash out). Yet in recent years, the industry has changed considerably. Today, it's a fast-growing field due to the expanded services agents can provide.

In addition to selling insurance, agents are now allowed to sell a variety of investment vehicles and related financial services such as annuities, mutual funds, and retirement plans. While they're not stockbrokers, some are qualified to sell similar financial products.

## What Will I Be Called?

You'll likely be an agent, broker, or manager. Other names on the investment side include financial planner, financial consultant, and registered representative. Each classification has its own qualifications and certifications that you must have in order to sell certain investment products (although an insurance agent can sell some investment-type insurance products).

## What Types of Insurance Are There? I Don't Want to Just Sell Car Insurance?

Different companies handle different products. The most common types of insurance people think of are property and casualty (P&C) and life. Sometimes agents deal in everything, but often they specialize in one or the other. Generally, P&C agents do not handle financial services.

There are several types of life insurance, but the two basic ones are "term" and "whole." Term insurance is when you pay a premium or fee to insure you for a set amount of time for say $500,000. If you die, it's paid. That's it, no questions asked. If you don't die during the period you paid for, you don't get the money back. Whole life is much more complicated. With whole life, you pay premiums as you do in term. However, the premiums build a cash value like a savings account. If after many years (twenty or thirty) you haven't kicked the bucket yet, you can withdraw the premiums you have paid in over time. It can be much more involved and has additional benefits, but that's the short version. The bottom line is that whole life acts as a basic investment. It's not a great investment, though. The rate of return will generally be less than a decent mutual fund. This was a problem many insurance agents had in the past. They were trying to sell whole life as a retirement package, but it couldn't compete with the stock market or mutual funds. Now agents have more options, and they can be more competitive.

A very different area of insurance you should consider is business insurance. Companies generally carry a variety of insurance. One example is liability insurance, which protects the company against a variety of things such as lawsuits, theft, fire, and loss of a shipment. Business insurance can also entail health or disability, which can be sold to an individual or a corporation.

## It's a Great Business Background

The insurance industry can give you a solid business background. Client building, sales, relationship building, computer skills, financial planning, and management are all skills that can help you throughout your career, whether or not you choose to remain in insurance. You'll also gain exposure and understanding of many other businesses with which you deal.

## Who Will I Deal With?

It depends on what type of insurance you go into. If you deal with companies, you may meet with executives and high-level managers. You may deal with small-business owners and entrepreneurs. In P&C or life insurance sales, you'll be dealing with individuals or families. It's a relationship business. You're talking about things that are precious to people and anxiety-provoking subjects that aren't fun to talk about, like death and who gets your money.

> Some insurance agents specialize, which determines who they deal with. Bart specializes in life and health insurance as well as Medicare supplements. As a result, he has many elderly clients.

## What's the Biggest Misconception?

Dennis Stork, executive vice president of the General Agent and Managers Association, says the biggest misconception about this field is that it's an easy and quick buck. Earning a client's trust takes time. You're selling peace of mind to your clients. You're also asking them to trust you with their money. "When you're just starting out, people are hesitant to trust you with their family and finances," says Jeff, an agent for State Farm.

## How Stable Is It?

In the beginning of your career, it's not at all stable. "If you can't make it in six months, you can't make it in this business," says Corky, an independent life agent. "The big agencies hire young people right out of school, give them a few weeks of training, and then send them on their way. They're given a small guaranteed salary for about six months, and if they aren't producing enough to cover their salary in six months, they're either fired or asked to go on straight commission, in which case they starve."

There's a huge wash-out period in the first two years where people leave for financial reasons or realize they hate the job. Those who make it past that period can do very well. Later in their careers, people either leave companies or choose to become independent agents and represent different lines.

## What Will I Do?

You know how boxers' ears are deformed from being beaten up? Get ready for that, because not only will your ears be sore from being on the phone more than you ever have in your life, you'll probably be beaten and boxed about by prospective clients who say, "Thanks, but no thanks." You'll do a lot of prospecting for leads, going through mailing lists and databases, cold calling, setting appointments, preparing quotes, meeting with prospective clients in their homes or offices, producing paperwork for new sales, and helping clients settle claims.

With a large company, new employees will have quotas. "You're told to make 150 calls a week and expected to see at least four people a week," says Jason, who works for one of the major insurance companies.

In P&C, you'll spend a huge amount of time servicing the client. According to one survey, up to 93 percent of a P&C agent's time is spent in service work. This means changing the coverage for an existing client, helping with a claim, and answering questions, which leaves only 7 percent of your time to pursue new clients. And new sales is where you make your money. The commissions are much smaller in P&C than in group one/life. "In P&C, you're spending most of your time on maintenance instead of selling, so you make less. That's why fewer people are going into P&C," says Corky.

In life and health insurance, you don't have as many maintenance issues and can spend more time selling.

## How Much Will I Make?

Veteran agents say that insurance is the easiest $100,000 and the hardest $20,000 you'll ever make. This means that once you're established and have extensive experience, a reputation, and sizable client base, you can live quite well off your residual income—if you don't starve to death before you get there.

You'll likely start out with a small guaranteed salary of around $2,000 a month for six months or until your training is complete. Be careful. Some companies consider this a draw against your future commissions. This means you owe the company the money that was paid to you during your training. This is common for some sales positions. However, it can become a dangerous practice, because you're borrowing from the future to pay for the present. So when you finally have a big payday, the money is already spent.

It's not like you'll be making money right off the bat. You'll have to get some clients. This can take a while, especially if you're young and don't have many connections. In your first year, you can expect to make in the low to mid-twenties. The average agent makes between $40,000 and $60,000, while experienced top agents can make over $100,000.

When taking an insurance job, make damn sure you understand your compensation package. You should have some money put aside as a safety net. The majority of these jobs are commission based, which means that you take a percentage of everything you sell. The good thing about insurance is that you have residual income. Here's how it works. You make the majority of your commission from the first year of premiums. In life and health, the agent can collect as much as 40 to 100 percent of the first year's premiums. In P&C, it's much less, 15 to 25 percent. In year two, it's reduced by about half and decreases every year after that. But you'll be paid a commission every year as long as that client holds the policy. That means that when you're in your fifties, you'll still be paid a commission every year on the policy you sold to someone when you were twenty-five, as long as that person renews the policy. The hard part is building up enough clients to get to that point.

## What's the Best Thing About Working in Insurance?

Agents cite the ability to really help people and provide a valuable service. If you can survive the first few years, the money is good. You also get the chance to meet different types of people. If you're successful, the perks can be nice. There are often bonus trips and awards for top performers. Independent agents say they love the freedom to choose the companies they work for and people they work with.

You're in a service industry, so you're always helping. You also have a lot of independence and responsibility early on. "Sometimes that's good, other times it can be overwhelming," says Kevin. "Look for a company that provides a good training program and doesn't just leave you out in the woods."

## What's the Worst Thing About It?

"They want slaves," says Corky, who began his career with a large company and is now an independent agent. "There are incredibly unrealistic

Tim, a former MONY sales associate, tells of having to make his quota of demonstrations. "I'm in my fraternity brother's first apartment. We're sitting on a used couch. He has been working for about three months, and I'm talking to him about planning for his retirement. It sucked."

quotas, and the big companies just want you to produce. If you can't, they'll get a new person in there who can." Others say working for a large company was like a dictatorship because of the bureaucracy and politics that can go on in a large organization.

If you're just coming out of school or are new to an area, you don't know anyone with any money to spend on insurance. Rookie insurance agents have two choices to obtain new clients: They can cold call from prospect lists or they can hit up everyone they know. This means contacting your friends, family, and all of your acquaintances. (Try selling life insurance and retirement plans to your fraternity buddies who have less money than you do.) This is a problem that many rookie stockbrokers go through as well.

The most successful people are those who come into it from other industries and have plenty of contacts. This means that many insurance agents tend to be older. They also have money saved up to tide them over during the rough starting period.

## What's It Like?

It's a professional environment with an office setting, but you'll sometimes spend a lot of time in the car or in someone's home. Starting out for a young person is stressful. There's pressure from headquarters to meet your quotas, there's a lot to learn in a short amount of time, and you're trying to make some money so you don't end up on the street. As you become more established, it gets easier. You're essentially your own boss and can make your own schedule as you get the hang of things.

## What About Education?

Hiring requirements vary from manager to manager, but a bachelor's degree is generally more than enough. In many cases, it's not necessary. There are several industry certifications and training courses that may be required in order to sell certain products. You can take insurance classes in school to help you understand the technical elements.

Agents must be licensed in their state or region. To sell life or health insurance, you must have a group one insurance license for your state. To sell property and casualty insurance, you must have a P&C license. You obtain these by passing a state exam. It's a tough test that over half of the agents fail the first time. To prepare for it, there are companies that provide training classes. Call your state's insurance board to learn more about the exam and preparation courses.

## What Sets Me Apart?

This is a business of connections and relationships. The better your people skills, the more successful you'll be. Your reputation is very important, too.

## How Do I Get Hired?

Most of the major insurance firms actively recruit on college campuses. Others hire people from recommendations or "nominations" from people in the industry. They also advertise heavily in the papers. You might also contact an insurance company's regional headquarters and ask if they're taking new agents.

It's not very hard to get hired. "They're looking for warm bodies," said one agent. "If you don't work out, you're gone and they get someone else." This is why there's so much turnover. Almost a third of insurance agents are self-employed.

---

### Actuaries

You might read a lot about actuaries or hear how it's a "hot job." It is in demand, but it's still a relatively small field with fewer than 20,000 actuaries in the United States. What is an actuary? In the most basic terms, it's an odds maker for the events, circumstances, and probabilities that occur in life. They calculate the risk and likelihood of certain events occurring. Their statistical research and findings help determine the potential financial risk and loss to an insurer. This affects the rates and premiums you pay. They calculate the probabilities for death, sickness, accident, disability, unemployment, or property loss.

Actuaries are often employed by major insurance companies and frequently specialize in life, health, property, or investments and financial planning. They have broad knowledge of the insurance industry, financial and economic issues, and health news and trends. They can work in various departments such as underwriting, investment, or pension planning.

How do you train to become an actuary? Let's just say you can't skip any math or stats classes. There are fewer than sixty accredited actuarial sciences programs in the United States. A degree in actuarial sciences is not required, but if you want to pursue this field, you should major in math or statistics. To become an actuary, however, you must pass several of the professional certification exams given by the professional societies. These are a series of exams given by the Society of Actuaries and the Casualty Actuarial Society. Actuaries start in the low thirties and can ultimately make over $100,000. Several studies show that the average salary for actuaries is between $47,000 to $65,000.

---

## Where Can I Learn More?

National Association of Life Underwriters
1922 F Street NW
Washington, DC 20006

National Association of Professional Insurance Agents
400 N. Washington Street
Alexandria, VA 22314

American Academy of Actuaries
1720 I Street NW
Washington, DC 20006

Society of Actuaries
475 Martindale Road, Suite 800
Schaumburg, IL 60173

Casualty Actuarial Society
1100 N. Glebe Road, Suite 600
Arlington, VA 22201

You should also contact your state insurance board.

## Who Are the Major Players?

Prudential
Met Life
Liberty Mutual
Chubb
State Farm Insurance
Travelers Property and Casualty
Progressive Insurance
Nationwide Insurance

## Where on the Web?

www.connectyou.com/talent—Insurance Career Center
www.connectyou.com/ic—Insurance Connections!
www.pianet.com—National Association of Professional Insurance Agents
www.ambest.com—A.M. Best Company
http://iiaa.iix.com—Independent Insurance Network
www.agents-online.com—Insurance Agents Online Network

# 32

## Journalism

**Some Common Positions**
- Reporter
- Desk clerk
- Copy editor
- Editor
- Designer
- Columnist

**Other Opportunities You Might Consider**

Journalists can be found working in newspapers, magazines, television and radio, and increasingly online. They can also work as freelancers. However, this section will focus on newspaper journalists. If you want to learn more about broadcast, check out the "Radio" and "Television" chapters.

Despite the popularity of the Internet, print is not dying, but the way newspapers deliver information is certainly changing. Many newspapers are developing online counterparts on the World Wide Web. Some papers have created entire interactive media departments.

You should also look for opportunities outside of the newsroom. There are marketing departments that create "niche" publications and special sections that add value to advertisers. Some media companies are even buying separate companies whose business is related to or even supports the newspaper. One major paper recently bought an outdoor advertising company to give their advertisers another medium. Don't forget about sales, information systems, graphic design, and photography opportunities.

## How Do I Get Hired?

This profession is all about networking, experience, and talent. Just because you have a journalism degree doesn't guarantee you a job or even mean you're qualified for a job with a newspaper. "The most important thing any student can do is to have several paid or unpaid internships before they graduate," says Sheila, an editor at the *Charlotte Observer*. Most

### Should I Specialize?

Some pros recommend that you specialize in one type of writing and become an expert in it. For example, if you're an entertainment writer, you might specialize in television or theater. If you're a sports writer, you might have the high school or college beat. In business, you might cover technology or personal finance.

newspapers have internships available, and some offer scholarships with them. This allows you to get hands-on experience in a newsroom and maybe even get some "clips" for your portfolio. Some papers bring in unpaid interns and pair them with reporters to be their shadow and learn the basics.

## How Do I Find Out About Internships?

Your best bet for finding opportunities is to contact the newspaper directly. Start by calling the human resources department or the newsroom. Some newsrooms have one individual who handles interns. A few (very few) newspaper pros said to check your campus career office, since papers will sometimes post internship opportunities there. However, if you're going to use your college's resources, the smartest way to learn about opportunities at papers as well as establish contacts is through the journalism department. Papers are much more likely to have a relationship with the "J" school than the career center. Talk to one of your professors and ask if he or she can help you get your foot in the door. Even after you graduate, don't be shy about using your college contacts. Remember, though, that networking and establishing contacts in this field begins early, before you graduate.

## What About Getting Hired for a First Job?

The first step is to decide what area of the paper you want to work in and what size paper you want to work for. Be realistic. No one starts out at the *New York Times*, the *Washington Post*, or the *Chicago Tribune*. You're more likely to start out covering high school sheep showing for the *Abilene Reporter News*.

Pick a section you want to write for. Hopefully, this matches the experience and clips you have. For example, are you a sports or entertainment writer? Do you want to work in features? Every paper is broken into sections and generally has an editor who's responsible for that area.

Once you've chosen your area of interest, go to the library and look in the *Editor & Publisher* yearbook. It is an annual guide that lists almost every paper in the country, along with the contact information for various section editors. Make sure you have the proper contact person and their correct title. There can be a lot of turnover in the industry, and if you send your information to a person who is no longer there, you're sunk. "Hi, I would like to be a reporter, but I can't even research who the right person is at your paper." Do your homework and get the right name and title.

Once you find the right person, you might send a résumé and sample clips to the editor without any advance contact or preparation. However, the smarter move is to call the managing editor and department editor before you send your information. You may not get through. If you can't, ask their assistant if there are any openings, what you need to do to apply, and what the boss looks for. Then send a letter and clips to both the managing editor and department editor. "You shouldn't just write and follow up. Call first," recommends Sheila.

## How Else Can I Learn Who the Decision Makers Are?

If you don't have a contact name, call the newsroom and ask for the managing editor or city editor. Some large papers even have hiring directors.

You can also contact the journalism associations and use their mailing lists. If you don't belong or don't know what the associations are, contact someone at the local paper and ask for names of the major groups.

## What Are Clips?

Clips are samples of your previously published work. They are stories you've written or edited that were published in a magazine or newspaper. It can be a campus newspaper, as long as it is representative of your writing style and ability. It is very similar to a portfolio or "book" for an artist. This is as important, if not more important, than your résumé, because this actually shows what you can do. When sending clips, think quality over quantity and show diversity in your writing and what you've covered. "Because there are so many good students coming out of school who have experience, clips are one of the few things to set people apart," says Danielle of the *Denver Post*.

## Where Will I Start?

Unless you've been an intern at a major newspaper, you will likely start in a small market. Your first position may be as a beat reporter. Some papers start people out as clerks. A clerk is a step below a reporter and does a lot of the fact-checking and grunt work. However, it can be a great chance to gain some writing experience, sometimes even under your own byline.

## Do Your Homework

Amy of the *Arizona Republic* tells of how one applicant impressed her by simply doing her homework. "I had interviewed many people for a position that was to help produce a special section for the paper. The girl I ultimately hired had plenty of journalism experience, but what impressed me about her was a comment she made about recent trends in newspapers. I asked, 'Where did you pick that up?' She replied that she had read an article written by our CEO in one of the trade publications. I could instantly tell she understood what we were trying to accomplish at the paper and was smart enough to do her homework."

## What Sets Me Apart?

Amy, of the *Arizona Republic* in Phoenix, says, "When I am recruiting, I look for initiative. I want to know that this person is self-motivated. I want someone who can generate ideas and won't wait for the editor to give them an assignment."

Jannelle, of the *Minneapolis Star & Tribune,* says, "It all boils down to really good writing, wanting to be part of a team, and being able to work with a variety of people. Good writing will get you in the door, but you still have to work well with others."

You should also understand the role newspapers play both in the community and in the financial world.

## Everyone Is Connected

Journalists are an incestuous bunch. They all seem to know one another. For as many papers as there are, it is still a small and closely-knit community. Your connections will not only help you land a first job, but will help you throughout your career. The pros recommend joining a local press organization or press club, which you'll find in most large cities. Call your local newspaper to learn of one in your area.

There are also special professional groups and associations such as the American Association of Sunday and Feature Editors (AASFE), the Professional Journalist Society, Sigma Delta Chi Professional Journalism Society, and the International Association of Business Communicators (IABC). Additionally, there are organizations for almost every minority group, such as the National Association for Hispanic Journalists.

## You Might Also Consider

Marketing and new business development is a growing area for newspapers. Newspapers are looking for ways to add value for their advertisers and expand their reach. Through marketing and business development, many are creating online services and electronic communication, television shows, and specialty publications targeted to niche groups. These activities and new businesses support the vendor and sales area of the newspaper. Anita, who works in the business development area of a major newspaper, says, "I get to feel like an entrepreneur."

## What Departments Have the Most Job Openings?

The number of job openings varies from paper to paper, but there are certainly some departments that are in need of writers more frequently than others. "Everyone wants to write features," says Ned of the *Daily Oklahoman*. "Sports never seems to have a problem finding writers, either." The area with the greatest need for writers is business. "There aren't that many people who can understand a financial statement and make it interesting," says Amy.

## Does My Education Matter?

Journalists are generally very well-educated. While a journalism degree certainly helps, it is not a requirement. There are journalists who have business or English backgrounds. Grades don't matter that much, either. What counts more than anything else is experience and talent. The best way to get experience and produce clips is to work for your campus paper. Regardless of where you write, just produce work. For fee or for free, it doesn't matter, just write.

## What Will I Do?

In addition to actual reporting, you will gather information from press releases and check facts, spelling, and names. There is a lot of phone work involved, according to Sheila. You may think of reporters as working out in the field and on the scene, but many do much of their work on the phone.

## What's the Career Path?

Very uneven. The days when a reporter came in and worked his or her way up the editorial food chain are gone. Today, you can come right in as a copy editor, but most mid-level editors started as reporters. The common path in a newspaper is reporter, copy editor, mid-level editor, senior editor, and managing editor. Some people choose to stay in reporting.

There are many unconventional opportunities for journalists today. Many are only interested in the online side and others are walking away from newspapers and beginning their own online services. Yet the interesting employer of journalist's this year will be the high-tech companies who want content for the Web. During a panel discussion on career opportunities for journalists at the most recent Association of Sunday and Feature Editors Conference, a Knight Ridder executive claimed that the largest employer of journalists this year would not be a newspaper or media company. It would be Microsoft, which is hiring journalists and writers left and right to produce content for Web sites.

## What Are the Pros and Cons?

If you like change and chaos, journalism is for you. It is not the same job every day. Journalists also cite that they enjoy working with lots of different people. They like seeing things from behind the scenes, from a perspective that the average person never sees.

As much as people like to beat up the "liberal media," it's actually a very conservative industry. Amy in Arizona says, "There's a real can-do culture, but it is also very slow to make changes."

The downside of journalism is that there's never enough time. It seems you're always on deadline. David of the *Boston Herald* says, "This is a real twenty-four/seven type of job. There's news every day of the year. The wicked hours can definitely affect your family and social life."

While many journalists said the money isn't great, they weren't moaning about it like other low-paying industries. As Jannelle says, "You really have to want to be here."

## How Much Will I Make?

It totally depends on the size of the market you're in. Entry-level reporters average around $23,000, while clerks generally start at $18,000. Reporters for a medium-sized newspaper such as the *Charlotte Observer* can expect around $700 a week. There's a lot of opportunity for growth, but you won't get rich doing this job.

Unless you rise to the top as an editor or in management, the maximum a reporter will make is around $65,000. The majority of reporters at any level make between $25,000 and $55,000. Your pay can also depend on a guild or union. The newspaper industry is highly unionized.

## What Are Some Misconceptions?

Not everybody that works in a paper is a writer. The newsroom only makes up about a third of the newspaper. Oddly enough, the newsroom doesn't always run the paper.

This also used to be thought of as a very male-dominated field, but lately there are more opportunities for women and minorities.

## What's the Environment Like?

It depends on what department you're in. Reporters mentioned several stereotypes, saying sports writers are loud and male, while feature writers tend to be laid back. Journalists are fervent readers and have a deep interest in people.

This is a stressful and constantly changing job. You're constantly working to meet a deadline. You must always be ahead of the game. This is not a nine-to-five job where you're chained to your desk. Reporters' hours vary, because they have a beat. You may have a shift from 2:00 to 10:00 P.M.

## What the Pros Read

*Presstime*
*Editor & Publisher*
*The Columbia Journalism Review*

## Where on the Web?

www.mediainfo.com—*Editor & Publisher*
www.igc.apc.org—Institute for Global Communications
www.spj.org—Society of Professional Journalists
www.poynter.org—Poynter Institute for Media Studies
www.charlotte.com—*Charlotte Observer*

# 33

• • • • • • • • • • • • • • • • • • • • • • • • • • • • • • •

# Law

**Some Common Positions**
> Lawyer/attorney/counsel
> Litigator
> Tax attorney
> Corporate/in-house counsel
> District attorney/prosecutor
> Criminal attorney
> Personal injury attorney
> Weasel

**Other Opportunities You Might Consider**
With a law degree, there's not much you can't do. Related fields and careers include politics, sports, and entertainment agent. You certainly don't have to practice law in the traditional sense. A legal education is great preparation for any business, especially one involving complicated contracts or transactions.

In the wake of the OJ trials, the legal profession has taken a beating. Law school applications are down, and there are fewer jobs available. Not to mention American's growing disgust as attorneys grandstand for the cameras and, in some cases, become news stories themselves.

This is a big switch from a few years ago when people were flocking to law school in record numbers in hopes of the successful and glamorous career portrayed on *LA Law*. However, like television shows, bull markets, and weekends, the explosive growth in the legal profession had to come to an end. And with the cancellation of *LA Law* several years ago, the legal profession entered a recession, resulting in a glut of attorneys. Yet despite its perceived demise, the legal profession is still a lucrative, prestigious, and rewarding career path.

## A Crash Course on Law School

In a nutshell, sometime during your senior year or after you graduate, you take the LSAT (a standardized entrance exam to law school) and then pray that you're accepted to a decent school.

It's recommended that you choose a school that is located where you think you want to practice after graduation, unless you go to one of the top law schools in the country. This is so you can start making connections in the area and studying that state's laws while still in school, hopefully making it a little easier to pass the bar exam. If you want more information regarding law school, there are plenty of books covering the application process in-depth. Kaplan, Princeton Review, and Peterson's all have good books on law schools and the LSAT.

## How Do I Get Hired?

The most common way is through your school. Every decent law school should have a placement center. Traditionally, law firms interview on campuses to hire first- and second-year students for summer internships. Your internships are very important. This is not the time to go backpacking in Europe. Summer internships or clerkships often serve as a serious recruiting period, with the top firms wining and dining interns, not to mention paying them embarrassingly well. It's almost like some courtship ritual or Greek rush. Your goal is to have a positive internship and make connections so you're offered a permanent position upon graduation. At least that's the idea. Not every internship is like this. If you work with a small firm, it may be quite different. In any case, you'll be doing research and might get to prepare briefs. You should try to intern for a firm that practices the area of law in which you want to specialize. The next most common way to get hired is the tried-and-true networking and schmoozing.

## What If I Choke on the Bar Exam?

You can take it again and again until you pass. The only problem is that if you're working, your employer will probably drop you if you fail it twice—or sometimes even once. Before you start freaking out, don't worry. Even big studs like John Kennedy, Jr. failed the bar the first time.

## Why Do You Want to Be an Attorney?

This should be the first question you ask yourself. You should ask it early and often. Law school has become an escape for many graduates who see

After graduating from Southwestern School of Law, James planned to move to Dallas from his hometown of Houston. James did a very smart thing after taking the bar exam. He talked with his family, friends, and professors and asked if they knew any influential people in Dallas he could meet with to establish some contacts in the community. After getting the names and numbers of some CEOs and wealthy individuals, as well as permission to use the relevant contact's name, he spent a week setting up lunches, dinners, and appointments for drinks. He told them he was moving to the area and wanted to talk with them about the best way to get started in the area and who he should contact. He ended up making great connections, many of whom were able to get him an audience with partners at some of the main firms in town.

it as a three-year pit stop on their way to finding something they really want to do. Law schools are filled with people who don't have a great love for the law or don't want to practice when they graduate. There are tons of lame excuses for pursuing a law degree: "It was law or business school," "It made my parents happy," "It sounded better than getting a job."

Three years is a long time to spend pursuing a career in which you don't plan to work, not to mention the money you'll spend on tuition.

Before you consider a legal career, ask yourself why you're going to law school. Is it to escape the job market? Is it because you don't know what you want to do? Have a reason for going to law school. Ask yourself if you really want to be an attorney. If so, what kind? Are you going for the legal education in hopes of applying it to another field? That's fine. Or do you want to work for a firm and try to make partner some day? If so, do you know what it takes to get to that point? Are you willing to make that sacrifice? Maybe you want to hang your own shingle and have your name on the door? Whatever your reason for wanting the degree, remember that law school is difficult and expensive. Make sure you have a reason for going before you embark on the three-year journey.

## It's a Profession, but It's Also a Business

A recent report by the American Bar Association concluded that attorneys today need a better understanding of how to develop a practice. The lawyer is now looked at as the "deal maker." Money making skills— "rainmaking"—is a priority among both students and firms. For this reason, some law schools are beginning to teach the business side of the law. Florida State University offers a "deals" class that covers topics ranging from entertaining clients to closing deals. At the University of Southern California law school, business executives are invited to tell students what they look for when hiring an attorney. The executives help students understand the importance of marketing, and they advise students on everything from firm brochures to fee schedules to what the lobby should look like.

## Opportunities for Non-Attorneys

Many firms are developing marketing departments to promote and enhance the firm's image and attract business. These departments are generally run by marketing specialists and people with public relations and communications backgrounds. Today, large firms usually either have marketing departments or hire individuals who contract or freelance their services.

## How Do Lawyers Make Money?

Lawyers make money quickly, if you consider that partners can charge anywhere from $325 an hour on up. Way up. Remember that, for the most part, law is a time-based profession. They charge an hourly rate, and they don't do anything unless it can be billed to the client, right down to copies, postage, and phone calls. Whenever an attorney talks to you on the phone, thinks about something related to a client while she is driving down the highway, or performs research (which is what most new associates will do), the client is billed for the time, generally in fifteen-minute increments. In large firms, there's constant pressure to bill a certain number of hours per week.

The other way attorneys make money is by taking a case "on contingency." When you see those obnoxious lawyers that advertise on TV saying, "I don't get paid until you get paid," they're talking about contingency fees. That means an attorney takes on a case and collects a fee contingent on the outcome of the case. If an attorney wins the case or obtains a settlement, he gets paid a percentage from the total amount of the judgment or settlement, often 30 percent or more of the total amount. If he loses, he gets nada. Actually, he gets his expenses (phone, copies, etc.) paid for, but not his fees. While 30 percent is the rule of thumb, details can be negotiated for each client and case.

Rob wanted to work in financial services after graduation, but didn't get the job he wanted right out of school. Weighing his options, he thought he could go to law school and reapply with the investment firms after he graduated. He never wanted to practice law, but thought the degree would be valuable. By the time Rob graduated, he had some pretty big student loans and needed to make some significant money quickly. He couldn't afford to take an entry-level financial services position. The natural solution was to practice law and work for a firm, which he did. Five years later, he is still with the firm working insane hours. He is miserable. "I got caught up making great cash, and now I'm used to the lifestyle. I can't take a financial hit and start from scratch."

● ● ●

Matt had only been married a few months and was happy working in a sales position when his father-in-law pressured him into going to law school. His father-in-law made it a sweet deal by saying he would pay for Matt's law school and help support them while he was in school. What a guy. Right? In the middle of Matt's second year, a family squabble caused Matt's father-in-law to cut them off, and he was forced to pay his own tuition to finish a degree he wasn't crazy about getting in the first place. After graduation, Matt couldn't find a job with a private firm, so he went to work reviewing contracts for the city of Tulsa. After two years, he left the profession and today is a sales manager for a steel firm.

Sometimes attorneys will waive their fee in exchange for equity positions or ownership rights in a company, product, investment, etc. Sometimes this can be more lucrative than charging an hourly fee.

## You Can Do It Anywhere, Anytime

Once you have your legal training and have passed the bar, no one can take that from you, as long as you keep up with your CLE (continuing legal education) credits. The law has proven to be a great career for some people who want to pursue other interests but still practice on a limited basis. You can work without being with a firm. Joyce, an attorney specializing in contracts and the mother of three small kids, says, "I've done the big firm thing and now I want to spend time with my family. I work when I want, and I can be selective with the clients I take on. I have none of the stress of being in a firm."

## A Great Place to Start

Philip and Trent met while they were associates at a large firm. Early on, they realized that spending the next twenty years in a conservative law firm trying to make partner like every other associate wasn't for them. They decided to look at what business they could do that would allow them to use their legal training. They decided on the entertainment industry. But Hollywood and New York were already full of young attorneys trying to break into entertainment as agents. They decided to do something different. They quit the law firm and moved to Nashville, because the growth in country music appealed to them. They opened Rogers & Thomas, and now land deals and manage the careers of country musicians and other entertainers.

## What Type of Law Do You Want to Practice?

There are many different types of law, but two basic distinctions are criminal and civil. Most attorneys specialize. Just because you're an attorney doesn't mean you know about criminal law if your specialty is tax. If you're a transactional attorney, you might not know anything about a highly specialized area such as intellectual property.

In civil law, there are many different kinds of law to practice: Tax, bankruptcy, corporate, real estate, contracts, intellectual property, and labor are just a few. Criminal law has two distinctions: prosecution and defense.

## How Long Before I Get to Be in Front of a Jury?

Yeah, yeah, *LA Law*, *Murder One*, and the OJ fiasco. We tend to picture attorneys as arguing in court before a jury. However, the truth is that some attorneys never step inside of a courtroom during their entire careers.

If you really want to be a trial lawyer, the best and fastest way for you to get experience in front of a judge and jury is to start your career in the public sector. In the private firms, most litigation is handled by the big-gun partners. It could be years before you get to handle anything on your own. But on the criminal side, there's a better chance of you trying a case much earlier. However, it's getting tougher to obtain trial experience. According to twenty-eight-year-old Trey McClendon, an assistant DA in Lubbock, Texas, "Traditionally, people who wanted to get trial experience, which is so difficult to come by, would start at a district attorney or prose-cutor's office, then move on to work for either a criminal defense attorney or plaintiffs attorney. Court experience counts the most, so people would get it and move on. But now more attorneys are choosing to become career prosecutors. It has made rising through the ranks in this part of law much more difficult because of increased competition."

## How Much Can I Make?

Now we get to the main reason many people become attorneys. If you want idealism, work for the ACLU. But if you were to ask the majority of law school students what they want after graduation, most would want to say, "Show me the money."

According to the U.S. Census Bureau, there are over 850,000 attorneys in the United States, with the typical partner making $168,000. The median base salary for attorneys is $86,730.

## What About Rookies and New Associates?

Salaries for young lawyers had been going up for years. They are now beginning to stagnate or dwindle. A study of starting salaries of law graduates by the national Associa-tion for Law Placement found the median salary for all types of attorneys to be $37,000. Is the money any better in one area? Attorneys in private practice traditionally make

**Median Starting Salary for Attorneys**

Private practice: $50,000
Business and industry (corpo-rate attorneys): $42,000
Government: $32,500
Public interest: $28,000

more than anyone else. Corporate attorneys or civil attorneys make more money than criminal attorneys. An assistant district attorney might start at between $30,000 to $35,000, depending upon location. Top U.S. attorneys might make close to six figures.

Not every attorney makes a lot of money. There are many who scrape by month to month or case to case. You might read or hear about trial lawyers or successful personal injury lawyers obtaining huge multimillion-dollar judgments, but for every one of them, you also have plenty who are hustling on several cases hoping that one settles before it's time to pay next month's rent.

## Where Are the Jobs?

Everywhere. You can live where you want, although you must be licensed by the state to practice. That buckskin-jacket-wearing-Daniel-Boone-wannabe Jerry Spence, who is always on CNBC commenting about every high profile case, lives in Montana of all places. All you have to do is pass the bar exam in your state of choice. However, many states have reciprocity, which means if you pass it in one state, you're exempt from taking the test in other states with whom they have an arrangement. For example, if you pass in Oklahoma, you're automatically barred in Kansas.

Traditionally, people think of attorneys as working in a law firm with eight names on the door and lots of wood furniture. But attorneys can work for any city, county, state, or federal government agency or department.

Corporations in every industry also have legal departments and attorneys who may work in the human resource department. Sometimes an attorney will gain experience in an area or industry while working for a firm and then move in-house for a client or company within that industry. Some corporations, such as publishing houses, entertainment companies, insurance companies, and hospitals, have teams of lawyers in-house.

## What Are Some of the Misconceptions About Attorneys?

The biggest misconception is that all attorneys are rich. They aren't. There's the potential to make big bucks, but it depends upon the type of law you prac-

---

### What Attorneys Make Around the Country

| REGIONS WITH THE HIGHEST MEDIAN SALARIES FOR ATTORNEYS | CITIES WITH THE LOWEST MEDIAN SALARIES FOR ATTORNEYS |
| --- | --- |
| 1. Phoenix—$134,400 | 1. El Paso—$45,891 |
| 2. New Jersey—$128,500 | 2. Portland—$52,320 |
| 3. North Carolina—$128,040 | 3. Austin—$59,912 |
| 4. Cleveland—$120,509 | 4. Minneapolis—$ 62,562 |
| 5. Alaska—$118,973 | 5. Columbus, OH—$ 66,360 |

tice. A prosecutor will never make as much as a top corporate attorney. There are assistant district attorneys who make less than $35,000. The trade-off is that they might actually be trying cases.

Another misconception is that all attorneys spend time in a courtroom. If you're with a big private firm, there are attorneys who specialize in litigation and handle all cases that go to trial. Many attorneys never ever step foot in a courtroom. And if they do, it's only after years of being a second stringer to a main partner. If you really want trial experience, you should consider criminal law.

There's also the perception that lawyers are unethical weasels. Not true . . . well, not entirely true. Sure, there are low-life attorneys, just as there are unethical salespeople, accountants, and doctors. Unscrupulous people can be found in virtually every industry.

## What's the Best and Worse Thing About Being an Attorney?

As an associate, the hours are exhausting. You'll easily work sixty hours a week, and you'll be doing this for a long time. "Law has changed," says Philip. "Partners are having to do more. They can no longer just sit on their asses or play golf while associates do all of the work, although it feels like that sometimes. You also have to play the firm's political games and suck up to the partners."

As a corporate attorney, Linda says the hardest thing is "knowing that I am the person it stops with. If the CEO calls me with a crisis, I am the person who must get the answer right, and a lot rides on that answer. Sometimes I run into situations with which I'm not familiar, and I have to learn on the fly or figure it out. That's frustrating."

Jeffrey says, "Being around other attorneys is a negative. We can be cocky assholes sometimes. And it gets annoying after a while. I also hate playing the politics and participating in the ass-kissing that can go on in a big firm."

Sherry Wong says that, despite advances, it still can be a "good ole boy's network." "As a minority woman, sometimes it's very hard."

As far as positive things about the profession, cash was at the top of the list, followed by the challenge and variety of the work. Oth-

## You Still Don't Know If You Want to Be an Attorney? Be a Paralegal

If you don't want to go to law school or want to test the waters to see if the law profession is right for you before making a three-year commitment, you might think about becoming a paralegal.

Also called "legal assistants," they do a lot of the research and prep work for attorneys. They may help gather or investigate facts, prepare reports on information they collect, maintain the legal files, and draft documents.

While it's a great way to gain exposure to the legal profession to see if it's right for you, many people make a career out of it or become specialized legal secretaries.

Paralegals can expect to earn a salary in the mid-twenties. But you can easily make another $10,000 to $20,000 a year in overtime at many firms. There are no mandatory certification requirements, but it's common for a paralegal to have at least a bachelor's degree. There are, however, certified paralegal training programs, which some firms require their employees to attend. These are mostly two-year degrees, but if you already have an undergraduate degree, you can complete them within a few months.

ers say that they enjoy helping others accomplish what they want or need. It could be anything from starting a company, closing a deal or transaction, obtaining a settlement, or solving a problem.

## What's the Career Path?

If you're in private practice, you pay your dues doing work on cases for senior attorneys and increasingly taking on more responsibility. Eventually, after a number of years, you can make partner, which means that you share in the firm's profits and might even get your name on the door. However, it's often a move-up-or-move-out policy. If you're passed over for partner several times, it's recommended that you find work elsewhere.

Mike, a bankruptcy attorney, knew his job, but did not have good people or rainmaking skills. He was passed over for partner and was told that he had one year to find a job elsewhere. The problem was that he had been an attorney for ten years and was making $100,000 a year. Other firms asked, "Why didn't he make partner? What's wrong with him?" It took him exactly a year to locate another job halfway across the country, at a 30 percent pay cut. Many in this situation simply start their own practices.

## Where Can I Learn More?

*How to Start and Build a Successful Law Practice*, by Jay Foonberg
American Bar Association
National Association for Law Placement

## Where on the Web?

www.foonberglaw.com—Jay Foonberg's page
www.abanet.org—American Bar Association

# 34

**Marketing**

**Some Common Positions**
- Marketing manager/director/VP
- Marketing assistant/coordinator
- Analyst
- Market researcher
- Product manager
- Brand manager
- Product development
- Direct marketing consultant

**Other Opportunities You Might Consider**

Marketing is closely related to several fields. It is practically joined at the hip with sales. Actually, one supports the other. Many people in marketing begin in sales and then make the transition to marketing. Other fields you want to check out are public relations and advertising.

Even if you are an engineer or have a technical background, there are opportunities for you in the product-development side of marketing. If you are a researcher, economist, demographer, or statistician, there are opportunities as a researcher or analyst.

While marketing is not sales in the literal sense of being in the field selling product to a customer, marketing is every other related activity that makes it possible for a sale to be made. This can include the development and design of the product or service, the packaging, the advertising, promotions and communication strategy, as well as the research that goes into determining who the buyers or markets are.

Virtually every industry and profession markets in some capacity. Even businesses that have never traditionally marketed (like law and accounting) are beginning to establish entire marketing departments.

There are a number of different types of marketing positions. Your options depend on your background, education, and interest.

## Where Will I Start?

Next to "I want to be in management," the most overused phrase used by job-hunting graduates is "I want to be in marketing." If you have a marketing degree and want to work in the marketing department of a major company as a brand or product manager, I've got good news and bad news. The good news is that there are plenty of opportunities in marketing and a number of ways for you to reach your goal. The bad news is that armed with your fresh marketing degree, the chances of you starting your career in the marketing department of a major Fortune 500 consumer products company or in product development helping to create the next hot new product are pretty slim.

Many people start as a marketing coordinator. This can be hands-on or it can be a gopher- or assistant-type of job. You may gather materials, conduct research, or run errands. Otherwise, people often make a transition from another area into marketing only after they understand the business or have acquired special knowledge such as product design or development.

## What Is the Career Path?

The good news is that marketing is one of the most valued and influential departments in most companies. It's a great background. According to a survey by executive search firm Korn Ferry, marketing is the fastest way up the corporate ladder.

If you have success in marketing, you may be in demand and get lured away by another company to try to revive their marketing efforts.

The path from entry level would be to product manager to brand manager. In some cases this may take a short time—two to five years, although it most often takes five to ten years.

## What Types of Marketing Are There?

Every industry or product has its own special way of being marketed. In addition, there are different methods for getting the message out: telemarketing, direct marketing, event marketing, cause-related marketing, or business-to-business marketing.

## I Want to Be in Product Development

Many people pursue careers in marketing believing they will be the ones dreaming up and creating new products. While that responsibility often falls under marketing, there is much more to product development than MBAs in an office conceptualizing the latest new product for your grocery store shelf. Product development is often technical and handled by scientists or engineers. Terry, director of product development at Gerber Foods (yes, the baby-food people), says he leads the team that develops new products, packages, and process designs for Gerber products. "Only about 15 to 20 percent of our time is in product generation. The remainder of the time is spent developing that idea into a product and then ramping up and implementing the product's release." Terry says that in a company like Gerber, it can take up to a year for a product to make it from idea to shelf. "We have developed hundreds of products in one year, and we have only released three during another year."

## How Can I Stand Out?

Experience is going to be the key. If you are a student and can obtain a position as a student rep for a company, do it. You will gain experience at devising a campaign and putting it into action in your own market.

Get an internship. Many marketing departments hire summer interns, and many of the larger companies such as Gerber use this opportunity to check out future graduates to see if they want to extend an offer after graduation. Mike, a marketer with Catalina Marketing, an electronic promotions company, says they hire most of their employees through internships.

If you are already with a company, you may use your product experience and knowledge to move into marketing. Sales, advertising, and public relations are the positions that are easiest to make the transition from.

## How Much Can I Make?

Entry-level marketing positions start in the mid-twenties to low thirties. Top brand and product managers average between $80,000 to $120,000, with top-level marketing directors and vice presidents earning much more. Most marketing positions offer insurance and standard benefits.

## What Are the Pros and Cons?

On the positive side, it is exciting to help create something and see it from start to finish. Alex, a brand manager with one of the top beverage companies, says, "It's cool when you walk into a store and see something on the shelf that you and your team thought of and saw come alive."

As for negatives, it is difficult to get started, and it is very competitive. Another downside is that it is not always as glamorous as one might expect. As Steve with Catalina says, "I deal with a lot of numbers, figures, and statistics." Other marketing specialists say it can be tough coordinating all of the necessary departments. "You have to be a great communicator and delegator," says Krista, marketing manager for a telecommunications firm.

## Where Can I Learn More?

The best resource is the American Marketing Association. They are one of the top trade groups around. They also have a fantastic student chapters.

AMA—American Marketing Association
250 S. Wacker Drive # 200
Chicago, IL 60606-5816
312-648-0536

Promotion Marketing Association of America, Inc.
257 Park Avenue South, 11th Floor
New York, NY 10010

Direct Marketing Association
1120 Avenue of the Americas
New York, NY 10036–6700

Bank Marketing Association
1120 Connecticut Avenue NW
Washington, DC 20036

Food Marketing Institute
800 Connecticut Avenue NW
Washington, DC 20006-2701

Sales and Marketing Executives International
Statler Office Tower, Suite 977
Cleveland, OH 44115

## Where on the Web?

www.ama.org—American Marketing Association
www.yahoo.com/business_and_economy/companies/marketing

There are hundreds of marketing-related Web sites.

∙ ∙ ∙ ∙ ∙ ∙ ∙ ∙ ∙ ∙ ∙ ∙ ∙ ∙ ∙ ∙ ∙ ∙ ∙ ∙ ∙ ∙ ∙ ∙ ∙ ∙ ∙ ∙

# 35

# Odd Jobs: Careers Off the Beaten Path

Not everyone wants to wear a suit and tie to work. I recently went to a dinner party at a friend's house. My friend is a successful fashion designer (not your run-of-the-mill job). He has an eclectic assortment of friends, to say the least. At this dinner party of about fifteen people, there were publicists, a reporter, a geologist, a doctor, a federal judge, an architect, and an astrologer. Who do you think everyone wanted to talk to?

Once in a while, you will run across people who do something that is so out of the ordinary that you are drawn like a moth to flame. "How did you get started? How do you make money? What do you do?" As my friend Jon, a former producer at *The Maury Povich Show*, says, "At parties, people aren't surrounding the bankers to learn about their jobs. They want to talk to me to learn about the phone sex operators and other weirdos we've had on the show."

Below are a few people who march to a very different drummer. Perhaps you can be inspired by their stories and follow your own nontraditional career path. You will notice that all of the people have one thing in common: They're in these careers because they love them and are passionate about what they do. Their current businesses often grew out of a hobby or personal interest, and they often sacrifice time or a big paycheck.

## Golf Etiquette Coach

Suzanne began her career as an attorney in San Francisco. "I went to law school primarily because it was a dream of my father's, but I practiced for several years." After college, she started playing golf with her brother and father. She was hooked and wanted to pursue learning the game. The problem she found was that while many women play, it is still a "good ole boy's" sport. "Many businesswomen are getting active in the game for business reasons, but it is not a welcoming sport for women. Most people are taught the mechanics of the game, how to hit the ball, but no one teaches the etiquette, rules, and finer points of the game that can actually help you do business on the golf course." As a result, Suzanne developed a workshop to provide that type of information. It has been incredibly successful. "There was nothing like this out there for women," says Suzanne. After some favorable media coverage, she was swamped with requests and decided to pursue golf etiquette rather than the law. "I can always and still do practice a little bit, but I came to this career because of my dissatisfaction with the law and because I discovered something that allowed me to do things I was passionate about: golf and travel." Today, she travels the country and has been to several other counties teaching golf etiquette primarily to women. She is hired by companies who want their executives to learn the rules and proper ways to do business on the course. She is also hired by travel-and-tour companies to perform her workshops at resorts.

## Image Consultant

How would you like to get paid to go shopping with people. Have you ever wanted to tell someone that something they are wearing makes them look dumpy or their hair needs to be cut? Can you imagine getting paid for that? Jana does. Jana began her career as a copywriter for an advertising agency and later freelanced. "I have always been involved with appearance, clothes, and I love to shop. When I became burnt out with advertising, I wanted something to do that I was excited about. That's when I decided to marry my interests and enrolled in a two-year art program to study lines, color design, and art."

Janna doesn't like to be called an image consultant. "Image consultants impose their image on a client. I find out who the person is and help them convey that in their dress."

Jana says she works with many entrepreneurs, entertainers, people who have undergone divorces and are looking to start over with a new look, and people who, as Jana says, "need to have congruity between who they are and how they look."

Jana performs several services ranging from going through your closet to weed out things you don't wear to analyzing your color and body structure and recommending which styles would look best to actually going shopping with you to select clothes. Jana charges her clients an hourly rate (approximately $100 an hour) or a package fee for her service. Her business is largely word of mouth and through media events at which she performs.

## Assistant to the Assistant of Robert Redford

While Alex was in college, a professor told him of a summer opportunity in New York to work on the set of the movie *Quiz Show*, which was being directed by Robert Redford. Alex spent the summer working on the set as a production assistant doing any odd job that needed to be done—running errands, grabbing lunch, etc. While on the set, he made some great contacts with Redford's production staff. He maintained contact with them during his senior year, and after graduation, he contacted them. Moving to Los Angeles, he got a job in Robert Redford's production company. He began as the assistant to the assistant of Robert Redford. (Could you think of a lower title?) "I did everything from professional to personal stuff. I would respond to mail, read scripts, and be a gatekeeper. I would also do personal stuff like take care of his car, answer phones, get stuff out to his house. I had to remind myself that I have a college degree as I'm waiting in the dealership for his car, but this is how you get started in the business and there are a million others out there like me."

The perks certainly outweigh the money. "I was paid horribly. There is no way I could live in LA on what I make without help from my parents."

(Just in case you were wondering, I asked Alex if he called him Robert or Mr. Redford. "Oh, it's just Bob to everyone.")

## Butt-Sketch Artist

Krandel was trained as an engineer and began his career working for Westinghouse. He had always been interested in art, and early in his engineering career, he decided to begin painting and drawing for fun. "I had painted several things, and on weekends would go to downtown Dallas to the arts district and try to sell my stuff on the corner. One day, I was watching a parade and was sketching the line of people from behind. I was going to paint the scene, but had to do the basic outline first. I had just drawn the silhouette of some people, so it looked like it was their bodies from behind." A person approached Krandel as the picture was not even near being completed and offered to buy it from him. Krandel said, "I'm sorry, this isn't finished. This is just a sketch." It didn't matter; the person really wanted the drawing of the parade watchers' butts. A lightbulb went on in Krandel's head. People pay for caricatures all the time.

These pictures are professional and tasteful, despite the "butt" name. Krandel devised a way to sketch people from behind in two minutes. While he is drawing them, he is entertaining and making jokes that come naturally when you are drawing someone's butt.

Krandel now has a studio in Dallas and employs three other artists who travel the country with him drawing butts for people at conventions, trade shows, and parties. He easily makes six figures. Check out his work at www.buttsketch.com.

## Beware of Titles

When I first stared my career, I thought I was so cool (I still think I'm pretty cool, but my wife and friends disagree). My first title was account executive. That's right, *executive*. It only took me a few weeks to realize that account executive was actually Latin for salesperson. So much for cool titles. A year later, I became a senior account executive, which meant I get new cards and more responsibility for the same amount of pay. Go figure.

Don't get caught up in what you will be called. Titles are great, but if they don't have any responsibility with them, they're useless. When I was vice president of a multimedia company, we had a vice president of snacks and drinks (a.k.a. receptionist who made sure that the 'fridge was stocked with plenty of soda).

## How About This Job Description?

Chief Technology Officer (CTO): No, this is not something out of *Star Trek*. According to one CTO job description, the CTO helps decide how to apply new technology most effectively. He synthesizes the broad array of alternatives and integrates new technology into a company's systems. Did you get all that? My head hurts.

# 36

. . . . . . . . . . . . . . . . . . . . . . . . . . . . . . . .

# Performing Arts

**Some Common Positions**
>Performers (actor, dancer, singer)
>Front office manager
>Director
>Lighting director
>Costumes and props
>Front of the house/tickets
>Unemployed
>Waiter

**Other Opportunities You Might Consider**
If you aren't a performer but have an artistic need and desire to be in the arts, this may be a great outlet for you. There are many opportunities for people who aren't performers. You can be on the business side of the arts, such as in administration, fund-raising, public relations, or ticket sales.

## What Can I Do?

There are many opportunities in the performing arts other than being an actor, dancer, or performer. The field of performing arts is broken into three categories, the first being administration. Here you may become a company manager, house manager, audience manager, public relations or marketing rep, bookkeeper, business manager, or fund-raiser. You might also work in box-office sales. Production is the second component, which includes everything from the creating, moving, and designing of costumes, sets, props, lighting, wardrobe, and more. The final element most people think of is performing. Of course, here you may be an actor, director, choreographer, musician, dancer, singer, or conductor.

## Where Are the Jobs?

Even though most jobs are found in either New York or Los Angeles, you can still have a promising career in other parts of the country. Outside of

New York or LA your best bet is to work in a major metropolitan city such as Chicago, Boston, or Washington, D.C. However, there are even theater and dance companies in cities like Cleveland and Salt Lake City. Most local communities have arts groups; some of them may be nonprofit organizations that must raise funds and obtain government funding or donations, others are privately funded groups.

## Biggest Isn't Always the Best

Many performers don't want to join a large or prestigious company. Yvonne, a professional dancer for the past nine years, says, "In a large company, you can get lost and won't get to do as much work. In a smaller company, you can perform more and be more innovative."

## How Do I Get Hired? How Do I Learn About Auditions, Tours, and Openings?

Much of the hiring is done through auditions, word of mouth, and being in the right place at the right time. If a dance or theater company is casting for a national tour, they always hold auditions in major cities. Yvonne says, "Dancers are always saying, 'Did you hear about this opening, or that this company is casting.' I obtained one tour because a person I used to dance with heard that a Canadian dance company was looking for someone with classical training who could dance modern and looked American Indian. They called and told me to send in a tape."

Sometimes, you can just contact a company and ask if they're holding auditions. In the dance world, you may be asked to come "take a class." This is a type of audition. It means you'll participate in one of the classes or practices so they can see how you move and take instruction. You may be asked to take only one class or stay for the week.

A video is very important. A résumé only tells of your experience, training, and credentials, but in a visual art, it's important for the director, producers, or choreographers to see how you perform, look, and move. Yvonne says she was hired for Cirque du Soleil exclusively off of her video.

## Where Do I Start?

It varies for each discipline. If you're a performer, you should have a pretty good idea early on that this is what you want to do. This is so you can start your formal training, which is critical in voice and dance. Professional dancers say that you should know by fourteen—while you're still in junior high—that this is the career path you want to take, so you should begin your summer training and classical dance camps. If you want to get into theater or musical theater, you don't need to know as early. Go ahead and have a life.

After artists graduate from high school, they often face several choices. They can attend college or move to New York or LA and begin auditioning. More and more artists are attending college to get a formal education and enhance their skills, not to mention that they may not be emotionally ready to start auditioning full-time.

## Is It Best to Go Straight to New York or Los Angeles?

It depends upon how good and how mentally and emotionally tough you are. Can you handle the competition and rejection? These are the most competitive places, where you will be fighting for jobs with the best of the best. These are also the places with the most opportunities.

## What's It Like?

This is a difficult way of life. You must be strong—physically, mentally, and emotionally. It's an extremely competitive and insensitive life. The cliché of the starving artist or actor/waiter is true in many cases. You will experience a great deal of rejection and there may be periods of time where you don't work, at least as a performer. You have to have a thick skin and be able to handle the rejection and blows to your ego.

Yvonne says, "Directors don't really care if you feel bad. The minute you aren't feeling well, you're compared to the next person who isn't sick or injured, and the next thing you know, they take your place."

Claire, a singer who auditioned for musical theater in New York for a couple of months, says, "I couldn't handle the lifestyle. I needed more structure."

> Yvonne, a classically trained dancer who performed with Cirque du Soleil in Las Vegas, says there was something very hedonistic about working in Vegas. "I performed twice a night. We would get through late in the evening, go party, and then sleep until noon. It wasn't the best lifestyle for a serious dancer. I fell into some bad habits."

## What Will I Do If I Am Not a Performer?

If you aren't a performer you might start out as a volunteer or intern in production, marketing, administration, or sales. As an intern or volunteer you will be asked to do a number of things that may seem beneath you, but this is the best way to get noticed. You will become a jack-of-all-trades and learn all aspects of putting on a production. Some of the things you might be asked to do, or should ask to do, include writing proposals for a fund-raiser or grant, writing press releases and handling publicity, helping to design and build sets, blocking scenes, orchestrating rehearsals, and, of course, cleaning up.

## Will I Be a Starving Artist or Just a Very Skinny One?

Let's just say you'll never be burdened with worrying about your investments. The starting pay can be incredibly low. As Elyse, a theater major who now works in administration for a children's theater, remembers, "When I started I was paid $75.00 a week. After I proved myself, I got a raise to $175.00 a week, but that was after three months. No one goes into the theater to get rich." Salaries vary according to where you live, the company you are with and whether you are a performer, are in production, or are in administration, but generally starting salaries range from free (zip, nada, nothing—suffer for your craft just so you can get your foot in the door) to approximately $15,000 a year.

In major companies, the pay can be good, but you might not perform throughout the entire year. For example, a company like the New York City Ballet might have a full season and pay their performers for the entire year. But others might not perform from November through January. That means you don't get paid. Keep in mind that getting paid "well" for a performer means that it sucks in another profession. Yvonne said that Cirque du Soleil was the highest paying job of her career, and it was only $800 a week. That is still under $30,000 a year.

In addition to low pay, which many say is the worst thing about working in the arts, there is no guarantee that you will get insurance benefits. Unless you are with a larger professional company, you are often considered an independent contractor and are responsible for your own taxes and insurance. However, pros in the field say the intangible benefits such as a creative, relaxed work environment and the opportunity to do something you love make up for the low pay. "I love what I do," was a comment echoed by people on- and backstage.

While there are various performers' unions, health benefits are still rare. They are only found in the major companies.

Of all of the arts, performers say that if you want to make money, you should go into musical theater or become an actor.

## What's the Career Path?

There really isn't one. It is transient and infrequent work that may require you to move between companies, productions, and even cities in order to advance and find work. Pros recommend that you volunteer for a local production to decide if this is the career and lifestyle for you. David, who has been in several traveling musical productions, says, "Not everyone is cut out for this way of life."

The way you advance your career is by developing a body of work and solid reputation. It is not uncommon for people to go back and forth between working as a performer and as a production person. "As long as you are working, it is good," says David.

## What Skills or Education Do I Need?

You're supposed to have talent, but, of course, that is not always the case. (Just watch MTV.) Many people have bachelor's degrees in either theater, music, or dance, but it's often not a requirement. There are also plenty of classes (many outside of college) that you can take to study other aspects of the performing arts, such as costume and set design. Regardless of what side of the curtain you are on, you will constantly be studying, taking classes, and striving to improve your technique.

If you decide to go into the business or administration side of the arts, a liberal arts degree is a great background. You will need to be a good communicator and problem solver. Every day and situation is different so you must be flexible and be able to adapt. You also have to have a little salesperson in you, because you might be called on to raise funds from board members and the community.

## A Successful Career Is a Long Career

Many people burn out, need to make real money, or become injured or too old to be competitive. The length of your career depends upon your discipline and how well you take care of yourself. Actors, musicians, and singers can have longer careers and perform at almost any age. Dancers have a limited shelf life. Yvonne, who just reached thirty, says, "It used to be that if you were thirty, you were at the end of your career. Today, if you're smart and take care of your body, you can last longer."

## What's the Best Thing About Working in the Performing Arts?

You're constantly surrounded by creative, artistic people. Performers say that even though you have directors or choreographers, you really don't have a boss. You're in control of how much better you can become. You also have freedom that other people only dream of. Artistic freedom. Personal freedom. "It's a great life, when it works," says David, an actor in Chicago.

## Where Can I Learn More?

The Theater Communications Group, based in New York City, publishes a newsletter called *Artsearch*. In it you will find nationwide job openings in the performing arts.

## Where on the Web?

www.theatrejobs.com—Theatre Jobs

# 37

• • • • • • • • • • • • • • • • • • • • • • • • • • • •

# Photojournalism

**Some Common Positions**
Photographer
Photojournalist
Cameraman/camerawoman
Director of photography

**Other Opportunties You Might Consider**
A number of varied organizations hire photographers on staff or as freelancers. As a photojournalist, your best staff opportunities outside of a newspaper or a television newsroom are with a magazine. Although photojournalists may frequently freelance for other types of work, they tend to specialize in journalism.

If you want to explore opportunities other than journalism, you should consider working as a studio, portrait, commercial, or artistic photographer. This may involve taking pictures for portraits, weddings, bar mitzvahs and the like. It may also mean that you shoot products for an advertising agency or corporate brochure.

Do you like photography? Do you enjoy news and journalism? Are you a little bit of an adrenaline junkie? If so, this might be the right job for you? We all pick up a newspaper to read the words, but in many cases, what speaks to us the most are the pictures: the images that tell the story in a different and often more compelling way than the words on the page. If you have ever been moved by a picture in a magazine, newspaper, or even images on the television news, then you have experienced the work of a good photojournalist.

Any dork with a Kodak can take pictures of an event, but photojournalists don't see themselves as technicians merely operating a camera. They see themselves as storytellers who communicate the joy, sadness, and emotion often found in news, human interests, sports, entertainment, and disasters. The story that a photojournalist communicates is just as important and requires as much skill as the person with the byline.

# What Are Some of the Best and Worst Things About Being a Photojournalist/Shooter?

Pros say it's like having a backstage pass to many different events. "You get to see many different ways of life, from the famous and wealthy to the poorest of the poor. You see little glimpses of it all," says Kerri of the *Arizona Republic*. "You learn a little bit about lots of things. That's what I like the most."

# What's the Toughest Thing About Being a Photojournalist?

Sometimes you get put in difficult situations where you're not always welcome. People already have ideas about the media being biased, slanted, or liberal. Others just don't want to be in the newspaper. As a journalist you're obligated to cover what's going on, good or bad.

You also see a lot of sadness, pain, and tragedy to which you wouldn't normally be exposed.

# Do I Need to Study Photography or Get a Certain Degree?

Many photographers train specifically to become photojournalists. Often they study journalism in school with an emphasis on photography. School will teach you a lot of the "how to's": how to work a camera; how to make a print; how to handle lighting, contrast, and color. But the best training a photojournalist can get is just being out there. Nothing beats actual experience.

# What Makes a Good Photojournalist?

Your pictures are important, but how you deal with people counts more than people realize. You have to relate to people on a very personal level. You must learn to be sensitive and make your subjects feel comfortable. Communication skills and the ability to get along with people are two things seldom taught in classes. They are critical to becoming a good photojournalist.

## What's the Difference Between a Photographer and a Photojournalist?

While both types of photographers may deal with people, photojournalists are often dealing with a highly charged human element and constantly changing conditions that few studio or commercial photographers encounter.

One shooter told me, "People who do art photography or studio photography won't touch photojournalism, because they don't like dealing with people."

Another newspaper photographer said studio photographers would rather be in a room where they're in full control of the lights. "They're working with inanimate objects, like a product for an advertisement, because they don't want to have to be out in the field where every day your subject matter is different." Why didn't he come right out and call them recluses?

Photojournalists have to be able to work well in high-pressure situations. Every day and every situation is completely different. Your light is never the same and your subject is never the same. Every day you're solving a whole new set of problems.

> You never know what you'll be covering. Kim of the *Dallas Morning News* was on her way to cover a high school athletic event when she was paged and told to immediately go to an accident scene where a television tower had collapsed. Other than the rescue crews, she was the next person on the scene. She witnessed the destruction first-hand, including seeing the three dead men. Her shot was on the front page the next day.

## What's It Like?

It's a very stressful, high-pressure job. There are always deadlines to meet. Sometimes you might only have three minutes, where a different kind of photographer might have three weeks to work on one shot. You have to go into a place, get a good picture as quickly as possible, and run back with it.

## How Much Can I Make?

The salaries are not high. Your standard photographer at a medium-sized city paper averages in the mid-twenties. If you're starting out or are located in a smaller market, it would be much less. It depends on your experience, seniority, reputation, and, most of all, the type of paper you work for. Salaries vary from market to market. Naturally, the larger papers in the country pay the highest, but they're also the toughest to get into. Some established photojournalists at major papers make over $50,000.

## Do Photojournalists Often Take Freelance Jobs?

Certainly. Many photojournalists freelance on the side to supplement their incomes. Photojournalist do all types of freelance work for magazines, companies, and individuals. Photojournalists don't normally work much with advertising agencies, because advertising agencies usually have big budgets and tend to go with more established commercial photographers. An advertising photographer will usually have a day rate of around $1,000. Companies that hire freelance photojournalists either have a low budget (photojournalists will usually work for less money than commercial photographers) or are looking for a journalistic style.

## What Will I Do? What's a Typical Day Like?

You'll generally have an eight-hour shift with your assignments laid out for you ahead of time. In a newspaper setting, up to 90 percent of your stories are planned in advance. But you always have to be on your toes, because assignments might pop up. When that happens, you may be diverted from an assignment to cover breaking news or a more important topic.

## How Stable Is It?

Most photojournalists are constantly working up to a better position. People who've reached a certain level, such as working at a major paper, seem happy and tend to stay put. However, shooters are always looking for their ideal job. In many cases, it means relocation to a larger market.

## What Sets One Shooter Apart from Another? Is It Your Attitude or Your Work?

Both. The quality of your photography and your skill as a shooter is important, but as the director of photography at the *Dallas Morning News* says, "It's not the hottest shooter that we want to hire, it's the person who's going to get along with staff and the person who's going to professionally represent the paper."

If you're on an assignment and have a bad attitude, you'll quickly get a reputation and no one will want to hire you. This may mean acting like everyone's got to get out of your way, not being sensitive in delicate situations like memorial services or accident scenes, or only being concerned with getting the shot. Being a respectful and caring human being is as important as being a hot shooter. But of course, the quality of your photography is the first thing people are going to notice.

## How Do I Get Hired?

Getting a foot in the door is critical. An internship is the best way to do this. Regardless of whether you're applying for an internship or a full-time job, you need to have a portfolio with slides. This portfolio should include samples of your work, such as portraits, features, or news. It doesn't even have to be published work, just make sure it's your best work.

"A lot of times our best stuff doesn't get published," says Kyle of the *Charlotte Observer.* "You can take a really great photo and there may not be room in the paper that day. Or a bigger story may take priority." Don't worry too much about it, though. You can still put it in your portfolio. Portfolios are starting to change due to electronic and digital photography. You're beginning to see more portfolios on disks.

Once you have your slide portfolio and résumé, begin to contact newspapers. The director of photography is a great place to start. Like most media positions, you stand a better chance in a smaller market. You may also have to intern or work part-time for a while to prove yourself. "I worked part-time and freelanced for a year until a full-time position became available. Since they were already familiar with my work, it made it that much easier for me to get the job," says Kim.

## Where on the Web?

www.poynter.org—Poynter Institute for Media Studies
(The Poynter Institute is one of the premier training grounds for all types of journalism. They also offer educational programs.)
www.mediainfo.com—*Editor & Publisher*
(*E&P* is the trade journal for all newspaper journalists. It has news, current events, and job openings. The print version is great, but the Web site will blow you away. This is the future of newspapers.)

# 38

$$\cdot\ \cdot\ \cdot\ \cdot\ \cdot\ \cdot\ \cdot\ \cdot\ \cdot\ \cdot\ \cdot\ \cdot\ \cdot\ \cdot\ \cdot\ \cdot\ \cdot\ \cdot\ \cdot\ \cdot\ \cdot\ \cdot$$

# Professional Speaking

**Some Common Positions**
> Keynote speaker
> Lecturer
> Motivational speaker
> Seminar leader
> Trainer
> Facilitator
> Late-night infomercial pitchman

**Other Opportunities You Might Consider**
The speaking business is closely related to training and development, which is often found in corporate HR departments. Companies hire people on a contract basis or keep them on staff to train employees in various subjects. Meeting and special-event planning is also closely related to speaking, in that meeting planners often utilize speakers and presenters in their conferences and events. Many speakers also work as consultants in their specialty area.

Let's just get this straight. There are many different types of speakers. Just because someone is a professional speaker doesn't mean they're a "motivational" speaker. When I think of motivational speakers, I think of Tony Robbins and his plastic hair jumping up and down, walking on fire, and invading my TV like some sort of late-night poltergeist. Or Zig Ziglar preaching motivation and positive thinking as if it were old-time religion. This is one type of professional speaker.

## What Kind of Speakers Are There?

There are humorous speakers, business speakers, keynote speakers, after-dinner speakers, and celebrity speakers, as well as seminar leaders, trainers, and facilitators. All are speaking and presenting, but each is very different in content, delivery, and how they're used by clients.

## Who Do They Work For?

Most speakers work for themselves. They're individuals who have special knowledge obtained in a field or through some experience. They may have an assistant or small staff assisting them with booking events and managing their office. The staff may also help conduct research.

Trainers and seminar leaders often work for a company in the human resources or training department. They're creating programs constantly on a variety of subjects or hiring speakers and experts to present to their employees.

## Who Hires Speakers?

You name it: companies, organizations, colleges, schools, and conventions. There are as many markets for speakers as there are types of speakers. The main markets are associations that hire speakers to present at conventions and corporations that bring speakers in for meetings and events.

## How Do I Get Booked?

Praying helps. Besides that, most speakers are booked a) by their own marketing efforts (telemarketing, direct mail, etc.) to a particular target audience, b) by reputation, or c) by bureaus, agents, and meeting planners.

## What Training or Skills Do I Need?

There's no specific training, education, or certification needed, although most serious speaking professionals belong to the National Speakers Association (NSA), which bestows its own titles and certifications. An NSA membership is pricey, running several hundred dollars annually. This alone weeds out the beginners from those who are making a living at it. The most important skill is to be "interesting and good." In many ways, you are selling sizzle as much as steak. People want to be entertained. They want to laugh. They don't want to sit through a lecture or be talked at or down to.

## How Much Can I Make?

It depends on your reputation, what market you are in, how good you are, how interesting your topic is, and how hard you work. You can make

According to the National Speakers Association, only 10 percent of professional speakers charge over $10,000. More than half charge between $2,000 and $10,000, and 20 percent charge under $500.

The problem with many speakers is that they aren't experts in their field, don't have a compelling topic, or are covering an area that everyone on the planet already addresses.

Reengineering and teamwork are a couple of such topics. You can't walk into a room without bumping into a speaker that bills himself as an "expert in change management."

**Top 10 Most-Requested Speaker Topics**

1. Change
2. Customer service
3. Global opportunities
4. Future strategies
5. Quality
6. New technologies
7. Productivity
8. Diversity
9. Legal issues
10. Health/fitness

(Courtesy of the National Speakers Association)

anywhere from less than $10,000 to several hundred thousand dollars. If you're good, making over $100,000 is not difficult. It's hard work, but it's not difficult.

Many speakers have an established fee that may be per presentation or per day and can range from a few hundred dollars (if you are a beginner) up to $10,000 a day. Many celebrity speakers like Colin Powell get $40,000 plus to speak for an hour. In addition to your fee, the client pays for your travel expenses, though sometimes it's worked into your fee.

## What About Benefits and Insurance?

You're on your own. As a self-employed person, you're responsible for everything—taxes, insurance, etc.

## What's the Biggest Mistake Rookies Make?

The biggest mistake is to quit your full-time job too early. You should decide to make this a career only when your speaking income starts to consistently become more than your salary.

The other mistake rookies make is to not pick a subject and become an expert on it. You can tell a rookie speaker—or just a bad speaker—by asking what they speak about. If they say, "I speak about anything," you have a rookie. There's no way you can effectively speak on every topic under the sun. People pay you for your knowledge and expertise. Don't fake it.

## Be Yourself

Pick a topic you believe in and are knowledgeable about. Don't fall for the latest trend. The worst type of speaker is someone you don't understand. For God's sake, speak English, not buzz-speak. For example, I've run across speakers who, when asked what they do, reply, "I'm a change agent. I help people reach their peak potential and discover their true calling." Sounds great Yoda, but what the hell does that mean?

## How Do I Get Started?

Like the Nike slogan says, "Just do it." Start speaking for free any chance you get. Get up in front of people and do your thing. Rarely does someone start out in this business with the intent of being a speaker. Those who do generally fall on their asses. The majority of speakers come into it from other fields. They acquire special knowledge or experience somewhere else, and at some point, they were asked to share that knowledge. When you begin to develop a reputation or get more requests than you can handle, you may begin asking a fee.

When you begin to consistently speak for a fee, you should develop good promotional and marketing materials and a demo video of yourself in action. These should be quality materials, not running a brochure off on your laser printer.

> I began speaking when I was asked to address a class of business students at the University of Oklahoma. It was well received, and they asked me back the next semester. I was working full-time and was flattered that I was asked, so I did it for free. Some of the faculty started telling other people about me, and I was then asked to speak at other schools. After several months, I had developed a reputation. Someone then asked me to speak at their function and asked, 'What's your fee?' 'Fee? What fee?' I said a number and they said okay without flinching. That was the start of things. It got to the point where I was being asked so much I was taking vacation time to speak around the country.

## What Are Speakers Bureaus?

They're organizations that find speakers for companies, events, and organizations. Some bureaus represent speakers exclusively, although the majority handle a large variety of speakers and will try to find the best speaker for their client, regardless of whether or not they represent the speaker.

When a bureau books a speaker for an event, it makes all arrangements and handles all the billing. In exchange, the bureau usually takes a commission/finder's fee, which is often equal to 20 to 30 percent of the speaker's usual fee.

Bureaus can be great, but the problem is they won't touch you unless you have a very marketable topic, excellent promotional materials, and a proven reputation.

## What Are Some Misconceptions About Speaking?

That it's easy money. You might get paid thousands of dollars a day, but you don't work every day. When you aren't speaking, you are researching, writing, marketing, or traveling. It might seem that I work for an hour or two when I'm speaking, but there are hours and hours of prep work before a presentation, not to mention the effort in marketing, scheduling, and follow-up.

Another misconception is that it's all glamour and excitement. About half of it is. Let me tell you how glamorous it is to sit in a Holiday Inn in the frozen tundra of Cedar Falls, Iowa, during the middle of January.

## How Can I Stand Out?

Being there for every audience, large and small. There are too many prima donnas in this business. It takes the same amount of time to be nice to someone as it takes to be a jerk. The idea is to be asked back.

## What Are Some Pros and Cons?

When you work, the money is great. When an audience clicks, it's great. It's also a wonderful feeling when someone who has heard you or benefited from something you have said lets you know how you have made a difference in their life.

On the downside, there's a lot of travel. You are often away from your family and friends. It's not the sort of travel where you can actually see the city. You might arrive in the morning, have meetings with your hosts in the afternoon, eat dinner, and then speak at night. You don't always go to the best places in the world, either. Yeah, Tony Robbins does his thing from the beautiful island of Fiji, but others spend their winter months trekking in the snow of Wisconsin.

## Where Can I Learn More?

*Speak & Grow Rich,* by Dottie Walters. She is the goddess of professional speaking. She owns Walters International Speakers Bureau in Glendora, California. She knows her stuff, and her book is the Bible for beginning speakers.

National Speakers Association
1500 S. Priest Drive
Tempe, AZ 85281
602-968-2552

(It's expensive to join, and it's a good thing. The cost alone weeds out wannabes or people who speak once a year to a bunch of drunken Rotarians. If you're serious about it as a career, join. You have everything from big-name authors and not so big-name authors [like me] to executives and consultants.)

Toastmasters International
P.O. Box 9052
Mission Viejo, CA 92690
714–858-8255

(It's not a breakfast club. If you are just starting to speak or need practice, join Toastmasters. There are weekly meetings in almost every city. Be warned: They can be extremely dorky, but it's a great practice for learning to present on an extemporaneous subject.)

## What The Pros Read

*Sharing Ideas*
*Professional Speaker*
Anything related to their field of expertise, along with newspapers, magazines, and trade journals. Good speakers read at least one book a week. Speakers have to be on top of their field.

## Where on the Web?

www.mpiweb.org—Meeting Planners International
www.nsaspeaker.com—National Speaker's Association
www.astd.org—American Society for Training and Development (ASTD)
www.toastmasters.org—Toastmasters International

# 39

Professional Student: Pursuit
of a Graduate Degree

People go back to school for any number of reasons. Some go to increase
their marketability and salary, while others are bored in their current jobs,
but don't know what their next career move should be. You can never
have too much education. Having an extra degree and the knowledge that
comes from earning it is definitely a good thing. However, regardless of
whether you are deciding between an MBA program, law school, a master's in education, or a graduate degree in any field, you should first ask
yourself some basic questions.

- Why am I going back to school? Do I need the degree? Am I bored?
  Am I escaping the job market? Am I hoping to make myself more marketable with a degree?
- Does my profession require that I have a graduate degree?
- Will having a degree make a significant difference in my salary?
- Am I going for knowledge, certification, prestige and respect within
  my field, or to increase my earning power?
- If I have to take out student loans to obtain my degree, will my
  increase in salary make up for the amount of debt I'm incurring?

These are all very difficult questions that can only be answered by you.
You know your ultimate career goals and motivations. I don't want to discourage anyone from going to graduate school. I just think you should go
for the right reasons and get the most for your money and time invested.

Being JobSmart means planning each step of your career carefully and with purpose. Too many graduate programs are full of students, career changers, and aimless moochers who look to graduate school as if they are crawling back to the womb, a safe place where things are good and no one can harm them. Graduate or law school can seem like a refuge from the cruel realities of the job market, where someone can wait peacefully until lightning strikes and their divine career path is laid out before them. Okay, maybe a little melodramatic, but you get my point. Have a reason for going. Otherwise, you are flushing money down the toilet.

## Is a Graduate Degree Worth the Money?

Only you can answer that. It depends on your goals and the industry you're in. What's more valued in your industry: education or experience? Of course, there are certain fields like psychology where a master's is the minimum requirement and doctorates are common. In some professions, an MBA is required, while in others, it's nice to have but not a necessity. Some professions just don't care if you have a graduate degree.

Will the payoff be worth the investment? According to *Business Week*'s annual ranking of the top MBA programs, the average starting salary for grads of top-tier schools is $67,067. Not bad coin just starting out, but notice that this was for the top graduates at the top schools. There are some MBA graduates who make only $5,000 more than they made before they went to graduate school.

### What Can I Do with an MBA?

The career choice for most MBAs is consulting, followed by marketing and investment banking. Hot on their heels is entrepreneurship. Randy, a second year MBA at SMU's Cox School of Business, says, "I'm getting my MBA so I can reduce my learning curve when I start my own business."

## Should I Go to Grad School Right After Graduation or Should I Work for a While?

I recommend that you work for a while, or at least take a break. The main reason is that you have likely been going to school for at least sixteen years in a row. You need a break.

You might think, "Why not just march right on and finish?" That's a good argument, except that grad school is often very different from being an undergraduate. It can be more intense, more like a real job. Allen, an MBA candidate at Vanderbilt, says, "If you worked between undergrad and graduate school, you're less likely to get burned out with school and will approach your graduate school in a more business-like manner."

The other reason you work for a while before returning to graduate school is that you will simply perform better if you have work experience and a frame of reference. MBA programs are a great example. Many MBA programs won't accept a candidate unless he or she has worked for at least two years. This is so you can have something intelligent to add to the class discussion. MBA programs often work in teams and groups, just like in many companies. If you are in the middle of a group discussion and someone says, "When I was at Andersen, we did this," and another person says, "Yeah, at my company we had a situation like that, too. Here is what we did," you can't add, "Well, I was in campus activities, and we once had a situation where . . ." Forget it. Many MBA programs use case studies to discuss and solve real business problems. How can you intelligently contribute if you haven't been through anything. Work first, then go back if it's necessary.

## Does Your Degree Make You Too Expensive to Hire?

In fields like engineering and the sciences, undergraduates are finding themselves in demand, while engineers with master's and doctorates are finding themselves unemployed or dramatically overqualified for what they are doing. According to the National Science Foundation, there is an oversupply of Ph.D.s in electrical engineering by 41 percent, civil engineering by 33 percent, and math by 32 percent.

"There are only so many teaching and research positions, and many companies can hire candidates with bachelor's degrees much cheaper and bring them up to speed," says Jason, a Ph.D. candidate at the University of Nebraska. "Besides, engineering and technical fields are changing so quickly that the only way to keep up is to be in the field doing it every day."

## Should I Work While in Grad School?

Absolutely. It will not only help you gain experience and keep up or even improve your skills, it is critical to your finding a job after graduating. In law and increasingly in business, internships are used as a test drive for both candidates and companies. Do anything, even if it's teaching as a graduate assistant. Work experience counts at all levels. Classroom knowledge is useless unless you can put it into practice.

## Does It Matter Where I Go to School?

It depends on your profession and degree. If you are simply going for the education, the name of your school doesn't matter and won't influence whether or not you get hired after graduation. If you're going to enhance your promotability based upon the reputation of your school, you should really go to a top-ten school or don't bother going. Don't get me wrong, there are many fine programs that will never make the *Business Week* or *U.S. News & World Report* rankings that offer a fantastic education. But I'm saying that if you're choosing an MBA or any other graduate program in hopes that the school name will impress people enough to hire you, it should be a top-ten school. If someone graduates from Wharton, Harvard, or Northwestern business school, you say, "Wow." Outside of the top ten, there are no "wow" schools, just ones that give you a good education.

## Can You Afford to Go Back to School?

I don't mean do you have enough money in the bank or do you can qualify for financial aid. I mean is the cost of obtaining the education more than the education is worth after graduation. According to the College Board, 1996 was the third straight year that tuition rose 6 percent. This is more than the average rise in income. As a result, students have to borrow more. Student borrowing is up an average of 17 percent annually since 1990.

You should also consider your opportunity costs. For example, if you are earning $40,000 a year and decide to quit your job to pursue a graduate degree, you will automatically be down $80,000 in lost income over those two years, plus your tuition and living expenses during that period. If your salary after graduation isn't significantly higher than the $40,000 you were making before your degree, it might not be a smart move for you to go back to school.

Brent decided to attend a prestigious private law school. He had to take out student loans close to $100,000. Yet after graduation, he decided that he didn't want to go the large private-firm route, which is where the big money is. Instead, he took a government job. His law school loans will be paid off when Brent is fifty-two.

## Where Can I Learn More?

*Business Week* Annual Ranking of Top Business Schools
*U.S. News & World Report* Annual Ranking of Graduate Programs

## Where on the Web?

www.princetonreview.com
www.kaplan.com
www.petersons.com
www.businessweek.com

# 40

· · · · · · · · · · · · · · · · · · · · · · · · ·

# Public Relations and Communications

**Some Common Positions**
> Account executive
> Publicist
> Public affairs director
> Media relations/media affairs representative
> Press agent
> Speechwriter
> Image consultant
> Communications consultant
> Communications director

**Other Opportunities You Might Consider**
Public relations and communications positions are closely related to advertising, marketing, special-events and meeting planning, and the media. Communications positions can be found in virtually any industry, organization, nonprofit, or the government. It encompasses anything dealing with a public image, message, or communication of an individual, company, association, event, or product.

Have you ever wondered how newspapers and television programs get ideas for stories? Sometimes, it's just great reporting, but other times, it's because an idea was pitched to a publication or program. It could be a press release or a phone call, anything to nudge the media and say, "Hey, this is newsworthy. You might want to cover this." You might think people would want to volunteer this information out of the kindness of their hearts, but their enthusiasm is more likely related to the size of their client's check. Publicists and PR agencies are paid to create news about a client.

# How Does Public Relations Differ from Advertising?

In public relations, you're trying to convince news and media sources that your story is newsworthy and deserves to be written about rather than buying space or time to present your commercial or ad. One of the main responsibilities of PR professionals is to get a client's point or message across to the media and the public.

Public relations experts issue press releases, set up press conferences and media opportunities, and handle the media during a crisis. Another big part of the job is developing solid media contacts. Good relationships with the media help to ensure that your client receives favorable coverage. Often you will issue a press release or pitch a reporter on your client's announcement, and the reporter will determine if it is newsworthy or if he wants to include the information in another piece he is working on.

## What Can I Do?

The main opportunities in public relations are with an private or government agency, freelancing, or in-house staff for a company or organization. Almost any organization that deals with the public utilizes public relations and communications experts to some extent.

## Where Do I Start?

The most common, and some feel best, place to start is at an agency. It is not uncommon for someone to gain contacts in the industry and then go to work in-house for a company. The typical starting position is that of a low-level (junior or assistant) account executive. Some people try to start their career in-house, but it is much more difficult to find entry-level positions with a company than with an agency. Most companies require that you have experience in their industry or at least experience dealing *with* their industry. "As recent as last year, you did not need a high-tech background to work in this department. Today, a high-tech background is required," says Shannon Bounds, senior public relations specialist for US Robotics.

In-house PR and communications falls under several categories: corporate communications, community relations, investor relations, government affairs, and public affairs and crisis management, to name a few. Each group handles a different specialty. For example, media relations staff is responsible for responding to questions from the media. Investor relations help prepare annual reports, financial reporting, and is responsible for any communication involving investors. Community relations handles any type of goodwill campaign or sponsorship in the community.

## Are All Agencies Alike?

No, the larger agencies represent a variety of clients and can perform most of the activities mentioned above. Many small agencies tend to specialize. The most common specialization is by industry. There are firms that only deal with healthcare companies or high-tech companies, etc. Other firms are known for the type of communication they specialize in, such as crisis communication.

## Will I Have Any Responsibility?

It depends on the agency. In some agencies, you will be given very limited client contact. Kristen, an account executive for a small New York firm specializing in healthcare, says junior executives at her agency are not even allowed to address a client for fear of giving wrong information. (Seems like her boss might need a little decaf.) "There are definitely some major league egos in this business," she says. But all shops aren't like this.

In many professions, if you want experience early on, you go to work for a small shop and then move to a larger one. This is not always the case in PR. If you can get in with a large firm, you're likely to get some real experience early on. "There's so much turnover, you can get a shot at some real work pretty quickly," says Jana, a former Hill & Knowlton AE. The tough part is getting in with a big firm.

## How Do I Get Hired?

This is an incredibly competitive industry at the entry level, since people are disillusioned and don't understand what the job is about. Simply sending in your résumé won't cut it. You need to have clips, samples of your previous work, and an understanding of the industry. A lot of hiring is done by word of mouth and contacts within the industry.

Kelly began her career as a temp in the communications department at American Express in Miami. It turned into a full-time position. There, she helped determine what events American Express would sponsor in the area and helped coordinate and publicize AMEX's participation in those events. Kelly did a lot of work with the Ft. Lauderdale Museum of Art, and as a result, when the museum needed a new communications director, they offered Kelly the position.

## How Can I Stand Out?

Be a good writer. Be persistent and have a knowledge of the agency's clients or industry. In the interview, show that you are comfortable with people, enthusiastic, and a good communicator.

## Who Are the Top Firms?

Among the largest public relations agencies are Hill & Knowlton; Burson-Marsteller; Daniel J. Edelman; Fleishman Hillard; Manning, Selvage & Lee; and Ruder Finn Rotman. The top firms are in New York, Chicago, Washington, D.C., and Los Angeles, but there are agencies large and small all over the country.

## What Will I Do?

Contact with major clients is usually left to executives with more tenure and experience. Janice, who has spent time on both the agency side and in-house as a communications specialist for a Big Six accounting firm, says, "In the beginning, you will do a lot of gopher and grunt work like making press packets, updating media lists, making follow-up phone calls, and writing press releases. Later, as you get some experience under your belt, you will begin to deal with the press, write speeches, plan events, and learn how to present your client's story." Your day-to-day activities might include planning a trade show, writing and running press releases, and calling journalists to see if they are interested in your client.

You might help publicize and promote an event internally, such as a wellness program or safety campaign within your company. Your company might do the same thing in the community. Your responsibility will be to organize the event, alert the media, and make sure it goes off without a hitch.

There are also a lot of numbers and reporting involved. "The hardest part of what I do is justify my work to the client," says Geena, a former Burson-Marsteller account executive who now has her own firm in Pittsburgh. "The client wants to know, 'What am I getting for my money.' If I get a placement for my client, I have to find out the reach to let him know how many people were exposed to the message."

## What's the Career Path?

Some people develop an interest in certain industries and want to capitalize on the relationships and contacts they have made, so they start their

---

### Open Access

Beth Shilling is public relations director for Beauticontrol Cosmetics. She works side by side with the CEO to help create the company's message and image. Beth sits in a powerful position. If you want to interview the CEO for a story, you go through Beth. Beth has worked to set up magazine articles, television appearances, even a book deal for the CEO. She also frequently deals with fashion magazines pitching stories attempting to promote Beauticontrol's line.

• • •

Have you ever watched *Entertainment Tonight*? If so, you know that they show clips and reports from the sets of movies currently being filmed. This is often months before the film is even completed. Why? To create hype, buzz, and awareness around the movie or its stars. There are publicists for studios, production companies, and even the stars themselves who might put together a package for *ET* or invite one of the entertainment shows to cover it.

Shannon Bounds started editing newsletters and publications for an Arizona-based company that provided reports, magazines, and books to the high-tech industry. She became familiar with the media and the technology and was able to turn that into a position as one of the public relations directors at US Robotics, the fastest-growing modem manufacturer in the world.

own firms. If this is what you want to do, it's best to have some clients in hand to help cover your bills before cutting the cord with an agency. Another option is to move in-house with a company in an industry you're familiar with.

## How Is Working In-House Different from an Agency?

In an agency, you're being pulled in many different directions. You may be working on several different accounts or several divisions of the same account. For example, at Edelman Public Relations, which represents AT&T, they handle several divisions, products, and promotions. "It can be confusing mixing several messages for the same client," says one former staffer.

Agencies have revolving doors. People don't stay in a big agency for long, says Jana, a former Hill & Knowlton staffer. "I got their experience, which was great. I put it on my résumé and I was gone." Geena says, "People leave all of a sudden or are pulled off of projects. You get thrown into a project you know nothing about."

In-house is a little slower and gives you a chance to focus, says Shannon of US Robotics. "Even when you're not concentrating on one product, you're concentrating on one message—the company message—and you can supplement that with other product messages. I think it's a lot easier and more focused. You can really dedicate your time to one client and become an expert on the products that you're focusing on rather than being spread so thin on different clients and different products."

## What Skills Do I Need?

Many people graduate with a degree in public relations and think they are armed and ready. Actually, a journalism or English degree might be more valuable. You have to be a strong writer and know how journalists think, since your job is essentially pitching stories to them or persuading them to be kind to your client. Regardless of your academic background, the primary skill you need is to be a good verbal and written communicator. "Graduates don't realize the amount of writing that is involved," says Jana, who left Hill & Knowlton to work for the communications department of a record company.

You must also be energetic, a fabulous networker, and creative. Other things that will add to your success is an understanding of the media and journalism and general business with an emphasis on marketing. Much of the aim of public relations and communications is to create awareness of and "sell" the person, product, event, or cause you represent.

More and more, public relations is becoming but one part of an integrated communications message. This means that you will be working closely with experts in marketing, advertising, and public relations. You must be a team player.

Experience, more than your degree, will make you stand out from the crowd. Most people gain experience through internships or by writing for a newspaper or magazine while in school. It is important that you save any work you have published. These clips will play a valuable part in your portfolio, which most employers will want to see.

> "You have to be a good listener as well as a good writer," says Shannon of US Robotics. You'll have to learn the vocabulary of your client's industry. "I must also do a lot of technical writing, because we make modems. Technical writing is not easy, because you need to approach an engineer, programmer, or technical-support person and interview them about this technology that you don't understand and then put it into terms a journalist will understand."

## Crisis Communications

Another form of communications that experts frequently have to deal with is crisis communications. This means that you rapidly develop a strategy to address a disaster or potentially damaging situation. An example of this would be the TWA or ValuJet crashes. Each airline had a spokesperson to address the media and provide them with information. In cases where a CEO or individual is to address the media, it's the PR person or communications director who will coach an executive on how to best handle the situation.

## In Need of Crisis Communications

An example of bad crisis communications is when Dallas Cowboy Michael Irvin was told it was a good idea to wear a full-length mink coat to his felony drug trial.

## What Are Some Misconceptions About PR?

Some people think PR is schmoozing, going to parties, and talking on the phone. Well, one out of three isn't bad. Sure you will schmooze a little bit and go to some parties, but get ready to talk on the phone more than you could ever imagine. At times, much of your day will be spent pitching stories to the media.

Another thing many people overlook is the amount of writing involved. "Good writing will set you apart from everyone else," says

Kerry, a former Hill & Knowlton AE. "So many people want to enter this profession thinking, 'I want to do special events,' and that's really only one small piece."

Shannon says, "I see some people who come into high-tech public relations thinking they can get by without knowing the technology. It's not true. Maybe five years ago, but now you have to understand the technology. Journalists and the public are too savvy. You have to understand what it is that you're publicizing." You're often the point person or spokesperson for the media. You're the contact when someone wants information about your company, client, or product, and you have to know these things so you can speak intelligently about them.

## How Much Will I Make?

This is one of the lowest paying professions at the entry level. Regardless of location, you can expect to make between $15,000 and $20,000. At least your insurance benefits are taken care of in most cases. Public relations is one of those professions where your perks and fringe benefits, such as meeting cool people and going to great events, make up for your anemic salary. It is not unlike television in that people think you make more than you really do.

Traditionally, the pay is better in corporate positions than in an agency, and agencies pay much better than the government or nonprofits. Top account executives in government or nonprofits with at least five years experience can make between $30,000 and $50,000, depending on location. Top executives in an agency or a corporation can make six figures.

## What's It Like?

It's a professional environment, but the hours are long, the work is hard, and you will experience rejection. Jana says, "Sometimes you get it from both sides. You get beaten up by the client and the reporters."

## Is It Stable?

Not in an agency environment. People job-hop to make more money and get more experience. Like an ad agency, if a budget is cut or a client moves, you can begin to look for work.

## What Are Pros and Cons?

On the positive side, the challenge and getting to see work or a project you were involved with succeed is very gratifying.

The pay and the long hours have to top the list of negatives. Jana says, "In many ways, it's a sales job. You're selling someone on your client. Some people like that element of it, but I don't."

## Where Can I Learn More?

PRSA—Public Relations Society of America
33 Irving Place
New York, NY 10003
212-995-2230

(They also have a student chapters around the country. The PRSA is one of the best student professional groups around. Contact the headquarters to see if there's a chapter near you.)

"Why the hell should I make someone else rich?" is what Tom Landers thought. "So many people get caught up in the lure of a big-name agency, they don't realize they are grunt labor while the client is paying big bucks and some partner is getting fat and rich." As an account executive with a major agency in the South, Tom was working with some prestigious clients. Although he was entry-level, the agency was charging the client $120 an hour for Tom's time. "When you calculate my hours, I am only getting about $20 of that. I made $20,000 my first year on the job," Tom said. According to Tom, "It's common for large agencies to obtain clients based on their reputation and name and then send in entry-level employees, yet charge the client a high rate." After two years of this, Tom decided he had had enough. He left and started his own firm, approaching some of his former clients. He had big agency experience and was doing the same work, but charging considerably less than the big agencies. His first year after leaving, he made over $100,000.

## What The Pros Read

*O'Dwyers Newsletter*

## Where on the Web?

www.prsa.org—Public Relations Society of America
www.hillandknowlton.com—Hill & Knowlton
www.edelman.com—Edelman
www.bm.com—Burson-Marsteller

# 41

• • • • • • • • • • • • • • • • • • • • • • • • • •

# Publishing

**Some Common Positions**
   Editor
   Agent
   Publicist
   Editorial assistant
   Copy editor
   Graphic artist and designer

**Other Opportunities You Might Consider**
There are opportunities in publishing for salespeople, attorneys, artists, public relations specialists, agents, and freelancers. You should also check out the "Journalism" chapter, which is a related form of publishing.

A career in publishing typically means working for a book publisher, newspaper, or magazine. (This section will focus on book and magazine publishing.) The job possibilities are endless, because it takes so many people to produce a magazine or book. You can be a writer, an editor, a researcher or fact checker, or an artist or designer. Publishing houses and magazines also have departments devoted to sales, publicity, legal issues, art, and more. You can be on the other side of the publishing arena by becoming an agent.

## Where Do I Start?

When people think of publishing, they think of editors. It is probably the most common position in publishing. However, before you reach editor status, you will most likely start out as an editorial assistant. Don't think because you have a degree (or more) that you are above being an assistant. Everyone pays their dues in publishing and starts at the bottom, regardless of how bright they are. Publishing is considered an apprenticeship industry. There are some very talented young editors in both books and magazines, but they have accumulated great experience early in their careers. This is a business with a lot of tedious dues paying. Editors recommend that you only choose this career if you can't imagine life without working in publishing. It is so tough in the beginning that you have to be completely devoted to it.

You can rest easy in the fact that almost everyone starts out this way. In publishing, it's rare for people to have secretaries. They have assistants instead. Typically, you will start as an assistant or editorial assistant to an editor or group of editors. You can rest easy in the fact that most everyone starts out this way.

The duties of an assistant include answering phones, proofreading, making copies, writing letters, and any other secretarial type of task. Your tenure as an assistant should be used to learn by osmosis. Try to pick up everything that your boss does and learn as much as you can.

Advancement in book publishing is painfully slow. You can expect to be an assistant for at least two years. Use that time to make contacts in-house and in the industry. Have your boss be a cheerleader for you to other people in the company to help you advance. If after a couple of years you can tell that your boss can't or won't help you become promoted, you should start looking for another job.

In magazine publishing, the low man on the totem pole is often the fact checker or researcher. You will make numerous phone calls, learn how to locate people and information, and double-check facts and stories. While it may seem like grunt work, it can be a valuable position and teach you a great deal.

## What Will I Do?

Eventually, you will advance to some form of editor. There are several levels of editors, each indicating seniority. Some common examples in magazine publishing are copy editor, assistant editor, associate editor, managing editor, and senior editor. In book publishing, the typical track is editorial assistant, assistant editor, associate editor, editor, senior editor, and executive editor.

As an editor, you will work closely with authors, writers or freelancers, and agents. You will review manuscripts, proposals, or queries and act as a coach or guide to the writer. Editors of both books and magazines have these activities in common, but there are some differences between magazine and book editors.

In book publishing, an editor's job is to find important new books and authors to acquire for their house. They then work closely with the author in developing the manuscript. Editors also act as liaison between the various departments that help produce the book. These may include art, production, publicity, and sales. You are like a project manager helping to guide the book through all steps of creation, publication, and promotion.

(Although the promotion is done by the publicity department, the editor is still heavily involved with the author.) And you will be working on several projects at once.

Book editors do a staggering amount of reading, at least five to ten manuscripts or proposals a week, although editors don't necessarily read them all the way through. The offices of every editor I've ever met looks like a war zone, piled with stacks of manuscripts at least a foot high. You might think that editors would spend their days reading, but oddly enough, that is not the case. Reading is done almost exclusively at night or on weekends.

During the day, there are meetings and lunches regarding the production of the current book. Editors may meet with an author or agent about purchasing a future project. There is also an unbelievable amount of paperwork and forms that editors must complete. Some editors estimate they spend at least twenty hours on paperwork and forms alone just to complete one book.

Hot editors are judged according to how many high-profile authors they bring in to the publisher and how successful their authors are. Relationships between editors and authors can be close, with some authors being more loyal to their editors than their publishers. It is not uncommon for an author to change publishers if her editor moves.

In magazine work, you rarely begin editing or writing. You begin as an assistant or editorial assistant, similar to book publishing. You will do some basic clerical activities and small assignments such as researching and writing a small box for a story or writing captions for photographs. If you are on the fast track, after about a year you may begin to do a little editing, and if you're really good, you will get to write or edit a small story.

## I Don't Want to Be an Editor. What Else Can I Do?

If you want to work in publishing, but don't feel you have what it takes to be an editor, you might consider sales, publicity or even working for an agent. But even here you might still begin as an assistant.

## What Do They Do?

The main job of a publisher's sales staff is to represent the publisher and sell the publisher's new releases to bookstores and booksellers.

If you work for an agent as an assistant, you will do some mundane activities like answer the phone and write letters, but you will also get to read manuscripts. You are the gatekeeper in many cases. If your boss trusts you, you might be able to read and recommend which manuscripts the agent should read. You will also make some great contacts within the publishing industry. Working for an agent is a great way to enter the business. (To learn more about agents, see the writer/author chapter.)

## What Skills Do I Need?

While there are no special degree requirements to become an editor (or really any other job in publishing) a liberal arts or English degree can be very helpful. Editors and others in publishing have a wide variety of backgrounds. Publishing is a tough career to train for, because it's not as if you can easily get a degree in it. Schools like NYU, Pace, and Columbia offer Masters degrees in publishing, but such programs are not commonly found at most colleges. There are also several special programs or courses in book publishing around the country that teach you the basics about the business and offer a placement service. Many editors have attended such a program. These programs are offered through various colleges and universities and often last several weeks. One of the most popular is a six-week summer program at Radcliffe College in Cambridge, Massachusetts (617-495-5678). This program introduces you to every department in a publishing house and informs you about agents. You will eat, sleep, and breath publishing for six weeks. In addition to the skills you learn, you will develop contacts. It's the perfect way to get into the business.

As far as actual skills are concerned, you must love to read. You should have excellent English skills, both written and verbal. You're constantly communicating with authors, agents,

---

### On the Job with Book Publicists

Craig, an executive at one of the major publishing houses, says, "Publicity is the last stop for an author before his or her book goes out to the world. Essentially, we are the mouthpiece of the publishing house."

In ensuring that a book finds its market, the book publicist develops a media plan that targets and caters to the intended market for the book (i.e., you wouldn't target *Modern Maturity* for an article on a rock star's memoir or send a book on menopause to *Rolling Stone*). Typically, the publicist will produce a press kit that can include a letter summarizing the content of the book, the author's credentials, and why the book's information is groundbreaking, exciting, and important. The press kit and book are mailed to newspapers, magazines, television and radio shows (these kits often contain suggested interview questions), trade journals, professional organizations, and a variety of other companies or groups that have been targeted in the market strategy for the book. After a mass mailing has been sent, the publicist will spend many hours following up and trying to book reviews, interviews, and in-store events.

Another major aspect of a book publicist's job is booking, scheduling, and coordinating an author's tour, in addition to holding the author's hand through the entire process. A book tour will visit five to ten cities, in which the publicist tries to book radio and TV interviews, a bookstore event, and newspaper coverage. This also entails booking the flight, hotel, car, and escort arrangements. Shari, a publicist at one of the top houses, summarizes her job this way. "Once the author and then editorial, art, and production have given birth to the book, it's my job to throw the party."

and coworkers. You *must* know how to type. More and more editing and communication is done via computer and e-mail.

## How Do I Get Hired?

People get hired in all the traditional ways, such as sending out résumés or temping in hopes of turning it into a full-time job. Since publishing is such an incestuous industry, most positions are found through networking and relationships.

Many people, particularly in magazine publishing, are hired through internships. Shannon, a columnist for *Glamour,* recommends finding out who the internship coordinator is at the particular magazine you want to work for. If the magazine does not have an internship coordinator, contact the magazine and ask who would be the best person to contact. Gregory, a former editor at *Business Week,* says there is never one standard contact person or title. "Every magazine is different. You have to have a contact name or else your information will sit on someone's desk."

You can also contact your alma mater to ask if there are any alumni who work in publishing or editing. There are temporary and placement agencies that specialize in publishing. One of the best is the Lynn Palmer Agency in New York City—many editors recommend it. Editors say the jobs they offer are the less appealing ones, but it is a great place to start.

## And You Thought Book Reports Were Only for School

Often in interviews for editorial assistant positions, applicants are put through small tests. One common test to write a reader's report (a mini book report that describes the book's strengths and weaknesses and offers a recommendation for passing or pursuing) on a manuscript that you take home overnight. Such reports are something you will have to do as an editor or editorial assistant. Employers can see if you understand the industry and books by your report. A great way to prepare for this situation is by researching the industry. In your report, you can compare the book you are covering to others in the market that succeeded and failed.

## Will I Work on All Types of Books?

Maybe, but most editors tend to specialize or have a niche they work in. An editor may specialize in business books, children's books, romance novels, or contemporary women's issues. If you know that you want to work in a particular field, you may begin by determining not only which publishers produce those types of books, but which imprints do as well.

An imprint is often a division within a publishing house. It's like a brand that specializes in a certain genre such as mystery, science fiction, business, or children's.

Jaime, an editor at a major publisher, says that most applicants just coming into the industry want to be literary fiction editors. "Literary fiction is a very crowded and competitive niche and is usually handled by seasoned, accomplished editors."

## What Will Set Me Apart from Other Candidates?

Knowledge of the publishing industry and that particular publisher will help you stand out from other candidates. Determine who publishes the books that you are interested in and research their list, including their high-profile books and authors. Most of the larger publishers have Web sites. Read *Publishers Weekly* and the *New York Times Review of Books* so you can be current on industry activities. "You have to be a book lover," says Jaime.

You need to be a good communicator, politician, and marketer. You will need to lobby for book projects that you want to buy. You must also be tactful when dealing with authors, agents, and people inside of your own publishing house. Editors aren't traditionally thought of as master marketers or salespeople, but those who are on the fast track tend to be more aggressive.

If you are trying to break in to the magazine business, you should be very focused. Shannon says to be passionate about the type of magazines you approach. "You have to believe in it. Study the magazine like a manual so you can know everything about it before you interview."

## What's the Career Path?

On the editorial food chain, there are many different levels that all do pretty much the same thing. The difference is the seniority and responsibility involved.

It takes a long time to advance as an editor, much longer than other areas like sales. People tend to stay in their own area and don't move laterally, for example someone doesn't start in sales and then become an editor. Advancement is based largely on talent and experience.

Publishing is an industry based on relationships and connections. Who you know cannot only help your career within the publishing house, but can help you learn about projects before your competition. It is important to cultivate relationships inside your own publishing house as well as with agents and authors. When someone leaves one publishing house for another, it is common for them to take many of their contacts with them.

Some people start their career in publishing and then realize that they aren't cut out for it, or don't have the patience to pay the dues required to advance, so they go to graduate school. As one editor says, "If someone is still there after a couple of years, he will make a career of publishing."

Gregory says that in magazine publishing, "At the entry level, [managers] don't expect you to stay, and they like that you won't stay. There is a lot of turnover, and the ones who make it are truly impassioned by the magazine business."

## How Much Can I Make?

In the beginning, not much. The entry-level pay is among the lowest of any industry. The entry-level salary varies from publisher to publisher, but ranges from approximately $16,000 to $20,000. One copy editor said he was offered $13,000 by a major publisher. Publishing is not a job you can leave at the office. There is always something to read and something to do. Both rookies and pros cite the low pay as a negative, but most realize this before going into the field. You should also remember that it is likely that you will be working in New York, where apartments can run well over $1,000 a month. In addition to your salary, most publishers and magazines offer insurance and retirement benefits.

Once you are established (about ten years at the minimum) and reach an executive level, you can make six figures. Editors-in-chief at the major publishers can make well over $200,000, and superstars at the top houses can make even higher.

## What Are the Pros and Cons?

One of the great perks of book publishing is that you get free books (although you are probably so sick of reading at work that you don't read for fun). You are also constantly surrounded by bright people, and the projects you work on can be very interesting. Shannon says, "The best thing is that you are always dealing with ideas. I also like how publishing is so influential. Millions of people will read what I had a hand in creating." You can also meet influential and famous people.

On the negative side, the hours can be long. One editor says, "It is like being in school. You always have reading and work to do. This is not a job you can leave at the office at 5:00 P.M." Another negative is the low pay, but again, people don't get into this business for the money.

## I Hope You Like New York

The center of the publishing universe is New York, where most major publishers are located. There are a few places where regional publishers or magazines are located, but most of the big players are in New York.

## What the Pros Read

*Publishers Weekly*
*Editor & Publisher*
*New York Times Book Review*
*Folio: The Magazine for Magazine Management*

## Where Can I Learn More?

*Literary Market Place*: The *LMP* can be found at most libraries, and it's a great resource, because it lists contacts, addresses, and phone numbers of publishers of books and magazines as well as agents.

## Where on the Web?

www.bookwire.com—Book Wire
www.harpercollins.com—HarperCollins Publishers
www.simonandschuster.com—Simon & Schuster
www.randomhouse.com—Random House
www.mcgraw-hill.com—McGraw-Hill
www.amazon.com—Amazon.com (the largest online bookstore)

### You Might Check Out

One rapidly growing area of publishing is online or electronic publishing. Many topical Web sites like parentsoup.com, aboutwork.com, tripod.com, or the Microsoft Network are loosely structured like publishers. In fact, they hire many editors from magazines and book publishers.

# 42

. . . . . . . . . . . . . . . . . . . . . . . . . . . . . . . . . . . . . . . .

# Radio

**Some Common Positions**
  On-air talent
  Reporter
  Producer
  Program director

**Other Opportunities You Might Consider**
  Public affairs director
  Advertising sales
  Promotions director

There's much more to radio than just playing music or being able to talk a lot. Radio, like television, is broken into three general categories: on-air talent, production, and sales.

On-air talent is just that—the talent or voice you hear when you are driving in the car. On-air talent includes reporters; talk show hosts; morning show hosts; DJs; weather, sports, or traffic reporters; and announcers.

The production side is made up of the behind-the-scenes folks who produce, research, and engineer a show. This may include fielding calls, scheduling guests, researching topics, or running the soundboard.

It's important to remember what the main goal of a radio station is: to sell advertising. It's a ratings-driven business, and good ratings drive advertising sales. The shows and the station must become well-known to local businesses and the community. This business side is made up of sales reps and promotion directors who sell advertising, write ads, and handle special promotions and public relations.

## Where Will I Start?

You'll probably start as an unpaid intern or an assistant producer, regardless of which side of the microphone you want to be on. This is a field where experience counts more than your degree. The best way to learn is simply by doing it.

As an intern or AP, you'll help the regular producer do whatever needs to be done. Gradually, you'll get more responsibility as you fill in for producers who are on vacation or sick. Some people continue on this production track, while others gradually make the move to on-air personality. Rarely does anyone start out on the air.

You also won't start out in a major market. You're likely to begin in a small market at a small station in an undesirable time slot, like the graveyard shift. No one, including Howard Stern, Don Imus, Rush Limbaugh, or Dr. Laura, started out in a great time slot at a top station. The most desirable time slots are drive time, approximately 6:00 to 9:00 A.M. or 5:00 to 7:00 P.M.

## How Do I Get Hired?

The best way to get experience is through an internship while you are in school. It doesn't matter whether your internship is through a campus or a commercial station. The most important thing is that you get experience being around radio, whether it's for free, credit, or minimum wage.

Kelly, a morning host in Dallas, says, "I worked for free basically for two years with different organizations. And even if I wasn't actually participating, I gained a lot of experience just by observing. I also got to know the right people."

Radio is a business of relationships. It's very important to stay in touch with people and make an impression. Kelly says, "Someone has always told me about every job I've ever had. A friend working at some station says, 'We have this opening coming up. Maybe you should talk to so and so.' And I then pursued it."

## What Will I Do?

Sherri, who has been in radio for ten years and is now a producer at KSFO in San Francisco, says, "I got lucky. I only licked envelopes for one day. I was put in the newsroom right away, so I was actually writing traffic reports and doing research on stories and setting up guests to interview. But I got lucky."

Other interns, primarily at music stations, will do a lot of phone research talking to people about what they listen to. You might also go to remotes to help set up the site or prepare the give-away prizes. "It may appear like crap work," says Rick, a morning show host at KNRB in Oklahoma City. "You may go to a concert that your station is sponsoring and give out T-shirts or bumper stickers.

## What Does a Radio Producer Do?

Basically, you take care of all of the host's needs. Sherri of KSFO says, "You're basically their baby-sitter." Producers make sure all the loose ends are tied up so the show operates smoothly. In smaller markets, the host may actually double as producer. You'll do everything from working the control board during a show, screening callers, researching and setting up interviews with guests, and establishing contacts and leads for stories. Producers organize many of the show's logistics and work closely with the promotions department to make sure the show is promoted properly.

## How Much Can I Make?

It depends on which side of the microphone you're on and the market you're in. Producers don't make as much as on-air talent, and salespeople in TV traditionally make more than those in radio. Producers may start in the low twenties. A couple of producers in major markets who have ten or more years experience said they are only now making in the high thirties. The big money is with major or syndicated shows, but those are few and far between. "You won't get rich in this job," says Sherri.

For hosts and on-air personalities, the pay varies wildly according to your station and market. At major stations, hosts can make an average of $50,000 to $60,000. Superstars in their regional or local markets can do very well. If you have a top-rated morning or drive time show in a good market, it's not unreasonable to make in six figures, but only two or three people in a market make that. Hosts and DJs at the beginning of their careers can expect a rough climb up the financial mountain. Scott in Oklahoma City has been in radio for five years. He has been a host for three years and still only makes around $20,000. Most DJs and news reporters with considerable experience average $60,000 to $80,000 a year.

## What Do You Like Best About Radio?

Radio is fun. It allows you to be crazy, creative, and spontaneous. Sherri, morning producer at KSFO in San Francisco, says, "I did a couple of internships in television when I was in college, and it just wasn't as fun as radio. Radio is on a much smaller scale than TV, so you get your hands in many different pots. I screen calls, I get to talk to listeners, I get to do production, I get to do research, I get to do everything. Whereas, if I were in television, I would just run the camera or Chiron machine or I would just research stories."

Other radio professionals say the instant gratification of radio is exciting. You make a phone call or get someone on the air, and within minutes, you are seeing results of your work. Radio is a great job for information junkies, because it lets you stay informed and learn about the news before anyone else does.

## What's the Culture and Work Environment Like?

People in radio come from a wide variety of backgrounds. Radio tends to attract the eccentric, so it's never dull or boring. You'll always find something interesting going on.

Radio has also changed considerably in the past few years. It used to be a much more freewheeling and loose culture. Today, since large corporations have purchased many stations, there's more bureaucracy and a corporate feel to radio. Consolidation is the future of the broadcasting industry.

## What's the Difference Between FM and AM?

The main difference is in format: FM is music and AM is talk radio. Music is a much different atmosphere than talk. Rick says, "Music is more laid back. People are crazier and it's more of a party mentality. It's a lot wilder, I guess." Music stations are generally much smaller, because it doesn't take as many people to produce a music format. People who have worked on both AM and FM say that FM can be more intimate and you might get to know your coworkers better.

## What About Education? Does It Help to Have a Degree or Be a Broadcast Major?

Formal education doesn't matter much in radio. Actually, many people on the air don't have college degrees, and there are many people with degrees in journalism who can't find jobs. This does not mean that there are dumb people in radio. The people are very bright, well-read, and informed, but they might not have much formal education.

The thing that matters most in this business is who you know. And like any business, being in the right place at the right time doesn't hurt.

Sherri in San Francisco says, "I do some hiring, too, and I don't look at people's education. I look at their experience, who they know, and where they've worked. It's all about networking."

## What Are Some Misconceptions About Radio?

As a listener, you may have a certain image of what the hosts look like or what the studio is like. (A common joke is that some people have a face for radio. Think about it.) It's not glamorous. It's a lot of garbage work, and there are a lot of little things that need to be taken care of in order to make a radio station work.

Radio studios are probably much smaller and messier than you think. They are incredibly compact and often look as if a tornado came through the studio. Some are ordered and neat, but the majority of studios are a mess.

Don't go into radio because you think you have a cool taste in music. Chances are you won't get to play everything you want. Most stations have play lists that dictate what you can play. So realize you may be forced to play the "Macarena" every hour on the hour. Radio, even at a music station, is about much more than simply following a play list. The challenge of radio is to constantly come up with a shtick and keep people interested so they don't switch the dial.

Being a show host takes much more than being funny or playing cool music. It takes a great deal of writing, research, and rehearsal. The DJs and hosts who come across as real, spontaneous, and funny are the ones who start in when the song ends. It sounds like they are walking by and have something interesting to say. It takes a whole lot of work.

Rick, who is the morning host of KNRB in Oklahoma City, says, "I never really knew how many hours I would work. I do the morning show, so I get here around four in the morning, and I am here until four or five in the afternoon writing the next day's show."

## What About Job Security? Is It a Stable Environment?

Not at all. In fact, it's not a good place to be if you're interested in job security. Stations are sold all the time, and it's very common to fire the entire staff. Stations basically clean house when they bring in new management.

---

### If You Want to Move Up, Move Around

Mark was an advertising sales rep at a large FM music station in Atlanta. He received an offer to become sales manager at a station in Seattle, so he and his wife moved to the Pacific Northwest. Three months after they moved, he received a better offer from a major station in Chicago. Thinking he and his wife would be in Chicago for a long time, they bought a house and became pregnant. To make matters worse, his wife's parents moved to Chicago to be closer to them. Ten months later (you guessed it), Mark was transferred by his station's owner to become the general manager at his original station in Atlanta. Advancement can happen quickly, but you must be prepared to go when it calls.

---

People also tend to hop around from station to station in order to advance or increase their salary. It's not uncommon to relocate several times in your career or move to different stations in the same market.

Radio is a ratings-based industry, and if the ratings aren't there, stations are quick to change formats. That means you might be out of a job the next day.

Sunny 95 was an all-country FM station when it was purchased by another company. The new owner decided to change the call letters and format. Three weeks after the purchase, the station went to an "all news, all the time" format. It hired an entire staff of news professionals from around the country. Six months into the station's new format, the radio station was sold again, and the new owner immediately changed formats. Within two weeks of the purchase, everyone was gone.

> ### How One Person Got On the Air
>
> As an intern, Scott was trying to find time to make his air-check tape. Since the studio was booked all the time except early in the morning, the only time he could come in was around four or five in the morning. "No one else wanted to do this, so I looked pretty good. The current morning host was the only person who saw me do this and gave me some pointers on my tape. When the program manager left the station, the morning host got the job. He had seen me hustle and show up early in the morning, so he gave me a chance at a show."

## How Does Someone Get On-Air?

Résumés are important, but the main thing every on-air personality must have is an "air check" or "demo" tape. This is a sample of what you sound like on the air. If you haven't been on the radio before, you have to go into a studio and make a tape of you pretending to be on the air. This should not be an hour-long mock show. Your air-check tape should be no longer than seven to eight minutes and should be a mix of different material. You should also have your best material at the beginning of the tape, so the program director will want to listen to the remainder.

One of the great things about working at a college station or as an intern is that you have access to a recording studio and equipment. Take advantage of this opportunity to make a professional demo tape.

Another way that people get on the air is to be a regular guest. Many stations have a frequent guest who may be a local columnist or person of interest. These people often fill in for a vacationing host and then develop a following. Many hosts and producers say it's whoever bugs the program director the most without being obnoxious. It's all about persistence, who you know, and being in the right place at the right time.

## Where Can I Learn More About Jobs in Radio?

Many cities have media networking organizations and clubs that meet regularly to discuss industry happenings or job openings. Check with one of your local stations to see if such a group exists in your area. The Broadcast Skills Bank and Media Alliance are two such groups in San Francisco. Also check out:

National Association of Broadcasters
National Association of College Broadcasters
American Federation of Television and Radio Artists (AFTRA)

## Where on the Web?

www.broadcastjobs.com—BroadcastJobs.com
www.nab.org—National Association of Broadcasters

# 43

• • • • • • • • • • • • • • • • • • • • • • • • • • • • • • • • • • •

# Real Estate

**Some Common Positions**
 Broker
 Appraiser
 Developer
 Property manager

**Other Opportunities You Might Consider**
Real estate is closely related to the finance and investment industry, as well as construction and building.

Hold on. Don't think that a career in real estate means wearing a gold Century 21 blazer and selling homes. There are two types of real estate—residential and commercial—and they couldn't be more different.

Selling homes is certainly one potentially lucrative career choice, although not many young people go into residential real estate. While changing, it is still a field dominated by "mature" women. (Is that politically correct enough?)

The focus of this profile will be one of the fastest growing and exciting career opportunities: Commercial real estate.

## What Does Commercial Real Estate Mean?

It is the building, buying, selling, leasing, and management of properties or land for retail space, office space, and warehouse or industrial use. It also includes the sale of raw land for investment purposes or development.

## What Can I Do in Real Estate? Buy It? Sell It? Develop It?

All of the above and then some. Commercial real estate companies can perform several functions. They can develop land by building a retail center or office building and then sell or lease it to tenants. They can negotiate or broker a lease on behalf of a tenant and receive a commission. They can broker the sale of a property. They can also represent the landlord and manage the property (office building) for him by handling all of the details from physical upkeep to administration and leasing. Brokerage is one of the more common areas for people to go into.

## Where Do I Start?

If you decide to become a broker, you will likely start out as a "runner." Many of the larger commercial real estate firms have a "runnership" program. It is a great opportunity to get into the business. You start by working under a senior person in the industry for anywhere from six to eighteen months. You will learn the ropes as you earn a small subsistence salary until you are good enough to work on straight commission.

## What Skills Do I Need?

"You should have discipline and drive and be motivated by money," says Michael, a broker with Grubb & Ellis in Atlanta. "You can make unlimited amounts of money in this business, although the 80/20 rule applies: 80 percent if the sales are generated by 20 percent of the salespeople."

It's a sales position, pure and simple. There's prospecting, cold calling, cultivating client relationships, and closing deals—all the elements you find in any sales position. That means that there can be a long sales cycle, which is the time it takes from the beginning of the deal to the actual closing. "It can be months, sometimes even over a year," says Terry, a broker with Cushman & Wakefield. "You have to be patient and manage your time well. You always have to have something in the pipeline, because you could spend months on a deal and have it blow up in your face. If you haven't worked on anything else or built up your leads and put deals [prospects] in the works, you are sunk."

You also have to have thick skin, because there is a lot of rejection. "You may talk to 100 people to get 1 to actually see you," says Terry. In addition, it can be devastating if a deal "blows up," and you have spent a lot of time on it. "You have to be balanced and even."

Since most people right out of school have no experience, employers would prefer that you get experience in another field before making the move to commercial real estate. People who have been in sales or in a team environment do very well.

## How Much Will I Make?

The potential is truly unlimited, but for the first eighteen months, it's hello Ramen noodles. As a runner, salaries are between $18,000 to $25,000. Top brokers easily make six figures.

Your income will never be the same from one year to the next. One year might be better than another. "Don't buy anything until you get paid," says Michael in Atlanta. "People come in and out of this business pretty frequently, because they can't manage their money or they can't wait until the deals start closing, which can take months. This is not the business to go into if you need money quickly." He recommends that you have at least $15,000 put away to live on until you can get things going.

## How Are Commissions Figured?

They can vary and are negotiable, but brokers usually receive between 4 and 6 percent of the total sale or lease. It works like this: You determine the monthly rent and multiply it by the number of months of the lease. Let's say you negotiated a five year (sixty month) lease, and the tenant's monthly rent is $1,000 a month. That total lease is worth $60,000. If your commission is 5 percent, you would be paid $3,000. Don't worry, this is just an example. The numbers most brokers deal with are often *much* larger than this.

## Georgia on My Mind and in My Wallet

Atlanta is the only city in the country that pays brokers a procurement fee in addition to their regular 4 to 6 percent commission. This procurement fee is equal to the first month's rent. This bears repeating: The agent gets to pocket the first month's rent on top of his commissions.

## What Is Property Management?

Just picture yourself, a mop, and some blue overalls. Just kidding. Property management, however, can include the physical upkeep of a building, but it does not mean that you are "Mr. or Ms. Fix-it."

If a building owner or landlord needs someone to run the building or handle leasing and administrative duties, he would hire a property management company. Some large commercial real estate companies have property management companies or divisions to serve as profit centers. One such company, Axiom, which is owned by Grubb & Ellis, manages over 80 million square feet in the United States.

## How Do I Find Clients?

Plan on doing a lot of cold calling. Brokers have their ears to the ground in the local business community and are constantly trying to find out what companies are moving to the area, whose lease is about to expire, and who is growing and needs more space.

There are also companies in each city that produce databases and directories of the commercial real estate climate, including what the square footage is, what their current rate is, when their lease expires, and whom to contact.

There is also a lot of networking and connections. "It is a lot easier to meet someone at a function and then get together with them later once they have met you than it is calling them cold on the phone when they don't know who the hell you are," says Terry.

## What Type of Background or Education Do I Need?

You really only need a college degree. Traditionally, your major is not important. However, the trend is moving toward having an MBA, preferably with an emphasis in real estate. As Michael says, "If you are talking with an executive at a major company about moving, he wants you to be as well-educated as possible."

A financial background can be helpful as well, since the deals can be very complicated. While you won't handle the financing end, you need to understand it. While unrelated to education, a strong sales background or experience will make it easier for you to be successful. Many brokers tend to have at least a few years of business experience or come into it from a different industry where they learned how to sell.

There are many professional designations, although there is not one all-encompassing certification like the CPA for accountants. Every state has their own licensing requirements and exams that all brokers must pass. There is also ongoing continuing education throughout your career. In some states, if you graduate with a degree in real estate, you can forgo certain portions of the tests.

There is a huge learning curve. This is a field where you learn by doing. "To truly get up to speed, you need at least three to five years experience," says Michael.

## Who Are a Few of the Major Players?

Cushman & Wakefield, Grubb & Ellis, and Coldwell Banker are a few of the larger international firms. Every city or region has firms that are excellent, but specialize only in that area. To learn who the commercial real estate companies are in your area, contact the Chamber of Commerce or local business journal.

## How Do I Get Hired?

Most people come into commercial real estate after working in another profession for a few years, although some enter straight out of school. Traditionally, these companies do not recruit on colleges for brokers. Some MBA recruiting is done, but not much.

The best way to enter the field is by contacting the district manager or regional vice president of the company in which you are interested. Call first before sending a résumé.

## What Are the Pros and Cons?

The pros are that you can make a ton of money if you are in the right city at the right time. It is fun and exciting—if you're successful. You are your own boss, but you still have access to the resources of a huge company. "You have complete control of your schedule and can do it from anywhere. All you need is a phone," says Terry.

The negatives are that it is a very competitive business. In any hot real estate market, there are tons of brokers competing for deals. In Atlanta alone, it is estimated that there are 50,000 commercial realtors.

Real estate is a high-stress environment with roller-coaster highs and lows. It's frustrating when you work on a deal for months and it falls apart. Since it is sales, which involves cold calling, there is a great deal of rejection.

It is also tough not having a consistent income. John, a broker at Trammel Crow, says, "You can make a lot of money, but it may be months in between pay checks. You will get a check for $20,000 and then not get paid for four months. You have to be careful not to blow it all."

## Is It Stable?

There is very high turnover. Some people leave the industry because they aren't successful. Others change companies. John at Trammel Crow says, "An account is loyal to the individual broker as much as it is to the company. When a broker leaves, he will try to take that client with him to his new company."

The industry is cyclical. According to brokers, commercial real estate markets tend to move in three-to-five-year cycles. Michael says, "Some brokers are wise enough to have a three- or five-year plan, where they might move cities and try to get in on the next big market."

## You Are an Independent Contractor

Sure, you may work for a large company such as Grubb & Ellis, but you are still an independent contractor. When you reach the point where you are making straight commission, you will not only be responsible for your insurance and taxes, you will be charged a fee for the use of the office you're in. Every broker is charged a "desk fee" (the name can vary). You are provided with support staff (secretary), research materials, an office, and phones. Then these office expenses are calculated and each broker is charged a percentage of those expenses. The percentage is based upon the revenue he or she generates. Terry says that with this system, you can see who is pulling their weight and who is a drain on the office. "You are here to produce, period, and the numbers don't lie. You can tell early on who will make it and who won't."

## What The Pros Read

*Commercial Property News*
*National Real Estate Investor*
*Real Estate Forum*

They also read the local business journal. Most generally have good coverage of the commercial real estate community. To find the journal in your area, check out www.amcity.com.

## Where Can I Learn More?

National Association of Realtors

## Where on the Web?

www.realtor.com—National Association of Realtors
www.sior.com—Society of Industrial and Office Realtors
www.ccim.com—Commercial Real Estate Network
www.nacore.org—International Association of Corporate Real Estate Executives

# 44

. . . . . . . . . . . . . . . . . . . . . . . . . . . . . . . . . . . .

# Retail and Merchandising

**Some Common Positions**
   Sales associate
   Buyer
   Merchandiser
   Manufacturer's representative

**Other Opportunities You Might Consider**
Retail is much more than hawking merchandise on a sales floor. There are elaborate departments and systems behind the scenes to make it all happen. There are opportunities in advertising, human resources, training, accounting and credit services, distribution and logistics, facilities management, information systems, auditing, and promotions, not to mention catalog services and direct mail for merchants like L.L. Bean and J. Crew.

It seems that many recent graduates and their parents equate working in retail with failure after graduation. I've even heard the media chime in by describing a tough job market as one where "there are college graduates working in retail." Well, that might not be such a bad thing.

Think about it. At almost every suburban strip mall in America, you will find a Gap, a Starbucks, and (thank God) a Barnes & Noble. Sure, there are legions of teenagers, college students, and aimless souls working behind a counter to pay the bills or biding their time until something they think is better comes along. But they aren't seeing the big picture: Retail and merchandising is a huge business with plenty of opportunity beyond the cash register.

## I Don't Want to Work in a Store. What Can I Do?

Think about it. Someone has to find real estate for the store locations. Someone has to train new employees and manage their benefits. Someone has to handle the accounting and financial concerns of the company. More than any other industry, retail and merchandising is related to almost all other businesses.

## Excuse Me, I Earned a Degree, So I Don't Have to Work Retail

If you still think retail is something you did while in college or on summer break to pay the bills, too bad. The five largest retailers are going to hire over 3,000 graduates this year. And these are not cashier McJobs. These are management track positions.

## What Is Merchandising?

Merchandising is one important part of retail. It can happen at both the store and the corporate level, and involves all aspects of selecting, buying, and getting products to the point where they can be purchased.

## What Does a Merchandiser Do?

Merchandisers determine which products will be carried and put in the stores. This is different than a buyer. At a company like Famous Footwear, merchandisers determine which shoes will be sold in certain stores. Each merchandiser is responsible for a certain product category. At some companies, merchandisers are responsible for a particular region, while others handle selections for the entire country. Susan, a merchandiser for Famous Footwear, a division of Buster Brown, says that her merchandisers get to know the buying habits of customers in each store. Products sell differently in certain stores. "If a store is located near a college campus, we carry a different selection than in a suburban setting."

Merchandisers do a great deal of analysis. They analyze how stores are performing, how certain products are selling, and which colors and sizes are the most popular. You need to know if a certain product is selling quickly, so you will be able to get more of it and have it shipped from the warehouse or manufacturer in time. Merchandisers also spend a lot of time on the phone dealing with stores, buyers, manufacturers, and just making sure that things run smoothly.

## What Does a Buyer Do?

Buyers are the people who directly purchase products from the manufacturers or representatives so that they can be sold in a store. Buyers work with a variety of people in the company to determine what they should buy. They consult with salespeople and marketing managers to determine elements such as price, marketing, advertising, and even distribution. Some buyers at larger retailers such as Target or WalMart may have a buyer who specializes in a particular product or line, such as men's shoes or ladies' belts. A buyer at a retailer like Crate & Barrel or Pier 1 Imports might be responsible for a wider group of merchandise, such as furniture or dishes.

## What Skills Do I Need to Be a Buyer?

Buyers not only have to be knowledgeable about their products, they must also be good communicators and negotiators. Some buyers might travel a great deal to go to wholesalers or showrooms to view a product and then negotiate a price. As a buyer you will have to be up on current trends, so you will read a great deal.

Because you might be dealing with people from around the world in person, via fax, or on the phone, you need to have excellent communication skills. You will have to track many figures and perform a great deal of paperwork. You will likely track sales figures, make sure that the stores have information about the product, and follow a product as it goes from the warehouse to the store.

## Where Do I Start?

Starting positions may vary from company to company, but typically you will start out as a merchandising assistant or assistant buyer. Buyers generally are quite experienced or have gone through an extensive training program.

Assistant buyers or merchandisers act as a go-between and share information with the sales, advertising, and distribution departments. JCPenney claims that their management trainees immediately start with three responsibilities as merchant, personnel manager, and operations manager.

You might start out on the floor in a store or unit. Don't let this upset you. Some companies like JCPenney make managers and executives from headquarters spend time in the store. How can you effectively run a retail operation and buy products that your customers will buy unless you are in the trenches.

## What Skills Do I Need?

Many colleges offer merchandising degrees, and they are helpful, but the best background for this profession is experience. You can gain experience very early and easily by working in a retail setting. If you are currently working retail, don't think of it as a dead-end position to simply pay your bills—use it to your advantage. There is so much that goes on behind the scenes to make sure that products get into and, most importantly, out of your store. It is common for people to work their way up from being on the retail floor to becoming a manager and eventually move into a larger position such as a buyer or department head at the company headquarters.

In addition to understanding merchandising and retail, you should also have a solid communications background and a good understanding of business, primarily marketing, sales, and promotions.

Many large retailers such as Nordstrom or Neiman Marcus have training programs for their buyers, while others start you out as an assistant and then let the leaders emerge from the pack.

## What Is the Career Path?

Different positions mean different things from company to company. At some companies, you will start as part of a buyers training program and then move to buyer. At others, they want buyers with previous experience. If you are an assistant buyer or merchandising manager, you can usually expect to have a review after six months. Once you are in corporate headquarters, you can be a buyer or move to another department such as advertising, visual merchandising (creating the displays), or distribution and shipping (handling logistics and moving product from the manufacturer to the store).

Your career path depends upon the store and which area of retailing you want to pursue. If you want to be in sales or store management, the best way is to begin on the floor learning the store. The natural path is to become a department head and eventually a store manager. You may have to transfer stores or locations to acquire that experience or enter a training program.

## How Much Can I Make?

The pay can vary, but in a training program you are looking at a salary in the low to mid-twenties, plus insurance, 401K, stock purchase plans, and, best of all, a merchandise discount.

## How Do I Get Hired?

Many of the major retailers hire for their management, merchandising, or buyers training programs. A lot of retailers

Sabrina, a rep for Karen Kane, got her job while she was working as a sales associate for Dillards. She said, "I spoke with everyone that came in the store. Every rep that came in, I would introduce myself and say, 'How did you get started?' The company approached me, because I was selling a lot."

actively recruit on college campuses. They also recruit for accounting, auditing, catalog, and information systems positions. It takes a lot of people to run a retail organization. Other positions are commonly filled through word of mouth.

Experience is the key to succeeding in this field. Age does not really matter, although it takes a lot of energy.

For manufacturing rep positions, it is mostly word of mouth. If you have experience, you can approach a company, but for manufacturers rep positions, you must have retail experience.

> Kim, who has worked retail for Dillards for six years, says, "I finally had to leave. I had not been able to spend a relaxing Thanksgiving or Christmas holiday with my family in years. The last straw was being scheduled until 7:00 P.M. Christmas eve and at 8:00 A.M. the day after Christmas. I never got to see my family when they were in from out of town."
>
> Kerri, a retail manager, says there is no way she could continue working in retail if she had a family. "As a manager, I'm there from either nine to six or twelve to ten. It runs your life. It's not an eight-to-five job, and you really take it home with you after a while."

## What Are the Pros and Cons?

If you like behind-the-scenes and analytical work, then you will like merchandising. You will also get the opportunity to work closely with stores in developing strategies. A potential downside to merchandising and buying, especially for someone who comes from a store environment, is that it is an office job, so it is much slower.

"Other than the fact that you have no life, it is okay," says Jarrod, who runs a retail clothing store. Ask most people in retail and they will tell you that the hours are the worst. Kim says Dillards only closes two days a year, Christmas and Easter.

You will get about two weeks of vacation time, which you can use after about six months to a year, but be careful, because you can never take your vacation around the holidays. You can only take it between February and October.

## What About Stability?

There is massive turnover. People get burned out easily.

## Who Are Some Major Employers?

The largest retailers are :

JCPenney
Sears
Macy's
Dayton Hudson
WalMart

# What the Pros Read

*STORES* (the official magazine of the National Retail Federation)

# Where Can I Learn More?

National Retail Federation
7th Street NW, Suite 1000
Washington, DC 20004
202-783-7971

Merchandising is not just clothing or department stores and mass merchants like WalMart and Target, but food, electronics, hardware, books, home supplies, and computers.

Take a look at a Barnes & Noble, Home Depot, or Comp USA.

The largest retailing association in the world. The NRF also publishes a free booklet entitled *Careers in Retailing*. It includes a list of schools that offer degrees in retailing.

If you want a list of the top 100 retailers and the top 100 specialty stores, the July and August issues of the NRF's *STORES* magazine offers these rankings. Call *STORES* at 202-626-8201 to order these issues.

If you are interested in careers in visual merchandising and displays, you should contact the National Association of Display Industries at 212-661-4261

# Where on the Web?

www.nrf.com—National Retail Federation

# 45

• • • • • • • • • • • • • • • • • • • • • • • • • • • • • • • • • •

# Retail Manufacturer's Representative

**Some Common Positions**
>    Sales associate
>    Marketing representative
>    Customer service representative
>    Account manager
>    Retail image consultant
>    Manufacturer's representative

**Other Opportunities You Might Consider**
There are many things you can do in the clothing and apparel industry, from design to sales to manufacturing. This section will deal primarily with the sales end of working for a manufacturer such as a company like Levi's. Other sections of this book you might check out are the "Retail and Merchandising" chapter.

With the big push for TQM (total quality management), some industry experts say that there are great opportunities for quality-control inspectors. These are generally people with a fashion, textile, or sewing background. This is a great place to start if you ultimately want to design, because you can learn how clothes are constructed and manufactured in large quantities.

Another great opportunity to consider is merchandising assistant or production assistant. These are entry-level positions that help obtain materials for production. They find the best price, order materials for production based on sales forecasts, and find the best factory to produce it.

Have you ever wondered how things get to the store? There is a whole world outside of retail that we never see, a whole world that get products from the factory to the store and on our backs. Here are a few great opportunities in the clothing and apparel industry that don't require you to be a designer or fashion model.

## What Can I Do?

Each manufacturer has a whole team that takes care of manufacturing the product, selling the product to buyers in various department stores, and maintaining a good relationship with the store to ensure their products are displayed properly.

## Where Will I Start?

There are several places you can start. Your first job should be in an area where you can learn all elements of the business and products. A great place to start is as a sales associate or customer service representative. You will likely start as part of a support team working with a national account sales manager. You will help order, enter, and follow up customer service research.

Don't think customer service is a dead end. Pros in the industry say this is the most comprehensive education you can receive. It's a crash course in the apparel industry, and it will prepare you for anything else you want to do. As a customer service rep, you must learn every part of the business. You are exposed to many different departments and learn the business inside and out. There is a lot of turnover because customer service reps become hot properties. Jaime, who began her career as a customer service rep for Levi's and later became director of marketing for Bugle Boy, says, "You have a full knowledge of the company, plus sales ability."

Another starting position is retail marketing rep. In this job, you travel from mall to mall working from the grassroots level in educating sales associates on the floor about the product and giving them incentives. (Whoever sells the most on Saturday wins a backpack.) Your job is to rally support among sales associates and effect change in a store.

Some people begin by working in a retail store as a sales associate and make contacts with the reps who travel to the store. There is so much turnover in the field that some reps, when leaving their jobs, will recommend individuals from stores as candidates for their positions. It is a natural fit, since the person in the store already knows the product.

## What Will I Do?

You will do a lot of problem solving and communicating with sales reps, stores, and buyers. Accounts like JCPenney place orders with a company. A customer service rep would take the orders over the phone and handle any problems.

Customer service reps search for merchandise, follow an order through the systems, and handle requests for return merchandise or buybacks. "You must be able to placate the other person and solve their problem," says Ken, a customer service rep for Levi's.

## How Do I Get Hired?

Most positions are found through networking, the newspaper, or by actually contacting the customer service or sales department of a company. There is very little campus recruitment done for these positions. Once you have a reputation, you will easily be snatched up by competitors. One rep said there is a lot of stealing of employees in this field. A manager will go into a retail store and see that a competitor's display is fantastic or is outselling their line, and she will ask the store department manager for the name of the competitor's rep.

## What Else Will I Learn?

Selling is the key to anything you do in this field, regardless of whether you are on the floor or dealing with a department store. You are trained to "up-sell." For example, a person calls in, and you say, "Let me take care of this problem, but by the way, we also have this fantastic new product." Jamie says, "Every new problem that comes into a company is an opportunity. If you solve problems quickly, you will advance quickly."

## What Skills Do I Need?

Your people and communication skills are the most important things. You will need to be able to think quickly and handle a customer or buyer who is angry. You are a problem-solver and salesperson above all. You will also need computer and basic office skills. Jamie used to test people she was hiring by putting them in different scenarios to see how they would respond. For example, she would ask, "Bette bought twelve dozen blue pants. We sent her pink pants. What would you do?"

## What Will Set Me Apart?

Companies are looking for someone young who is enthusiastic and can be passionate for the brand—a major cheerleader. Working retail is a good background.

## How Much Can I Make?

Customer service reps make between $8.50 and $13.50 an hour and generally work forty-plus hour a week. Retail marketing reps start at an annual salary of around $25,000, and good reps with a hot line can earn over $60,000.

## What Is It Like?

As a marketing rep, you may call on department stores door-to-door and then write a report on what the floor looks like, how much stock there is, and what the sales associates are doing.

It's also a physical job. You are in the stockroom folding clothes and moving fixtures. There's a lot of travel. Most reps are gone at least half of their work hours. For some, the travel may cover the entire country, while others may just do day trips in their state or region. Most reps work from home and have a laptop. Kimberly, a rep for Karen Kane, says that there is a lot of paperwork, but your hours are flexible.

## What's the Career Path?

Retail marketing reps can move up to district or regional manager. The other career path for marketing reps is to move into sales. Many marketing reps report to the sales rep who handles the account, so a networking relationship can be easily established.

## What Are the Pros and Cons?

Some people think that working in the apparel industry is glamorous, but it can be pretty tedious. As a sales associate, you could put together a sample line, which may have 100 samples that must be ironed, steamed, and hung.

On the positive side, Kimberly says, "It's great that your age and tenure really don't matter, just your experience and how good you are." Others say that the amount of experience you get early on is fantastic. Jaime says, "Where else are you going to be exposed to departments like credit, shipping, accounts receivable, traffic, as well as learn how to trace shipments and allocate inventory in an entry-level position?"

## What The Pros Read

*Womens Wear Daily*
*STORES*

Publications devoted exclusively to their type of product (shoes, menswear, etc.)

## Where Can I Learn More?

National Retail Federation
325 7th Street NW, Suite 1000
Washington, DC 20004
202-783-7971

## Where on the Web?

www.nrf.org—National Retail Federation

# 46

· · · · · · · · · · · · · · · · · · · · · · · · · · · ·

# Sales

"Everyone is selling something."
—ANONYMOUS

**Some Common Positions**
    Account executive
    Sales associate
    Sales representative
    Pest

**Other Opportunities You Might Consider**
When people say they want to be in marketing, they often overlook sales. The two are joined at the hip. Many sales reps go into management, marketing, product development, or customer service. Sales departments in many organizations are among the largest and most influential groups in the company.

Companies and organizations are in business to make money. They do this by selling a product they produce or service they perform. The types of companies that have sales forces, regardless of industry, are virtually endless. Companies in high tech, financial or information services, insurance, food, fashion, office equipment, industrial equipment, consumer goods, and the media all have sales forces.

Sales positions aren't limited to a certain geographic region or degree. They also don't require special certification, although there may be some industry specific exceptions. (Most sales certification is to enhance the person's reputation or credibility.)

## What Will I Be Called?

Account executive, sales professional, sales representative, sales associate—they all mean roughly the same thing. If you're in real estate, insurance, or financial services you might be called a broker. If you're in retail sales, you might be called an associate. If you are selling used cars you might be called a weasel . . . sorry, salesperson. The bottom line is that in every industry at every level, there are people who are selling products, goods, and services in the marketplace. Regardless of title or industry, they are all in sales.

## Where Will I Start?

Where you start and how you train will vary from company to company. Some organizations have extensive training programs that can last from several weeks to a year. In these you may be given a thorough overview of the product or services before you are allowed in the field or to have contact with a client. Xerox, Proctor & Gamble, and some of the major consumer goods companies are known for their training programs. Graduates of these programs are often in demand because of the excellent training they receive.

Other companies give you a crash course and then throw you right into the field to let you sink or swim. People also get started by being assigned to a sales support position. By supporting a sales staff, you can see what they need and the problems they encounter. You may only be in this role for a short amount of time. You may also be partnered with or "shadow" a more senior sales person for a while to learn the ropes.

## What Will I Do?

Regardless of what you are selling, the basic duties of a salesperson are similar. Among your basic activities will be prospecting, or looking for new leads (potential clients). Some sales reps are provided with leads by the company. Others have to find prospects on their own. This means doing research to learn about a company and determine who the contact person (buyer or decision maker) is. It may involve a lot of reading, surfing the Web, and making phone calls.

You'd better pack your bags, because travel is often a big part of the job. You may have to travel to the next town or across the country to make a sale or take care of a customer. Traveling up to eighty percent of the time is not uncommon for some reps.

Another big part of your job, besides making the sale, is taking care of your customers' needs no matter how insignificant they seem. This type of follow-up after the sale requires a lot of paperwork, correspondence, and phone calls. You will also need to stay on top of current events within the industry and the activities of your competitors.

## Where Will I Work?

You will likely be assigned a territory. This may be a market or area that you are responsible for. Territories can be assigned by geography, client size, alphabetically, by the type of business the clients are in, or other criteria. Some sales reps have hundreds of clients they are responsible for, while others may only deal with a handful of major clients that need special attention.

You might work in an office on the phone, a retail outlet, or the field at a client's location.

David, a drug rep for Ciba-Geigy, says, "I can go weeks without talking to my manager. I just fax my weekly reports to headquarters, and as long as I have good numbers, no one says anything."

● ● ●

Angela, a rep for Oscar Meyer, spends her days going to stores in her market, checking inventory, preparing displays, and taking orders. "I spend most of my time in my car or on the road. When I get back home, I spend a couple of hours a night filling out paperwork."

## What Is It Like?

Some sales reps have schedules that allow them to work flexible hours. This doesn't mean the hours are easy, though. Some people keep regular office hours, but salespeople work long hours and sometimes weekends.

You may get lucky and work in a nice office with an assistant or support staff. However, some reps must do everything for themselves and work in a noisy cube or open bullpens with other people.

## How Much Can I Make?

As much as you are willing to work for. If you want to be "shown the money," this is where it is going to happen. As you saw in the "How Much Do People Really Make?" chapter, only a small percentage of the population makes over $100,000 a year. Of those people, more than half of them are in some form of sales. Your potential income is truly unlimited.

However, your total income depends on many factors, such as the quality, price, and reputation of the product or service you are selling, the commission structure of your company, and, of course, how good you are. Salespeople who make over six figures are not uncommon, but there are others who have a tough time making it month to month.

Entry-level salaries vary greatly, but can range from the mid-teens to just over thirty thousand dollars. It depends on the industry and the company. Some companies compensate their reps with a combination of base salary plus commission and bonus. The trend is to offer a small base salary that allows you to make enough to pay your bills, but doesn't leave any room for fun, extravagance, or the expensive brand of macaroni and cheese. This is done to motivate you to earn hefty commissions. The majority of your income will come from commissions instead of salary. Commission fees are often based upon a percentage of the amount of goods sold, targets reached, or quotas met.

Insurance and retirement packages are frequently offered, but some reps are considered independent contractors and must pay for these things themselves. Sometimes sales reps have other benefits, besides salary or commissions, that can increase their income or at least improve their lifestyle. These may be generous expense accounts, or a car and gas allowance.

## What About "Commission-Only" Sales?

This means you don't get a salary. You are *only paid* when you sell something. Since the commissions are usually a high percentage, this is great if you are selling. Have a bad month, and you're eating Top Ramen. Have a series of bad months, and you're selling plasma just to get the free cookies.

Actually, if you don't make any commissions, you're allowed to take a "draw" or advance against future commissions earned. If you're having a rough patch and keep taking draws against anything you make in the future, you can get way behind. The next thing you know, you've made a big sale and are expecting a big commission check, but it has to go toward paying back your advance.

Both straight salary and commission-only sales have their benefits, but some experts say for entry-level sales, the best form of compensation is a mix of salary and commission. "This lets our people not have to worry abut how they are going to pay their bills, so they can focus on selling and making commissions," says Greg, a sales manager for a company that sells software to banks.

If you are looking for a job where you know what you will be making one year to the next, this is not it. Your income will vary from one year to the next. Some months and years are better than others. Smart sales reps are disciplined with their savings. Marty, a sales rep for an information services company, says, "I may have a huge month and then go two months where I don't make anything."

## What Skills Do I Need?

First and foremost, you must be a good communicator. This includes being a fantastic lis-

Don't get too excited about the car. I mean, it's a great perk. Not having a car payment is wonderful, plus the company generally picks up your insurance and gives you a gas allowance. But before you picture yourself cruising around in a new Ford Explorer or even a Mustang, you might want to lower your sights a little bit and realize that most company cars are four-door sedans such as the Ford Taurus.

Another fun car fact is that you are the *only* person who can drive it, unless you're married. No friends, no brothers or sisters, and certainly no girlfriends or boyfriends.

## A Great Place to Start

Acquiring sales skills and experience is one of the hardest things to do, but once you have them, you're marketability is incredible. In a world where experience is as valued as education, gaining that experience early is a real key to success. Many students are learning incredible sales skills (and making great cash) while still in school through a company called Southwestern Book Company.

Southwestern, based in Nashville, Tennessee, has been in business for over 100 years and hires over 3,000 college students each summer to sell books door-to-door in suburban and rural communities nationwide. No, this is not a door-to-door cult, and before you turn your nose up at the idea of selling door-to-door, realize that it is not uncommon for Southwestern reps (who are all college students) to make well over $10,000 in a summer. In addition to this, the Southwestern reps are put through intensive sales training that rivals that of Fortune 500 companies. Some very influential people put themselves through school selling for Southwestern, including Tennessee governor and former presidential candidate Lamar Alexander.

Lee McCloskey, sales director and self-described "corporate anarchist," says that Fortune 500 companies approach him all the time asking to recruit Southwestern reps after graduation because of their excellent real-world sales experience. "Southwestern reps know how to ask for and close the sale."

If you are a student and want to learn more about sales training and selling with Southwestern Book Company, check out their Web site at www.southwestern.com.

tener. Your livelihood will depend upon your people skills and persuasiveness.

You must also be assertive. People often confuse this with being obnoxious. While some salespeople are certainly pushy and some industries are known for high-pressure tactics more than others (automobiles and insurance), the best salespeople see themselves as consultants rather than peddlers or venders.

Shelly, an account executive for a medical supply company in Los Angeles, says, "You need to be persistent and have a thick skin. Rejection is a way of life in this business. It's a law of numbers. The more people I talk to, the greater my chances are of reaching someone who will say yes."

## What About Education or Background?

Generally, there are no special degree or educational requirements, but some organizations may have their preferences. "Education isn't as important as experience and talent," says Eric of Bear Stearns. There are many people in sales with business degrees, but this is also a great field for liberal arts majors. In most sales companies, you will start out on even footing with your coworkers. You will be taught what you need to know. At this point, you just have to be bright. Your degree or grades don't matter," says Angela.

Because you're often working on your own and there may not be much direction, self-discipline and motivation are something you must posses.

You must have patience. Certain sales cycles can take longer than others. Some salespeople work for over a year just to close one deal. And sometimes that deal can blow up in your face after you have spent so much time and effort working with someone.

Some industries require that you have sales backgrounds in similar fields or sales environments before they will hire you. Since many undergraduates want to work for pharmaceutical companies, most drug manufacturers want you to have at least two years experience in outside sales, working for a company that has a product (not a service). "Drug companies love people who worked at Xerox, Pitney Bowes, or another office equipment or consumer goods company," says Eric of Ciba-Geigy.

## How Do I Get Hired?

There isn't one certain way to get hired. Some organizations actively recruit on campuses or through career fairs, while others use the classified ads. If you want to contact a company regarding a sales position, your best bet would be to contact the director or vice president of sales or the sales manager. This is much more effective than going through personnel or human resources.

Once you have a track record with solid results (consistently meeting your quotas and targets) and between three to five years experience, you might be contacted by a headhunter or sales recruiter. Headhunters are quite common in this field, but they only want to talk with you if you have experience.

## How Can I Stand Out?

Your people skills are the most important asset you have. The best salespeople are great listeners. Sure, you must be persuasive, but how can you persuade someone unless you know their wants and needs. Ben, a sales rep for a financial services firm, says, "You have to listen to the client. They will tell you what they want or what their objections are, maybe not directly, but if you listen you will know how to help that person."

This is also a business of results. Make sure you keep track of your results, and realize that your "hitting" your numbers, meeting your quotas, and making the sale are how you will be judged.

## Aren't Salespeople Supposed to Be Sleazy and Unethical?

I'm sorry, you must be thinking about attorneys. Some people have an image of the salesperson as the shady used-car salesman. The truth is that you have sleazeballs in every industry, and yes, there are unethical salespeople just as there are unethical doctors.

## What Are the Pros and Cons?

The money and the freedom are the top reasons people go into sales. "I feel more in control of my future," says Greg, who works for a company that sells software to banks. It is that independence and self-reliance that draws many people to this profession. "I would rather let my income depend on my abilities rather than wait for someone to notice my work and hope I get a raise," says Greg.

The downside is that you will experience a lot of rejection. I mean *a lot* of rejection. Lee, sales director for Southwestern, says that a big problem for young salespeople is that they become disillusioned when they don't have immediate success. "It becomes easy to dwell on it when you keep getting rejected. Instead, young sales reps need to look at every rejection as a learning experience and discover how they can improve."

## What Is the Career Path?

There really isn't an established career path, because some people want to go into sales management and be responsible for a larger territory or have several reps report to them, while other reps pass up management opportunities so they can stay in sales. In some situations, reps can make more than sales managers because of the commission structure. Mike, a former sales rep and now a sales manager for a software company, says, "I like the responsibility, and it's good for my career long-term, but I lost money when I became a manager. My paycheck now depends on my reps meeting their quotas. The reps can make more than I can."

Some sales pros use their connections, industry knowledge, and product experience to go into other areas like marketing or product development. Others become entrepreneurs.

With sales experience and a track record of consistently reaching and surpassing quotas and setting records, you are very marketable. Companies are always seeking experienced salespeople who have a successful track record. You can choose to stay in one industry, or you can take your sales skills (which include closing sales, getting orders, and establishing a rapport with clients) to other companies in a different industry. If you are a good salesperson, you can learn the specifics of a product or service.

## Is Sales Competitive?

Yes. Sales is an extremely competitive field. There is competition for the great positions, although other fields like the media and financial services are harder to break into. Once you are hired, you will face competition in the marketplace from other companies vying for your customers and from inside your own organization as people try to break records, win contests, and achieve bonuses.

Salespeople are competitive by nature, so many companies often have rankings, incentives, and sales contests among coworkers. Sometimes, it may be for nothing more than a parking spot or plaque, but it might be for merchandise, trips, or cruises. During my sales career, I won trips to Mexico, merchandise (yard tools), and golfing vacations, but the best prize was always cash.

## What the Pros Read

In addition to reading the trade journal for their particular industry, sales pros read:

*Sales & Marketing Management*
*Selling*

## Where Can I Learn More?

Sales and Marketing Executives International
Statler Office Tower, Suite 977
Cleveland, OH 44115

Direct Selling Association
1666 K Street NW
Washington, DC 20006

## Where on the Web?

www.ama.org—American Marketing Association
www.nasp.com—National Association of Sales Professionals

Ron was one of the top salespeople at a software company. He was known as a bit of a maverick and bent the rules a little bit. Because his sales numbers were so good, no one seemed to care. Ron was also one of the highest paid sales reps. After three years on the road, he was promoted to manager. As a manager, he was no longer in the field selling, so he was not making high commissions. His income was cut by 20 percent. Ron was used to being in control of his own future. "I didn't have to depend on anyone else to reach their quotas."

# 47

· · · · · · · · · · · · · · · · · · · · · · · · · · · · · · · · · · ·

# Television

**Some Common Positions**
    On-air talent
    Show host
    News reporter/correspondent
    Anchor
    Producer
    Production assistant
    Floor manager
    Editor
    Director
    News director
    Program director
    Assignment editor
    Camera operator
    Researcher
    Production manager

**Other Opportunities You Might Consider**
If you like broadcasting and entertainment but don't have great TV hair, there are similar opportunities in radio and film. If you enjoy reporting and writing, you should consider the many opportunities with newspapers and magazines. Even public relations and advertising—especially the media side—are fields that are related to the television business.

Working in television gives you three choices: talent, production, and sales. When most people think of a career in television, they think it means being in front of the camera. The on-air staff are often refereed to as the talent. These are the hosts, reporters, or anchors. While these may be the most high-profile positions, there are only a few available. The majority of positions are available behind the camera in production. Since television is, after all, a business, there are marketing, publicity, and advertising departments as well.

On-air talent means being an anchor, reporter, or host. These are the most coveted and competitive jobs. Think about television news programs or talk shows—there can only be so many hosts. The bulk of opportunities in television exist behind the scenes in production. It seems that there are a million and one titles, but the main positions include producers, directors, editors, writers, and camera and sound people.

Television stations make their money by selling advertising space, or airtime, to sponsors. Like any other business that needs to market, advertise and promote their company, television stations promote their shows, news, and station to advertisers and the community. Television advertising sales is very similar to any other sales position, and is almost identical to radio sales. Traditionally, there's more money in television sales. Opportunities in publicity, public affairs, marketing, and sales are often overlooked, because they don't have the glamour of being in front of the camera.

Early on, you should decide at what type of station or network you want to work. There are several types of television stations: news, entertainment, cable, and networks. Cable stations and networks may produce some news, but they also run syndicated entertainment or educational programs and produce their own original programming. Examples would be MTV, E!, A&E, ESPN, USA, TNT, and CNN.

News stations are what most of us are familiar with. These are the local affiliate stations of the major networks—ABC, NBC, and CBS. Fox stations used to be entertainment only, but they are developing a heavy news presence. Obviously, what makes a news station different from the rest is that they have a newscast and reporting staff. This is often the largest expense of a station, but it is also one of the greatest revenue generators.

Some stations are independent—not affiliated with a network. Some independent stations have news operations. WABU in Boston—the official station of the Boston Red Sox—is an example of an independent station with a large news and sports staff.

Entertainment stations are just that. They don't have a news staff and might only run syndicated programs or reruns. These are your basic *Baywatch* and *Dukes of Hazzard* stations.

Catherine, an anchor for the ABC affiliate in Oklahoma City, started her reporting career in hopes of being a respected journalist. Her first assignment was a hard-hitting, cutting-edge segment called "Wednesday's Pet." You know, the segment that shows a homely dog or cat hoping that you'll call in to adopt it. Catherine spent a year as "Pet Girl," constantly bugging the news director for a better assignment. She then became the consumer reporter. After another year or so, she began filling in for the weekend anchor. She finally got her big break during the Waco standoff. She did several live spots and tape packages for the network and other stations that didn't have a remote crew available. This gained her credibility back home, and she was soon on her way to bigger stories and more guest anchor spots. Today, after six years, she is now the morning show anchor.

● ● ●

Most television stations have a public affairs director that helps with any type of public event, cosponsorships with local companies and organizations, and special community programs and projects. There are also FCC regulations that state how much programming for children and special groups a station must air. The public affairs director usually addresses these issues and may even host a public affairs program. You might not have known this because these shows generally air at horrible time slots like Sundays at midnight.

# Where Do I Start?

This is an extremely competitive field on either side of the camera. If you think your fresh mass-communications degree and a burning desire to be the next Peter Jennings or Chris Berman are enough to get you a job in a major market, give it up. This can be a cut-throat industry, especially in the beginning. No one starts out in a major market, and even small markets won't give you a chance if you are unpolished or lack experience. In television, maybe more than other industries, you have to pay your dues. Most people interested in being on air start their career at a small station or affiliate.

If you want to be on camera, your best shot is to move to nowhere Montana and cover high school water volleyball for a year. Start with a small local station or affiliate. You'll find many small or rural television stations staffed with young people, all trying to get experience and airtime. Your goal should be to get experience and material for your demo tape. Some people start out in a production role and then make the leap to on-air talent, although this path is probably more common in radio than in television.

In production, or behind the scenes, you'll most likely start out as an unpaid intern. Don't worry about the pay. Just get experience anyway you can. If you're lucky enough to get a paying position, you'll probably start out as a production assistant, researcher, fact-checker, associate producer, or grunt. You should try to learn about all aspects of the newsroom, from writing to producing and editing. Some of your activities might include making phone calls to research facts or book guests, writing copy, going on shoots with a reporter, carrying equipment, or even getting lunch.

During an internship, make sure you get your hands on everything you possibly can. A lot of it'll be grunt work, but you'll learn through osmosis. Some of the things you might do as an intern, runner, or production assistant (the main entry-level positions) might include: making phone calls, faxing, carrying cable and other gear, sweeping, delivering mail, and getting lunch and coffee. It's the usual grunt work

## Did You Know?

Many television programs and networks have research departments. Ever wonder where shows like *Rikki Lake* or *Maury Povich* get story ideas or discover random facts about transvestite truckers and the women who love them? There's either a department or staff member whose sole function in life is to surf the Web and search databases like Lexis-Nexis discovering facts the hosts and producers can use. At the networks, there are entire libraries or information centers that provide this information. Where do you think ESPN gets their stats? From a roomful of people searching every wire, ticker, and database under the sun. Local stations also use these services. *NewsTalk TV*, a cable program, has a talk show with a host who sits to the side pulling up information from the Internet as guests are speaking live about a topic. I know, I was on the show.

You never know what you'll be asked to do. Tracy, a former associate producer for the now canceled *Current Affair*, developed a reputation around the studio as the local expert on serial killers. Whenever the show wanted to schedule an interview with someone on death row, she was the one to research it, contact the prison, and arrange the interview. She even spoke with Jeffrey Dahmer and Charles Manson from prison.

found in most internships and entry-level jobs, but if you get lucky or are a big enough pain in the butt, you might get to go on shoots with reporters and producers or learn to write, edit, and run the board or camera. You might even get to do a voice-over. It depends where you are and how you take advantage of opportunities. The key is to remember that nothing is beneath you. Everything around you is an opportunity to learn, even if it means just being around it and seeing how things are produced, how people act, how they find information, and what the successful people are doing. You're also making contacts that you can use in the future.

## What Does a TV Producer Do?

The best description I've heard came from a producer who said, "Producing is like planning a birthday party. You have a basic idea, and you put everything together so the party matches your idea of how it should be. You make sure there's a clown, cake, streamers, balloons, whatever it takes to make the party happen. It's the same thing in TV, except instead of cake and ice cream, you're putting together video footage, interviews, and sound bites to make a finished product.

Ashley, a reporter for an NBC affiliate, was in the second year of a three-year contract when she received an offer to become the anchor of a station in Alabama. This was a big chance to move from reporter to a full anchor. Her current employer would not release her from the contract, and she had to turn down the offer.

Others, primarily production staff, are sometimes hired as contractors on an indefinite, temporary basis. (I was confused, too.) "Permatemping" is very common in television production. You're not a full-time employee or eligible for any insurance benefits, yet you're expected to show up every day and act as a regular employee. This is okay, except most temporary positions last a certain period of time and then the job is over or you're offered a permanent position. Permatemp jobs don't have a time limit, and there's no prospect for a permanent position. Doug, who is now a full-time employee with benefits, was a permatemp producer at MTV for two years. The plus here is for companies who don't have to offer benefits or pay taxes, because you're considered an independent contractor.

## How Do I Get Hired?

Don't worry about campus recruiting, because it's almost nonexistent.

If you want to be an on-air personality, your demo tape or package is more important than your résumé. A demo tape is a video of your best clips, segments, or stories. It shows you in action. Many people create their demo tapes while serving as an intern or while working at their campus station. It should be edited very tightly and have your strongest work at the beginning. Once you have a tape and a résumé, you should send it to news directors and keep following up.

The most effective ways to get hired are word of mouth and networking. This is true for talent, but especially for production. Doug, a producer at E!, says, "The hardest part about production is getting in. It's a very tight community, but once you're in, you can be set." Some in TV say that you can expect a 90 percent or more rejection rate. The major shows and networks get hundreds of résumés a week.

Once you're established, there are headhunters and placement services that deal exclusively with broadcasters. These companies are usually hired by a station's management to conduct a search for a new on-air talent. The station calls and says, "We need a brunette female anchor." The search firm has a database and a collection of tapes of brunette female anchors to choose from. You can send your tape to one of these firms, but only if you have a professionally edited tape. Call first to learn if they have any requirements. One of the largest of such firms is Don Fitzpatrick & Co. in California.

Another way established broadcasters find work is through an agent. This is similar to an actor, musician, or author. TV agents represent on-air talent and either help find them work or negotiate the contracts for their clients. Although, one correspondent who has an agent says, "I don't know of anyone whose agent actually found them a job, but everyone has an agent anyway, so they can cut a better contract." An agent's commission is generally 5 to 10 percent.

> Brandon Bryce worked his way through school as a radio host for an alternative radio station. He then landed a spot as a weekend weatherman on a local CBS television station. As part of the deal, he was asked to use a stage name. He became Bo Brandon.
>
> C'mon, it's the weather, not *The Young and the Restless*. Why not just call him Buck Naked? I'm still trying to determine if there's a service that comes up with stupid TV and soap opera names.

## What Skills Do I Need?

You have to be creative, patient, a good writer and communicator, and know how to type. If you're on the production side, you need to have technical experience and be familiar with the equipment. If you have a strong accent or regional dialect, you had better lose it. Newscasters and on-air talent are told to sound nondescript, like they are from the Midwest. A lot also depends on your looks and voice.

## Does Education Matter?

Many people have degrees in television, broadcasting, or mass communications, but your degree doesn't really matter at all. Your degree and education are helpful only if you're able to use it to get hands-on experience at your college station.

Amy, a correspondent for *Good Morning America*, says, "I don't think anyone has ever asked me if I went to school, let alone what my degree was." Experience is what counts. Need more proof? Peter Jennings, often thought of as the most intelligent man in television, did not go to college.

## What's the Career Path?

There really isn't an established career ladder or path. Advancement comes by gaining more exposure, responsibility, better (higher profile) assignments, and better time slots. Being the weekend or noon anchor is not as good a gig as the weekday 11:00 P.M. anchor. To advance in television might mean moving frequently. People commonly move between stations and markets to get more money and exposure. Connections count for a lot in television, so start building your Rolodex early.

> The worst thing about looking for a job on television is that it can often feel like video dating. You send a demo tape of yourself to someone and hope they like what they see. "You're judged on how you look, how you speak, how you put the piece together. It can make you feel very vulnerable," says Amy Atkins of *GMA*.

## What Makes Someone Stand Out?

Experience, experience, and more experience, preferably at an early age. One producer said, "If I see a recent graduate who has three years of experience at her college station and has edited, written, produced, or directed, the light goes on that says this is an aggressive person who wants to make it in this business."

## How Much Can I Make?

Entry-level salaries in television (both in front of and behind the camera) are about as low as you'll find. As I mentioned, your best bet of even finding a job is in a small market. One rookie reporter in Montana started at the mind-numbing salary of $13,500 a year—yes, that's before Uncle Sam took his cut. Amy of *Good Morning America* says when she started her career in Bakersfield, California, she made $16,000. The upside is that you'll probably love what you do and will be glad to pay them to let you do it, because you're having a blast. Even though it's hard work, the extras are nice and you're building your career.

Talent and production staff are sometimes initially employed on a contract basis rather than as full employees. This usually serves as a trial period. If a station wants to hire you permanently, you may be asked to sign a multi-year contract. This can be a good thing, unless you want to move or are made an offer by another station.

Some production staff may be on contract for the length of a project. It's not uncommon for production staff to change jobs frequently, much more than talent. This is especially true outside of news. People job-hop all the time for advancement or out of necessity. If your show is canceled, so are you.

## On the Job with Doug Goodstein, Producer at E! Entertainment Television

Experience really is the difference between those who get hired and those who don't. The earlier you can get started, the better. By the time Doug Goodstein graduated from the University of Hartford, he had already been an intern at four different stations and programs, including WABC and WNBC in New York, as well as for *Geraldo* and a cable company. By the time he graduated, Doug had a job offer with *ABC World News Tonight*. "I was really fortunate in my internships, because I was allowed to get my feet wet, really wet. At WABC, I was the community services intern, which was in the public affairs area. I learned to write PSAs [public service announcements]. I wrote the bios of the reporters, and when they had a shoot, I was allowed to tag along with the producers as a PA."

At WNBC, Doug was on the assignment desk for the local news, answering phones, faxing, and doing other grunt work, but he was also able to go out on shoots with reporters and watch how stories were edited.

When Doug graduated, he worked as a runner and PA at the 1992 Democratic and Republican National Conventions for ABC. Doug then went to work as desk assistant for *ABC World News Tonight*. "It was a staff job. I helped assignment editors with phone calls, running scripts, filling up wire copy, and helped the reporters and producers research stories and send copies of local newspapers all around the world."

Doug had a strange encounter during his first few days on the job. "I met a director from one of the shows and he said, 'Welcome, but my advice to you is to get out of here. The last thing someone young should do is be in a network, because it will take forever for you to move on. You should be at a cable network where you can move up and then finish your career at a network.'"

Doug stuck it out at ABC and left exactly two years later. Did he agree with the director's advice or was the director just jaded? "I realized I was qualified to do so much more, but the status quo prevented me from doing what I really wanted to do.

## What's It Like to Work in Television?

Do you think TV is glamorous? Newsrooms and television studios are often very casual. I've been on news sets where the weatherman was in a suit with tennis shoes and no socks. Another anchor (who always sat behind a desk) wore shorts with his coat and tie. But that is where the casual atmosphere ends, because there are often tight deadlines and changes to the script that happen as you are on the air. It can be very stressful (not unlike the movie *Broadcast News,* where Holly Hunter is screaming profanities at everyone.)

A career in television may appear glamorous, but it is far from it. "Oh, there are times when it is like that," says Carmen, a reporter for a small station in Florida, "It can be pretty cool getting recognized in the grocery store, but I have also missed countless weddings and family events because of my schedule." In the beginning you will make a number of personal sacrifices and your family and friends might not understand. You might have to work holidays, because as a common saying around newsrooms goes, "The news doesn't stop on holidays."

The hours and schedule are also erratic. You may work Wednesday through Sunday from 2:00 to 11:00 P.M. Catherine in Oklahoma City did not have a weekend off during her first three years as a reporter. This really screws up your social life if your friends or spouse have regular jobs with weekends off.

Ashley says, "It's nice to be a local celebrity, but it also means that you give up some privacy. Sometimes people will feel that they know you and that gives them the right to say things you would not say to a stranger. I've received letters and calls from viewers commenting on my hair, my weight, or why I covered a certain story. I get some sweet letters, but I also get some spooky things like a guy who sent me underwear."

I hope you have a thick skin, because it's not just concerned viewers who offer constructive criticism. Stations often hire image and broadcasting consultants to help enhance the look or image of a station and its personalities. You may be asked to change your look, cut or dye your hair, lose weight, change your clothes, change how you speak, even change your name. You may lose out on a job for a reason that has more to do with your hair color than your journalistic skills. If they are looking for a blonde from the South and you're a brunette from the Northeast, there's not much you can do about it. It's like acting, you have to look right for the part.

Right or wrong, TV is superficial. Your reporting and news gathering skills are important, but your career depends a lot on your looks and how your looks fit into a certain market or show. And I am not talking about *Baywatch*, either. Many news shows want the right look. And that often means trying to look as much like a Benetton ad as possible. If management has a certain look in mind or needs to round out the look of its news desk or staff, they'll actively search for that look. Stations may hire an agency or headhunter to find an African American female anchor or an Asian male meteorologist.

A TV studio is a weird mix of talent in suits and makeup and others who look as if they are in the same clothes as the night before. Reporters may take a cameraperson or crew with them on a shoot, or they may be alone and end up lugging a camera themselves and doing physical work.

Once you reach a certain level, it changes. One reporter for a major network says, "The main difference between working for a local station and the networks is that there are so many people here who can help me with my job and make it easier for me. I've never been in an editing room

## On the Job with Doug Goodstein, Producer at E! Entertainment Television (*cont.*)

"It was great working there, but you're dealing with the top people in the business, and for someone twenty-four and right out of college, it's impossible to compete with people at the top of their field. Even if you're eager, aggressive, and good at what you do, chances are you won't rise as quickly as you could at a cable network."

Doug also says his character didn't fit in with hard news. "I needed a looser environment. That's when I decided entertainment might be a good choice." He applied to about twenty New York shows and networks.

The whole process took about eight months until he landed a job at E! One reason it took so long is that E! has such a small production staff in New York. There simply wasn't an opening. Doug stayed in touch with the E! producer during that time and kept his name fresh on his mind. When an opening became available, Doug was called in. "I didn't know what show they wanted to hire me for when I went in." Imagine Doug's surprise when he learned that he was being hired as an associate producer for one of E!'s top rated shows. (I'm not allowed to say which one, other than that it's a daily show hosted by a major syndicated radio personality with long black hair. You figure it out.)

Today, after two years with E!, Doug is a full producer. "I do much of what I did as an AP, like produce shows, act as field producer, and set up the location on remote shoots. I even make props and shop for wardrobe. I also coordinate our internship program. Hiring people is now my biggest thrill."

People tend to think that TV is glamorous, but you need to realize how much work goes into producing material for TV. Every minute of what you see on TV may have taken several hours to produce.

You'll find your share of weasels in every business, and TV is no different. Josh, a rookie at a major network, tells of how he had prepared a story proposal for a news show's producers. The document had been laying on Josh's desk. As Josh returned from lunch, he saw a peer reading the proposal and the research. The next week, Josh discovered that the weasel had stolen Josh's idea and created a slightly different version. He turned it in to other show producers at the network.

since I've been here, but in my first job, I edited every piece I did."

Some people perceive news anchors as empty talking heads. Well, some anchors really are—probably much more than you could ever imagine. Don't get me wrong, there are many well-prepared, informed, thoughtful, and professional journalists. But just because someone is hosting a show or sitting behind a news desk does not make them intelligent, informed, or prepared. There are people behind a news desk or sitting in the host's chair who wouldn't know what to do if didn't appear on the Teleprompter or if it wasn't being told to them by the producer through the earpiece.

It's often the producers and directors who determine the direction of the show, the guests, what spot goes where, and what you'll talk about. On the other hand, many reporters and people in the field do everything, including all of the writing and editing of their work.

Have you ever noticed how some hosts look so prepared when they are talking to a guest on a quick news segment? I've been on several news programs where the host rushes in thirty seconds before we go on air, looks at me, and says, "Thanks for coming. Now who are you and what are we talking about." True story. However, when the cameras roll, you would think that we had gone to high school together and they had read my book three times. Truth is, they have a card with four questions on it or the producer is telling them things through the earpiece. Look for it next time you watch the news. You can tell who's really prepared and who isn't.

A staffer for a major talk show said you would be surprised to learn how many broadcasters simply take the easy road and read whatever is put before them. "There are some national anchors and household names who wouldn't think twice about asking a guest if monkeys flew out of his butt, as long as it was written on the card in front of them."

## Where on the Web?

www.nab.org—National Association of Broadcasters (NAB)
www.vine.org—The Vine
www.broadcastjobs.com—BroadcastJobs.com

# 48

• • • • • • • • • • • • • • • • • • • • • • • • • • • •

# Temporary and Contract Careers

With an estimated 5 million people downsized, laid off, or fired since 1990, the way people work has certainly changed. Companies have chosen to outsource certain jobs and even entire departments. The result is a new type of employee—one that is hired only when needed. Contingent workers and temporary employees now make up 25 percent of the U.S. private sector workforce, according to the Bureau of Labor Statistics. What was once thought of as a last resort for people who couldn't find anything else has in fact become a permanent career path.

While there are pros and cons, both employers and workers seem to love this new work arrangement. Companies love it: Although they may have to pay a higher hourly wage, they aren't burdened with paying workers a full-time salary or costly insurance benefits. As for workers, they like the fact that they are constantly developing and acquiring new skills and won't fall victim to downsizing or layoffs. Regardless of what you call it, temping, contracting, and freelancing are here to stay.

## Aren't Temp Jobs Just for Secretaries?

Until recently, most of the temp jobs were clerical, and even today almost 40 percent of positions are clerical or administrative. But temping is often far from grunt work and advanced coffeemaking. Temp firms now specialize in a number of professions that cater to companies with special needs or those that outsource certain projects. The fastest growing area of temporary and contract assignments are in the technical and computer fields. Industrial or skilled technical positions are the next largest groups.

Types of temporary assignments may include:

Clerical/administrative
Industrial
Technical
Professional (accounting, bookkeeping, financial, law)
Healthcare
Marketing

## Why Would I Want to Temp?

Obviously, earning a paycheck and gaining experience is better than sitting on the couch eating Doritos and watching *Melrose Place* reruns. Fifty-four percent of temporaries work to pay the bills, but there are also many who see temping as a way to create an opportunity and turn it into a full-time job.

## How Can I Turn a Temp Assignment Into a Full-Time Job?

Temp assignments are a great way for you to test-drive a company and let them see you in action as well. Almost 40 percent of temps have been offered full-time employment at the company/organization they were on assignment with, according to National Association of Temporary Staffing Services (NATSS). If you are on a temporary assignment you think you might want to pursue as a full-time position, learn about the business and make contacts throughout the organization. Don't be shy. Let it be known to your supervisor and others in the company that you are interested in a full-time position if one were to become available.

Being a temp increases your odds of getting a job for several reasons. One is that you can bypass the personnel department and all of the initial screening that goes on in many companies. As a temporary employee, you have an advantage that most job seekers don't: You are already in the door and have a chance to show an employer what you've got. It's your chance to shine and demonstrate what you can do. That's better than an interview anytime.

Jeanette got her start as a temp in the marketing department at Pepsi's headquarters. She did a good job and let the department head know that she was interested in working there if something ever came up. It did, and now she is working in the marketing department.

Temping can also help you land a job at the company of your choice. Bruce Steinberg of the NATSS says that if you have a certain company in mind and are having trouble getting in to meet with anyone, you might try contacting the human resources department and asking which temporary service they use. Next, contact that temp agency and tell them you are able to go on assignment and that you want to go to company X. You may not get placed there, but Steinberg says it is a savvy way to increase your odds of getting in the door.

## What Will I Do?

You may do anything from administrative and clerical work to accounting and bookkeeping to writing proposals or even writing code. The variety of temporary work today is incredible. The variety is one of the things that most temps say they like the most about temping.

## Temping to Help Your Business

Is your small business going through a slow period or an off-peak season? It is becoming more common for small-business people in certain fields to sign up with various temporary agencies. It's common among freelancers or editors, who may temp as a way to remain working when they don't have a project or client. Some people use the temp opportunities as a way to meet new clients and promote their services. Donna, a freelance editor, says, "It is a great way for me to build my business and obtain clients whom I otherwise would never have learned about."

## How Much Will I Make?

That too can vary according to the type of temporary you are, the work you are doing, and the contract you are working under. If you are a clerical or administrative temp, you may earn between $12 to $20 an hour. For a technical position such as a programmer, that fee may be $75 to $200 per hour. Many people with technical skills love working as a temporary or contract employee, because they can make much more than someone working for a company full-time. Greg, a contract programmer in San Jose, says, "I can make about $130,000 a year, while someone doing the same thing who works full-time for a company is only paid $90,000, and they still worry if they will have a job next year."

---

### Did You Know?

It's not just clerical and high-tech workers. Everybody is temping these days; even professionals such as attorneys and accountants are temping. Accountemps and Co-counsel are two temporary firms that specialize in placing professional accountants and attorneys. They are national organizations. Check for a branch in your local area.

---

## What About Benefits?

Generally, temps do not receive benefits, because they are either considered independent contractors *or* employees of the temporary firm, not employees of the client company where they are assigned. That bothers some temps like Anita, "I'm doing the same job and working the same hours as the person next to me, but I don't have insurance, a retirement plan, or any other perk of working for a company."

Although some temp and personnel firms are beginning to offer insurance benefits, it's still pretty rare and only offered to employees who have been on an assignment or with the firm for a significant amount of time, generally over twelve weeks at a minimum. The demand for quality part-time and temporary help is so great that many companies are offering insurance benefits to contingent workers that were long reserved only for full-time employees.

## How Long Are Assignments?

Fifty-five percent of temporary assignments last eleven weeks or longer according to the National Association of Temporary and Staffing Services. However, some can be for only a few days to as long as six months to a year.

## You Are the Ultimate Free Agent

Some people choose to remain temps. Almost 40 percent of the temps surveyed by the NATSS say they would like to work as temporaries on an ongoing basis. It's not uncommon for temps to make more money than full-time employees (if they're working consistently), plus they don't have to deal with the politics and BS that full-time employees contend with.

Mike in Nashville says, "I like it, because I can get experience in different fields and am constantly learning new skills, where if I were in one position, I might get stuck doing the same thing over and over and never grow."

## How Do I Know Which Temp or Personnel Firm to Use?

There are several established companies, as well as some reputable smaller shops. You can check your local listings or contact the local business journal in your city to obtain a list of the largest temporary or personnel firms. You can also contact your Better Business Bureau or the National Association of Temporary and Staffing Services. You want to make sure that you will be paid promptly, fairly, and accurately. Most importantly, you want to be sure that they will find work for you.

## Who Are Some of the Largest Temporary and Personnel Firms?

Kelly Services, Manpower, Accountemps, and Snelling are a few of the top national firms. Look in your city's listings for a ranking of the largest temporary agencies in your area, or contact the NATSS.

## Where Can I Learn More?

National Association of Temporary and Staffing Services
119 S. St. Asaph Street
Alexandria, VA 22314-3119
703-549-6287

## Where on the Web?

www.natss.org—National Association of Temporary and Staffing Services
www.napsweb.org—National Association of Personnel Services

# 49

· · · · · · · · · · · · · · · · · · · · · · · · · · · ·

# Travel

**The Most Common Position**
   Travel agent

**Other Opportunities You Might Consider**
Being a travel agent is certainly not the only thing you can do in this enormous industry. The travel and tourism industry itself generates more jobs than any industry except healthcare and business services. The Department of Commerce estimates that by the year 2,000, it will be the number-one industry in America. But this doesn't mean we'll have several million travel agents running around. There are many elements that make up the travel industry. Among them are hospitality (hotels, resorts, casinos) and food service (restaurants), which are both covered in this book, as well as airlines, cruise ships, conventions, car rentals, and attractions such as Universal Studios and Sea World. Tour companies market "all-inclusive" vacation packages that include accommodations plus air, land, and cruise travel. FunJet, Adventure Tours, Affordable Vacations, Kingdom Tours, MLT Vacations, and TransGlobal are some tour companies. Many operate similarly to any other business. In this chapter, the focus will be on where it all begins: the travel agent.

Often people pursue a career in travel because it appears glamorous (unless you are snowed in at the Boston airport for a weekend or have to stay at a Motel 6 because your company is too cheap to pay for a hotel with shampoo). Others want to become travel agents because of the fantastic perks such as discounted or even free travel to great locations. The travel agency business has changed rapidly in the past three years, and after talking with pros in the field, I don't know if it's for the better. Before you decide to leap headfirst into becoming a travel agent, consider what follows.

## Is It Just Working in an Agency?

No. There are essentially three types of travel agencies or organizations in which to work. The first is for an in-house or on-site agency arranging business travel for its employees. These are on-site private agencies. The second is as an in-house corporate travel employee for a large company or corporation. Here, you'll arrange travel solely for company employees. The third is in an independent or franchise travel agency writing both business and leisure travel. Business travel is travel arranged for people or corporate employees traveling for business purposes, and leisure travel includes non-business travel and travel for vacation or leisure purposes. This includes travel and accommodations at resorts, cruises, and tours. Both may include arranging ground transportation or rental cars for clients.

Some agencies handle everything, but more and more people are specializing in one or the other (business or leisure). You can also work for one of the airlines or tour companies in reservations and sales.

Recent cuts in commissions are forcing many agents to choose leisure over business travel.

## What Will I Do?

Being a travel agent is essentially a sales and service position requiring a great deal of knowledge and organizational skills. You'll sell airline, rail, and cruise tickets; lodging; car rentals; and travel packages, as well as educate travelers about destinations, services, and costs.

You'll spend most of your day on the phone and the computer researching fares and availability and taking bookings. You'll also troubleshoot when something goes wrong. And it will. Jeff of Carlson Travel says, "I'm often the first person my clients call when something bad happens. If they're stuck somewhere, missed a flight, or if the reservation gets lost, I'm the one who has to fix it."

Doug of Seagrave Travel says, "There are days when I don't get up from my desk or talk with anyone else in the office, because I'm so busy. The job of travels agents has been made easier because of programs like "Bargain Finder," which automatically looks for the cheapest fare. Before these were available, agents had to painstakingly search each combination.

## What Sets Me Apart?

"Many agents are getting away from service," says Betty of Journey House Travel. They feel that because their commissions have been capped, they don't have to serve the customer as well. I still have to look that traveler in the eye, so I want to do the best job I can."

"Everyone has relatively the same equipment and the same access to information, so service is what'll keep them coming back to you," says Doug.

# What Education or Training Do I Need?

There's no special undergraduate degree requirement, but there is a lot to know. Take a look at a travel agent's computer screen one day. It's amazing how many codes and configurations he or she must know. Most airlines have their own proprietary machines or reservation systems that you must learn.

Some colleges offer a two- or four-year curriculum in travel, but most people choose to take a short six- to eighteen-week basic course in travel. These are frequently offered at community colleges or continuing education programs. You can also take travel courses directly from the airlines or at special training schools. American Airlines is thought to be one of the best travel schools around, plus they own the Saabre System, widely used as the universal reservation standard. These courses can sometimes be expensive, but some agencies will sponsor their employees and pay for training.

There are additional certifications and credentials offered, but as several agents said, "They look good on your résumé, but they don't buy you anything in your career." Meaning that it won't increase your salary.

## How Do I Get Hired?

Most larger agencies ask for five years of experience. Great catch-22, huh? But don't worry, increased competition and the commission cap have forced many small agencies and mom-and-pop shops to hire beginners fresh out of school or a training program. "The training programs are so good that it doesn't matter as much," says Betty. "Plus, the small agencies can get a young person right out of school for much less than someone with experience." (Much less is all relative, because this is one of the lowest paying careers around.)

There's no college recruiting for these positions. You must pound the pavement yourself. Agents recommend contacting various agencies and sending résumés. (How is that for revolutionary job search advice?) One thing you might think about is working with a temp

---

## What If I Want to Start My Own Travel Agency?

Great. Go for it. You still need the training and coursework to understand the reservations systems. In addition, you must have an "appointment" by the Airline Reporting Corporation (ARC). ARC serves as a coordinating body and clearinghouse for the airlines. While this appointment is not required, it's virtually impossible to do business with the airlines without it, since the ARC makes it possible to collect commission from the airlines as well as get ticket stock and discounted tickets. They're the closest thing to a governing body. They protect the agents and the airlines. To get an appointment, you must apply and obtain a bond or irrevocable letter of credit in the amount of $20,000. (This does not mean that you have to come up with $20,000.) It's a financial screen to protect the carriers and guarantee that you are not a bad credit risk. It also demonstrates that you are "for real" and intend on operating as a travel agent. Otherwise, anyone would become a travel agent just to get the discounts. For more information, contact:

Airline Reporting Corporation (ARC)
1530 Wilson Boulevard, Suite 800
Arlington, VA 22209
703-816-8000

agency. There are temp firms specializing in the travel profession. Betty says it's a profession about relationships and that each agency is different. "Temping lets you work for someone to see if you like them before you try to pursue them for a full-time job."

Once you're established, there are headhunters and placement agencies that deal exclusively with travel professionals. Kerry, who has six years experience, says, "I get at least two calls a week from placement agencies." Contact ASTRA (American Society of Travel Agents) to get the names of placement and temporary agencies in your area.

## What Are the Pros and Cons?

The commission cap is a big negative for many. The atmosphere is stressful and fast-paced. Phones are always ringing or someone needs to be called back. You're also the person taking the heat when things go foul. "Sometimes there are things that are beyond your control, but it's still up to you to fix your clients' problems," says Betty.

The hours are another tough thing. "Sometimes I'm on the phone all day and then I still have things to get done," says Doug.

"I'm here until 7:00 P.M. consistently. I can't tell someone who is stuck in a city that I will get back to him tomorrow," Betty says. "You get used to it. You know that someone is out there depending on you."

The benefits? The discounted travel, of course. Resorts and airlines are always making it easy to go places for free. Resorts constantly lure agents to properties in hopes that agents will recommend them to their clients. "I have plenty of free tickets, it's just a matter of finding time to use them," says Doug. Agents also say they enjoy keeping clients happy or making sure they have a problem-free trip

## How Much Can I Make?

Well, at least you get free travel. Even with experience, you won't make much. Managers make only in the thirties. Starting salaries are between $18,000 to $22,000 and don't escalate much from there. Some agents with ten years or more experience are only making in the upper twenties. One former manager with fifteen years experience said, "I just stopped,

### What's All This About a Commission Cap?

Agents make their money from commissions, based on the sale price of any ticket or package they sell. Commissions are paid back to the agent by the airline or service provider. Traditionally, this commission was 10 percent of the total price. If an agent sold a $1,200 ticket, the agent made $120. Last year, the airlines decided they would cap the amount of commission they would pay. Today, the commission structure is a flat $50 on any ticket over $500. That means that even if an agent sells a $600 or $1,200 ticket, she still makes only $50. Anything below $500 is still 10 percent. It has cut many agents' salaries in half and put many mom-and-pop shops out of business or forced them to go all leisure, which does not have a cap for cruises or international air travel.

because the extra hours on weekends and the extra stress weren't worth it." Some agencies offer insurance benefits. Salaries and benefits will be higher and more plentiful with the larger agencies such as American Express or Carlson. For the amount of knowledge and work involved, these salaries are ridiculous.

## Why Do It?

For the travel benefits. Betty says, "We go into it for the glamour, and when we realize there isn't any, we do it for the free travel."

## What About Stability?

If people are with large agencies, they tend to stay for a while, but there can be a lot of turnover in the business. "It depends on the atmosphere at the agency," says Betty. People go from agency to agency. It's a large industry, but it's closely knit. People tend to know one another. Many people get in the business and then leave for a while before getting back into it.

## Where Can I Learn More?

American Society of Travel Agents (ASTRA)

## Where on the Web?

http://astanet.com—American Society of Travel Agents
www.nbta.org—National Business Travel Association
www.iacvb.org—International Association of Convention and Visitor Bureaus

# 50

● ● ● ● ● ● ● ● ● ● ● ● ● ● ● ● ● ● ● ● ● ● ● ● ● ● ● ● ● ● ● ● ● ● ●

# Web Site and Internet Developers

**Some Common Positions**
> Webmaster
> Web designer/developer
> Graphic artist
> Custom programmer
> Software developer
> Internet marketing specialist
> Editor/publisher

This field has a lot to offer even if you aren't a programmer or don't know how to write HTML. People are scrambling to figure out if advertising, commerce, or content will control the Web. So right now, there are opportunities for people with marketing, advertising, financial, journalism, and art backgrounds.

**Other Opportunities You Might Consider**
Working for an advertising agency's interactive unit, helping a major company market its services online, or freelancing your writing, artistic, or programming skills. Don't forget newspapers. Print is not dead, but they're shaking in their boots. Many newspapers have developed online counterparts.

Five years ago, if you had told someone, "I'm a Webmaster," he would have looked at you as if you're some sort of Dungeons and Dragons freak that needed to get out more often. Today, a Webmaster is one of the newest and most highly sought after positions around.

It seems that every major company, mom-and-pop shop, and special interest group wants to be on the Web, not to mention the many wannabe publishers hoping to take control of the new medium. With over 150,000 sites on the World Wide Web and hundreds more being added daily, you can bet that it's a mad sprint to figure out how to make a buck off of the Web.

# What Is a Webmaster?

A Webmaster is the person who develops and maintains a site on the World Wide Web. He or she generally works with a graphic designer and a writer or client who produces the content (art and text). The Webmaster then does the coding (programming), as well as maintaining the links and upkeep of the site.

Webmasters and the entire production staff of writers, graphic artists, designers, systems administrators, and software developers may work for a small Internet or Web site developer, for a major company or large advertising agency, or freelance.

# Where Are the Jobs?

They're virtually everywhere. You'll find one-person shops, small companies with a skeleton staff of contract employees, and major companies like Sprint, Microsoft, and Texas Instruments employing people to produce content or maintain sites on the Web.

Geographic boundaries don't matter at all. However, it's commonly thought that the San Francisco Bay Area is the headquarters for any technological developments regarding the Web and New York is the content capital, with its number of writers and artists.

# Are You a Journalist?

Last fall at the American Association of Sunday Feature Editors (AASFE) Conference, a panelist from Knight-Ridder said that the largest employer of journalists in the next year would not be a newspaper or even a publisher. It would be Microsoft. They're hiring journalists, writers, and editors to help create content for their many Web offerings.

# Don't Bet the Farm

As much opportunity as this field promises, people are still experimenting and trying to find what works and, most importantly, what consumers are willing to pay for. As quickly as Microsoft is hiring journalists and people for their Web offerings, it has been reported that they and other companies are quick to pull the plug on sites that aren't popular, fail to capture an audience, or, more importantly, aren't paying advertisers quickly.

There are many small Web site developers in every city. These are the training grounds for most people. Then there are larger companies developing major sites on the Web for corporate clients or content-oriented developers such as tripod.com or i.village, which created and maintains the parent soup and about-work sites on the Web.

## It's Not Just Technical Positions

You can have the coolest site in the world, but if people don't know about it or they visit once and never come back, your site is ineffective. Increasingly, a business background or understanding of marketing is proving helpful to anyone entering this field.

## What's the Career Path?

This field is so young that you can really blaze your own trail. No one knows what the career path is, so you're free to make your own. Generally, people have obtained experience on their own or working for a small developer. After you have some experience, one option is to open your own shop. This is a great industry for young entrepreneurs. The relatively low start-up costs allow many bedroom entrepreneurs to sprout up.

However, the most common path so far has been for people to get experience and training working for a smaller Web developer in hopes of selling their skills to a large corporation that has an in-house staff. Lori Barber, owner of NetSuccess, a Web site developer with several major corporate clients, says, "We end up hiring a lot of young people and giving them a chance. Yet as soon as we train them, larger companies like Sprint and Northern Telecom come by and recruit them." It's great for the employees, because they're usually doubling their salaries when they move to a large company. Roger worked for a small developer part-time while he was in school, and after graduation he walked right into a job with Sprint for $40,000.

## What Are the Pros and Cons?

It's an exciting industry. It's constantly in the media. There's growing competition, but it's exciting and constantly changing. People are making fortunes all the time. Age doesn't matter. Experience and background don't matter. Anyone can do it, and many people are doing it. This leads me to the negatives about this field.

No one knows where this thing will go. There's no career path, job security, or training program. "Technology is changing so rapidly that we have to learn as we go," says Lori. If you can't fly by the seat of your pants, you need to become an accountant or something more grounded.

So far, it looks like the Internet will continue to be a success, but as with many things, there may be a shake-up that leaves only a few large companies on top.

People are trying to decide if the Web is a medium, art, commerce, or all three. At its core, it's a business. Otherwise people wouldn't be flocking to it like ants to a picnic.

## Where Do I Start? How Do I Learn It?

There are few training programs for this, although the number is growing. The problem is that the software, plug-ins, and other tools are changing so rapidly that the schools and courses are behind. On a basic level, most people simply go to Barnes & Noble and buy a book on how to write HTML.

## How Much Can I Make?

There's a lot of debate about this. There's a ton of hype around guys like Marc Andresson, founder of Netscape, and Jerry Yang and David Filo, the two "twentysomethings" who founded Yahoo! They are both worth over $100 million. They're the queen bees. Meanwhile, worker bees might make $7 to $15 an hour. A systems administrator might make $22 an hour. It depends on the demand, your skills, and the company you're with.

Companies report that Webmasters can make anywhere from $30,000 to $100,000. People I spoke with said they started at low salaries or did things for free until they learned some skills and had some work to show. Once they had some experience, many doubled or tripled their salaries overnight.

As a freelancer, you can earn from $50 to $100 an hour. There are no standards. People will charge all over the map—take whatever you can get and feel good about charging.

Unless you're with a major company or someone who has some bucks, you can forget about benefits.

## How Do I Get Hired?

Some people say just buy a book, learn it, and start doing it. There are not many schools that teach this. Things are changing so quickly on the Web that by the time you take a class, what you're learning is outdated.

The first thing is to have a Web site of your own or a sample of work you have done for others. This is just like an artist's or writer's portfolio. Employees want to see what you're capable of. Lori of NetSuccess says, "I look for typos and small errors. If you have a typo or your work looks bad, I don't want to talk with you." If you're an artist or a writer, the same thing applies. You need to have a portfolio or samples.

These are not the type of jobs you find in the newspaper. They're found by using the medium itself. Employers say they find most of their help through the newsgroups on the Internet. Try looking in the various newsgroups. You might try looking in the newsgroups for Web developers, HTML editors, and Internet presence providers. You can also contact the Web site developers themselves. If you're interested, call first, then send a résumé and tell the employer the address of your site.

## What Skills Do I Need?

Pieta Knook, who heads up microsoft.com, says, "It's pretty rare to find a lot of people with Web skills. Our experience is we can teach that quickly. Besides, the maximum experience anybody's going to have in this is what, a year?"

Oddly enough, you can't be a Web know-it-all. There's nobody who knows everything. It's moving too fast. Pick a specialty and do it well. "A couple of years ago, you could be a jack-of-all-trades, but now it's all about specialization," says Tony Manuro, Webmaster for Cyber Solutions.

You also need to be flexible. "We are constantly doing things we have never done before," says Lori Barber. She also says it's not just about writing code. "I want someone with a good attitude, because we are working as a team. I also want someone who can interface with the clients."

## What's the Biggest Mistake You See People Make?

Tony says the biggest mistake he sees is people who are extremely technical trying to play the role of the artist. "You can't do it all. Do what you do and we can make it work."

## Where on the Web?

There are many developers' newsgroups. Go onto your favorite search engine to discover more.

www.websitebuilder.com—WebsiteBuilder.com
www.wdda.org—Web Designers and Developers Association

# 51

● ● ● ● ● ● ● ● ● ● ● ● ● ● ● ● ● ● ● ● ● ● ● ● ● ●

# Working Abroad:
# International Careers

Living and working in a foreign country may sound appealing. As we become a more global society and technology makes it easier to conduct business across time zones and geographic boundaries, there are more opportunities for people to conduct business internationally. It can be a glamorous and rewarding experience. But don't pack your bags and grab your passport yet. Working in a foreign country is very different than being a tourist on holiday, and jobs are much harder to come by than in the United States. Once you begin looking for employment in a foreign land, the dream can quickly become a nightmare. In order to work abroad, there are a few things you should know first.

## You Can't Just Fly to Europe and Get a Job

Think how hard it is for foreigners to find work in the United States. There are a number of legal and government hoops that people must jump through in order become employed. Even then, many of the positions available are lower-level jobs. In my hometown of Dallas, there is a huge Russian population. There are people who were engineers or scientists in their homeland bagging groceries or working as nannies. In New York, it is rare to find an American taxi driver. When you go to another country to work, you will encounter much of the same political and bureaucratic red tape that foreigners experience here in the United States.

Simply put, your career options abroad are fairly limited unless you:

- Teach English.
- Work in a relief organization.
- Are in the military or government.
- Are willing to work lower-level service or labor jobs, which may be paid under the table.
- Are an entrepreneur and meet certain criteria.
- Work for a US multinational company or foreign company that is willing to sponsor you in another country.

I hate to be the prophet of doom, but the likelihood of your getting off of the plane in Paris and obtaining an entry-level position similar to what a graduate might have here in the United States is pretty slim. Further, it is not very likely that as an entry-level employee you will be hired by a multinational company to live and work overseas. While it can happen, it is considered a home run. One of the toughest realizations for many Americans is that your options working abroad are really quite limited.

## What Can I Do?

You can work in any number of businesses and professions, as long as you meet the requirements set forth by that country. American expatriates work in advertising, hospitality, financial services, and manufacturing. However, many of those who work for a US company abroad or even a foreign company obtained their positions before moving to that country. They may have been assigned to that post only after they had been working a while for the company. Rarely does a company hire an entry-level employee for an overseas assignment.

## Is a Degree in International Business an Advantage?

No. You are better off studying a foreign language. Just because you graduate with an international degree doesn't mean that you will work abroad. In a recent study of those who have graduated from American graduate programs with an international focus, only 20 percent of those employed are foreign-based. The consensus was that a degree can help you understand cultures and business practices, but as in the United States or Canada, it takes more than a degree to become successful.

Carrie graduated with a double major in business and Spanish. She wanted a Latin American assignment, but did not know what industry to pursue. She researched what kinds of companies did a lot of business in the region and discovered that many oil and gas companies were active in Central and South America, so she began to contact various oil companies. She also subscribed to a magazine called *Mexico Business* to learn about American companies in Mexico and Mexican companies in the United States. Her business degree was nice, but it was her Spanish skills that made her attractive to employers and ultimately helped her land a job with an exploration company.

Experience and good communication skills are something in demand all over the world.

## I Want to Work in the International Operations of a Major Company

All I have to say is good luck. You want one of the choicest jobs in most companies. It is extremely difficult for an entry-level employee to get an international assignment early in her career. It can happen, but more often than not, companies reserve these positions for more seasoned employees. Learning a corporate culture is tough enough without having to learn an entirely new culture in another country.

In America, most entry-level positions are based here in the United States. In mid-level positions, you may get to travel to other countries on business. It is usually only experienced or senior executives who get to live abroad.

## Why Do Companies Hesitate About Sending Younger or New Employees Overseas?

It is outrageously expensive. The cost of sending an employee overseas is so costly that it is a great a risk to send someone who is unproven, inexperienced, or doesn't grasp exactly how the business works.

Many companies prefer to hire foreign students who have studied here in the United States to work in their foreign operations. It is easier for a company to hire someone who is from that country, speaks the language, and understands the culture, not to mention the legal issues of citizenship and work permits.

## Are There Any Special Requirements or Permits Required?

Just like foreigners in the United States must have green cards or work visas to become legally employed, you must have proper documentation to have certain types of employment in most other countries. Contact that country's embassy or consulate in Washington to see if you meet the criteria. If you want to work in any European or EC country, you should contact the US embassy in that country. They often know what US companies in the region are hiring US citizens and for what positions you may qualify. Don't hold your breath, though. It is extremely tough to get a work permit. In France, less than 100 are issued each year.

Check with the embassy of the country you want to work in to discover what their requirements are. Some are more lenient than others. Getting a job anywhere in Europe is tough. Certain Asian countries such as Singapore make it easier for foreigners to work there.

In any European (EC) country, you must have the proper permits and documentation, unless you are one of the following:

- An employee of the US government
- A representative of a US firm having no branch, subsidiary, or representative in the UK
- A representative of the media
- A self-employed person, such as a writer or artist

Generally, if you are in a country on a student visa, you are limited to working on campus or in certain jobs, if you are allowed to work at all.

To work in another country you must be sponsored by your employer. If you go to work in Europe for Mobil Oil, Mobil would be your sponsoring company. Just as many Americans are territorial about foreigners coming in and taking jobs from Americans, people in other counties have that same fear, so you must have a company sponsoring you to work in that country. It is an expensive and complex process to sponsor an employee, so many companies are careful about whom they sponsor. If you move to the UK and want to work for a British company, that company would have to pay to sponsor you, assuming you meet the criteria for working in that country and there is no British citizen that could do the job. See why it's such a pain to work overseas?

## Can I Have an International Career Without Living Abroad?

Absolutely. Actually, this is smarter than trying to start out living overseas. Living here in the States and working on international accounts can be a great way to learn international business, other cultures, and gain the attention of your employer. When an overseas position becomes available, you can be considered.

Eric, twenty-six, works for a company that leases heavy equipment to companies all over the world. While based in Houston, Eric spends two weeks a month traveling to South America or Asia to meet with prospective clients. Even though he lives in the United States, Eric has an international career.

You may even choose not to live abroad. Companies large and small are going global and conducting business with clients all over the world without having a permanent employee in that country.

## What Are My Best Bets for Getting a Job in Another Country?

If you have your heart set on living and working overseas, your best bets are in the following areas:

- Teaching English: There is a huge need for English teachers, especially in the Pacific Rim. The majority of recent grads working overseas are teaching English as a second language.
- Grunt Jobs: Working odd jobs as a laborer or lower-level service worker is a great way to make some spare cash to pay for your Europass. (This is much easier than trying to get a corporate job, because you may not be able to obtain the proper permits to work in an office or professional setting.)
- A small, rapidly growing U.S. company that is expanding abroad: You may have a better chance of getting an overseas assignment by working for a small company that is growing rapidly and wants to expand overseas than you would with a huge multinational.

## What Skills Do I Need?

Obviously, language skills will set you apart. Remember that working abroad requires that you become more of a "world citizen." You are the foreigner. It takes a great effort to become accustomed to other cultures, even in English-speaking cultures.

Cliff started his career as an account executive for a small software company in Oklahoma—a far cry from Europe and international business. He later became a sales manager and was asked to head a new business unit in Europe. The company wanted to develop some relationships and begin to establish a presence in Europe, so it offered Cliff the chance to start a one-person office in London. "I never would have had this opportunity with a much larger company," says Cliff.

## What Are the Most Popular Languages for Business?

According to Berlitz, one of the leading instructors of foreign languages, French, German, Spanish, and Portuguese are the most popular Western languages for business. Korean, Chinese, and Japanese are the most popular Eastern languages for business.

## What About the Peace Corp?

In the past, people have pushed working in the Peace Corps as a great way to work abroad. Long thought of as the ultimate job for do-gooders, today's Peace Corp is not only highly competitive, but requires specialized knowledge often in highly technical areas such as biology, agronomy, or medicine. This is not an extreme Club Med. You are often in a developing country without the modern conveniences we take for granted. You will work to improve and often save lives. It is a rigorous application process. Each year thousands of people apply to the Peace Corp, yet only a few are accepted.

## Where Can I Learn More About Working Overseas?

Start by contacting the embassy or consulate of the country to which you are interested in moving. They can be located around the country, but the highest concentration are in Washington, D.C. You should also contact the US embassy in that country.

In addition, most countries and foreign governments have trade organizations or branches of their Chamber of Commerce located here in the United States. These can be found in many major US cities, especially port cities.

You can also contact:

### Don't Be the Ugly American

While we may think the United States is the greatest country on Earth and nothing can beat good old American know-how, when you go to Europe, Asia, or any other place in the world, you are the foreigner. All of the cultural and language problems that educated people from Asia, India, Russia, and Africa have when they come here will undoubtedly be problems for you.

Council on International Educational Exchange (CIEE): 888-COUNCIL
Peace Corps: 800-424-8580
Japan Exchange and Teaching Program (JET): 202-939-6772
*Transitions Abroad* (A magazine that lists international job resources): 800-293-0373

## Where on the Web?

www.jobsmarts.com—JobSmarts (for links or lists of a number of international newsgroups)
www.overseasjobs.com—Overseas Jobs Express
www.summerjobs.com—Summer Jobs
www.netmatters.co.uk/users/adiann—International Jobs and Expat Career Opportunities

www.bbbhou.org/consumin/money/jobscam.htm—Overseas Job Scams
    (run by the Better Business Bureau)
www.igc.org/worldteach—Council on International Educational Exchange
www.peacecorps.gov—Peace Corps

# 52

● ● ● ● ● ● ● ● ● ● ● ● ● ● ● ● ● ● ● ● ● ● ● ● ● ● ● ● ● ●

# Writer/Author

"Everyone has a book inside of them, and some of them should stay there."
　　　　　　　　　　　—ANONYMOUS

**Some Common Positions**
　　　Writer
　　　Author
　　　Freelance writer
　　　Columnist

**Other Opportunities You Might Consider**
Writers can make a good living doing a variety of things. Many people think of writing as a being an author (the main focus of this chapter), but you can also write for a magazine, newspaper, industry publication, or even an online service or Web site. You should also check out the "Journalism" and "Publishing" chapters of this book, since those are related careers. Public relations professionals also do a great deal of writing. These types of writers can have salaried or freelance positions. Some people also work as technical writers, creating training manuals or directions for a variety of products or services.

Every couple of weeks, I'm approached by someone at an event where I am speaking or receive an e-mail or letter that asks for advice on choosing a career. After a while, the person changes the conversation by saying, "But what I really want to do is write a book. How do I do it? How do I become an author?"

I'm always happy to share that information, because I remember when I was in their shoes and was asking various authors how they did it. I must tell you, it's very difficult to get published. There are many exceptional writers who never get published, while other hacks or anyone famous or infamous can make a fortune. Who knows why?

If you feel you have a story inside of you or something important that needs to be shared with others, the following information will give you a basic understanding on what it takes to become a published author.

# How Do I Get Published

Pray hard. It's extremely difficult getting published. This is an incredibly competitive business, because only a limited number of books are released each year. Actually, it's easier to tell you how *not* to get published.

While logically it seems that if you have a manuscript or book idea, you should send it directly to a publisher (after all, they are the ones who will buy your book idea and actually publish the book), sending an unsolicited manuscript to a publishing house is generally the sure-fire way to assure that your material will never be published. Publishers are deluged with manuscripts every week. Most unsolicited manuscripts and proposals end up in what is known as the "slush" pile. If someone gets around to reading it, great, but most likely it will be an assistant who is reading dozens of unsolicited manuscripts over lunch. In all probability, you will be sent a form letter or have your manuscript returned to you. Rarely is a book plucked from the slush pile and actually published.

> "Unsolicited" means that the publisher doesn't know you, has not contacted you, or was not handed the manuscript/proposal through an agent.

The most effective way to ensure that your proposal or manuscript stands a chance of being published is to obtain a literary agent who can sell it for you.

# Do I Really Need an Agent?

Absolutely. There are a few success stories of people who represented themselves or were discovered on their own, but these are the exception rather than the rule. Contacts, connections, reputation, access to decision makers, and, most of all, knowing what is going on in the industry are keys to success. A *good* agent has all of these things.

An agent will help take care of you in the marketplace. He or she will go to bat for you and sell your project to the right publisher. Your agent knows editors at various publishing houses and their individual tastes. Each editor is different and tends to want to work on projects that interest him or her. In addition to negotiating on your behalf with publishers, a good agent will help guide your career.

# How Do I Get an Agent?

Find an agent that is the right one for you. Many agents specialize in the type of authors they represent. Some may deal only in nonfiction, while others handle writers of a particular genre such as romance or science fiction. Some represent a variety of authors. Before you send your proposal or manuscript, call the agent and ask if he or she handles your type of material. Find out what they need to consider your project. Depending on the project, your credentials, and the agent's personal preference, some agents want to see an entire manuscript, while others want to see only a proposal and sample chapters.

Publishing a book is not cheap. There are far more expenses that go into it besides the author's advance. There are distribution, production costs, marketing, and publicity costs associated with a book. Publishers are willing to take chances, but it is best-selling authors like John Grisham that make it possible for lesser known or first-time authors to have a chance.

There are several ways to learn about agents. One is to look in the *Literary Marketplace (LMP)*. It can be found in your local library, and it lists various agents and publishers with their contact information. The annual *Insider's Guide to Book Editors, Publishers, and Literary Agents* by Jeff Herman is also an excellent resource. Another idea is to look in the acknowledgments of books similar to the kind you want to write. Any smart author will thank his agent in the acknowledgments.

When you call, it's unlikely that you will get to speak directly with the agent. You will probably speak with an assistant. Don't get upset and blow this person off. Being an assistant is how many agents start their careers. Assistants also have a great deal of power, because they are the first screen and will probably be the first ones to read your proposal or manuscript. If they like it or think it has promise, the assistant will pass it to her boss. But as Donna, assistant to one agent, says, "At least 90 percent of what is sent to most agents goes in the trash or is returned to the author. It seems that every plumber from Milwaukee thinks they are a novelist."

## Should I Write the Whole Book First.

If you are a fiction writer, agents and publishers generally want to see a manuscript or several completed chapters (approximately 100 pages). Nonfiction writers don't always need to have a complete manuscript. For nonfiction, agents and editors generally require a detailed proposal.

## What Is in a Book Proposal?

A book proposal is not unlike any other marketing or sales proposal. A proposal should include a very detailed outline with a summary of what each chapter will cover; a section that describes who you are and why you are the right person to write the book; a description of who the intended audience is for the book and how it's different from what is currently on the market; ideas for how the book can be marketed; and a description

Not all writers are full-time writers. Don was a geologist and worked for two oil companies before turning his personal interest in Abraham Lincoln into a best-selling book, *Lincoln on Leadership*.

and sample of the author's voice, writing style, or tone. The proposal can be as few as fifteen pages to over fifty pages.

## What Type of Education and Background Do I Need?

It doesn't matter, unless you are writing as an expert authority on a subject. You simply must know your topic. Many writers start out doing something very different from writing; they never expected to become writers.

Having an English degree is no guarantee of getting published. Being an English major is helpful if you want to be an editor, and it will make things easier for you technically as a writer, but otherwise it's unimportant.

## How Much Will I Make?

It can vary wildly and depends on the success of your book. When an author receives an offer for his book, he is paid an advance. This is an advance sum of money that counts against future royalties that the book is expected to earn. Once the book earns enough money to pay for the advance, the author begins to receive a royalty (percentage of each book sold). Advances can range from $10,000 to hundreds of thousands of dollars and beyond if you are a major celebrity or have a large following.

The advance can be paid several different ways. In some cases, the author is paid half of the advance upon signing the contract and the balance once the manuscript is completed and accepted by the publisher. If the book never makes enough money to cover the advance the author received, he never sees another dime from the book. He does not, however, have to pay back the advance. Not every book earns back its advance. If your book does "earn out" (earns more in royalties than the advance paid), then you will receive royalties on that book as long as it is in print. You will receive a check once or twice a year for your royalties on the sales of your book.

Royalties are negotiated by your agent and can vary according to the type of book you're writing (hardcover royalties are a higher percentage than paperback), your reputation and marketability, and the book's marketability. When you get to the really big money, fiction seems to make more than nonfiction, unless you are someone famous. We aren't talking about major percentages. Most authors receive between 7 to 15 percent, although that can be negotiated if you have an impressive reputation or large audience.

## What Is It Like?

Writers don't all sit around in tweed jackets and smoke pipes, if that's what you're thinking. Each writer is different. Some write full-time, while others write and perform other activities such as speaking or consulting. Some write in their free time, because they have full-time jobs.

Some authors start out part-time until they get a book deal or a major break. It's tough to say "I'm a writer" when you're just starting. Many begin as journalists or freelancers.

Some work from home while others may have an office. Your time is flexible, except when you have a deadline. Then it can be incredibly frustrating for you and your family. It can also be frustrating if you have writer's block.

The bulk of most writers' work is done alone. Although if you are conducting research for a book, you will meet many interesting people and may even learn new things as you become an expert in an area. When it is time to edit the book, you will work closely with your editor, who acts as a coach and guide. Some writers have an assistant, researcher, or even staff to help them.

Writing and publishing a book takes a long time. Publishers generally plan at least a year before a book is released. It can be slow going until you turn your book in, and then you will become very busy during the editing process. There are many steps to creating a book that don't initially involve the author, such as the sales, design, and advance promotion.

Once the book is released, authors may tour or promote the book for an intense period lasting several weeks to a couple of months. This may include travel and television and radio interviews.

## What Are the Pros and Cons

Having someone pay you to share your ideas sure beats working construction. Many writers say the freedom and flexibility it offers is what they enjoy. It's also a rush to go into Barnes & Noble and see something that you created. Having a published book can also lead to other career opportunities such as speaking and consulting. In some cases, writing a book enhances your credibility in an existing job.

On the negative side, writing is not secure or consistent. Some authors don't like it when they realize they will actually have to promote their books. "It seems so commercial," says one fiction writer. (Funny, I thought the idea was to sell books.)

Working from home can be both a pro and a con. It's nice to have the free time, plus working in jeans and a baseball cap beats wearing a suit (not to mention how much you save on dry cleaning). But there are also distractions. Your ego may take a beating, as well. Many writers are insecure. (Although there are plenty who let their heads swell to the size of pumpkins.) It can be exciting when you get good reviews, but you tend to take the bad reviews personally.

If you only write and have no other income, you have to budget. You may be making a lot of money, but after your advance, you might only get paid royalties twice a year—if you earn out your advance.

## How Do I Write a Book?

When I got my first book deal, I completely freaked out. I thought, "What am I going to do? I've never written a book before. For that matter, I've never written more than a twenty page paper before." I contacted my friend, Jerry Bowles, who often writes for *Fortune* and is the author of several business books. "What do I do?" I asked.

Jerry's sage advice was, "Just write. Do whatever works for you. There isn't a formula or right way to do it. Everyone is different." Clueless and still without direction, I took Jerry's advice and just started writing.

Every writer has their own method, regime, and style. What works for Jerry won't work for me, and what works for me may not work for you. I don't write all the way through from start to finish. I begin with detailed outlines; use idea wheels to match examples, statistics, and stories; then fill in the guts and piece things together. Other writers start at page one and go consistently through to the end without missing a beat. Some writers write for at least a few hours every day, while others research for a long time and then work furiously at the end, writing the book in a relatively short time. The best advice is to just begin. Find a system that works for you and makes sense.

## Where Can I Learn More?

Remember that people change jobs frequently in this industry, so be sure to consult to most recent editions available for each of these resources.

*Writer's Market*: An annual listing of the periodicals, newspapers, and publishers that you will approach to sell your work. The listings include addresses, contact names, and submission criteria.
*Literary Market Place*: An indispensable resource that offers contact information on publishers and agents. It can be found in your local library.

## Where on the Web?

www.wga.org—Writers Guild of America
www.bloorstreet.com/300block/3author.htm—World of Writing
www.amazon.com—Amazon.com (the largest online bookstore)
www.bookwire.com—Book Wire

# 53

• • • • • • • • • • • • • • • • • • • • • • • • • • • • • • •

# Your Perfect Job: Now It's Up to You

**The Most Common Position**
Whatever you want to do
**Other Opportunities You Might Consider**
Infinite Possibilities

There really are an infinite amount of possible careers available to you, only a handful of which could be described in this book. Now it is up to you to go out and conduct your own research. Talk to a professional in a career that sounds interesting. Try to ask the same types of questions that were asked throughout the career profiles. Anything you want to know, you should ask. Remember that your first day at work is too late to discover that a career is not right for you. Use this as a guide to conducting your own informational interview with an employer or professional in a certain field.

Some questions you might ask include:

- What is it that you do?
- How did you get started?
- How do most people get hired?
- Where will I start?
- What will I do?
- What is the career path?
- How much can I earn?
- Are there any misconceptions about this profession?
- What are the pros and cons?

- What is the culture and work environment like?
- What sets me apart from other candidates?

At the beginning of this book, I mentioned that I hoped it would serve as a map for your career. Now that you have a better direction and a better understanding of which roads to pursue and maybe which roads to avoid, go out and create your own path. Good luck, and always remember: Success is not only about working harder, it's about working smarter.

> Don't forget to thank everyone who takes the time to meet or talk with you. All you have to do is write a simple three-sentence note.

# Part III

## Resources

# 54

## Where Can I Learn More?

### Associations, Trade Groups, and Professional Organizations

The following are some of the main trade groups, associations, and professional organizations of the industries and careers profiled in this book. I recommend that you contact them directly to learn more about career paths in the field in which you are interested.

Many associations produce special materials, books, or brochures for job seekers. You might also ask if they have student chapters or activities for young professionals who are new to the industry. If so, you should certainly become involved, at least on your local level. Some may have discounted membership rates for students or young job seekers. You should also go on the Web to learn more. Many associations have their own Web sites.

## Research Tips

Sometimes, you might not know an organization's phone number. If you want the 411 on where to find any phone number, call (Area Code) 555-1212.

If are looking for a Web site and don't know the address, go to a Web browser such as Yahoo! (www.yahoo.com), Excite (www.excite.com), Infoseek (www.infoseek.com), or Alta Vista (www.altavista.com) and type in the name of the organization you are looking for.

Academy of Motion Picture Arts and Sciences
8949 Wilshire Boulevard
Beverly Hills, CA 90211-1972

Academy of Television Arts and Sciences
5220 Lankershim Boulevard
North Hollywood, CA 91601-3109

Advertising Council Inc.
261 Madison Avenue
New York, NY 10016-2303

Advertising Research Foundation
641 Lexington Avenue
New York, NY 10022

Aerospace Industries Association of America,
   Inc.
1250 I Street, NW, Suite 1100
Washington, DC 20005-3922

Air Transport Association of America
1301 Pennsylvania Avenue NW, Suite 1100
Washington, DC 20004-1707

Aircraft Owners and Pilots Association
421 Aviation Way
P.O. Box 863
Frederick, MD 21701

American Accounting Association
5717 Bessie Drive
Sarasota, FL 34233-2399

American Advertising Federation
1101 Vermont Avenue NW, Suite 500
Washington, DC 20005

American Association of Advertising Agencies
666 Third Avenue
New York, NY 10017-4056

American Association of Engineering Societies
1111 19th Street NW, Suite 608
Washington, DC 20036-3690

American Association of Individual Investors
625 North Michigan Avenue, Suite 1900
Chicago, IL 60611-3110

American Association of Insurance Services
1035 South York Road
Bensenville, IL 60106

American Association of Nurse Anesthetists
222 South Prospect Avenue
Park Ridge, IL 60068-4001

American Association of Occupational Health
   Nurses
50 Lenox Pointe
Atlanta, GA 30324-3176

American Bankers Association
1120 Connecticut Avenue NW
Washington, DC 20036

American Bar Association
750 North Lake Shore Drive
Chicago, IL 60611

American Booksellers Association
828 South Broadway
Tarrytown, NY 10591

American Chiropractic Association
1701 Clarendon Boulevard
Arlington, VA 22209

American College of Health Care Administrators
325 South Patrick Street
Alexandria, VA 22314-3510

American Corporate Counsel Association
1225 Connecticut Avenue NW, Suite 302
Washington, DC 20036

American Council for the Arts
One East 53rd Street
New York, NY 10022-4201

American Council of Life Insurance
1001 Pennsylvania Avenue NW
Washington, DC 20004-2599

American Council on Education
One Dupont Circle, Suite 800
Washington, DC 20036-1193

American Culinary Federation
10 San Bartola Drive
St. Augustine, FL 32086

American Electronics Association
5201 Great American Parkway, Suite 520
Santa Clara, CA 95054

American Film Marketing Association
10850 Wilshire Boulevard, 9th Floor
Los Angeles, CA 90024-4321

American Financial Services Association
919 18th Street NW
Washington, DC 20006

American Health Care Association
1201 L Street NW
Washington, DC 20005-4014

American Hotel and Motel Association
1201 New York Avenue NW, 6th Floor
Washington, DC 20005-3931

American Institute of Aeronautics and
   Astronautics
The Aerospace Center
370 L'Enfant Promenade SW
Washington, DC 20024-2518

American Institute of Architects
1735 New York Avenue NW
Washington, DC 20006

American Institute of Certified Public
   Accountants
1211 Avenue of the Americas, 6th Floor
New York, NY 10036-8775

American Institute of Food Distribution, Inc.
   (The Food Institute)
28-12 Broadway
Fair Lawn, NJ 07410

American Institute of Graphic Arts
164 Fifth Avenue
New York, NY 10010

American Insurance Association
1130 Connecticut Avenue NW, Suite 1000
Washington, DC 20036

American League of Lobbyists
P.O. Box 30005
Alexandria, VA 22310

American Marketing Association
250 South Wacker Drive
Chicago, IL 60606-5819

American Occupational Therapy Association
4720 Montgomery Lane
Post Office Box 31220
Bethesda, MD 20824-1220

American Physical Therapy Association
1111 North Fairfax Street
Alexandria, VA 22314

American Rehabilitation Association
1350 I Street NW, Suite 670
Washington, DC 20005

American Resort Development Association
1220 L Street NW, Suite 510
Washington, DC 20005

American Society for Clinical Nutrition, Inc.
9650 Rockville Pike
Bethesda, MD 20814-3998

American Society for Training and
   Development
1640 King Street
Box 1443
Alexandria, VA 22313

American Society of Appraisers
P.O. Box 17265
Washington, DC 20041

American Society of Chartered Life
   Underwriters and Chartered Financial
   Consultants
270 South Bryn Mawr Avenue
Bryn Mawr, PA 19010-2195

American Society of Cinematographers
1782 North Orange Drive
Hollywood, CA 90028

American Society of Civil Engineers
345 East 47th Street
New York, NY 10017

American Society of Composers, Authors and
   Publishers
ASCAP Building
One Lincoln Plaza
New York, NY 10023

American Society of Landscape Architects
4401 Connecticut Avenue NW
Washington, DC 20008-2302

American Society of Mechanical Engineers
345 East 47th Street
New York, NY 10017

American Society of Newspaper Editors
P.O. Box 4090
Reston, VA 22090-1700

American Society of Safety Engineers
1800 East Oakton Street
Des Plaines, IL 60018-2187

American Society of Travel Agents
1101 King Street, 2nd Floor
Alexandria, VA 22314

American Speech-Language-Hearing
   Association
10801 Rockville Pike
Rockville, MD 20852

American Symphony Orchestra League
1156 15th Street NW, Suite 800
Washington, DC 20005-1704

Association for Supervision and Curriculum
   Development
1250 North Pitt Street
Alexandria, VA 22314-1453

Association for Systems Management
P.O. Box 38370
Cleveland, OH 44138

Association of American Colleges and Universities
1818 R Street NW
Washington, DC 20009

Association of American Publishers, Inc.
71 Fifth Avenue
New York, NY 10003-3004

Association of Human Resource Systems
    Professionals
P.O. Box 801646
Dallas, TX 75380-1646

Association of Independent Television Stations,
    Inc.
1320 19th Street NW, Suite 300
Washington, DC 20036

Association of Operating Room Nurses, Inc.
2170 South Parker Road, Suite 300
Denver, CO 80231–5711

Association of Trial Lawyers of America
1050 31st Street NW
Washington, DC 20007

Bank Marketing Association
1120 Connecticut Avenue NW
Washington, DC 20036

Bankers Roundtable
805 15th Street NW, Suite 600
Washington, DC 20005

Building Owners and Managers Association
    International, Inc.
1201 New York Avenue NW, Suite 300
Washington, DC 20005

Business Technology Association
12411 Wornall Road
Kansas City, MO 64145

Commercial Finance Association
225 West 34th Street, Suite 1815
New York, NY 10122

Computing Technology Industry Association
450 East 22nd Street, Suite 230
Lombard, IL 60148-6158

Council for Exceptional Children
1920 Association Drive
Reston, VA 22091-1589

Council of Insurance Agents and Brokers
316 Pennsylvania Avenue SE, Suite 400
Washington, DC 20003-1146

Credit Research Foundation
8815 Centre Park Drive, Suite 206
Columbia, MD 21045-2158

Credit Union National Association, Inc.
5710 Mineral Point Road
P.O. Box 431
Madison, WI 53701-0431

Direct Marketing Association
1120 Avenue of the Americas
New York, NY 10036-6700

Direct Selling Association
1666 K Street NW
Washington, DC 20006

DPMA Association of Information Systems
    Professionals
505 Busse Highway
Park Ridge, IL 60068-3191

Electronic Industries Association
2500 Wilson Boulevard
Arlington, VA 22201

Employee Benefit Research Institute
2121 K Street NW, Suite 600
Washington, DC 20037-1896

Food Marketing Institute
800 Connecticut Avenue NW
Washington, DC 20006-2701

Food Service and Packaging Institute, Inc.
1901 North Moore Street, Suite 1111
Arlington, VA 22209

Futures Industry Association
2001 Pennsylvania Avenue NW, Suite 600
Washington, DC 20006-1807

General Aviation Manufacturers Association
1400 K Street NW, Suite 801
Washington, DC 20005-2485

Graphic Communications Association
100 Daingerfield Road
Alexandria, VA 22314-2888

Human Resource Planning Society
317 Madison Avenue, Suite 1509
New York, NY 10017

IEEE Computer Society
1730 Massachusetts Avenue NW
Washington, DC 20036-1992

Independent Insurance Agents of America, Inc.
127 South Peyton Street
Alexandria, VA 22314

Information Industry Association
555 New Jersey Avenue NW, Suite 800
Washington, DC 20001

Information Technology Association of America
1616 North Fort Myer Drive, Suite 1300
Arlington, VA 22209

Institute for Operations Research and the Management Sciences
940-A Elkridge Landing Road
Linthicum, MD 21090-2909

Institute of Certified Financial Planners
7600 East Eastman Avenue, Suite 301
Denver, CO 80231-4397

Institute of Internal Auditors
249 Maitland Avenue
Altamonte Springs, FL 32701-4201

Institute of Real Estate Management
430 North Michigan Avenue
Chicago, IL 60611-4090

Insurance Accounting and Systems Association, Inc.
P.O. Box 51340
Durham, NC 27717

Insurance Information Institute
110 William Street
New York, NY 10038

International Association of Convention and Visitor Bureaus
2000 L Street NW, Suite 702
Washington, DC 20036-4990

International Customer Service Association
401 North Michigan Avenue
Chicago, IL 60611-4267

International Food Service Manufacturers
    Association
Two Prudential Plaza
180 North Stetson, Suite 4400
Chicago, IL 60601

International Interior Design Association
341 Merchandise Mart
Chicago, IL 60654-1104

International Mass Retail Association, Inc.
1700 North Moore Street, Suite 2250
Arlington, VA 22209

International Newspaper Marketing Association,
    Inc.
12770 Merit Drive, Suite 330
Dallas, TX 75251-1215

International Personnel Management Associa-
    tion
1617 Duke Street
Alexandria, VA 22314

International Reading Association
800 Barksdale Road
P.O. Box 8139
Newark, DE 19714-8139

International Real Estate Institute
8383 East Evans Road
Scottsdale, AZ 85260–3614

Magazine Publishers of America
919 Third Avenue, 22nd Floor
New York, NY 10022

Marketing Research Association, Inc.
2189 Silas Deane Highway, Suite 5
Rocky Hill, CT 06067

Million Dollar Round Table
325 West Touhy Avenue
Park Ridge, IL 60068-4265

Mortgage Bankers Association of America
1125 15th Street NW
Washington, DC 20005-2766

Motion Picture Association of America
1600 I Street NW
Washington, DC 20006

Music Educators National Conference
1806 Robert Fulton Drive
Reston, VA 22091-4348

National Academy of Television Arts and
    Sciences
111 West 57th Street
New York, NY 10019

National Art Education Association
1916 Association Drive
Reston, VA 22091

National Association for Home Care
519 C Street NE
Washington, DC 20002-5809

National Association for Law Placement
1666 Connecticut Avenue, Suite 325
Washington, DC 20009

National Association for the Specialty Food
    Trade, Inc.
120 Wall Street, 27th Floor
New York, NY 10005-4003

National Association of Broadcasters
1771 N Street NW
Washington, DC 20036-2891

National Association of Health Underwriters
1000 Connecticut Avenue NW, Suite 810
Washington, DC 20036

National Association of Life Underwriters
1922 F Street NW
Washington, DC 20006

National Association of Professional Insurance
   Agents
400 North Washington Street
Alexandria, VA 22314-9980

National Association of Realtors
430 North Michigan Avenue
Chicago, IL 60611-4087

National Association of Registered Lobbyists
601 Pennsylvania Avenue NW, North Building,
   Suite 700
Washington, DC 20004-2611

National Association of State Boards of Accountancy, Inc.
380 Lexington Avenue, Suite 200
New York, NY 10168-0002

National Association of Television Program
   Executives
2425 Olympic Boulevard, Suite 550E
Santa Monica, CA 90404

National Association of Temporary and Staffing
   Services
119 South Saint Asaph Street
Alexandria, VA 22314

National Association of Theater Owners
4605 Lankershim Boulevard, Suite 340
North Hollywood, CA 91602-1891

National Athletic Trainers Association
2952 Stemmons Freeway, Suite 200
Dallas, TX 75247

National Business Aircraft Association
1200 18th Street NW, Suite 400
Washington, DC 20036-2506

National Business Travel Association
1650 King Street, Suite 401
Alexandria, VA 22314

National Cable Television Association
1724 Massachusetts Avenue NW
Washington, DC 20036-1969

National Computer Graphics Association
P.O. Box 660
Dunkirk, MD 20754-0660

National Council of State Boards of Nursing, Inc.
676 North St. Clair Street, Suite 550
Chicago, IL 60611–2921

National Education Association
1201 16th Street NW
Washington, DC 20036

National Family Caregivers Association
9621 East Bexhill Drive
Kensington, MD 20895-3104

National Food Brokers Association
2100 Reston Parkway, Suite 400
Reston, VA 22091

National Food Processors Association
1401 New York Avenue NW
Washington, DC 20005

National Grocers Association
1825 Samuel Morse Drive
Reston, VA 22090-5317

National Newspaper Association
1525 Wilson Boulevard, Suite 550
Arlington, VA 22209-2434

National Press Photographers Association, Inc.
3200 Croasdaile Drive, Suite 306
Durham, NC 27705

National Restaurant Association
1200 17th Street NW
Washington, DC 20036-3097

National Retail Federation Inc.
325 7th Street NW, Suite 1000
Washington, DC 20004

National Society of Professional Engineers
1420 King Street
Alexandria, VA 22314-2715

National Society of Public Accountants
1010 North Fairfax Street
Alexandria, VA 22314-1574

National Venture Capital Association
1655 North Fort Myer Drive, Suite 700
Arlington, VA 22209

National-American Wholesale Grocers'
   Association/International Food Service
   Distributors Association
201 Park Washington Court
Falls Church, VA 22046-4621

Newspaper Association of America/The
   Newspaper Center
11600 Sunrise Valley Drive
Reston, VA 22091-1412

North American Retail Dealers Association
10 East 22nd Street, Suite 310
Lombard, IL 60148

Point-of-Purchase Advertising Institute, Inc.
66 North Van Brunt Street
Englewood, NJ 07631

Promotion Marketing Association of America,
   Inc.
257 Park Avenue South, 11th Floor
New York, NY 10010

Property Management Association
8811 Colesville Road, Suite G106
Silver Spring, MD 20910

Radio-Television News Directors Association
1000 Connecticut Avenue NW, Suite 615
Washington, DC 20036

Regional Airline Association
1200 19th Street NW, Suite 300
Washington, DC 20036-2401

Sales and Marketing Executives International
Statler Office Tower, Suite 977
Cleveland, OH 44115

Securities Industry Association
120 Broadway
New York, NY 10271-0080

Semiconductor Industry Association
4300 Stevens Creek Boulevard, Suite 271
San Jose, CA 95129

Society for Human Resource Management
606 North Washington Street
Alexandria, VA 22314

Society for Marketing Professional Services
99 Canal Center Plaza, Suite 250
Alexandria, VA 22314-1588

Society of Professional Journalists
16 South Jackson Street
P.O. Box 77
Greencastle, IN 46135-0077

Travel Industry Association of America
1100 New York Avenue NW, Suite 450
Washington, DC 20005-3934

# About Bradley G. Richardson

At age thirty, Bradley G. Richardson is already a best-selling author, professional speaker, and consultant to Fortune 500 companies regarding career issues for young adults and entry-level employees. A former sales executive in the high-tech industry, Richardson is the author of *JobSmarts for Twentysomethings* and is currently president of the BGR Group, Inc., a Dallas-based training and consulting firm.

He speaks to thousands of young adults and job seekers each year at colleges, public seminars, and conferences, in addition to being a columnist for the *Charlotte Observer* and career correspondent for Paramount UPN Television in Dallas. His writing has appeared in *USA Today*, the *Wall Street Journal*, and *Rolling Stone*, and he has been a guest on *Good Morning America*. Richardson is a graduate of the University of Oklahoma. He lives in Dallas, Texas with his wife and daughter.

## How to Contact Bradley

Let me know what you think. I would love to hear from you. If there is a career you would like to see covered in future editions or if you have a comment, question, or story about working in one of the career paths covered in this book or just working in general, give me a call. Let me know what it takes to become JobSmart in your field.

---

### Get Smart!

Bring Bradley and JobSmarts to your college, company, or organization. If you want to know more about Bradley's JobSmarts speaking events, please contact us at:
800-JOBSMARTS.

Bradley G. Richardson
JobSmarts™
P.O. Box 704120
Dallas, Texas 75030
e-mail: info@jobsmarts.com
Visit JobSmarts™ on the web at www.jobsmarts.com

---